NEWCOMB COLLEGE
1886-2006

For Mary Jo –
whose heart expresses the knowledge
gained from a women's college education and
the wisdom earned from the ebb and flow of life's
experiences –

NEWCOMB
COLLEGE
—— 1886-2006 ——

Higher Education for Women in New Orleans

With love and great appreciation for our
lasting friendship,

EDITED BY

Susan Tucker and Beth Willinger

LOUISIANA STATE UNIVERSITY PRESS
BATON ROUGE

This book is made possible in part by the generous support of the Newcomb College Institute.

Published by Louisiana State University Press
Copyright © 2012 by Louisiana State University Press
All rights reserved
Manufactured in the United States of America
First printing

DESIGNER: Michelle A. Neustrom
TYPEFACE: Whitman
TYPESETTER: BookComp, Inc.
PRINTER: McNaughton & Gunn, Inc.
BINDER: Acme Bookbinding

LIBRARY OF CONGRESS CATALOGING-IN-PUBLICATION DATA

Newcomb College, 1886–2006 : higher education for women in New Orleans / edited by Susan Tucker
and Beth Willinger.
     p. cm.
   Includes index.
     ISBN 978-0-8071-4336-0 (cloth : alk. paper)— ISBN 978-0-8071-4337-7 (pdf)—
ISBN 978-0-8071-4338-4 (epub)— ISBN 978-0-8071-4339-1 (mobi)   1. Newcomb College—History.
2. Women—Education (Higher)—Louisiana—New Orleans—History. I. Tucker, Susan, 1950–
II. Willinger, Beth Ann, 1943–
   LD7105.N49 2012
   378.1'5420976335—dc23

                                                                              2011039035

The paper in this book meets the guidelines for permanence and durability of the Committee on
Production Guidelines for Book Longevity of the Council on Library Resources. ∞

Photographs and illustrations reproduced in this book are from the collections of the Newcomb
Archives of the Newcomb College Center for Research on Women unless otherwise noted.

In memory of Josephine Louise Newcomb, who, in her desire to remember her daughter, Sophie, bequeathed to thousands of daughters the gift of "knowledge, which is power, and can not be taken away"; to the Newcomb College administrators, faculty, staff, students, and alumnae who believed in this gift and magnified it through their lives and service; and to the future of Tulane University that all may remember.

CONTENTS

PREFACE

Newcomb's first and only president, Brandt Van Blarcom Dixon, concluded his book on the early history of the H. Sophie Newcomb Memorial College by noting that "the greatest achievement" of those years rested in the "Newcomb spirit" and in a new beginning for the College. The 1918 move to the "redbrick majesty" of the Broadway campus figured favorably in this new beginning, providing extensive room to grow and joining the established College "more closely . . . to Tulane." The later history of Newcomb, he wrote, "must be written by others."

This book is a response to Dixon's charge—it is a broad overview of the whole of the College's past as the first degree-granting coordinate college for women in the United States. Although nearly a century has passed since Dixon concluded his "brief history," only in the last thirty years did the College begin to attract scholarly attention. The essays reprinted in this volume by Lynn Gordon, Joan Paul, Jessie Poesch, and Karen Kingsley represent some of the first efforts to cast the College within the history of women's postsecondary education. Other efforts to document Newcomb's rich history and the history of Newcomb alumnae gained momentum with plans to celebrate Newcomb's centennial in 1986. A Newcomb Oral History Project was initiated by Adele Ramos Salzer (NC 1940), in collaboration with the Newcomb College Center for Research on Women, and a conference was hosted on the higher education of women. Memories of the College within various essays draw from several of the nearly one hundred interviews conducted with Newcomb's early graduates, alumnae, and deans and faculty of the College.

Most importantly, attention to the College's rich history grew from the creation of the Newcomb Archives in 1989. Until this time, the historical records of the College were long stored—some might even say hidden—around campus. The College records have been enriched by the donations of College papers, photos, scrapbooks, letters, and professional papers of more than fifty alumnae, and the Newcomb Archives has grown to 1,500 linear feet.

These resources have made possible the work of numerous scholars. Among those are the authors and interviewers whose research and perspectives form this anthology. Along with those mentioned above, these writers provide a foundation for future research. We do not intend for this historical overview of Newcomb to be the definitive work on the College. Newcomb College excelled in a number of arenas worthy of continued exploration: especially, the national prominence of Newcomb alumnae; Newcomb's contribution to the arts; and the loyalty of alumnae. This body of work places Newcomb among those coordinate colleges with a written history, including Barnard, Kirkland, Douglass, and Radcliffe colleges. Yet the coordinate college, important as one of three models of women's higher education in the United States, remains relatively obscure. One of our main objectives in compiling this anthology is to promote interest in the historical importance of the College; both to preserve existing College documents and memorabilia, and to encourage additional research. One particular area that deserves further exploration is how Newcomb's coordinate structure and student culture compare to those of other coordinate colleges. Perhaps more than in the case of the women's college or the coeducational institution, the precise form of the coordinate college was always locally defined—a reflection of the particular milieu in which the purpose of an education for women was considered. This book shows that accommodation within Tulane University—an institution that only slowly admitted women—and in the southern city of New Orleans.

The title chosen for our book underscores that accommodation by acknowledging the duration of the College; the privilege of a college education for women; and Newcomb's location in New Orleans. The essays bring an understanding of the relationship between the College and the University over time, and the reciprocal influences between Newcomb and the city; the local as well as national forces that shaped its evolution; and, finally, the way students, faculty, administrators, and, yes, even Mrs. Newcomb, acted. Over the years, the College changed from being often considered the domain of an elite group of white, southern upper-middle-class women. The essays show how the College was built around the need for this group to be educated; show that the city and the region could not afford to neglect these women; and show that very slowly the words, silences, and circumstances surrounding the exclusivity of this society were changed by the very act of educating these

relatively few women. Newcomb students and alumnae enjoyed a special status, if not from their families and centuries of segregation, then from their
own education at the College. The privilege of an education, "the knowledge
which is power" idea used by Mrs. Newcomb and repeated in our dedication,
was a Renaissance ideal that slowly became a democratic one. Newcomb College was part of this transformation. We intend, then, to open the discussion
to a spectrum of interpretations, to show the College's plurality as much as its
singularity.

The book is also a response to the undoing of this formal and yet fluid
configuration of a women's college within a university. In 2005, the University
addressed the challenges posed by the federal levee failures with *A Plan for
Renewal*. The plan adopted by the Administrators of the Tulane Educational
Fund called for a single undergraduate college to be named Newcomb-Tulane
College "in recognition of the missions, histories, and values of these colleges."
This later new beginning remains highly controversial, if only because change
is always difficult, and this change carries, for many, the weight of a broken
promise and another reinterpretation of how women will be educated within
the University. Yet, as the essays in this volume illuminate, such a change was
long predicted and was accomplished in increments over many years.

Dixon dedicated his book to the Newcomb alumnae, "whose constancy,
loyalty and intelligent help have been of the utmost value in the building of
Newcomb College." We, too, acknowledge the Newcomb alumnae, as well
as the Newcomb faculty, administrators, and staff, who, over more than 120
years, built and maintained Newcomb's national reputation of academic
excellence.

The essays are organized into three sections representing different perspectives on the College's mission. Part 1, "Beginnings," expands on Dixon's
history of the founding of the College in the years between 1886 and 1918
and considers how the philosophies of the early founders and the sociohis-
torical context in which the College was established gave form to the college
for women at Tulane University. Writers consider the events shaping Mrs.
Newcomb's plans and her relationship with administrators; ideas about the
appropriate role and education of women; and the design of College facilities
to address the growing educational needs of a college for women. Part 2, "Distinctions," focuses on the coordinate college system and several of the specific
programs that distinguished Newcomb among other educational institutions
and in the lives of its students. Part 3, "Lives," presents biographical and

autobiographical accounts, as well as memories of and about former students and faculty members, and invites consideration of the interplay between the College and the city of New Orleans in the life experiences and contributions of educated women. Found in these essays are replies to the age-old query: What is the purpose of an education for women? As in all anthologies, certain aspects of the past are overlooked, and we have tried to address some of these areas in an introduction to each section.

As this volume has been more than nine years in the making, there are many who have contributed to its production. First, we gratefully acknowledge the eighteen authors and two interviewers whose research on varied aspects of Newcomb's history give depth and breadth to this volume. It has been a joy and privilege to exchange ideas and share our mutual interests in the College with these scholars. Others have written, and are writing, on the College, especially Emily Clark, Sylvia Frey, Amy McCandless, and Meghan Freeman. We appreciate the work of Maggie Dittemore of the Smithsonian Institution in compiling, with Susan Tucker, an annotated bibliography on southern women's higher education that allowed us a beginning.

Our students and student workers at the Newcomb College Center for Research on Women have been of utmost assistance. We thank Kati Bambrick for her editing skills, and the 2002 "Research in the History of the Higher Education of Women" class for their ideas on many of Newcomb's customs and traditions. Help was also given by Renee Randazzo, Ann Marie Messick, Bridget Borel, Amy Lin, and Cristela Garcia-Spitz.

Thanks to Adele Ramos Salzer and her family, who gave so generously to a series of lectures on the higher education of women; to Amy Porter Stroh, who gave funds for the Newcomb Archives; and to the National Historical Publications and Records Commission, who first funded the Archives and the creation of a guide to the Newcomb records located all over the campus and city. For their friendship, vision, generosity, trust, and belief in building knowledge about women's lives, we are indebted to Florie Gale Arons, and her daughters Andrea Arons Huseman, Gina Arons, and Lisa Aldridge; Marla Custard; Loraine Despres Eastlake; Dana Zale Gerard, and the M. B. and Edna Zale Foundation; Eugenia Goff; Emily Schoenbaum; Gilbert Vorhoff and the family of Nadine Robbert Vorhoff; and Jesselyn Zurick.

Librarians Cristina Hernandez and Bea Calvert assisted always in helping us find pertinent sources. Archivist Mary Allen Johnson not only helped with Newcomb records but also proofread many articles. Thanks to Gillian

North, whose work for her dissertation at the University of Keele added to our knowledge of Newcomb's early library; to Marcie Ferris and Cathy Kahn, for their interest in Jewish students at the College; to Katy Coyle and Nadiene van Dyke, for their work on the history of early Newcomb; to Rosalind Hinton, Betsy Hemenway, and Joan Bennett, who commented on early introductions and essays of this book; to Gin Taylor McLure, Donna Pierce, and Janie Stone Christensen, who made vivid the memories of Newcomb in the early 1970s; to the memories of Betty Werlein Carter (NC 1931), Rosa Freeman Keller (NC 1932), and Mary Hunter Irvine (NC 1925), who exemplified what it means to be a Newcomb alumna; to Jean Bragg, who so often explored Newcomb art with us; to Judith Bonner, whose work on Newcomb's art faculty served as a continual reference point; to Tom Strider and Sally Main, always helpful colleagues; to Stephanie Bordy, whose interests in Newcomb embroidery and archival skills helped in our work; to Ann Die, Margaret King, Mary Ann Maguire, and Allison Raynor, for giving meaning to a Newcomb education; to our many students, who gave meaning to our lives; to Sylvia Collins, for her assistance on all matters; to Pat Stevens, whose kindness and friendship remain a touchstone for all that can be right in the world; to Adelaide Wisdom Benjamin (NC 1954), for love of Nursery School history; to Barbara Ewell and Jerry Speir for their encouragement and unfailing friendship; and in memory of Richard Collin, who used his great intellect to amuse, provoke, and make us think about the meaning of education.

We also thank our families, who have grumbled yet supported our hours writing and our conversations saturated with Newcomb facts and figures, particularly Franny Tucker (NC 2005), Kristen Calonico Chawla (NC 1990), Ian Lambert, and Susan Martin.

Finally, it is a privilege to have worked long years with all associated with the Center and the College in every way, and with colleagues today at the Newcomb College Institute. It is thanks to them that our work has been, and continues to be, situated within a place of both learning and friendship.

BEGINNINGS

I believe there are features of a woman's college which can be developed here better than anywhere else, i.e., the modern languages . . . [and] also for the *ladies,* industrial art and design," wrote Tulane University president William Preston Johnston (1831–1899). Johnston's plan for a college for women, separate from but still a part of Tulane University, had only a few months previously gained the support of someone he had long known, Josephine Louise Le Monnier Newcomb (1816–1901), who expressed "a deep personal sympathy with the people of New Orleans and a strong desire to advance the cause of female education in Louisiana." Weaving into his plans her desire to establish a memorial for her daughter, Harriott Sophie (1855–1870), "the H. Sophie Newcomb Memorial College, in the Tulane University of Louisiana" opened in the fall of 1887. In Johnston's long and successful tenure as president, 1884–99, the design and funding of the women's college may have been his greatest and most lasting achievement.[1]

Johnston's outline for the curriculum of the women's college differed from the curriculum of the all-male Tulane College, and also from the women's colleges of the Northeast that aimed to offer women the same classical education as that provided to men.[2] His plan would educate women and girls in the languages familiar to the city, French and Spanish, and provide a vocational education as well as an academic one needed for the economic development of the New South. The idea of the "New South" was more than an economic concept. It combined northern humanitarianism with southern paternalism in a move toward social reform.[3] Johnston's plan offering both liberal arts and vocational education was among a host of contrasting elements present in this New South ideal that would define the College at its beginning. Funded by a widow who chose New York as her residence yet entrusted the execution of her design to a southern gentleman, the memorial college was linked at once to the Victorian and the modern; reform and conservatism; racial segregation and religious tolerance; conformity to ideals of womanhood and challenges to gender restrictions.

Building a College on Contrasting Influences

Johnston was part product and part maker of this climate. A former Confederate colonel, Johnston was among the first faculty at Washington College (renamed Washington and Lee University in 1870), and in 1880, he was appointed president of the state-supported Louisiana State University and A&M College. Johnston left LSU in 1883, and in 1884, he became the first president of the Tulane University of Louisiana, a private institution created through the donation of Paul Tulane and the transfer of all properties of the state-funded University of Louisiana.[4] As a professional educator, Johnston felt passionately the need to develop an educated workforce of both women and men, and saw particularly the need for women as teachers. New Orleans in the 1880s, then the South's largest city, was still experiencing the toll of the Civil War and Reconstruction on the economy and education. The region in general lagged far behind the northern states in education, and Louisiana lagged behind even other southern states, with fewer than half the public school teachers employed in Kentucky, Tennessee, Alabama, Mississippi, or Arkansas.[5] Johnston's plan for the education of women emphasized a curriculum that would prepare them for employment.

While Johnston held pragmatic views on women's education and employment, he nevertheless honored the South's traditional gender ideals, including separate social spheres for women and men. Although New Orleans—then as now—was not always a recognizably southern place, the resistance to coeducation at the newly formed Tulane University was nuanced and idiosyncratic, yet pervasive. No legalities stood in the way of coeducation. The legislative act establishing "The Tulane University of Louisiana" specified that the University "be dedicated to the intellectual, moral and industrial education of the *youth* of the State." Paul Tulane's act of donation specified "white young *persons.*"[6] However, when Johnston was president of LSU, a group of young women asked for admission and were refused on the grounds that the inclusion of women would defeat "the manifest purpose of the state . . . the education of males."[7] As Tulane was to be tax-exempt, a form of state funding, Johnston perhaps carried such reasoning to the private institution. More likely, however, conservative social and moral reasons prevailed. Educating women and men together was still a novelty: only a handful of midwestern and western states offered coeducational opportunities.

As coeducation at Tulane was considered socially inappropriate, Johnston crafted a plan for the education of young men and women under one institution, but divided into "departments," or colleges.[8] This "coordinate arrangement" allowed a curriculum for women distinct from the curriculum for men, and opened the possibility of additional funding for the University's mission if a donor could be persuaded to finance the education of women. Funding of a separate women's college within Tulane would eliminate fears that the admission of women would deplete the University's resources and remove suspicions that monies marked for the education of men would be diverted to subsidize the education of women. Johnston's proposal was unassailable for establishing a separate female division as publicly and legally a part of the male institution of Tulane, yet financially self-supporting.

Within two years of assuming the presidency of Tulane, Johnston's search for a donor to fund the women's college led him to Josephine Newcomb. "Mrs. Newcomb," as she always was called, was left a widow and single mother when her husband died in 1866. Warren Newcomb's death had made her quite wealthy, and her own wise investments increased her inheritance many times over.[9] However, it was the death of her only living child in 1870 that would emotionally both cripple and motivate her for the next sixteen years. Mrs. Newcomb considered "many beautiful charities" before settling on "a memorial that would enshrine her [Sophie's] memory in a manner best fitted to render useful and enduring benefit to humanity."[10] Once the memorial was chosen, Mrs. Newcomb devoted her remaining years, and the commitment of her considerable wealth, to this purpose.

The nineteenth century in general was marked by many large commemorative efforts, but Mrs. Newcomb's first acts were actually quite modest. Her initial gift of $100,000 was not large enough to build an independent women's college with majestic buildings on sprawling "picturesque" grounds as Matthew Vassar had built.[11] Her donation was given with the understanding that the amount "was large enough in case of failure, and small enough to allow additions in case of success."[12]

The first true measure of success came in 1890, a mere three years after the beginning: the award to eight students of the baccalaureate degree, and to two others a degree in design. Their achievement was not the mark of individual effort alone; they stood together as the first graduating class of the first degree-granting coordinate college for women in the United States.[13]

REFORM AND CONSERVATISM

Three powerful forces agitating for women's higher education were well at work in New Orleans prior to Johnston's appointment as president. One was a group of women journalists. Among these women was the publisher of the city's largest newspaper (the *New Orleans Daily Picayune*), Eliza Jane Poitevent Holbrook Nicholson (1849–1896), who in 1876 became the first woman to head a major daily newspaper in the South. Nicholson, whose pen name was "Pearl Rivers," was an ardent supporter of the education of girls and employed a number of female journalists. The *Daily Picayune*'s most prolific writer was the brilliant Catharine Cole (pen name for Martha R. Field, 1855–1898), who reported often on the need for change in the status of women, especially in light of the economic conditions in the city.[14] Although Cole championed the "common woman," her articles most often were read by the city's elite women.[15]

Another local writer who advocated for the education of women and personally knew the power of education in one's ability to earn money was Jennie C. Nixon (1839–1917). As a young widow, Nixon went to Europe and there hired private tutors to educate herself and her children. She returned to find employment as the society editor of the *New Orleans Times-Democrat* and as a public school teacher. In 1887, she was hired as the first faculty member of the newly established Newcomb College and taught English and rhetoric until her retirement in 1907.[16]

Nicholson, Cole, Nixon, and other women journalists inspired mothers and daughters to begin educating themselves. In the 1880s, a number of clubs began with the goal of self-education—the Woman's Club, the Geographics, the Portia Club, and the Equal Rights for All Club.[17] These civic-minded organizations whose scholarly activities were well publicized grew into a cohesive group of white, middle- and upper-class women whom Johnston could identify as allies in the fight for women's education at Tulane.

The second powerful force on Johnston's side was another group of prestigious white women who had spoken on behalf of women's suffrage at the 1879 Louisiana Constitutional Convention.[18] Led by Caroline Merrick (1825–1908), these women joined in the national debate as proponents of women's education. In the early 1880s, Merrick opened her home to the Christian Temperance leader Frances Willard, who was on a speaking tour that included New Orleans. One of the main ideas Willard espoused was the admission of women to colleges and universities.[19] It was this knowledge about the coeducational opportunities open to women in some midwestern state universities that had prompted several women to request admission to LSU in 1881.[20] Though denied admission, the women remained ready for the time when arrangements would allow for the education of women in the city and state.

The third force supporting Johnston's efforts for the education of women was the 1884 World's Industrial and Cotton Centennial Exposition held at present-day Audubon Park.[21] Boldly, and still to the modern eye quite surprisingly, fair organizers chose a famous northern abolitionist, Julia Ward Howe, to head the Woman's Department at the New Orleans fair. Howe's lyrics to "The Battle Hymn of the Republic" had made her a celebrity, as had her charisma. Despite the wariness of many New Orleanians concerning Howe's appointment, her brief stint in New Orleans influenced generations of southern women.[22] One New Orleans woman succinctly described the full impact of Howe's visit: "For many years an earnest desire had possessed me to behold a genuinely strong-minded woman, one of the truly advanced type. Beautiful to realize she stood before me! And in a position the very acme of independence—upon a platform delivering a speech."[23]

Howe also was praised by community activists such as Merrick for arranging programs that broadly introduced the idea of middle-class women as wage earners.[24] New Orleans journalists proclaimed the Woman's Department as the place where "woman has first been recognized as a potential factor in the world's development."[25] Howe herself was pronounced the "embodiment of [the] Victorian ideal of womanhood," but equipped with "what used to be called 'masculine' competence."[26] The department advanced ideas among New Orleans women about participating in national and local debates on a range of issues and introduced women and girls to various types of education offered elsewhere.[27]

The exposition also offered art classes for women taught by Tulane School of Architecture professor William Woodward (1859–1939) and his brother Ellsworth Woodward (1861–1939). The classes were so popular that "ladies would arrive hours in advance. . . . Long lines formed outside the classroom in the hope that some would vacate their chairs and their places could be taken."[28] When the fair ended, the two New Englanders continued teaching the art classes and founded the Ladies Decorative Art League and the New Orleans Pottery. The Woodwards also established "Free Drawing" classes for women within Tulane in which more than one thousand women enrolled between 1884 and 1887.[29] It was from the enrollments in these art classes, as well as the "Home Study" and "Reading Society" classes established by the University, that Johnston could estimate the numbers of women who might be ready to seek an education within the University.[30]

With the re-formation of the University as a privately funded institution, these progressive women hoped Tulane would be a place where women could undertake collegiate work. The daughter of Caroline Merrick, Caroline Merrick Guthrie, wrote an open letter to Mr. Tulane in the *Times-Democrat* urging "that this great institution should be co-educational in its scope."[31] In fact, Tulane's act of donation gave the Administrators of the Tulane Educational Fund great freedom in determining the type of education that should be given.[32]

A less powerful force, but still an important ally in Johnston's plan, was an unorganized mix of New Orleans families with daughters. Some families followed an older tradition of southern planters and sent their children north for schooling.[33] However, as Ida Rittenberg Kohlmeyer (NC 1933) relates in her interview in part 3 of this volume, this practice was more common for sons than for daughters, and also required a larger financial commitment. Two rare examples of families who sent their daughters to northeastern colleges were the families of Clara Gregory Baer and Ann Hero. Baer, who attended Boston's Emerson School of Oratory, and Hero, who attended Vassar, returned to New Orleans to have stellar teaching careers at Newcomb.

Additionally, southern families who had lost family breadwinners understood that daughters, as well as mothers, might be called upon for economic support and therefore were in need of a practical education. The 1880s demographic data illuminate factors that may have contributed to parental concerns regarding the need for daughters to work. Whereas less than 6 percent of married women were employed nationally, approximately 43 percent of single women and 32 percent of women who were widowed or divorced were in the labor force. The loss of men and boys during the Civil War, coupled with the higher mortality rate for men due to disease and illness, meant that in New Orleans, as through most of the South, women outnumbered men, particularly in the age group fifteen years and older.[34] Moreover, in the late 1800s, the median age of first marriage was twenty-two years for women and twenty-six years for men. Thus there was a strong likelihood that a woman, particularly a woman in the South, would spend several years of her adult life as a single woman or never marry. If she were to marry, there was a likelihood of becoming a widow. This unpredictable life course often propelled women into the labor force as aptly illustrated by the experiences of several women already mentioned: Nicholson, Cole, and Nixon.

Further evidence of the need for educating women for gainful employment comes from Newcomb student enrollment records. In Newcomb's first graduating class (1890), of ten students, two students were the daughters of widowed mothers, and another student, an orphan. (All three of these students continued on to graduate school.) Among incoming students during the period 1890–1913, "mother," a designation that uniformly meant "widow," was exceeded only by "merchant" as the occupation of parents or guardians.[35]

Thus, for families who knew education to be important for suitable employment, and for those families who wanted their daughters to have the same liberal arts education as that offered by the northeastern women's colleges, the free evening courses in art and other subjects were not the answer. Rather, the ambitions of these families for well-educated daughters made them partners in Johnston's plan to establish a women's college as a part of Tulane University.

At the same time, mitigating factors worked against serious educational pursuits for young women. Namely, the city was not prosperous enough nor was Mrs. Newcomb's initial donation large enough to support an independent women's college like those in the Northeast. Second, very few New Orleans girls had received a secondary education preparing them for collegiate work.[36] Third, the antislavery movement, which in other parts of the United States had nurtured ideas about women's participation within a democracy, had no comparable foundation in New Orleans.[37] Few New Orleanians beyond the well-read followers of Merrick and Cole were concerned with women's status as second-class citizens or held strong convictions concerning education as a means of attaining political and legal equality for women.[38] Next, neither Protestant nor Catholic groups in New Orleans, as could be found in other parts of the country, argued outside the confines of their individual institutions for the education of women as preparation for intelligent motherhood or for reading and teaching the Bible.[39] Finally, even those parents who supported the idea of a college education for their daughters expected them to finish their education by age seventeen.[40] Parents were interested mainly in accomplishments, the "gentility" that the scholar Christie Farnham so aptly named, such as decorative painting and needlework, not in the acquisition of knowledge.[41] For most families, a daughter's route to adulthood was through marriage and motherhood.

There were other hindrances, especially New Orleans' social customs, that thwarted full support for the higher education of women.[42] The affluent families of the city were accustomed to bringing their daughters into society through the debutante season, and in this manner finding them suitable and well-to-do husbands. For most white, upper-class families in New Orleans, the debutante year remains de rigueur, especially since it ties not only daughters but whole families to useful business, political, and social networks.

Johnston sought to introduce a path less dependent on family heritage and more reliant on individual merit, but neither he nor subsequent administrators were entirely successful in this. One example of the perceived conflict between education and social attainment for women can be seen in the life of Henrietta Nicholls, a member of Newcomb's first class in 1887 and daughter of the governor of Louisiana. Supporting Johnston's ideas about the importance of the College for the future of the city and state, Governor Nicholls and his wife asked their daughter to consider education. As Henrietta Nicholls Garrett noted years later in her memoir: "Most girls in New Orleans didn't go to college, but made their debut in society. Father . . . thought if the governor's daughter went to college the other girls might follow her example, so he asked me to give up my idea of coming out and enter Newcomb."[43]

Later, other daughters began to choose education over social prominence. For example, the print artist Caroline Wogan Durieux (NC 1916), whose work is described by Earl Retif in his essay in part 3 of this volume, convinced her parents to apply the funds for her debut to the cost of her graduate education at the Pennsylvania Academy of Art.

CONFORMITY TO IDEALS OF WOMANHOOD AND CHALLENGES TO GENDER RESTRICTIONS

Brandt V. B. Dixon only reluctantly accepted the invitation of the Tulane Administrators to become the first president of Newcomb College.[44] He fully understood the challenges presented by the city's social traditions, the inadequate preparation of girls for college work, and the uncertainties of future funding for the women's college. Selected by the Administrators because of his success as a high school principal in St. Louis, Dixon had a vision of a college education for women based upon the example set by his alma mater, Cornell, the first Ivy League institution to admit women (1872).

Dixon's appointment proved a fortuitous one with regard to the realization of academic goals and the administrative management of the College. Tulane University historian John Dyer credits Dixon, "more than any other single person," with having "charted the future course of the H. Sophie Newcomb Memorial College." Dyer describes Dixon as "plump, bushy browed and ruggedly handsome . . . a captivating speaker, a man of broad culture, and an indefatigable planner and worker."[45] The tasks before Dixon—building an institution of higher education without precedent in the United States, hiring and developing a suitable faculty in a city with a meager educational system, establishing academic policies that would both provide an education of the first rank and allow young women to support themselves, designing and overseeing the physical facility, and gaining the trust and confidence of the College's benefactress—required these skills and more.

Not everyone shared Dixon's vision of building a women's college of high academic standing, including the president of the Tulane board, Randall Lee Gibson. Dixon recalled that Gibson told him frankly: "Mr. Dixon, you have a large imagination. I'm afraid . . . you'll never build such an institution for southern girls. It's entirely against all customs and traditions of the South— and the character for southern girls."[46]

Still, when the first students entered Newcomb in October 1887, New Orleans journalists wrote enthusiastically of plans for this unusual venture, one devoted not to "deportment" or "finishing," but to allowing "girls . . . to prepare themselves for professional life or high scholastic achievement." Illustrious women were named as models, such as Clotilde Tambroni, who in 1794 had taught Greek at the University of Bologna. Newnham College of Cambridge University was evoked as an example of a women's college, with a long description of the courses offered, and noting its setting within a prestigious institution that had educated only men since the thirteenth century. The new college in New Orleans would take time to grow into a place like Newnham, but, the journalists posited, such an experiment was well worth the effort.[47]

The early writers on Newcomb specifically articulated an advantage for girls in being "in a separate college of their own which, however, is to be a constituent part of Tulane."[48] From the beginning, then, Newcomb students were visibly attached to the male university and were encouraged to think of themselves as the peers of male students. While not physically classmates with men, Newcomb students, at least in principle, were seen as capable of attaining a college education equal to that provided to men. Thus, without challenging the all-male domain of Tulane, Newcomb stood as a challenge to ideas asserting women's limited abilities.[49] Dixon himself came to see in the students "a responsiveness to ideals, a growing persistency of purpose, and an initiative which I had not at first suspected."[50]

RACIAL SEGREGATION AND RELIGIOUS TOLERANCE

The story of Mrs. Newcomb, as told in the essays by Marcia Wedell and Harriet Swift, is important in uniting the various forces that came together to create the College. After her initial discussions with Johnston, Mrs. Newcomb wrote to the Administrators of the Tulane Educational Fund in 1886 about her "long cherished design" to find a suitable memorial for her "beloved daughter." Mrs. Newcomb determined that her daughter might best be remembered through some "work of the spirit that should go on year by year doing good." This work would be in the form of a college for "white girls and women."[51] Like Paul Tulane before her, who had stipulated racial restrictions on student enrollments, Mrs. Newcomb had a particular vision as to the race, social class, and feminine virtues of the females a college would serve. To her, the students would be girls like Sophie—young, white ladies who would be taught in a "respectable and moral neighborhood."[52] A college was to be "a credit and an honor to the name of" Sophie, a place reflective of Sophie's "gentle and pious life."[53]

Mrs. Newcomb requested that the institution "be in harmony with the fundamental principles of the Christian religion" and "have a chapel or assembly room in which worship may be observed daily for the benefit of the students"—though neither worship nor instruction were to be of a sectarian or denominational character.[54] Invitations to participate in the 1895 dedication of the chapel were extended to officials of the Presbyterian, Episcopal, and Catholic churches as well as to the rabbi of Touro Synagogue, thereby establishing Newcomb as a nonsectarian private college.[55]

VOCATIONAL EDUCATION AND THE LIBERAL ARTS:
THE PRACTICAL AND THE LITERARY

Mrs. Newcomb left little written evidence of her thoughts on women's education. Unlike the founders of the women's colleges of the Northeast, who had clear and specific visions of the purpose of an education for women, Mrs. Newcomb requested only that the new college bearing Sophie's name should "look to the practical side of life as well as to literary excellence."[56] This directive possibly came from her own knowledge of the need and right of women to be in command of their own money. At Warren Newcomb's death in 1866, his family challenged his will and fought to gain control of the estate that Josephine and Sophie had inherited. Only because Josephine Newcomb lived in New York, one of the first states to pass a Married Women's Property Act, was she able to defend her right to have and to control her (and Sophie's) legacy.[57]

Mrs. Newcomb's residence in New York also meant she was aware of the debates concerning the lack of higher education for women and for broadening the type of work available to girls and women of all social classes.[58] She owned and marked a copy of Lillie Devereux Blake's *Woman's Place To-day*, which describes the struggle for women's admission to Columbia. In this 1883 book, Blake replies to the Reverend Morgan Dix, who had written in protest to a petition signed by more than a thousand prominent citizens of New York advocating for the coeducation of men and women at Columbia. Mrs. Newcomb also had a copy of Reverend Dix's lectures, but she made no marginal notes in them.[59]

It is unknown if Mrs. Newcomb envisioned women's struggles to enter Columbia coalescing in a coordinate college arrangement as ultimately occurred in the 1889 founding of Barnard College. However, there existed a number of nineteenth-century "experiments" upon which Mrs. Newcomb and Newcomb's founders could base their aspirations for women's education within Tulane. In the period 1830–50, female seminaries and academies all over the United States expanded their teachings to include classical languages and to provide an education grounded in academics and self-reliance.[60] Students educated at these academies were prepared for the founding of Vassar (1865), Wellesley (1875), and Smith (1875). The early historian of women's education Thomas Woody identified two diverse goals for the beginnings of women's colleges: first, that women should be trained as teachers; and second, that women should be educated on the grounds of promoting religion and health.[61] Yet, Vassar, Wellesley, and Smith also offered something different since they sought to give women the same classical education as that given men: "the best methods to perfect her intellect." Sophia Smith's will, providing for Smith College in 1875, located this wish within a "design to furnish my [own] sex means and facilities for education equal to those which are afforded now in our Colleges for young men."[62] Smith's statement is not unlike the goal quoted in Newcomb's earliest bulletins, one likely crafted by Dixon. The college for women at Tulane aimed to offer "young women of Louisiana and the adjoining States . . . a liberal education, similar to that which is now given to young men by the Tulane University, and to young women also by other institutions of the first rank in distant parts of the United States."[63]

Dixon strove to develop and maintain a strictly defined collegiate educa-tion at Newcomb—one that came close to the standards of his alma mater. At the same time, he acknowledged Johnston's plan for a college that would offer industrial art and design and Mrs. Newcomb's request for an education both practical and literary. He addressed the educational needs of the majority of students who were unprepared for a rigorous program of study by offering the option of a partial course of study, or work in a single branch, and certificates for work accomplished.[64] He recognized that the new college should accom-modate the many New Orleans students who wanted to study only art, or who wanted to enroll in only one or two courses. In these various approaches, he drew upon his observation of other eastern schools to shape a college that would join the "culture of Vassar and the practicality of Pratt" in the southern city of New Orleans.[65]

Thus the College instituted what would today be called "tracks" for dif-ferent types of students. The few who were qualified and chose to pursue a baccalaureate degree were called "academic" (later "collegiate") students. Students who took only one or two of the literary classes were designated "special students." Students enrolled in the art classes predominated. In the first session, 150 students enrolled: 59 in the academic classes, and 91 in the special and art classes.[66] In 1888, a one-year preparatory grade was estab-lished, and by 1895, a full four-year high school was flourishing. Dixon's dis-appointment in the small number of students enrolled in the baccalaureate program continued as enrollments between 1887 and 1901 hovered around 65. Eventually, a prepared group of students entered the College from New-comb High School and from other girls' private high schools in the city that had adopted the educational standards established by Newcomb. In New-comb's last year on the Washington Avenue campus, 1917–18, 381 students were enrolled in the collegiate classes.[67]

Newcomb's total enrollments also rose. The special students outnumbered the academic students during the first two decades and, along with the high school students and the art students, accounted for a 65 percent increase in student enrollments in the early years, reaching a peak of nearly 300 students in the 1907–08 academic year.[68] In retrospect, it can be seen that the special and art students were critical to the establishment of the College. While special students could also be found in the male undergraduate college, "specials" at Newcomb provided needed tuition dollars, and their numbers helped to reassure Mrs. Newcomb of the success of the College. They also gave a certain assurance to the community at large that Newcomb could be many things to many people and would not change too radically how women in New Orleans lived.

A number of these special students became, or were already, primary and secondary school teachers. Early Newcomb catalogues advised that the special courses were "of value to those who intend to prepare themselves for teaching some particular branch, or those who, having completed their school or college career, nevertheless are unwilling to abandon further intellectual pursuits."[69] A four-year "Normal Art" program was immediately established to prepare teachers of art, and a one-year "Normal Physical Education" certificate program was begun in 1893–94, followed by a two-year certificate program in 1905, and a four-year degree program in 1909.[70] Dixon had proposed taking over the City Normal School from the school board in 1909 and offering a two-year certificate program for teachers in grammar grades and a four-year program for high school teachers. Orleans Parish often restricted where teachers who had not attended one of the normal colleges of the state could teach, and Dixon felt the merger would be mutually beneficial.[71] He noted the need for a school of education in addressing the city's inadequate provision of education in general, building closer relations with the public schools of the city and state, and offering better teacher training.[72] The proposed takeover was rejected, but Newcomb nevertheless opened its School of Education in 1909 with just thirteen students. The School was disbanded in the 1920s, a reflection of the ambivalent attitudes held by both Newcomb and A&S faculty about teacher training throughout their histories. The study of pedagogy would be offered in various special units over time, including the "University Department for Teachers," "College of Education," "Department of Education," "Division for Teachers," and "Courses for Teachers."[73]

Many prospective teachers majored in fields other than education, and Newcomb sent a number of leaders into the public school system of the city and state who are deserving of study.[74] Leslie Parr's essay in this volume tells of one such teacher, Sarah Towles Reed (NC 1904). Through women like Reed, school board leader Marion Pfeifer Abramson (NC 1925), and numerous others, Newcomb fulfilled several of Johnston's objectives for the women's college by preparing women as teachers and helping to raise the educational standards in the city and state. In addition, Trent Watts describes in his essay how Newcomb's most notable programs—in fine arts and physical education—promoted southern womanhood as preparation for women's duties in the New South. Moreover, by educating the educators, Newcomb extended its influence and scholarly reputation as these teacher-alumnae encouraged their own female students to enroll in the College.

Dixon's exacting requirements for the academic program and his desire to "make the A grade" resulted in success in 1903, when Newcomb was one of only three colleges—Randolph-Macon Woman's College and Baltimore College for Women (now Goucher College) being the others—to achieve the standards required for membership in the Southern Association of College Women. As late as 1916, Newcomb was one of only seven southern schools for women holding a standard college designation within the Southern Association of Colleges.[75]

Campuses and Integration into University Life

Dixon's success in building the College, especially in the numbers of students enrolled, is partially revealed by the move of the College from one campus—to another (1891)—to another (1918). The first Newcomb students attended classes in a converted two-story brownstone residential building on the corner of Camp and DeLord (now Howard Avenue) Streets, near what is now Lee Circle. While the Hale Mansion previously had been "a fine example of the southern home" and thus framed the feminine ideals of domesticity and virtue, Dixon deemed it undesirable from the first moment he saw it.[76] The campus was not far from an area increasingly plagued by crime and prostitution.[77] Moreover, its urban location lacked privacy. "Men loitered on the banquettes, watching the girls in their ankle-length skirts take their genteel exercises in the yard."[78] These unfavorable conditions likely contradicted the very reasons the Tulane board had selected the residential property. Just as Harvard administrators aimed to make Radcliffe students "as unnoticed as the daughters of any Cambridge residents," so, too, did Tulane administrators wish to protect and buffer the presence of women as college students.[79]

Recalling Mrs. Newcomb's desire that the students be taught in a "respectable and moral neighborhood," it is fortunate perhaps that she never visited this first campus. Her first visit to the College, in February 1892, occurred after she had been persuaded by Dixon and others to finance the purchase and renovation of "the almost palatial Burnside Place," a two-story Italianate mansion in the Garden District. This three-acre campus, bounded by Washington, Sixth, Camp, and Chestnut Streets, provided a setting more similar to the isolated academies and convents that served day students in other southern cities.[80]

Once Mrs. Newcomb observed the success of the College, she became a frequent visitor, and rooms were reserved for her in the Josephine Louise House, built in 1894.[81] In 1899, she bought a house in the neighborhood at 1224 Fourth Street, and upon her death in 1901, her home became a residence house for students called Newcomb House.[82] Mrs. Newcomb held a strong interest in the building of the chapel, and she personally employed the architect and determined the furnishings.[83] The campus grew to include Warren House at 1234 Sixth Street, the Pottery Building at 2828 Camp Street, the Music School at 1224 Sixth Street, and the Household Arts Building at 1238 Washington Avenue. These four buildings and Mrs. Newcomb's home still stand and are marked by commemorative plaques. The Tiffany glass windows from the chapel are now part of the Myra Clare Rogers Chapel and Woodward Way of the Woldenberg Art Center on the Broadway campus.[84]

When the College moved to its present site on Broadway Street in 1918, relative prosperity ruled. The location, adjacent to Tulane University, had the benefit of easy geographic access to collegiate life and the additional resources of the University. With Mrs. Newcomb's money, administrators and faculty oversaw the construction of the Administration Building (Newcomb Hall), Art Building, and the Josephine Louise Residence Hall. As Karen Kingsley explains in her essay, the architectural design of the Broadway campus was intended to emphasize domesticity and protection, features accentuated by the location of the College in a new, predominantly white, upper-class residential neighborhood. However, the grounds were soggy and had once been a field for grazing cows. Dr. Mildred Christian recalled: "We had many difficulties of a physical kind because the grounds were just nothing but mud. There was nothing solid. . . . It wasn't beautiful."[85] Flooding was more common than on the slightly higher Washington Avenue campus, a fact that would become especially important in 2005, when the levees were breached and the campus flooded following Hurricane Katrina.

The rituals, traditions, and moral tenor of the first two campuses continued on the Broadway campus, and for the first few years the College continued along as a "separate and distinct" women's college.[86] However, change was under way. Advances in communication and travel and the increasing acceptance of women as college students brought Newcomb students more into the mainstream. In group photographs of the student body, not one Newcomb student retained long hair; all had cut their hair in the fashionable bob. They began contact with women's colleges of the Northeast and other southern women's colleges, with whom they exchanged publications, joined national and regional organizations, and competed in debates. For example, Lynn Gordon's essay illuminates some of the ways the students and alumnae of Newcomb and Agnes Scott came together and diverged. Newcomb's Alumnae Association proudly measured their fund-raising efforts in sending a post–World War I Relief Unit to Europe against those of the women's colleges of the Northeast.[87]

However, the early Broadway period, 1918–30, also began a marked shift away from the separate women's culture and the administrative and academic autonomy that had developed over more than thirty years. Newcomb's deans and faculty members were to become, step by step, more integrated into the organizational structure of a college within a university. Some viewed these changes with distaste, but others believed that the move toward integration within the University was the point of the ever-evolving coordinate structure. Women proved themselves good students and that they, and their professors, were worthy of recognition, and also of the best education and co-curricular activities the University could offer. The fluidity of the coordinate structure seemed to offer these advantages.

Leadership and Issues of Trust

Much of Newcomb's early history was shaped by the interplay between Dixon and Mrs. Newcomb. Though Mrs. Newcomb was determined that the memory of her daughter would continue in a lasting manner, her trust in who should have oversight of the memorial college was less certain. Although her donations were given to the Administrators of the Tulane Educational Fund, Wedell describes in her essay Mrs. Newcomb's questioning as to whether her gifts should be given to the Administrators, directed to Newcomb separately, entrusted solely to Dixon, or transferred to some other new school. Wedell writes that Mrs. Newcomb had considered establishing a Newcomb board of trustees to oversee the matters of the College but was dissuaded from doing so by Dixon. Perhaps Dixon worried over his own conflict of interest in relation to a separate Newcomb board, as well as the certainty of conflict between such a board and the Tulane Administrators. Perhaps Mrs. Newcomb recognized that her power rested in controlling how and when her money was spent. The thought of donating her entire fortune to the College before her death appears never to have entered her mind. As revealed in Dixon's account, Mrs. Newcomb gave, and then often reconsidered, her continuing gifts. Ultimately, she trusted Dixon and the board. From 1886 until the time of her death in 1901, she donated a total of thirty-one gifts in amounts as small as $341.00 and as large as $125,000.[88]

The essays by Wedell and Swift in this volume allow insight into both Mrs. Newcomb's reasons for keeping such questions at the forefront of her mind and her decision to leave the money entrusted to the Tulane Administrators.[89] Above all, she feared that her family would claim legal rights to her fortune, and she took many cautionary measures to keep that from happening. In a letter to her attorney, James McConnell, dated May 28, 1890, she wrote to explain "the principal reason" she found it again necessary to declare the city of New Orleans her legal domicile:

> From various reports that have reached me, as well as knowledge, I regret to have to say I am apprehensive that there are among my relations some who, without the shadow of legal right or cause, but actuated solely by mercenary motives, may attempt to thwart the execution and fulfillment of my intensions as expressed in my last will and testament. . . . I have asked your professional assistance and have been guided by it in all these matters, in order that my estate may be settled here [in New Orleans] by my Executors under your advice as their counsel . . . and thus the benevolent purposes I have in view will be neither frustrated nor delayed in their execution.[90]

Concerns about her family's "mercenary motives" likely contributed to Mrs. Newcomb's feelings of being "alone and unprotected," as Swift reports. She lived in a world ruled by men where a woman's control of her own money was a novel and rather unpopular idea, and where a widow with a near constant travel itinerary and a seeming preoccupation with her estate was seen as odd or eccentric. Yet, her idiosyncrasies could also be read as prescient. Her "neurotic" indecision about the placement of her money with Newcomb College or with its parent body, Tulane University, could just as easily be understood as a valid realization of how women's money was removed from their control and dispersed.

Similarly, her fears about an imminent battle over her estate proved correct when her relatives contested her will in 1901. By placing her money within a large university, and not in an independent women's college, she secured the support of the Administrators of the Tulane Educational Fund—comprised of some of the most prominent and influential men in the region—and the counsel of practiced attorneys to fight for the memorial for Sophie. Note that her attorney, James McConnell, was at the same time a member of the Tulane board while her two executors, Brandt Dixon and her cousin Joseph Hincks, were board employees—as president of Newcomb College and secretary-treasurer of the board, respectively. Tulane won the legal battle, and Sophie's college continued for more than a century.[91] In 1909, when the University was awarded the full legacy of her estate for the College, Newcomb emerged as a leader among women's colleges, and a college more secure than Tulane itself in many ways. Ironically, in 2006, the measures she took to ensure that her will would be "executed and fulfilled" . . . "without embarrassment or contention of any kind" again failed.[92] This time her descendents came forward to challenge the Administrators to uphold Mrs. Newcomb's bequest leaving her estate for "the present and future development of this department of the University known as the 'H. Sophie Newcomb Memorial College.'"[93] A five-year legal battle to prevent Tulane University from closing the College and transforming it into the H. Sophie Newcomb Memorial College *Institute* ended February 18, 2011, when the Louisiana Supreme Court refused to hear an appeal of a lower court ruling upholding Tulane's closure of the College in the aftermath of Hurricane Katrina.[94] The Institute's official name today is the Newcomb College Institute of Tulane University.

Continuing Contradictions

Overall, the early influences on the College have continued into the twenty-first century: the evocation of memory, the location in the mix of modernity and conservatism that New Orleans accommodated, and the perpetual economic recovery of the city continually shaped the lives of students at Newcomb. Accommodations were made for those students desirous of a rigorous academic experience *and* for those wanting something more genteel than useful. For both types of students, Newcomb offered a home in a welcoming environment. As scholar Leslie Miller-Bernal suggests in the title to her work on coordinate colleges, Newcomb's administrative configurations nurtured this duality of an experience both conservative and liberating.[95] The circumstances that repeatedly redefined the College were such that Newcomb women learned to stand up for their rights as members of the University, just as Mrs. Newcomb had done to ensure their educations. Johnston lived to see nine graduating classes, the success of the pottery program, and the emphasis on French, Spanish, and German in the curriculum for the women's college within Tulane. These various forces forged what Dixon called "the Newcomb spirit."

NOTES

1. William Preston Johnston to Dr. Robert A. Holland (board member), May 4, 1887, in Dixon Papers, Tulane University Archives, Howard-Tilton Memorial Library (hereafter cited as UAHT).

2. Tulane College, 1884–94, had been named previously the "Academic department" or "Academical Department" from 1878 (and earlier) to 1884. In 1894, Tulane College was renamed the "College of Arts & Sciences (A&S)," a name it would bear for nearly a century. The merger of the Newcomb and A&S faculties in 1987 brought about the renaming of the College to "Paul Tulane College" in 1993. With the 2005–6 restructuring of the University, Tulane College and Newcomb College were joined as "Newcomb-Tulane College" (John P. Dyer, *Tulane: The Biography of a University, 1834–1965* [New York: Harper and Row, 1966], 46nn., 78; *Tulane University of Louisiana Catalogue, 1889–90, Announcement for 1890–91,* "Tulane University. Historical Statement" [New Orleans: 1890], 5 [hereafter cited as *Catalogue,* followed by year], Newcomb Archives, Newcomb College Center for Research on Women [hereafter cited as NA NCCROW]; and "Paul Tulane College," http://docs.google.com/gview?a=v&q=cache:A-oPVYFyij8J:www .tulane.edu/~admincat/pdfcat/section7/paultulane_05.pdf+tulane+college+hist). Hereafter, the College will be referred to by its long-held name: A&S.

3. Dyer, *Tulane: The Biography of a University,* 16.

4. Ibid., 38, 44. The University of Louisiana was comprised of the departments of medicine and law, the preparatory department (high school), and the recently established academic department (ibid., 26nn. , 35, 46, 48–49).

5. 1890 U.S. Census, table 7, "School Enrollment, Census of 1890: Public Common School, by States and Territories," www2.census.gov/prod2/.

6. Emphasis added. See Dyer, *Tulane: The Biography of a University,* appendixes 1 and 2, 301–11.

7. Minutes, Board of Administrators, University of Louisiana, December 8, 1881, quoted in Samuel Lang, "History of Tulane University," manuscript, chap. 16, p. 7, UAHT.

8. Johnston's idea for separate colleges was being discussed in various forms across the nation (Reuben Gold Thwaites, "Coeducation," in *History of the University of Wisconsin,* chap. 6, www.library.wisc.edu/ etext/wireader/Thwaites/Chapter06.html).

9. Dyer, *Tulane: The Biography of a University,* 55.

10. Brandt V. B. Dixon, *A Brief History of H. Sophie Newcomb Memorial College, 1887–1919: A Personal Reminiscence* (New Orleans: Hauser Printing, 1928), 5, 11, 13.

11. Helen Lefkowitz Horowitz, *Alma Mater: Design and Experience in the Women's Colleges from Their Nineteenth-Century Beginnings to the 1930s* (New York: Knopf, 1984), 23–37.

12. Dixon, *Brief History,* 9.

13. The Mississippi Industrial Institute and College for the Education of White Girls of the State of Mississippi in the Arts and Sciences, chartered in 1884 and opened in 1885, preceded Newcomb as the first degree-granting college for women in the Gulf South.

14. Lamar Witlow Bridges, "A Study of the New Orleans *Daily Picayune* under Publisher Eliza Jane Poitevent Nicholson, 1876–1896" (PhD diss., Southern Illinois University, 1974); James Henry Harrison, *Pearl Rivers: Publisher of the Picayune* (New Orleans: Department of Journalism, Tulane University, 1932); Elsie Farr, *Pearl Rivers* (New Orleans: Times-Picayune Publishing, 1951); Martha Field, *Catharine Cole's Book* (Chicago: Way and Williams, 1897); Thomas Ewing Dabney, *One Hundred Great Years—The Story of the "Times Picayune" from Its Founding* (Baton Rouge: Louisiana State University Press, 1944); Catharine Cole Papers, NA NCCROW.

15. Miki Pfeffer, "Exhibiting Women: Sectional Confrontation and Reconciliation in the Woman's Department at the World's Exposition, New Orleans, 1884–85" (master's thesis, University of New Orleans, 2006), 28–29; Elizabeth Bisland, "The Woman's Club," *New Orleans Times-Democrat,* November 30, 1884; Catharine Cole, "Personal and General Notes," *New Orleans Daily Picayune,* January 16, 1885; Catharine Cole Papers, NA NCCROW.

16. Faculty and Staff Biographical Files, UAHT; Dyer, *Tulane: The Biography of a University,* 177.

17. Patricia Brady, "Mollie Moore Davis: A Literary Life," in *Louisiana Women Writers: New Essays and A Comprehensive Bibliography,* ed. Dorothy H. Brown and Barbara C. Ewell (Baton Rouge: Louisiana State University Press, 1992), 109.

18. Carmen Lindig, *The Path from the Parlor: Louisiana Women, 1879–1920* (Lafayette: Center for Louisiana Studies, University of Southwestern Louisiana, 1986), 36; Caroline Merrick, *Old Times in Dixieland: A Southern Matron's Memories* (New York: Grafton Press, 1901), 153.

19. Lindig, *Path from the Parlor,* 36, 47, 60–61.

20. Elizabeth Seymour Eschbach, *The Higher Education of Women in England and America, 1865–1920* (New York: Garland, 1993), 60–119, 136–64; Irene Harwarth, Mindi Maline, and Elizabeth DeBra, "Women's Colleges in the United States: History, Issues, and Challenges," www.2ed.gov/offices/OERI/PLLI/ webreprt.html.

21. Donald Clive Hardy, "The World's Industrial and Cotton Centennial Exposition" (master's thesis, Tulane University, 1964), 46; Pfeffer, "Exhibiting Women," 2.

22. Pfeffer explores this idea in detail in "Exhibiting Women."

23. Belle Kearney, *A Slaveholder's Daughter* (1900; repr., New York: Negro Universities Press, 1969), 107–8.

24. Pfeffer, "Exhibiting Women," 21, 34, 45–48.

25. "The Department of Woman's Work," *New Orleans Times-Democrat,* March 4, 1885.

26. Grace King, *Memories of a Southern Woman of Letters* (New York: Macmillan, 1932), 54.

27. Lindig, *Path from the Parlor,* 36, 47, 60–61; Suzanne Ormond and Mary E. Irvine, *Louisiana's Art Nouveau: The Crafts of the Newcomb Style* (Gretna, La.: Pelican Press, 1976), 21; Pfeffer, "Exhibiting Women," 58–59.

28. Ormond and Irvine, *Louisiana's Art Nouveau,* 10.

29. Katy Coyle, "Pottery and Petticoats," April, 1993, 10, manuscript, NA NCCROW. In 1885–86, the "Free Drawing" classes accommodated "men and youths" in five classes; teachers (male and female) in two classes; and women alone in one "Woman's Evening Decorative Art" class (*Catalogue, 1885–86:* 55–56).

30. *Catalogue, 1885–86:* 56–60; *Catalogue, 1886–87:* 70–81. See also Ormond and Irvine, *Louisiana's Art Nouveau;* and Poesch's essay in this volume.

31. Merrick, *Old Times in Dixieland,* 153.

32. *Catalogue, 1884–85,* "Historical Statement" (New Orleans, 1885), 6–8. This is the first catalogue of the Tulane University of Louisiana.

33. Anne Firor Scott, *The Southern Lady: From Pedestal to Politics, 1830–1930* (Chicago: University of Chicago Press, 1970), 97; Catherine Clinton, "Equally Their Due: The Education of the Planter Daughter in the New Republic," *Journal of the Early Republic* 2 (Spring 1982): 52–53; Christie Anne Farnham, *The Education of the Southern Belle: Higher Education and Student Socialization in the Antebellum South* (New York: New York University Press, 1994), 2–3, 7.

34. U.S. Census Bureau, Families and Living Arrangements—Historical Time Series: "Estimated Median Age at First Marriage, by Sex, 1890 to the Present," www.census.gov/population/socdemo/hh-fam/ms2.xls; Statistical Abstract of the United States: 2003, "No. HS-30 Marital Status of Women in the Civilian Labor Force: 1900–2002," www.census.gov/statab/hist/HS-30 .pdf; and "Marital Status of the Population by Sex: 1900–2002," www/census.gov/stabab/ hist/ HS-11.pdf ; vol. 11: *Report on the Mortality and Vital Statistics of the United States as Returned at the Tenth Census (June 1, 1880);* "Table VIII—Mortality in 50 Principal Cities, by Grand Groups, Age and Sex, Etc., Grand Group 4— New Orleans, LA," www.census.gov/prod/www/abs/decennial/1880.htm.

35. Newcomb Student Records, NA NCCROW.

36. Dixon, *Brief History,* 28. Students were required to pass entrance exams in English grammar, U.S. history, rhetoric and composition, English and American literature, geography, and arithmetic. The curriculum allowed for three programs: Classical; Scientific and Industrial; and Literary and Modern Languages (see the Tulane University catalogues, 1887–91; and Barbara Miller Solomon, *In the Company of Educated Women: A History of Women and Higher Education in America* [New Haven: Yale University Press, 1986], 22–23).

37. Alecia Long, *The Great Southern Babylon: Sex, Race, and Respectability in New Orleans, 1865–1920* (Baton Rouge: Louisiana State University Press, 2004); Bridget K. Meyer, "New Orleans Businesswomen of 1880–1883 and 1905–1908" (bachelor of arts thesis, Tulane University, 1983); Donald E. DeVore and Joseph Logsdon, *Crescent City Schools: Public Education in New Orleans, 1841–1991* (Lafayette: Center for Louisiana Studies, University of Southwestern Louisiana, 1991).

38. Katy Coyle, "The Founding of H. Sophie Newcomb College: An Experiment in Southern Higher Education for Women" (master's thesis, Tulane University, 1996), 56. See also Horowitz, *Alma Mater,* 42–55, 69–81.

39. McCandless, *The Past in the Present,* 30–35, 123. See also Gordon on Agnes Scott in this volume; Anna Heubeck Knipp and Thaddeus P. Thomas, *The History of Goucher College* (Baltimore: Goucher College, 1938); Albea Godbold, *The Church College of the Old South* (Durham, N.C.: Duke University Press, 1944); Frances Griffin, *Less Time for Meddling: A History of Salem Academy and College, 1772–1866* (Winston-Salem, N.C.: J. F. Blair, 1979); and Jonathan

Sarnoff, "White Women and Respectability in Antebellum New Orleans" (PhD diss., University of Southern Mississippi, 2003).

40. Dixon, *Brief History*, 25, 29.

41. Farnham, *The Education of the Southern Belle*, 2, 28–29, 30–31.

42. Scott, *The Southern Lady*, 111–14; Nina Silber, "Intemperate Men, Spiteful Women, and Jefferson Davis," in *Divided Houses: Gender and the Civil War*, ed. Silber and Catherine Clinton (New York: Oxford University Press, 1992), 283–305.

43. Henrietta Nicholls Garrett, memoir, manuscript, n.d., 22–23, 30, NA NCCROW.

44. Dixon, *Brief History*, 22–24.

45. Dyer, *Tulane: The Biography of a University*, 58.

46. "A Dixonless Newcomb? Impossible Is First Thought of Alumnae," clipping, Scrapbook SCR 020, 1919, NA NCCROW.

47. "A University College for Women," *New Orleans Daily Picayune*, July 11, 1887; "Newcomb College for Women," *New Orleans Daily Picayune*, October 13, 1887. See also Josephine Louise Newcomb Clipping Scrapbook, UAHT.

48. "A University College for Women."

49. "Maiden Bachelors of Art," *New Orleans Daily Picayune*, June 18, 1890.

50. Dixon, *Brief History*, 33.

51. Ibid., 13, 10; Josephine Louise Newcomb, quoted in *Brief on Behalf of Respondent Brandt V. B. Dixon*, 251, Dixon Papers, NA NCCROW.

52. JLN to Johnston, from early Lent, 1887, cited in court case *Brief on Behalf of Respondent*, 246; Dixon, *Brief History*, 88–89.

53. JLN to Johnston, January 14, 1896; Surrogate's Court, New York Supreme Court, Protest Records, Law Library, Tulane University, 244; JLN to the Administrators of the Tulane Educational Fund, January 11, 1896, as quoted by Dixon, *Brief History*, 13.

54. JLN to the Administrators of the Tulane Educational Fund, October 11, 1886, as quoted by Dixon, *Brief History*, 10.

55. Dixon, *Brief History*, 10, 95.

56. Horowitz, *Alma Mater*, xvi–xvii; Dixon, *Brief History*, 10.

57. Dyer, *Tulane: The Biography of a University*, 53; see also Sandra Moncrief, "The Mississippi Married Women's Property Act of 1839," *Mississippi History* 97, no. 2 (May 1985): 110–25.

58. Louise Schutz Boas, *Women's Education Begins: The Rise of Women's Colleges* (Norton, Mass.: Wheaton College Press, 1935), 217; Mabel Newcomer, *A Century of Higher Education for American Women* (New York: Harper and Brothers, 1959), 17.

59. Lillie Devereux Blake, *Woman's Place To-day: Four Lectures in Reply to the Lenten Lectures on "Woman" by the Rev. Morgan Dix, D.D., Rector of Trinity Church, New York* (New York: John W. Lovell, 1883); Morgan Dix, *Lectures on the Calling of a Christian Woman: and Her Training to Fulfill It, delivered during the season of Lent, A.D. 1883* (New York: D. Appleton, 1883); Rosa Keller, "Josephine Louise Newcomb," manuscript, 11–14, NA NCCROW.

60. Thomas Woody, *A History of Women's Education in the United States* (Lancaster, Pa.: Science Press, 1929), 184, 187; Newcomer, *A Century of Higher Education for American Women*, 60.

61. Woody, *A History of Women's Education in the United States*, 149.

62. Sophia Smith as quoted in Horowitz, *Alma Mater*, 70.

63. *Catalogue, 1886–87* (Newcomb Announcement for 1887–88): 83.

64. *Catalogue, 1888–89* (Newcomb Announcement for 1889–90): 79.

65. Dixon is quoted on this wish in Mary Caroline Crawford, *The College Girl in America and the Institutions Which Make Her What She Is* (Boston: L. C. Page, 1905).

66. Dixon, *Brief History*, 29.

67. Ibid., 42–45, 65, 132, 197-98.

68. Lydia Elizabeth Frotscher, "A Brief History of Sophie Newcomb College," Album, NAB 029, NA NCCROW; Dixon, *Brief History*, 29, 116–17, 132–33; *Bulletin of the Tulane University of Louisiana, the H. Sophie Newcomb Memorial College for Women, Announcement for 1918–1919*: 151.

69. *Catalogue, 1888–89* (Announcement for 1889–90): 79.

70. See *Catalogue* for the years given.

71. Dixon, *Brief History*, 144–49; Laura Saunders Landry, Oral History Interview with Susan C. Thompson, March 13, 1985.

72. Dixon, *Brief History*, 144–47.

73. Dyer, *Tulane: The Biography of a University*, 204–5.

74. See Newcomb Archives, Collective Biographical Files, teachers.

75. Emilie W. McVea, "Women's Colleges and the Southern Association," *Proceedings of the Association of Colleges and Secondary Schools of the Southern States* (1922): 108.

76. Dixon, *Brief History*, 34, 26; Dyer, *Tulane: The Biography of a University*, 91. Mrs. Newcomb also had objected to this particular neighborhood (see JLN to Johnston, January 14, 1887, Surrogate's Court, 244).

77. Al Rose, *Storyville: New Orleans: Being an Authentic, Illustrated Account of the Notorious Red-light District* (Tuscaloosa: University of Alabama Press, 1974), 102.

78. Dyer, *Tulane: The Biography of a University*, 91.

79. Horowitz, *Alma Mater*, 95–104. See also George P. Schmidt, *Douglass College: A History* (New Brunswick, N.J.: Rutgers University Press, 1968), 17–18.

80. Dixon, *Brief History*, 81–82; Dyer, *Tulane: The Biography of a University*, 92.

81. Dixon, *Brief History*, 92.

82. Ibid., 104, 128.

83. Ibid., 89, 92.

84. Ibid., 89, 92–93; Tulane University of Louisiana, The H. Sophie Newcomb Memorial College for Women, 1903–1904 (New Orleans: Published by the University, April, 1904), map n.p., http://tulane.edu/nccrow/newcomb-archives/history-of-newcomb-college.cfm.

85. Mildred Christian Oral History Interview with Florence Bass, April 21, 1986, NA NCCROW.

86. "The New Newcomb and the Old," *Newcomb Arcade* 10, no. 4 (June 1918): 292–95, NA NCCROW.

87. Newcomb Relief Unit Records, 1918–1922, NAB 030, NA NCCROW.

88. Dixon, *Brief History*, 195.

89. See also McConnell family papers, Box 40 1723–1962, Manuscripts Collection 156, Folder 7 and Box 41, Folder 4, Louisiana Research Collection, Howard-Tilton Memorial Library (hereafter cited as LaRC).

90. Josephine Louise Newcomb to Jas. McConnell, Esq., May 28, 1890, McConnell family papers, Box 44 Folder 5, LaRC.

91. *Catalogue, 1887–88*, "H. Sophie Newcomb Memorial College for Young Women," 65; "Board of Administrators," 3, NA NCCROW. The sixteen-member Board of Administrators

included two U.S. senators, a justice of the Louisiana Supreme Court, a physician, a minister, and at least two attorneys.

92. J. Newcomb to Jas. McConnell.

93. John Pope, "Newcomb Suit Continues as Women's College Merged with Tulane," *New Orleans Times-Picayune*, June 30, 2006; John Pope, "New Suit Filed over Newcomb Closure," *New Orleans Times-Picayune*, August 21, 2008. Quote from Dixon, *Brief History*, 17.

94. Katherine Mangan, "Tulane U. Wins Donor-Intent Lawsuit over Closing of Women's College," *Chronicle of Higher Education*, February 21, 2011.

95. Leslie Miller-Bernal, "Conservative Intent, Liberating Outcomes: The History of Co-ordinate Colleges for Women," in *Gender in Policy and Practice: Perspectives on Single Sex and Coeducational Schooling*, ed. Amanda Datnow and Lea Hubbard (New York: Routledge, 2002), 156–71.

1

FOUNDING NEWCOMB COLLEGE

MARSHA WEDELL

Tragedy, philanthropy, and educational vision converged auspiciously to bring forth the H. Sophie Newcomb Memorial College. In 1870, Josephine Newcomb's daughter and only surviving child, Harriott Sophie, died in New York, where mother and daughter had been living since the death of Sophie's father, Warren. Josephine and Warren Newcomb had lost a son at birth in 1853, then Warren died in 1866, at age fifty-two, in New York, followed by the devastating blow of Sophie's sudden death only four years later.[1] Within this brief four-year period, Mrs. Newcomb had lost the two people closest to her in life, and her grief was deep and nearly overwhelming. Not until the founding of Newcomb College in her daughter's memory would Josephine Newcomb again find focus and purpose in her life.

Josephine and Warren Newcomb had been married for twenty-one years before Warren died, during which time they had become extremely prosperous. They had met in Louisville, Kentucky, and married in New Orleans, places to which each had come for different reasons. Warren Newcomb had been born in Bernardston, Massachusetts, in 1814, one of twelve children of Harriott Wells and Dalton Newcomb, but he left the family farm with two older brothers to seek his fortune in the Kentucky country.[2] About 1840, Warren became a partner in the wholesale grocery firm H. D. Newcomb & Brothers. The firm prospered, and the Newcomb brothers became known as outstanding businessmen in the rising West, and their company considered the greatest commercial house in Kentucky.[3]

Josephine Le Monnier had been born in 1816, to Alexander Le Monnier, a French gentleman who had settled in Baltimore, and Mary Sophia Waters, from a genteel Baltimore family of English background.[4] Upon the death of her mother, Josephine Le Monnier moved from Baltimore to New Orleans in 1831 to live with her older sister and brother-in-law, Eleanor Anne (Ellen)

and William Henderson.[5] The Hendersons were in the habit of spending summers in Louisville in order to escape the steamy and unhealthful climate of
New Orleans. It was there that Josephine Le Monnier met the enterprising
young businessman Warren Newcomb, who made frequent buying trips to
New Orleans. Known as a dignified and cultivated gentleman, he enjoyed the
social amenities and had a wide circle of friends.[6] As fate would have it, each
had also become acquainted at that time with a native of Louisville, William
Preston Johnston, later president of Tulane University.

On December 15, 1845, Josephine Le Monnier and Warren Newcomb were
married; Josephine was twenty-nine years old and Warren was thirty-one. The
Newcombs continued to spend some of the winter months in New Orleans,
where Warren bought commodities to be shipped to Louisville, but by the
early 1850s they were dividing their time between Louisville, New York, and
Europe, where, in Paris, Mrs. Newcomb contracted and survived smallpox.[7]
Both of their children were born in New York; their surviving child, Harriott
Sophie, was born on July 29, 1855, and bore the name of each grandmother:
Sophia Le Monnier and Harriott Newcomb. Warren retired in 1863, at age
forty-nine. The Newcombs spent the better part of the next two years traveling in Europe, spending six months in Paris, where Sophie became proficient
in French. Warren Newcomb began to long again for some business activity
and established Warren Newcomb & Co. in New York, trading in cotton and
tobacco. He remained active in the business until his health failed in the
spring of 1866; he died in August of that year of liver disease.

Although the Newcombs lived in New York during the Civil War and Warren was from Massachusetts, their sympathies were said to lie with the South,
and their New York residence was known as a gathering place for those with
southern leanings.[8] Warren much admired General Robert E. Lee. Shortly before his death Warren donated ten thousand dollars to establish the Harriott
Sophie Newcomb Scholarship Fund at Washington College, where Lee was
president, and where William Preston Johnston was just beginning his teaching career.[9] A letter from Warren Newcomb accompanying the gift stated: "I
desire my subscription to the Washington College should be regarded as an
expression of sympathy for the severe trials, afflictions and hopes my Southern friends have sustained in what they consider a just and patriotic cause—it
will be sufficient reward to me to have the privilege of donating to my friends
a scholarship for each thousand dollars subscribed, to stand on the records of
the institution as a perpetual memorial to my only daughter, Harriott Sophie
Newcomb, to whom I have given the disposal of the scholarships."[10]

Washington College, later Washington and Lee University, was for young men only, and what ideas Warren Newcomb had concerning women's higher education is not known. The mention of his daughter, in whose honor the scholarships were given, connects her to the college in a very specific way, but there is nothing to indicate any suggestion on the Newcombs' part that they believed women students should be considered.[11] About 1872–73, Josephine Newcomb added to her husband's gift with a donation of $20,000 to Washington and Lee University for a library in memory of her husband. At her request, Professor William Preston Johnston was entrusted with supervising the erection of the new building.[12] Years later, when Johnston had become president of Tulane University, his acquaintance with Josephine Newcomb and the high regard she had for him would unquestionably facilitate her decision to fund a women's college at Tulane.[13]

Sophie's own education had been mainly by private tutors, although she had attended a girls' seminary in New York just before her father's death. Warren Newcomb's death brought deep sorrow to both mother and daughter, and the two were said never to have been away from each other for a single day.[14] Sophie again resumed her education at home, presumably to be closer to her mother, and became the focus of Josephine Newcomb's life. In 1867, Mrs. Newcomb took Sophie to Baltimore, where she studied at the Eclectic Institute and generally excelled, despite several periods of illness. The two returned to New York in September 1868, where Sophie again attended the seminary run by Miss De Janon and Miss H. B. Haines, the latter noting the girl's sweet manners and gentle way.[15] Sophie was a very affectionate child and often composed poems in which she expressed her love and devotion to her mother. In an essay entitled "What I Desire in the Future," Sophie wrote:

> First I would like my dear and only parent spared to me in health and strength until my education is finished, and as long afterwards as it shall please my Heavenly Father to spare her to me. Then I desire to be a comfort to her, and to reward her for all she has done for me through life.
>
> I should like sufficient means, with my labors, to relieve the poor and suffering, . . . and to give all in my power to the aged, and infirm and the needy. . . .
>
> I wish much to travel and visit countries and places that I have learned and studied about, but would like most of all to visit the Holy Land . . . and lastly, I do desire to be a perfect Christian.[16]

For several years, Mrs. Newcomb and Sophie made the Clifton House, Niagara Falls, their summer home, returning to New York in the fall. In 1870, Sophie was again being instructed by a private tutor at home, as Mrs. Newcomb was reluctant to allow the child to be away from her. On December 9, Sophie suddenly fell ill with diphtheria, and seven days later she is said to have murmured faintly, "Mama take me on your lap. Mama, how dark it is." Sophie Newcomb died that day, December 16, 1870.[17] Josephine Newcomb was overcome by grief and for the remainder of her life dressed in dark colors, her subsequent actions revolving around the memory of her daughter. Sixteen years later she settled upon the idea of endowing a college for women in New Orleans, ending a long and anxious search for the most appropriate and enduring monument to the memory of her beloved daughter.

Josephine Newcomb's wish for a memorial to her daughter dovetailed perfectly with President Johnston's desire to do something for women's higher education in New Orleans, and their two wishes were brought together by a mutual friend, Ida Slocomb Richardson of New Orleans. Ida Richardson was herself from a family known for its wealth and generosity. Her brother, Cuthbert Slocomb, was said to have organized a Confederate battery of artillery at his own expense.[18] Paul Tulane, Judah Touro and others who gave much of their wealth for the city's benefit were among her acquaintances. According to Grace King, Ida Richardson was "reputed to be the richest woman in the city; a title, however, that she despised."[19] Coincidence and fate played a hand as Ida Richardson, privy to the dreams of both Josephine Newcomb and Johnston, proved an effective intermediary. Josephine Newcomb had discussed her vision of a memorial to Sophie with Mrs. Richardson, asking advice in the matter. For a time, Mrs. Newcomb seemed intent on founding an asylum for Protestant orphans in New Orleans to be called "St. Sophie's Home." She was making liberal gifts to a number of charities, many of which benefited children, but she continued her quest for the consummate memorial.[20] Johnston had also been talking with Mrs. Richardson, a friend whose opinion he frequently sought, ostensibly to enlist her help in persuading someone to endow a college for women, but perhaps Johnston had the wealthy and sympathetic Mrs. Richardson herself in mind. Recalling a recent letter from her acquaintance Josephine Newcomb asking again for suggestions for a memorial to her daughter, Mrs. Richardson related these communications to Johnston, but told him she did not suppose Mrs. Newcomb financially able to endow a college.[21] Josephine Newcomb's frugal lifestyle and penchant for secrecy apparently kept even close friends unaware of the extent of her wealth. Johnston decided to take the chance, and with Mrs. Richardson's permission to cite her suggestion, he wrote to his friend in March 1886 with a proposal for a women's college. Josephine Newcomb's immediate reply asked Johnston to inform her of the full amount such a college would cost. She requested information "in every way complete for the purposes you desire . . . I will consider the whole matter with care, and due consideration." She insisted on total confidentiality "from all and everyone," the same request, she explained, that had been made of General Custis Lee when she gave the funds for Newcomb Hall in Lexington, Virginia.[22] From there, events moved quickly. A college for women had great appeal. Josephine Newcomb invited Johnston to meet with her in New York, at which time they discussed the proposal. She reportedly told him, "If you think $100,000 will start it I will give you a check for it."[23] On October 11, 1886, Josephine Louise Newcomb wrote a letter to the Administrators of the Tulane Educational Fund announcing her intention of endowing the H. Sophie Newcomb Memorial College:

> In pursuance of a long cherished design to establish an appropriate memorial of my beloved daughter, H. Sophie Newcomb, deceased, I have determined at the instance of my friend Col. William Preston Johnston, to entrust to your Board the execution of my design.
>
> Feeling a deep personal sympathy with the people of New Orleans and a strong desire to advance the cause of female education in Louisiana, and believing also that I shall find in the Board selected by the benevolent Paul Tulane the wisest and safest custodian of the fund I propose to give, I hereby donate to your Board the sum of $100,000, to be used in establishing the H. Sophie Newcomb Memorial College, in the Tulane University of Louisiana, for the higher education of white girls and young women.
>
> . . . But I do not mean in this my act of donation to impose upon you restrictions which will allow the intervention of any person or persons to control, regulate, or interfere with your disposition of this fund, which is committed fully and solely to your care and discretion, with entire confidence in your fidelity and wisdom.[24]

Josephine Newcomb, like Paul Tulane before her, sketched out the broad outline of her intentions and entrusted the Tulane Administrators to carry out the details of the project, a fact that would take on great significance in later years. In addition to her stipulation that the college was to be for "white girls and young women," she requested that "Christian worship" be observed daily and that the "education given should look to the practical side of life as well as to literary excellence."[25] She also asked later that Sophie's birth and death be remembered annually with an appropriate memorial service.

The pleasure she felt about her decision was clearly reflected in a letter to Johnston not long after Newcomb's opening: "Such a memorial I consider better than statues or monuments, to be a benefit to so many in giving knowledge, which is power, and can't be taken away from you except through affliction and death."[26] Clearly Josephine Newcomb's personal quest for a suitable memorial to her daughter was over; and through her gift for the College, her own life was renewed. As Mrs. Newcomb later explained: "Until I thought of this work I was a very wretched woman . . . but in this college my daughter lives again to me. She does not seem to be dead, but lives again in this college and in these girls."[27]

While $100,000 was a significant sum in 1886, it was clear to Johnston and the administrators that larger amounts would be necessary to permanently fund a college. Johnston and Brandt Dixon, Newcomb's first administrator, took great care in their dealings with Mrs. Newcomb, fully realizing that the future of the College was largely dependent on her continuing goodwill and generosity, the maintenance of which often proved difficult, requiring great tact and diplomacy. For the first two years of his Newcomb presidency, Dixon was instructed by Johnston to refrain from contacting Mrs. Newcomb for fear that she would interpret anything he might say as a plea for more money and become offended. Johnston, well acquainted with her sensitivities, particularly where money was concerned, handled all correspondence with Mrs. Newcomb in that early period.[28] As he pointed out, Mrs. Newcomb, with "characteristic prudence . . . limited her first donation to $100,000." Yet, once she had observed the direction the school had taken, "she added her gifts freely and generously to the original endowment, meeting every need as it arose in the development of the college."[29]

Newcomb College became the focus of Josephine Newcomb's life, and while she derived much satisfaction and happiness from her involvement with it, the relationship between the benefactress and the Administrators of the Tulane Educational Fund—from the College's founding until her death— was not always smooth. Gradually, she came to place the greatest trust in Dixon, to whom she confided her innermost hopes, and sometimes fears, about the future of the College. She appointed him one of two executors of her estate, the other being her cousin Joseph A. Hincks, the secretary-treasurer of the Tulane Board of Administrators. Ultimately, Mrs. Newcomb would give the College approximately $1 million during her lifetime. At her death in 1901, the remainder of her property was to be transferred to the College as well. However, receipt of her final bequest was delayed by an attempt on the part of Mrs. Newcomb's relatives to break the will, which developed into a prolonged legal battle in the New York courts that was settled in 1909.[30]

Josephine Newcomb had been left a wealthy widow. Soon after her husband's death, however, she found that others had designs on her inheritance. Mrs. Newcomb was a generous person, but also a suspicious one with a tendency toward secrecy. The dogged pursuit of her money by those on both sides of the family seems certainly to have influenced her behavior and, one may assume, was a factor in coloring her worldview and affecting her relationships.

Warren Newcomb's estate at the time of his death in 1866 was valued at $513,112; of this, $200,000 was left in trust for Sophie. The remainder was left to his wife, which included a separate trust providing a life income of $10,000 per year.[31] After Sophie's death, her trust reverted to her mother, and the valuation of the whole estate in January 1871 had reached $761,913.[32] Not long after Warren Newcomb's death, some of his relatives had sued unsuccessfully to break his will, leaving bitter feelings between themselves and Josephine Newcomb. This was a rather grim foreshadowing of the intense ill-will that would develop between Mrs. Newcomb and her own relatives, which also stemmed from their disappointment surrounding an unrealized inheritance. The strained and unpleasant relations Josephine Newcomb had with her sister's family undoubtedly heightened her sense of isolation in the years after her daughter's death. She spent a good deal of time and effort protecting her assets from what she considered to be a grasping and ungrateful family.

In the weeks following Sophie's death, Josephine Newcomb's deep grief led to concerns about her mental condition. Her sister, Ellen Henderson, godmother to Sophie, went to New York after the girl's death and convinced Josephine to visit the Hendersons in New Orleans. Ellen Henderson's husband had died a few months before Sophie, so perhaps there was some thought of mutual consolation. However, Josephine Newcomb's visit with her sister in early 1871 turned out to be the beginning of the family's estrangement from each other. Before leaving New York for New Orleans, Josephine Newcomb gave Ellen Henderson, who found herself in financial difficulties following her husband's death, $50,000, and made arrangements for each of Ellen's four children to be sent checks of $25,000, for a total of $150,000.[33] This amount represented nearly 20 percent of Josephine Newcomb's net worth, a sizable gift, and she intended it to be their sole inheritance, an idea the Hendersons refused to accept. Mrs. Newcomb had decided to begin her search for a memorial to Sophie and to devote her life and the remainder of her money to charity. The Hendersons, however, anticipated that Mrs. Newcomb's gifts to them were but the beginning of a larger inheritance, which they continued to pursue during Mrs. Newcomb's lifetime and even more relentlessly after her death.

It was during Josephine Newcomb's visit to her sister's home in January 1871 that the infamous "carriage ride" incident occurred, souring the Newcomb-Henderson relations permanently and marking the beginning of Mrs. Newcomb's suspicions that her relatives were attempting to place her in an asylum. While in a carriage one day in New Orleans with her sister and her sister's son-in-law, Michael McCarthy, they passed Hotel Dieu, a hospital that also housed the mentally unstable. Josephine Newcomb later claimed that the conversation had implied that her relatives intended to commit her there, an accusation the Hendersons would vehemently deny. Demanding that the carriage return to the Henderson home at once, Mrs. Newcomb departed the city in great haste, and before the arrival of the much-anticipated checks for her niece and nephews. She left instructions that the mail was not to be opened, but when the letter arrived, Ellen Henderson opened it and distributed the checks to her children.[34] It appears that Ellen was well aware of her sister's intention to withhold her gift to Henderson's four children, and in subsequent letters and conversations with friends, Mrs. Newcomb left no doubt that that had been her intention. She was disappointed in the Hendersons and very angry at her sister. Subsequent attempts by the Hendersons at reconciliation failed.[35] After 1873, there was no direct communication between Mrs. Newcomb and the Henderson family. It must have been very clear that she did not intend to leave them any more money. When Ellen Henderson died in 1880, Josephine Newcomb's friend and financial advisor wrote: "She has gone to her final account where she must give account for all her base treatment to you. . . . Her ability to injure you is ended."[36]

Mrs. Newcomb remained firm in her belief that her relatives were ill-intentioned toward her and wanted to have her committed to an institution in order to gain control of her money, an idea that increasingly haunted her. She clipped articles from newspapers reporting incidents in which sane people were locked away in asylums by relatives or acquaintances with designs on the person's money, pointing out to her own friends how she herself had only narrowly escaped such a fate.[37] Her fears were no doubt intensified when some years after the "carriage ride" incident, Johnston told her that an acquaintance of his, Charles O'Connor, a New York lawyer, had been approached by H. Victor Newcomb and some of her Henderson nephews.[38] Johnston reported, in an account the Hendersons would later deny, that O'Connor was asked to initiate legal proceedings to have Mrs. Newcomb declared insane and incapable of managing her affairs, which O'Connor refused to do. Mrs. Newcomb regarded this as confirmation of her suspicions and low opinion of her relatives.[39]

Josephine Newcomb worried a great deal over the ultimate disposition of her assets, which, by 1895, she had decided to leave to Newcomb College. A will made that year left substantially all of her property to the College, but she fully expected her will to be challenged at her death and constantly worried that her relatives might succeed in blocking her intent. She consulted James McConnell, a New Orleans lawyer and member of the Tulane board, in whom she had confidence and trust, and in 1898, she executed a new will in New Orleans. This will, written in her own hand, was suggested by McConnell, who advised that a will in this holographic form "can never be successfully assailed and the disposition of which she will not be required to make known to anyone."[40] It was also at McConnell's suggestion that Mrs. Newcomb left her property directly to the Administrators of the Tulane Educational Fund with the tacit understanding that the sole use was to be for the benefit of Newcomb College. She expressed her "implicit confidence that the Administrators of the Tulane Educational Fund will continue to use and apply the benefactions and property I have bestowed and may give, for the present and future development of this department of the University known as the 'H. Sophie Newcomb Memorial College' which engrosses my thoughts and purposes, and is endeared to me by such hallowed associations."[41]

This was an important change from her prior will of 1895, in which her assets had been left in a trust specifically "for the benefit of the H. Sophie Newcomb Memorial College" under the direction of the Tulane Administrators.[42] The last will, as was the case with her original donation establishing Newcomb College, entrusted the Tulane board with complete control of all assets to be used at their discretion for Newcomb's benefit. In a memorandum to the Tulane board, Mr. McConnell outlined the assurances he had given to Mrs. Newcomb, explaining that he was "happy to be able to say that I dissuaded her from this [restriction], assuring her as I did that the Board of Administrators of the Tulane Educational Fund would devote the property bequeathed by her to them entirely to the benefit and development of the H. Sophie Newcomb Memorial College . . . and that she could rely upon my assurance in that respect; and I now and here repeat to this Board this statement and emphasize the assurance so given by me to Mrs. Newcomb in order that it may not be forgotten."[43]

However, McConnell made his memo known only to three board members, Robert Walmsley, Joseph C. Morris, and Joseph A. Hincks, and not to the entire board as he had originally intended. No doubt McConnell believed the board would act in Newcomb's best interests, but he clearly recognized the importance of complete control of the funds—which he made sure was given to the board without any encumbrances or caveats—and decided to keep knowledge of his role in effecting this confined to a small group of board members. Mrs. Newcomb's estate was enormously important to the future of the College, and McConnell was all too aware of her unpredictable temperament, as well as the play of uncertainties. He had been, for example, Paul Tulane's New Orleans lawyer and had drafted the codicil to Mr. Tulane's will that left substantial property to Tulane University. But when Tulane died in 1887, the will was never found, and the University received nothing from his estate. It was a heavy blow, a deep disappointment to the board that remained very fresh in their memories.[44] This unhappy incident for Tulane may well have influenced McConnell's thinking, impressing upon him the necessity of doing everything possible to assure that the Newcomb assets were securely under the control of the University.

At the time of writing her last will, Mrs. Newcomb's main concern and focus were her relatives, and her intention to protect her estate from them. By 1900, however, she was experiencing serious doubts about whether the Tulane board, to whom she had entrusted her funds, would comply exactly with her wishes. Age was taking its toll on the board, and several of the original administrators who had died or retired were replaced by men whom Josephine Newcomb did not know and who she felt did not heed her wishes. In 1899, Johnston died, and Mrs. Newcomb was indignant when Dixon—the man she most trusted and her choice as Johnston's successor—was passed over by the Board of Administrators. Throughout the summer of 1900, Mrs. Newcomb and her companion and confidant of many years, F. Walter Callender, corresponded with Dixon recommending that Newcomb College be separated from Tulane and have its own board, which Mrs. Newcomb would appoint.[45] "Vassar, Smith, Wellesley and other colleges are distinct corporations, why shouldn't Newcomb be the same?" Callender asked.[46] The idea of a separate charter had been germinating in Mrs. Newcomb's mind for several years. She had become uneasy about Newcomb's relationship to Tulane when, in the early 1890s, local politicians attacked Tulane as a rich man's school while other groups protested Tulane's tax-free status, and a resolution was introduced to annul the University's charter in the state legislature.[47] Further, as Tulane struggled with financial difficulties, Mrs. Newcomb became increasingly concerned about the possibility of Newcomb funds being diverted for general university use, in spite of past assurances from the Board of Administrators that this would never happen. In 1897, Mrs. Newcomb established a special endowment fund with Dixon as sole trustee. The special fund, yielding some $15,000 per year, was set up to cover Newcomb's operating deficits, and Mrs. Newcomb had insisted that it be kept separate, as well as secret, from the Tulane board. Dixon, however, managed to persuade her to include two Tulane board members as joint trustees with him, her friend Joseph C. Morris, and her cousin Joseph A. Hincks.[48]

Where Mrs. Newcomb's mistrust of the Tulane board could lead worried Dixon, his greatest fear was that she might withdraw further support from the College. He had managed to soothe her concerns in the past, but the mercurial benefactress had become obsessed by the idea of her funds being diverted from the exclusive use of Newcomb College. She also expressed concern that Johnston's successor and new president of Tulane, Edwin A. Alderman, might attempt to dictate to Newcomb. By the summer of 1900, she was considering a new will and wrote to Dixon, much to his distress, requesting that he ask the Tulane Board of Administrators to return to her all the funds and property she had already given. She proposed that these funds should be combined with the remainder of her estate in a trust for the benefit of Newcomb, with Dixon and her New York financial advisor, Pomroy Brothers, as sole trustees.[49]

Dixon placed this crisis before the board members present in the city that summer. He then made the trek to Richfield Springs, New York, where Mrs. Newcomb was spending the summer, to explain the position of the

University. The opinion of the board was that Mrs. Newcomb had made her gift to the people of the state, and thus the funds had passed into the realm of the public trust and could not be returned, except perhaps by legislative action, and even this was doubtful.[50]

Subsequent meetings with Josephine Newcomb and Callender required all the skills of a trained diplomat, as the future of the College hung in the balance. Mrs. Newcomb had one last bombshell for the beleaguered Dixon when she suggested that the board could keep what she had already given them, and she and Dixon could build a new college at Thomasville, Georgia, a place she had visited through the years. Mrs. Newcomb had already made inquiries there and expressed confidence that sufficient gifts of land and other advantages promised in Thomasville would offset that left behind in New Orleans. Dixon saw thirteen years of pioneering work passing before him, and that at a time when he felt the attitude in New Orleans toward a college for women was about to turn an important corner. All this was carefully spelled out to Mrs. Newcomb and Callender, but Dixon struck a chord deep within Mrs. Newcomb's heart when he argued that to abandon the college in New Orleans would be tantamount to "renouncing the love and esteem which was growing stronger year by year for the name of Mrs. Newcomb and Sophie."[51] The veneration of Sophie's name carried the day, and the Thomasville idea was dropped, but Mrs. Newcomb made one last attempt to circumvent the Tulane Board of Administrators.

Shortly after Dixon's return to New Orleans from Richfield Springs, he received a deed transferring Mrs. Newcomb's entire estate to him. A letter from her New York lawyer accompanied the deed, explaining that this gave Dixon complete power to draw upon both the principal and income, subject only to a modest amount necessary for Mrs. Newcomb's living expenses. Again Dixon found himself caught in the precarious middle ground between Mrs. Newcomb and the board. Above all, he wanted to secure the financial position of the College, but acceptance of such an arrangement would, he felt, amount to "something like treason to the board of administrators," who, he believed, "were earnestly intending to abide by their promise to preserve the Newcomb fund for the sole use of the College."[52] Again Dixon's diplomacy prevailed, and Mrs. Newcomb acquiesced in his refusal and left her will intact.

Illness prevented Josephine Newcomb's return to New Orleans in the fall of 1900. She stopped at the home of a friend in New York, where she remained until her death on April 7, 1901, Easter Sunday; she was eighty-five years old. Mrs. Newcomb was buried in Green-Wood Cemetery in Brooklyn, New York, where her husband and children had preceded her.[53]

Conflict concerning her money, however, was far from over; in fact, a new and bitter phase was just beginning. As expected, Mrs. Newcomb's relatives challenged her wishes and shortly after her death initiated a lawsuit to revoke and annul her will; a pitched battle ensued in the courts of New York.[54] The stakes were high, as Newcomb College was to receive some $2.6 million from the estate, an amount comparable to almost $70 million today.[55]

In July 1902, the Surrogate's Court of the County of New York appointed a referee, Robert E. Deyo, to hear evidence in the case. Several years of testimony and taking depositions ensued. The referee's report issued in March 1905 dismissed the plaintiff's claim for revocation of Mrs. Newcomb's will, and the Surrogate's Court ruled accordingly in January 1906. The Hendersons persisted, however, and the case went through two appeals. Finally, in April 1908, the court of appeals upheld the decisions in favor of Newcomb College.

An intensely private person, Mrs. Newcomb would surely have recoiled at the public airing of her life. The testimony took several bizarre turns as the Hendersons attempted to depict Mrs. Newcomb as a woman subject to "insane delusions" who "heard noises" and attended séances where she had conversations with her father and Sophie; they also testified that she had even been observed "jumping over the bedroom chairs one after another in rapid succession . . . tho [sic] she was not in the habit of taking any exercise whatever."[56]

James McConnell, the lead lawyer for the estate of Mrs. Newcomb, along with the estate's New York counsel, George Canfield, countered with a stream of witnesses and affidavits attesting to Mrs. Newcomb's rationality, generosity, and competence, with the court referee finally concluding that the mass of lay and expert testimony had left no doubt "that Mrs. Newcomb to the last was a woman of sound and vigorous mentality."[57] McConnell admitted to especially relishing the questioning of one of the plaintiffs as to how he could account for the remarkable increase in Mrs. Newcomb's assets over the years if she had been, in fact, insane?[58] The question remains as to who was responsible for the remarkable growth of Mrs. Newcomb's assets from the time of her husband's death in 1866 to her own death in 1901. Some believe that while Mrs. Newcomb was certainly frugal and quite meticulous where finances were concerned, it was not she, but the New York firm of Pomroy Brothers, who made the actual investment decisions that accounted for the impressive growth of her assets and funded her giving.[59] Others believe that Mrs. Newcomb participated as fully in the administration and management of her funds as she did in the affairs of the College, and that she herself had excellent business judgment and abilities.[60]

Unfortunately, contentiousness also plagued the aftermath of the "Newcomb Will Case," as the litigation became popularly called. Bitter controversy erupted within the Board of Administrators of Tulane and in the city of New Orleans over the amount of the legal fees involved. After many consultations with law firms in New York, McConnell and Canfield suggested a fee of $225,000–$250,000 to be divided between them. The New Orleans press declared the fee "grossly extortionate," and one board member was reported to have asked how the board could ever face the public and ask for money after paying such a fee?[61] Dixon expressed deep concern that "people of standing in the city" had suggested impropriety in the employment of a board member in the University's legal affairs, not to mention the misunderstanding among many in their belief that the whole matter of Mrs. Newcomb's will should have been settled in New Orleans instead of the courts of New York.[62] To complicate matters, only a few years before this dispute, the president of the Administrators of the Tulane Educational Fund, Judge Charles E. Fenner, had been at the center of a ferocious public controversy in which he was accused of using his board position for personal financial benefit. While Judge Fenner was ultimately shown to be innocent of any wrongdoing, he resigned his position on the Tulane board in order to protect the University from any potential embarrassment.[63] Dixon feared that the Newcomb matter, coming so closely on the heels of the Judge Fenner controversy, could escalate into a major public relations fiasco and prove harmful to the College. Thus a committee of the Board of Administrators was formed to deal with the issue of the disputed legal fees that resulted in a friendly suit by McConnell and Canfield against the board for payment. By this strategy, the board felt the matter was taken out of its hands and settled by a disinterested party—in this instance, by a court referee.[64] The *New Orleans Times-Democrat* printed an account of the whole issue, explaining that McConnell had been appointed counsel for the executors in accordance with Mrs. Newcomb's wishes and that the Board of Administrators had nothing to do with his selection.[65] A newspaper in Donaldsonville, Louisiana, chided the New Orleans press for not getting all the facts: "In the particular case it is entirely conceivable that the largest sum so far mentioned might be exceedingly moderate compensation for the services actually rendered."[66]

Ultimately, Canfield accepted $100,000 and McConnell $75,000 plus expenses, with the court referee characterizing their performances in the case as "a really signal professional achievement meriting a high standard of compensation."[67] Thus, at last, disputes over Mrs. Newcomb's estate were laid to rest, or so it appeared. Newcomb College had indeed received its inheritance as intended by Mrs. Newcomb, and the last vestiges of the troubled strands her money had spawned seemed to be settled. But Mrs. Newcomb's fears about her wishes being honored by the Tulane board seemed, almost eerily, to foreshadow the future.

In the ensuing decades, controversy within the University community concerning Mrs. Newcomb's intent and the use of her endowment would become the source of acrimonious debate on a number of occasions. There would be those in 1987—a century after the opening of Newcomb College and the year that bitter controversy between the College and the University administration reached an apex—who would contend that the University's reorganization of the faculties of Newcomb College and Arts & Sciences as the Faculty of the Liberal Arts and Sciences did indeed ignore and subvert the founder's intent. Perhaps the Newcomb alumnae, the self-described "daughters" of the founder who led the opposition to the changes, felt they were speaking on behalf of Mrs. Newcomb herself. Many continue to feel so today.

While Josephine Newcomb had been neither a social reformer nor an educational visionary, in her own way she had chosen well. She had survived personal tragedies and conquered grief, leaving at her death a women's college, the first of its kind, generously endowed and offering young women opportunities that death had denied her own daughter. Warren Newcomb would surely have been well satisfied with his wife's judicious use of his fortune; he could hardly have done better. His own Harriott Sophie Newcomb Scholarship Fund at Washington College had, in a way, evolved—part tragedy, part triumph—into the H. Sophie Newcomb Memorial College of Tulane University.

NOTES

1. In re Newcomb's Estate, 192 N.Y. 238, 84 N.E. 950 (N.Y. 1908); Newcomb Case, N.Y. Supreme Court, Appellate Division, Record on Appeal, vol. 1, 46-47 (among bound volumes of James McConnell), Special Collections, Tulane University Law Library.

2. "Newcomb Family File," University Archives, Howard-Tilton Memorial Library, Tulane University (hereafter cited as UAHT).

3. Bethuel Merritt Newcomb, *Andrew Newcomb and His Descendants* (New Haven, Conn.: privately printed for the author by Tuttle, Morehouse and Taylor, 1923), 493; "Brief on Behalf of Respondent Brandt V. B. Dixon," New York Supreme Court, Appellate Division, First Department, 124–25, Brandt Van Blarcom Dixon Papers, 1888–1941, Newcomb Archives, Newcomb College Center for Research on Women (hereafter cited as Dixon Papers, NA NCCROW); In Newcomb's Estate, 84 N.E. 950 (N.Y. 1908); Newcomb Case, vol. 1, 32–34; John P. Dyer, *Tulane: The Biography of a University, 1834–1965* (New York: Harper and Row, 1966), 53–54.

4. "Opinion of Robert E. Deyo, Referee," Surrogate's Court, County of New York, "In the Matter of an Application for the Revocation of Ancillary Letters Testamentary Granted in the Matter of the Estate of Josephine Louise Newcomb, Deceased," 6, Dixon Papers, NA NCCROW.

5. Ibid., 6–7.

6. Samuel Lang, "History of Tulane University," chap. 17, manuscript, UAHT.

7. Clipping, *New Orleans Times-Democrat*, April 11, 1901, Scrapbook, Mrs. Warren Newcomb, UAHT

8. Ibid.

9. Ten thousand dollars for the cost of goods and services in 1866 would be the current equivalent of $142,000 (see Samuel H. Williamson, "Five Ways to Compute the Relative Value of a U.S. Dollar Amount, 1790 to present," MeasuringWorth.Com, 2011, www.measuringworth.com). Dollar-value translations are based on the MeasuringWorth.Com Consumer Price Index calculations.

10. Bethuel Merritt Newcomb, *Andrew Newcomb and His Descendants*, 274.

11. Washington and Lee University did not admit its first female undergraduates until 1985.

12. "Opinion of Robert E. Deyo, Referee," 49. The referee dates the building of the Newcomb Library to "about 1872 or 1873" (Dixon Papers, NA NCCROW). However, Dyer dates the building to ten years later, 1882, as does Washington and Lee University at http://ir.wlu.edu/factbook/AboutW&L/history/chronology.htm.

13. Johnston dedicated his second book of poems, *Pictures of the Patriarchy*, "To Mrs. Josephine Newcomb[.] This little book of verse is dedicated as the memorial of an ancient friendship and of her beneficence and wisdom shown in gifts for the higher education of the women of New Orleans" *(New Orleans: F. F. Hansell & Bro., 1895)*.

14. "In Memoriam: Harriott Sophie Newcomb," n.p., n.d., Louisiana Collection, Tulane University Library.

15. Ibid.

16. Ibid.

17. Ibid.

18. Grace King, *Memories of a Southern Woman of Letters* (New York: Macmillan, 1932), 330.

19. Ibid.

20. Josephine Newcomb founded a school for poor girls in Charleston, South Carolina, and gave $20,000 to the Confederate Home there. She also gave to a school for the deaf in New York City and endowed a bed in the Eye, Ear, Nose and Throat Hospital in New York in memory of Sophie. She looked to the South as the location for her "major work" for Sophie, as the Newcomb fortune had its origin in southern commerce. She was particularly fond of New

Orleans (see Dyer, *Tulane: The Biography of a University,* 55). In Newcomb's Estate, 84 N.E. 950 (N.Y. 1908); Newcomb Case, vol. 3, 1048, 1063; Law Library, Tulane University; "Opinion of Robert E. Deyo, Referee," Dixon Brief, 49, Dixon Papers, NA NCCROW.

21. Dyer, *Tulane: The Biography of a University,* 75–76; King, *Memories of a Southern Woman of Letters,* 330; Ida Richardson to Brandt Dixon, June 21, 1890, Dixon Papers, NA NCCROW.

22. Josephine Louise Newcomb to Col. Johnston, Letter, dated "8th day in Lent, 1886," UATU.

23. "Opinion of Robert E. Deyo, Referee," 52. Measured by the Consumer Price Index, $100,000 in 1886 would be the approximate equivalent of $2,390,000 in 2010 (Measuring Worth.Com, 2011).

24. Minutes, Administrators of the Tulane Educational Fund, November 9, 1886, 266, UAHT.

25. Ibid.

26. Quoted in "Brief on Behalf of Respondent Brandt V. B. Dixon," 251, Dixon Papers, NA NCCROW.

27. Clipping, "Opinion in Will Case," *New Orleans Times-Democrat,* May 26, 1908, 5, Dixon Papers, NA NCCROW.

28. Brandt V. B. Dixon, *A Brief History of H. Sophie Newcomb Memorial College, 1887–1919* (New Orleans: Hauser Printing, 1928), 36–37.

29. Edwin Fay, ed., *The History of Education in Louisiana* (Washington, D.C.: Government Printing Office, 1898), 221.

30. Dixon, *Brief History,* 195. Her total gift was $3,626,551.68.

31. The comparable current dollar amounts follow: Warren Newcomb's estate of $513,112 in 1866 would be roughly equivalent to $7.27 million; Sophie's trust of $200,000 approximately $2.83 million; and a $10,000 per year income approximately $142,000 annually. The value of Warren Newcomb's 1871 estate is comparable to approximately $14 million. (Measuring Worth.Com, 2011).

32. In Newcomb's Estate, 84 N.E. 950 (N.Y. 1908); In re Newcomb's Estate; Newcomb Case, vol. 3, 1042.

33. Current comparable dollar amounts for Mrs. Newcomb's 1871 gifts would be: $50,000 = $921,000; $25,000 = $460,000 (Measuring Worth.Com, 2011). Ellen Henderson's four children were: William Henderson, Warren Newcomb Henderson, Howard Henderson, and Victorine Henderson McCarthy (wife of Michael McCarthy). On the tangled relationship between Mrs. Newcomb and her sister's family, see "Opinion of Robert E. Deyo, Referee," 38–40, Dixon Papers, NA NCCROW.

34. One of Ellen Henderson's sons resided in Louisville at the time, and his check was sent directly there.

35. "Opinion of Robert E. Deyo, Referee," 22–27; In Newcomb's Estate, 84 N.E. 950 (N.Y. 1908); In re Newcomb's Estate; Newcomb Case, vol. 3, 1042.

36. A. H. Pomroy to Josephine L. Newcomb, August 3, 1880; In re Newcomb's Estate; Newcomb Case, vol. 3, 1181–82.

37. In re Newcomb's Estate; Newcomb Case, vol. 3, 1038, 1065–66; see also Susan Wittig, "Reflections of Sorrow and Hope." *Newcomb News* 5, no. 11 (1981): 2–11, NA NCCROW.

38. H. Victor Newcomb was the son of Horatio Dalton Newcomb, Warren's brother. Maury Klein, "The Strategy of Southern Railroads," *American Historical Review* 73, no. 4 (April 1968):1058–59, www.jstor.org/view/00028762/di951355/95p00045/0.

39. See "Opinion of Robert E. Deyo, Referee," 27.

40. Ibid., 69–70.

41. Josephine Louise Newcomb's will executed in New Orleans on May 12, 1898, in Dixon, *Brief History,* 17

42. Memo, James McConnell to Tulane Board of Administrators, McConnell family papers, 1723–1962, Manuscripts Collection, Howard-Tilton Memorial Library, Tulane University, 70118 (hereafter cited as McConnell Papers, LaRC).

43. Ibid.

44. Dyer, *Tulane: The Biography of a University,* 47, 60–63.

45. Concerning her philanthropy, he wrote: "The noble soul of Mrs. Newcomb is a blessing to our times, not only as fact but also by example. She has done more than she realizes" (F. W. Callender to Brandt Dixon, September 19, 1890, Dixon Letters, UAHT). Callender himself made several gifts to Newcomb College, notably marble busts of Warren, Josephine, and Sophie, on exhibit at NA NCCROW.

46. F. Walter Callender to Brandt Dixon, July 10, 1900, Dixon Letters, 1887–1901, UAHT.

47. Dyer, *Tulane: The Biography of a University,* 86–89.

48. Dixon, *Brief History,* 103–4.

49. Ibid., 110–12.

50. Ibid.

51. Ibid., 112.

52. Ibid., 112–13.

53. In re Newcomb's Estate; Newcomb Case, vol. 1, 21, 44–45, 47.

54. The Hendersons claimed that Josephine Newcomb was a resident of New York and therefore had died without a will; that she was not of sound mind; and that there was a conspiracy on the part of Tulane Administrators, who unduly influenced her decision. A transcript of the trial is located in the Law Library of Tulane University.

55. There was also an attempt on the part of some relatives of Warren Newcomb to claim the trust he had left to Josephine Newcomb, from which she had been receiving a life income. The claim was denied (see McConnell Papers, Box 16, Folders 10 and 12, LaRC).

56. In re Newcomb's Estate; Newcomb Case, vol. 2, 300–305, 315, 333.

57. "Opinion of Robert E. Deyo, Referee," 47.

58. James McConnell to Charles E. Fenner, February 20, 1903, McConnell Papers, Box 16, Folder 1, LaRC.

59. A. H. Pomroy was a trusted friend of Josephine Newcomb. He died in 1881, and his son, William, and nephew, Henry, continued the firm, with Henry becoming Mrs. Newcomb's main advisor.

60. "Opinion of Robert E. Deyo, Referee."

61. Clipping, *New Orleans Item,* November 7, 1908, McConnell Papers, Box 16, Folder 8, LaRC.

62. Brandt Dixon to James McConnell, November 6, 1906, McConnell Papers, Box 16, Folder 4, LaRC.

63. Dyer, *Tulane: The Biography of a University,* 123–25.

64. Joseph Hincks Jr. to George Canfield, October 28, 1908, McConnell Papers, Box 16, Folder 6, LaRC.

65. Clipping, *New Orleans Times-Democrat,* November 20, 1908, McConnell Papers, Box 16, Folder 8, LaRC.

66. Clipping, *Donaldsonville (La.) Chief,* November 14, 1908, McConnell Papers, Box 16, Folder 8, LaRC.

67. Edward M. Shepard to H. B. Walmsley, May 23, 1911, McConnell Papers, Box 16, Folder 10, LaRC.

2

"BEING ENTIRELY ALONE & UNPROTECTED"

Mrs. Newcomb in Letters

HARRIET SWIFT

L ittle is known about the woman named Josephine Louise Le Monnier Newcomb. College and university lore portrays her as eccentric and difficult. University historian John Dyer introduces readers to Josephine Newcomb through her letter of donation to the Administrators of the Tulane Educational Fund. He then dismisses her generosity as "sentimental" and writes: "Revealed in this letter is the story of a precocious and sickly child and of the pathetic, overprotective attachment of the mother for that child. It is the story of a wispy, lonely little woman who combined in one mind and personality the astute business sense of a Hetty Green and the sentimental, ethereal qualities of an Elizabeth Barrett Browning."[1] Tulane University president William Preston Johnston initially advised Newcomb's president, Brandt Dixon, to direct all correspondence with Mrs. Newcomb through him. Otherwise, "however carefully the letter might be worded, she would possibly look upon it as a plea for more money, and somehow take offense."[2]

Dixon eventually met and corresponded with Mrs. Newcomb and, over a ten-year period, became one of her most trusted advisors. His straightforward description of Mrs. Newcomb offers a view of a complex woman: a woman possessing wit, intelligence, generosity, and great resolve who was, at the same time, frail, frugal, and apprehensive.

In stature, Mrs. Newcomb was somewhat below the average height, and quite slender. For many years her health was most uncertain, but such was her energy and force of character that it was difficult to realize how ill she often was. Her memory of people and of facts, her ability to quote what she had heard or read, her wit and ready repartee gave constant surprise and pleasure to those

44

of us who knew her well, but with strangers she was most reserved. Like many elderly people, she had acquired certain peculiarities of thought and practice easily misunderstood. . . . It was her disposition to be quite exacting in little things, but she was most generous and sympathetic in affairs of greater moment. She dressed in the simplest manner, spent dollars and dimes most carefully, but, when convinced of a genuine need with which she sympathized, gave away checks freely. Mrs. Newcomb was a timid woman, careful not to intrude on any occasion.[3]

More recently, as the study of women's lives emerged as a serious field of inquiry, interest in Mrs. Newcomb's life beyond that revealed in these sparse accounts and College lore took on scholarly importance. Susan Wittig, Newcomb College dean from 1979 to 1981, examined Mrs. Newcomb's personal library for its "insight into the life and the ideas and the personal hopes of the woman who owned it."[4] Rosa Keller (NC 1932), New Orleans philanthropist and voice of social justice, explored University and College archival collections in search of evidence about Mrs. Newcomb's financial acuity and beneficence. "There is quite a bit more of mystery than of history in her biography," Keller wrote. "If she kept diaries, none have come down to us. Her letters could illuminate Mrs. Newcomb for us, but these, too, are nowhere to be found."[5]

Quite serendipitously, however, letters written by Mrs. Newcomb have been found. While researching the family of Gustavus Schmidt (1795–1877) during 2002,[6] I discovered among a collection of some 1,274 items, many written in French, an entry in the finding aid for Box 2, Folder 15: "1876, July 11, Charles Schmidt, New Orleans, to Mrs. Warren Newcomb, New York." While the Schmidt collection focuses mainly on Gustavus's work as an attorney in early Louisiana, "hidden" are five letters between his son Charles Schmidt (1832–1891), Josephine Louise Newcomb, and Mrs. Newcomb's second cousin Léda Louise Hincks (1835–1908), who married Charles in 1869.[7]

Similarly, a letter in the James McConnell Papers is addressed to Tulane University president "Col Wm. P. Johnston" from "Jo L. Newcomb." James McConnell served as an Administrator of the Tulane Educational Fund from 1882 until the time of his death in 1914, and also as Mrs. Newcomb's personal attorney. Among the documents in the McConnell collection are materials used by McConnell to thwart the legal challenge to Mrs. Newcomb's will brought about by her relatives.[8]

This essay examines several of these letters to better understand Mrs. Newcomb as a friend, relative, and neighbor. In contrast to the formality of her letters addressed to the Tulane Administrators, her letters to family and friends are often quite chatty and punctuated with abbreviations and underlining for emphasis. Her letters illuminate her intellect, reveal her sensitivity to the joys and sorrow in the lives of others, and unapologetically express her own sadness and fears.

The first letter in the Schmidt collection was written to "Mrs. Newcomb" by Charles Schmidt to announce the birth of his and Léda's daughter.[9] Charles's affectionate tone coupled with the fact that he wrote immediately to notify Mrs. Newcomb of this special event speaks to the closeness of the relationship:

New Orleans, July 11th 1876

Dear Mrs. Newcomb,

Léda gave birth to a girl yesterday at about 1 o'clock A.M. Both mother and child are doing remarkably well. Of course, Léda cannot hope to see you this summer in New York, but she trusts the time is not far distant when she will have the pleasure of introducing her daughter to you. After mature deliberation, it has been determined that the young lady's name is to be Louise. She is also to bear that of Marie. As you might suppose, the child is found to be physically faultless. She is strong and healthy, and there is no telling how near she may eventually reach perfection. I cannot be considered an impartial judge, and can therefore only give you the opinions of my wife's friends.

Meanwhile, no Centennial excursion or Northern or European trip for Léda this year. She says that later in the season she will allow me to absent myself for a few weeks, in which event I will not fail to do myself the pleasure of calling on you.

Léda and the family beg me to send their love to you.

Believe me,

Very respectfully and sincerely yours,

C. E. Schmidt

It is unclear how this letter made it back to the Schmidts and into their collection. As Mrs. Newcomb's letter of October 16, 1876, recognizing the birth of Louise is written specifically to Léda, without mention of Charles, it's possible that Mrs. Newcomb was traveling and the letter was returned to

Charles, having never reached her. Her letter, written with a steady hand in brown ink on 4 ⁶⁄₈" × 5 ⁵⁄₈" folded ecru writing paper with an embossed *N*, is copied verbatim:

Mrs. Warren Newcomb

P.O. Box 2846

New York

Oct 16th/76

Dear Léda,

By Mr. Zacharie who is now in New York, I send you a set to keep for your sweet babe_ it has been admired by all who have seen it _ On New Year, 1871 Sophie was to have put it on for the first time but I trust she was in Light of Peace with her Heavenly Father, who took her from me I would also send you her picture in blue velvet frame & Ma's [her mother] in Steel & Gilt armor & Mr. Newcomb's set in gold & black enamel (as I have promised them all to you) if I could part with them now, but it is a mournful sadness to have them before me & this will prove they are to be yours. I also have a set of Garnet & gold sent to dear Ma from some of Pa's family in Paris. I want Lucie [Léda's sister] to have. The recent cruel efforts of your Cousin Ellen & the constant threats I hear, of her son-in-law W. M. McCarthy & her children[10] make it necessary, my advisors tell me to be very particular; & oh Léda (being entirely alone & unprotected) I am so crushed by a severe insult I received from the present Proprietor of the New York Hotel, which took all my faith, all my fortitude & my prayers to accept it with resignation & submission; but such is life _ made up of trials & disappts. Do Léda, when you see Mme. Rost make my souvenirs to her, as I was compelled to leave without saying goodbye & she is always so kind to me, with love remember me aff'ly to your Pa, Lucie, & husb & kiss your dear babe for Cousin Jo

[PS] When you hear of my death write to Mr. A. H. Pomroy 54 Broad St New York.

In this letter written nearly six years after the death of her daughter, Sophie, Mrs. Newcomb conveys her warm affection for Léda by gifting to Léda's baby daughter the set of jewelry that was to have been worn by her deceased child. This affection and generosity stand in sharp contrast to her feelings toward her sister's family, whose "cruel efforts" were to serve as a constant reminder of the need to protect her assets against their efforts to seize them,

including the gifts that she here bequeaths to Léda to "prove" her intentions
as suggested by her advisors. While some considered Mrs. Newcomb's concern with family matters to be an unfounded obsession, time proved that she
well understood the motivations of her sister's son-in-law and children. In
fact, as a widow in the late nineteenth century, she may have experienced being "entirely alone and unprotected" more often than suggested in her mention of the crushing "severe insult" received from the hotel proprietor.

Then, not two weeks later on the same stationery, a very short note to
Léda:

Mrs. W   PO Box 2846   New York NY
Oct 30th 1876 [but postmarked October 29th]
Dear Léda,
On Oct 15th I sent you by Mr. Jas L Zacharie a letter & a box for your sweet
babe, & I have had no ansr. I fear as she is yet so young you do not like it.
therefore feeling I can take the liberty with you return it to me at once by
express & I will send you something I prefer you to have for yourself & her, &
will also send the set I have for Lucie. Please direct the package thus, "Mrs.
W.N. Care of A.H. Pomroy 54 Broad St NY." With Souvenirs to you & yours &
a kiss to your babe
Cousin Jo

What was the "set" that Mrs. Newcomb sent? This may have been as small
as a necklace with a pendant hanging and matching earrings; or as large as
a set that included five or six pieces. As Sophie was to have worn it for the
first time at age fifteen, it seems likely that this was a small set and more
appropriate for a young lady than the garnet set that Mrs. Newcomb sent to
Lucie.[11] Considering the slowness of the mail in the nineteenth century, her
consternation over Léda's lack of response seems an example of Mrs. Newcomb's alleged impatience. However, it also seems to indicate a desire to send
the "perfect" gift, something that would be a meaningful and appropriate
commemoration of the birth of her cousin's first child.

We never learn Léda's thoughts about the gift, but her "sweet letr" of response would seem to indicate that the relationship was equally important to
both cousins and any offense quickly forgotten. Mrs. Newcomb's third letter
to Léda describes the family significance of the jewelry she is sending to her,
and again references other possessions she wishes for Léda to have in the
future. In subtly contrasting her cool relations with her sister's family and

the warmth and love among Léda's family members, Mrs. Newcomb appears preoccupied with keeping her possessions out of reach of her sister's family. Consider however, the possibility that these letters are not representative of a lifetime of letters between Mrs. Newcomb and Léda but were saved by the Schmidt family precisely because of their potential use as legal documents in an anticipated dispute over her will.

> New York Nov 25th /76
> Dear Léda
> The box & yr sweet letr I have received all safe, & return by my good friend Mr. Ed Pillsbury what I think you will like better _The bracelet I send you, will be of double value to you, when I tell you it was ordered & made for me by your "Cousin Warren" whom you knew & which you can leave for your dear child as I wrote, but wear it Léda & wear it often for the worth & taste combined. The set of Garnet of my dear & Sainted Mother's for Lucie was often worn & valued by her therefore like the bracelet I wish them to remain in your family. These Souvenirs Léda are gifts of pure friendship & not from anything I have received or expect to receive & only wish I could send the pictures I have promised you but they are marked for you. Many long years of happiness to your dear Papa & all knowing how you all love another & with my best wishes & love to each one & yourself & kiss to your sweet babe.
> Cousin Jo
> Mrs. Warren Newcomb
> PO Box 2846 New York NY

Three years later, on a 3" × 2 ½" note card dated December 24, but postmarked December 23, 1879, "Cousin Jo" writes from New York about the discord with her sister Ellen and her family:

> Chere Laida, [a phonetic spelling, one of Mrs. Newcomb's few spelling errors, although her capitalization and punctuation were erratic]
> In these sad days I know you will rejoice with me My Exr [executor] has recov'd from your Cousin Ellen my darling's picture, for wh[ich] Mr. A. H. Pomroy wrote to her for, & you & yr dear hus'd [husband] read her severe letter to him, in ansr which he still holds. A lady wrote me from Louisville, Mr. McCarthy said, I had sent for it, wh[ich] I have never done, or said a word, know'g yr Cousin Ellen could prove nothing, she wrote to Mr. A.H.P. & I would yet have the picture before very long.[12] Last sumr Mr. A.H.P. met

the Rev W Norton, who is the clergyman of the Church, yr Cousin Ellen &
her family attend. Mr. P had a long talk with him, told him everything all I
had done & given to Mrs. Wm H'son and her four children, & were indebted
to me for all they possess'd & enjoy, & all her cruel treatment to me, & their
ungrateful returns to me. The Clergyman was struck at such revelations_ Now
my Ex'rs & my lawyer speak openly of the whole affair to anyone. You see I
have written to you first, feeling I have the sympathy of you & yr dear hus. I
inclose two little cards for Louise do kiss her for me, with love to Cousin John
[Léda's father] & Lucie; & for yrself & yours,[13] all you desire; Nine years the
16th of this month, was I made motherless & alone.
Aff'ly Cousin Jo
Dec 24th 1879

This was the last letter from Mrs. Newcomb in the Schmidt family papers.
Surely others were written and perhaps discarded or saved, someday to be
found "hidden" in the collection of other family members.[14] Even if the events
Mrs. Newcomb writes about are too obscure to piece together (her sister,
Ellen Henderson, refused to return to Josephine a portrait of Sophie; she
generously had given monetary gifts totaling $150,000 to Ellen and her four
children, but their relationship had soured when Mrs. Newcomb surmised
that Ellen and her son-in-law, "Mr. McCarthy," were attempting to institution-
alize her), her feelings of betrayal and the vindication of having that betrayal
recognized by persons of importance are clearly communicated. Moreover,
in this letter, Mrs. Newcomb's habit of underlining words for emphasis is
given an emotional edge by her use of red ink to underscore her position. One
could speculate that she literally was "seeing red."

A Different Focus

That righteous indignation, coupled with a desire to memorialize Sophie, was
brought to bear on one goal when Mrs. Newcomb was approached by Tulane
University president Johnston about establishing an allied women's college as
a memorial for her daughter. Instead of focusing her considerable energy on
the misdeeds of her estranged family, Mrs. Newcomb searched for and found
her lifework in the H. Sophie Newcomb Memorial College.

When Newcomb College opened its doors in October 1887, Mrs. Newcomb was seventy-one years old. Johnston wrote to Mrs. Newcomb and

enclosed a newspaper article about the opening. Shortly thereafter, Mrs. Newcomb responded. This letter, located in the collection of attorney James McConnell, was possibly given to McConnell by Johnston. Her letter reveals a comfortable friendship with the president, whom she addresses as "Colonel," as it moves quickly from her change of residences, to the opening of the College, to the offer to furnish and provide for a College chapel, to news of New Orleans acquaintances and sympathy to the president for the loss of his uncle:

14 of West 15th St _   N.Y.   Oct. 31st/ 87

Col Wm. P. Johnston,

Dear Col

Your two last letters of Sept 19th from Staunton, and Oct 15th (my dear husband's birth day) from N.O. was only received a few days since, as you directed it—"39 Broad St <u>N</u> Orleans La" was only received a day or two since [sic] as it was sent back to <u>your</u> city, and was returned to me again. I arrived from Lime Rock on the 13th, the very day the H.S.N.M.C was opened; and have been very busy in getting fixed for the winter, but do hope all will be well. The person I lived with at 13 West 22nd St, did not want any invalids, or delicate persons in her house. While I know I am delicate, I am <u>not</u> an invalid, as I am <u>not</u> helpless.__ I received the newspaper you sent me with a half dozen others, and am so happy to know all is so satisfactory to you it is so encouraging and spiriting. __ I read Catharine Cole's account, but Col[onel] are there no rooms to be appropriated for a Chapel and a reception room; as I have two portraits I intended for the H.S.N.M.C., one taken at four years of age, and one at the time of her death; and also a very excellent photograph of Mr. N[ewcomb], and other pictures, and many books, and some ornaments. The Chapel I will furnish & finish, as I wish it simple but very pretty, & would like to know from you, all that is required. I was in hopes to have seen Mrs. Richardson before her return South. __She had my true sympathy for her two nieces; her Bro's only child, renounced her Church, her country, & her fortune, to become the wife of a R.C. [Roman Catholic] Italian Count & reside in Rome Italy. The other her only sister's child, Mrs. I. B. Potter, commenced an engagement at the Fifth Ave Theater Oct 31st. I am told Bishop H. C. Potter feels deeply for his Bro Howard, who is the Father-in-law of Mrs. I.B.P. —

I am most happy you are so truly encouraged, at the opening of the Tulane University.__ I do pray <u>both</u> may ever give you all the comfort & success you ever desire.

What a glorious triumph was the close of your Uncle's life, such a solace to his relatives and friends. To see our dear ones so resigned to go, & so filled with Faith & Hope, relieves & soothes the last parting, but nothing but His Love, & care & time, can heal the wound of the broken heart.

Our weather is clear but cold.

Very truly & Sin'ly, Jo L. Newcomb

There are several curious aspects of this letter. First, in Mrs. Newcomb's habit of abbreviating, she refers to the College by its acronym, H.S.N.M.C., never mentioning Sophie's name or expressing her own satisfaction with the establishment of the memorial she had long anticipated. Perhaps she was withholding her enthusiasm for a time when she was certain of its success, a caution expressed by her donation, and by her reluctance to visit the College until February 1892. Rather than mentioning the triumph of the College opening, she draws attention to what is missing, the College chapel. Further, she refers to the opening of Newcomb College as "the opening of the Tulane University." An oversight on her part, perhaps, for she then writes in hopes that "both" will give Johnston "comfort & success," meaning apparently both Newcomb College and Tulane University. In this letter, she defines herself in words any biographer would remember: "delicate" but not an "invalid."

The McConnell Family Papers contain an additional file of letters offering insight into Mrs. Newcomb's life. In a thick folder are the letters solicited from her friends and neighbors as evidence in the court case that would last from 1901 to 1908, challenging her donation to the University. These letters address the grounds of the lawsuit, attesting to her sanity and independence of thought (i.e., not under the control of the Board of Administrators), and corroborating New Orleans as her legal domicile. In the letters handwritten on engraved writing paper, most with Garden District addresses, the women who knew and admired Josephine Newcomb stepped into a public arena in her defense. The letters following are typical:

New Orleans

May 29th, 1902

This is to certify that I lived next to the Josephine Louise House on Washington Avenue, opposite the H. Sophie Newcomb College, and have resided there since 1893. The Josephine House was built after the purchase of my own home.

Mrs. Newcomb spent her winters there, the last one being 1898.

In 1899, she established a home on Fourth Street, directly back of mine. Just before leaving for the North, in the spring of 1900, Mrs. Newcomb sent for me, wishing to show me "her beautiful home," as she called it. We went over the entire house. I saw much of Mrs. Newcomb when she lived in the Josephine Louise House, her apartments being next to my home. We held almost daily conversations through the open windows, the intervening space being something like 18 feet. During 1898 and 1899, Mrs. Newcomb frequently visited me in the evenings at my residence.

During all my acquaintance with her, I had opportunities to judge her, as one person would another. She often told me that her time was mostly spent in looking after business affairs, as she attended to those matters herself. From my knowledge of her during the last few years of her life, I can positively affirm that Mrs. Newcomb was perfectly sane and that all of her mental faculties were normal and unimpaired.

Respectfully,

Mrs. M. M. Suthon

And:

. . . During these twelve years Mrs. Newcomb was frequently a guest at dinner parties at my home and discussed matters of general interest as intelligently as any woman friend & I have heard businessmen say of her that she was thoroughly cognizant of the most minute details of her affairs, allowing nothing to be done unless previously explained by them. . . . Mrs. Newcomb always impressed me as a woman who knew her own mind & was perfectly capable of disposing of her property understandingly.

Very truly,

Margaret Avery Johnston

And again on Mrs. Newcomb's intelligence:

This is to certify that I, Julia C. Logan, was personally acquainted with Mrs. Josephine Louise Newcomb for nearly twelve years, and that during the above stated time she ever commanded my respect and admiration for her great good sense, judgment, and rare intelligence. . . . I beg further to add that Mrs. Newcomb was a woman whom it was a privilege to know, and that I never left her presence without feeling that I had been personally benefitted by the contact with a woman of such rare greatness of heart.

Addressing Mrs. Newcomb's sanity and independence of character:

> . . . As to the question of her sanity it is absurd to question it. No one who knew Mrs. Newcomb could do so. She was a woman of her own mind—very strong & decided anything but weak & uncertain.
> Very sincerely,
> Mattie M. Austin

The letters exhibit an underlying sense of reserve, no doubt a product of their intended use as legal testimony. However, the formality also may reveal that no one became terribly close to Josephine Newcomb. She lived in a number of places throughout her lifetime—New Orleans, New York City, and various resort cities, staying mainly in residential hotels—and had not built the friendships enjoyed by longtime neighbors. We see this peripatetic life when she mentions in her letters that her mail hadn't reached her or had been delayed. Moreover, she was isolated by widowhood and by choosing, within her particular society, a different life from those of these women so similar to her in background and class. In a very real sense, Mrs. Newcomb worked. As her neighbor Mrs. Suthon put it, "her time was mostly spent in looking after business affairs, as she attended to those matters herself." Though Mrs. Newcomb's accounts were managed by brokers, she was knowledgeable about her financial investments and thought a great deal about how money could be entrusted to one individual or one institution over another. The letters written on her behalf reflect upon her knowledge and cautious trust that served her well in managing and protecting an increasing fortune.

For the court case in Tulane's defense of the College, there were thirty-eight testimonials in all, twenty-eight of them from Mrs. Newcomb's friends. Though the tone of these testimonials lacks the intimacy of letters such as those between Mrs. Newcomb and the Schmidts, they are uniform in their admiration and possibly envy of Mrs. Newcomb's ability to take care of her business affairs and to be "a woman of her own mind." Most of the letters were written by women who had property and resources of their own and who most likely had experienced the difficulties of controlling their own wealth. Recall that in Louisiana, as in many other states, male relatives had extraordinary legal powers over women's property and even hired advisors, such as accountants and attorneys, could easily ignore the intentions of their female clients.

While the location of Mrs. Newcomb's letters—"hidden" within the collections of prominent men—illustrates one of the difficulties for scholars studying women's lives, the letters themselves define Josephine Newcomb as a woman who set her own course and was treated seriously by her advisors and by the men and women who were her friends and acquaintances. This was no small achievement for a widow of the nineteenth century. Her letters and those about her are a rich source of knowledge for those interested in how, although "entirely alone and unprotected," she eased her way into protecting herself, befriending others, and leaving a legacy that was to benefit thousands of women.

NOTES

1. John P. Dyer, *Tulane: The Biography of a University, 1834–1965* (New York: Harper and Row, 1966), 53.

2. Brandt V. B. Dixon, *A Brief History of H. Sophie Newcomb Memorial College 1887–1919* (New Orleans: Hauser Printing, 1928), 36–37.

3. Ibid., 14–15.

4. Susan Wittig, "Reflections of Sorrow and Hope." *Newcomb News* 5, no. 11 (1981): 2–11, Newcomb Archives, Newcomb College Center for Research on Women, Tulane University (hereafter cited as NA NCCROW).

5. Rosa Keller (1911–1998) "Josephine Louise Newcomb." n.d., NA NCCROW. See also Rosa Freeman Keller Collection, Amistad Research Center at Tulane University.

6. Schmidt family papers, Manuscripts Collection 207, Louisiana Research Collection, Howard-Tilton Memorial Library, Tulane University, 70118 (hereafter cited as LaRC).

7. Léda's father, the Honorable John W. Hincks, and Mrs. Newcomb's mother, Sophia Waters, were first cousins (personal correspondence of Winifred Delery Hills and Beth Willinger, January 4, 2011).

8. McConnell family papers, Manuscripts Collection 156, Box 15, Louisiana Research Collection, Howard-Tilton Memorial Library, Tulane University, LaRC.

9. The four letters are located in Schmidt family papers, Box II, Folder 15, LaRC.

10. "Cousin Ellen" is Josephine's sister, Eleanor, and her four children, a daughter and three sons.

11. Waldhorn & Adler (New Orleans), representative correspondence, July 2005.

12. The Hendersons moved to Louisville, Kentucky, in 1872.

13. It is notable that Mrs. Newcomb doesn't mention Léda's brother, Joseph A. Hincks. J. A. Hincks was one of her executors and as secretary-treasurer of the Administrators of the Tulane Educational Fund figured prominently in representing Mrs. Newcomb's interests to the board both prior to and after her death.

14. Since the writing of this essay, a file of letters written by and to Josephine Newcomb has been located in the McConnell family papers.

3

SOPHIE NEWCOMB AND AGNES SCOTT COLLEGES, 1887–1920

From Dutiful Daughters to New Women

LYNN D. GORDON

Editors' Note: Lynn Gordon's essay, excerpted from her book *Gender and Higher Education in the Progressive Era* (Yale University Press, 1990), tracks the second generation of American women to attend college, from 1890 to 1920. Gordon is especially interested in noting how these students addressed some of the political and intellectual boundaries faced by the women who had preceded them. Her work is important as one of the few studies to compare the experiences of women at different types of institutions. She draws upon the writings of female students at the coeducational universities of Chicago and California, the women's colleges of Vassar and Agnes Scott, and the coordinate college of early Newcomb. She found differences in the areas of voting rights and expectations, interests in careers, and relationships between students, faculty, and alumnae. Vassar, for example, had more opportunities for faculty and student interaction, but Newcomb students had a greater chance for interaction and planned activities with alumnae. Gordon's article is one of the few studies comparing Newcomb to another southern college. In the original work, Gordon's essay begins with the founding of Newcomb College; that account is omitted here as a thorough discussion of Newcomb's founding is provided in the introduction to part 1.

Agnes Scott College in Decatur, Georgia, began as a seminary and high school established by a philanthropist and evolved into a college. Although [the college was] located only three miles from Atlanta, its origins and educational philosophy drew on traditional Christian values rather than more modern urban concerns about women's needs for self-support. Founded in 1889, through the efforts of Dr. Frank Henry Gaines, pastor of the Decatur Presbyterian Church, the school offered a primary education that year to sixty-three young women and six small boys under the age of twelve. In 1890, Colonel George Washington Scott gave $40,000 to the Decatur Female Seminary, the first of many such donations eventually totaling $112,500. To express their gratitude for Scott's gifts, the trustees renamed the school the Agnes Scott Institute, honoring the colonel's mother. Intending from the first that the institute should grow to be a college, the trustees named Dr. Gaines president; he served in this position until his death in 1923.[1]

The mother of seven children and stepmother to another five, Agnes Irvine Scott symbolized, to her son and the school's trustees, the ideal Christian wife and mother. Devoted to Shakespeare and the poetry of Robert Burns, she taught intellectual and spiritual values to her children. As her son John put it in the ceremony dedicating Agnes Scott Institute to his mother: "She met the duties of her sphere with the sublimest faith and trust in the goodness of God. . . . She was a Presbyterian and loved her church. . . . She . . . saw to it that no child of hers should go out into the world ignorant of the Shorter Catechism."[2]

The founders and trustees of the institute adopted the Agnes Scott Ideal, thereby proclaiming their desire to educate young women who would follow in the footsteps of Colonel Scott's mother. Printed each year in the institute's catalogue, the school's goals were: "1) A liberal curriculum, fully abreast of the best institutions of this country. 2) The Bible a textbook. 3) Thoroughly qualified and consecrated teachers. 4) A high standard of scholarship. 5) All the influences of the College conducive to the formation and development of Christian character. 6) The glory of God the chief end of all." Additionally, early leaders of the school formed a covenant, agreeing to offer daily prayer for the school, its unconverted students, and the glory of God.

The president and trustees of the institute were all required, by the terms of the charter, to be Presbyterians (by the 1920s, the board had eleven trustees representing the synods of Alabama, Georgia, and Florida); and teachers, practicing Christians. No rules limited the student body to Presbyterians, or even to Christians, but required Bible study, chapel services, Sabbath observance, and vesper services were all part of the Agnes Scott experience. On Sundays, students rose at half past seven, breakfasted at eight, had Sunday School at nine, church at eleven, a special Sunday dinner, meditation time, supper, Christian Band meetings, evening services, and hymn singings. For many years, faculty gave no assignments for Mondays, so that classwork would not tempt students from their prayers.[3]

Between 1889 and 1906, when the institute officially became Agnes Scott College, the trustees struggled to raise both money and academic standards. Although the college elected to remain independent of direct church control, southern Presbyterian churches contributed heavily to Agnes Scott's support, helping the institution match funds donated by the General Education Board. When Gaines died in 1923, the college owned twenty acres and eighteen buildings. To achieve collegiate academic status, the trustees gradually eliminated the lowest grades and added higher ones. This made it difficult for some students, who, for example, might spend four years as seniors without graduating. As James Ross McCain, second president of the college, noted in his history of Agnes Scott: "It is a small wonder that of the 1663 students who attended Agnes Scott Institute, only 68 received diplomas."[4]

In 1906, the institution officially renamed itself Agnes Scott College and conferred its first bachelor's degrees. Like Newcomb, the new college continued to offer preparatory work; the Agnes Scott Academy remained open until 1913. The number of residential students reached 130 for the year 1906–7, with an additional 31 nonresident students (figures refer only to the college, not the academy); by 1918–19, 335 college students lived on campus; an additional 53 were day pupils. In 1898–99, resident students paid $127.50 per term; by 1910–11, the college charged $325 to $350 a year for tuition, room, and board. The college assured parents that: "Every effort is made to give . . . the character of a Christian home. Teachers and students constitute one household. Care is taken to render the home life of the student not only attractive, but conducive to the cultivation of those graces which mark refined women. . . . Instruction in manners, and etiquette is given by the Lady Principal."[5]

The Student Government Association (SGA) of Agnes Scott printed the social regulations at the beginning of each school year for the benefit of freshmen, and as a reminder to upperclasswomen. In the handbook of 1912–13, the SGA cautioned students to observe the 10:00 p.m. lights-out rule, register for a chaperone when leaving Decatur, avoid soda fountains, moving pictures, and talking on the street when in the company of young men, obtain the dean's permission for any campus visitors, and of course, maintain silence and decorum on Sundays. When visiting friends, the handbook cautioned: "Follow the rules of the lady of the house, but receive no permissions from her not in accordance with college rules."[6]

The number and quality of faculty grew with the college. In 1913–14, the faculty roster listed four men, all with PhDs, fourteen women with undergraduate degrees from prominent colleges and universities, and three women who did not have bachelor's degrees but had studied at normal schools, colleges, and universities. The faculty also included two Agnes Scott alumnae: Alice Lucile Alexander (BA, Agnes Scott; AM, Columbia University), adjunct professor of French; and Margaret Ellen McCallie (BA, Agnes Scott; PhB, Chicago; and graduate studies at universities in Berlin, Heidelberg, and Paris), adjunct professor of German. Gaines and the trustees took great pride in the school's rapid acceptance into the Southern Association of Colleges and Secondary Schools in 1907.[7]

While administrators, trustees, and faculty sought to make Newcomb and Agnes Scott the academic equivalents of Vassar and Wellesley, students at these institutions carefully considered the nature, meaning, and effects of their college years. Like college women in the North, they found that higher education, even when designed to preserve tradition, conflicted with family claims and created new imperatives. As southerners, however, they defined those imperatives somewhat differently and more conservatively.

The Newcomb Spirit and the Meaning of Women's Higher Education

Newcomb's success brought public acclaim. New Orleans newspapers praised both the College and the women who attended it, assuring readers that higher education did not destroy the charm of southern ladies: "The *Picayune* hails the fair bachelors of Sophie Newcomb. Bachelors of science and of arts they are withal girls, gay, bright, tender, and sweet. And what if their pretty little heads be stuffed with philosophic theses and parallelopipedons and Greek prepositions. There is just as much room as ever for thoughts of flounces, frills, and furbelows and all the charming frivolities of girl life." Although Newcomb designed its art program to prepare women for careers, the *Picayune* ignored this promotion of female independence, commenting: "Art design and decorative work are fully in the reach of the gentler sex and well adapted to the strength and condition of females."[8]

Newcomb's commencement speakers, usually ministers, disapproved of "the charming frivolities of girl life." They stressed instead the connections between higher education and domesticity and assured seniors and their parents that men found educated women attractive and marriageable.

No man likes a fool for a mate; a bright clever intellect counts for much in moral training. . . . Good intelligent men believe in sensible intelligent women. . . . Sentimental slenderness and delicacy have gone out of style. . . . Men like a girl who can eat a good hearty dinner and enjoy it.

The college for the higher education of women is the pride and glory of New Orleans and in fact of the whole South, for it is the only one in the South that ranks with Vassar and Wellesley. . . . It has been proven conclusively that a woman's mind is as capable of taking as high an education as man's and to this noble end the college is doing a lion's share.

If you prefer to pass what you call domestic life with a woman who is distinctly ignorant so be it. You have the right, and may God have mercy on your soul.[9]

Tulane president Edwin Alderman agreed that college women should concentrate their efforts on domestic matters: "The old time woman had a charm, a definite charm. . . . Like the woman of today, the old time woman wanted to do great things, but did not trouble herself much about reform in the world without; she tried, first, to get things right around her, in her own home . . . [to] hold fast to that essential charm, homemaking genius."[10]

The bankers, professionals, and government workers who sent daughters to Newcomb were pleased to educate them under Tulane's auspices, thereby ensuring their capacities for self-support. Despite the middle-class status of Newcomb parents and the relatively low tuition, 25 percent of the students went to college on scholarships. Besides the traditional bachelor's course, the College offered degrees in art, music, education, and domestic science. Although each department or school had a four-year course combining liberal arts work with professional training, most students stayed two years, received a certificate of proficiency, and went on to teaching jobs in elementary and secondary schools. The prestigious Newcomb Art School produced graduates able to support themselves as independent craftswomen. The school offered instruction in embroidery, brasswork, jewelry, and bookbinding but was best known for its pottery. Using the blue and brown college colors and depicting southern flora and fauna, the pottery won prizes at the Paris Exposition of 1900 and at similar exhibitions in the United States. Orders poured in, and art school students filled them. Graduates who set up their own shops and kilns earned forty or fifty dollars a month.[11]

Relationships with Tulane men reinforced views of Newcomb students as charming, marriageable girls. Until 1918, when the College moved to the

University campus, three miles separated the institutions, and poor public transportation prevented informal social contacts. Fearing distractions or worse, Newcomb faculty and administrators strictly controlled access to their campus, discouraging males from strolling around the grounds or waiting for women in the halls. Thus, in contrast to the situation on coeducational campuses, Tulane men did not have to deal with the constant presence of women. They invited Newcomb students to their campus for plays, lectures, and dances, but as guests; women did not threaten masculine prerogatives. In 1896, a writer in the *Jambalaya*, Tulane's yearbook, celebrated the charms of college women with a limerick:

My Pearl Is a Newcomb Girl

I've met all the girls in the city,
Some wild, some gay, and some free,
Though mine won't be out till next winter,
I tell you she's in it with me,
She's bone-ing her studies at Newcomb,
And learning whatever she shall;
She's the best-looking girl in the College,
Is my little Newcomb gal.[12]

Newcomb students reached out to young men. Perhaps because they had little interest in independent professional careers, student authors found no incompatibility between romance and a college degree. Short stories published in the *Tulanian*, a joint publication of Tulane and Newcomb societies, had a standard boy-meets-and-wins-girl format. In one example, "According to Cable," a Newcomb freshman fooled and charmed an arrogant northern college man into thinking that she was a young Creole girl fresh out of the "convent on the Rue Royale." The young man discovered her ruse but did not hold it, or her college education, against her. They planned a wedding and a home in the South, where "college girls" were more feminine than those the bridegroom had seen back home. The Newcomb student had no qualms about quitting college for marriage. In another story, a Newcomb student en route to visit a college friend arranged to meet the friend's brother on the train. They agreed to wear blue ribbon bows to recognize each other. A series of mishaps followed because other passengers had adopted similar schemes.

Toward the end of the trip, the student met a handsome Cornell man who asked to see her again.[13]

This widespread social acceptance of Newcomb College, and public approval of higher education for southern women, actually masked serious familial tensions. Parents expected that their daughters' lives would continue as before, even though they were going to college. Although he won the battle to restrict entrance to women seventeen and over, President Dixon had to assert the College's claim to students' time and efforts. In a letter to parents, he noted:

> The College and Faculty solicit the cooperation of the parents and guardians in securing for the students the fullest opportunities for uninterrupted study. It is not possible for the young ladies to devote themselves to social entertainments and at the same time perform their college duties in a satisfactory manner. . . . The standing of many of our students has been seriously affected by the social distractions of the past quarter, their energies impaired, their interest and faithfulness in their work greatly lessened. It is therefore urgently requested that such disturbing influences be more carefully avoided in the future.[14]

On another occasion, the president resorted to sarcasm: "Your letter is received asking that your daughter be excused from gymnastic exercises on the ground that she has sufficient [exercise] during her summer vacation for the demands of the whole year. Permit me to ask the following: I presume that she has a hearty Thanksgiving dinner; is she excluded from later dinners on that account?"[15] As Dixon and his faculty contended with the family claim on students' attention, he blamed the difficulties on traditional southern attitudes toward women:

> The Southern girl has been accustomed to the most solicitous care, and has learned to expect every attention and courtesy from her associates and others; in consequence she is inclined to be self-willed and exacting, but not self-reliant; alert and quick-witted, but not persistent and steady, eager for novelty and possessing a fine initiative, but changeable and dependent upon others for results. She lacks the discipline which comes from interest in that which requires hard work. . . . She has not been required to fend for herself, is guarded and supervised continually.[16]

Students may have entered Newcomb with the habit and attitudes Dixon described, but they came to share his concerns. The 80 percent of Newcomb women who lived at home had difficulty combining family and college responsibilities, as students' stories demonstrate. In "The Gospel of Work," Jessica's family continually interrupted her attempts to finish an essay. With her father away on business and mother feeling her rheumatism, Jessica had to help her sister Marion perform household chores and look after the younger siblings. Domestic life became particularly hectic when Uncle Daniel dropped by and her mother wanted to prepare a special meal. Frustrated and angry, Jessica exploded: "What was work? Wasn't her essay a noble work? Wasn't it greater work than beating eggs, or setting the table, or putting tin soldiers into a rickety pasteboard box, or putting a dolly with a broken head to bed? Wasn't the paper she had written a month ago, pleading for children's playgrounds, of value? Had it not helped a good cause? Wasn't that work and service? Really, it seemed a very much greater, far-reaching service."

Jessica became reconciled to her situation only when Marion explained their mother's gospel of work: "She said that when we helped her about the house, whenever we straightened things up, or mended clothes, or swept, or did anything like that, no matter how little it seemed, it helped her, and then she could help father all the more, and he could get more done, and would be doing his part better, and then we'd all be doing something to help the world along, and then . . . we'd all be happier." A reformed Jessica rose at six to prepare the family's breakfast, so that she would have time to write her essay on the value of different kinds of work.[17]

In another story, when senior class president Eliza Rotfield went home for the holidays, she found her younger sister Barbara ill with pneumonia. Mrs. Rotfield asked Eliza to remain home, but the latter refused, explaining the honor and importance of being senior class president. After graduation, Eliza said, she would return home, get a job, and devote herself to helping her family. With assurances from Mrs. Rotfield that no immediate danger existed, Eliza kissed Barbara good-by and returned to college. Once back in school, she became involved in defending an innocent student from a charge of cheating on a French examination. Just before Eliza's turn to present her case to the Student Council, she received a telegram from home and grimly decided not to open it: "She had worked up for this great moment and she felt that she had to do her part, her duty at once. She went to the meeting. . . . She conquered." After the successful conclusion of the case, Eliza read the telegram, which told her of Barbara's death that morning. In both stories, the student authors presented sympathetically the claims of college life. Yet in these two cases at least, protagonists found it impossible to combine family responsibilities and the demands of higher education.[18]

Like parents who wanted their daughters educated but not involved with college life, Tulane men also expressed ambivalence about women's higher education. They admired Newcomb women from a distance but had difficulty dealing with them as fellow students. Newcomb and Tulane occasionally shared activities; when they did so, men assumed leadership, just as male students did on other, fully coeducational, campuses. The *Arcade* contained some serious writing, but women contributed only gossip columns to the University's papers, the *Olive and Blue* and the *College Spirit*. Newcomb women entered and won the annual Carnot debate competition in 1911 and again in 1912. Tulane men thereafter refused to compete, saying they were "too much taken up with their daily work." Clearly, Newcomb's status as a coordinate women's college won its students autonomy they could not have received as coeds. And so long as they did not work or compete with men, Tulane students continued to regard Newcomb women as suitable recipients of their romantic attentions.[19]

Eventually, Newcomb women established some distance from their families and participated more freely in college life. After the move to Washington Avenue and the establishment of a real campus, students founded chapters of national sororities, class and self-government associations, a dramatics club, a debating society (the Agonistic Club), and basketball teams. These activities and work on student publications kept nonresidents at the college afternoons and evenings, fostering friendships and institutional loyalties. Excited by the change in students' attitudes, Dixon revised his views of southern womanhood: "I was obliged to recognize in them a responsiveness to ideals, a growing persistency of purpose, and an initiative which I had not at first suspected." Through these activities, Newcomb students developed new identities as college women and self-consciously sought the meaning of their education.[20]

New Orleans of the Progressive Era had a social reform–settlement–suffrage network working through women's clubs. At Kingsley House, head resident Eleanor Laura McMain, a student of Jane Addams and Graham Taylor, spearheaded programs for public health, education, and labor law reform. Nationally known reformers Kate and Jean Gordon founded the Era Club, a women's suffrage group. They urged passage of child labor laws, reorganized community welfare activities, and Jean Gordon became Louisiana's first state factory inspector. These women all had connections with Newcomb College: they spoke on campus; Jean Gordon judged student debates; and in 1913, Eleanor McMain offered a course in social settlement work.[21]

Just as southern progressivism was more conservative, less widespread, and less successful than the northern variety, so Newcomb students responded differently to reform imperatives than their counterparts at Vassar. Writings in the *Arcade* did not deal with social reform or politics and denied any student interest in suffrage. When the College offered its first economics course in 1911, the journal reassured the community that the study of political economy would not produce suffragists:

> This course in Political Economy was offered at the special request of the girls themselves. Certainly this is a sign that Southern women, too, are becoming interested in those things that were once thought of as strictly "men's affairs." Woman's Suffrage has had very little support or encouragement among Southern women—the majority of us knew little and cared less about it. The fact that at Newcomb Political Economy is studied does not mean, however, that Newcomb girls are to become suffragettes—or even suffragists. Far from it! I can see mothers and grandmothers holding up their hands in holy horror and letters from dear old aunts and god-mothers advising the parents not to send their precious children to be demoralized. No, but a course in Economics and Sociology does mean that the girls at Newcomb are taking an intelligent interest in, not politics in the narrower sense of the word, but in political economy.[22]

Although conservative in their political beliefs, Newcomb students felt themselves to be different from their "dear old aunts and god-mothers." The public continued to see them as "southern belles," but they fashioned new self-images, asserting their intellectual capabilities. When Agnes Scott students came to an intercollegiate debate on compulsory military training dressed in formal evening clothes, Newcomb women, who lost the match, accused their opponents of using feminine wiles on the judges.

In a satiric skit printed in the *Arcade*, Newcomb debaters wore military costumes, while Agnes Scott wore "Mary Pickford curls, a fluffy frock with a large sash, and carried some knitting." The Newcomb student took her task seriously: "Ladies and gentlemen, in this world crisis when America finds herself plunged into dangers on every hand, does not every condition, every situation point to the absolute necessity of military training for every man and boy in America?" The Agnes Scott debater looked up from her knitting and responded: "Well, I think nothing could be worse than compulsory military training. In the first place, the poor boys would be bored to death, you know they would. Then, they'd have to do their training in the summer, mostly, and can you imagine a vacation without any boys?" In the skit, as in reality, the negative won, and the *Arcade* writer added a speech in which judges proclaimed the "superior womanly intuition" of Agnes Scott.[23]

As college women, Newcomb students accepted public social and educational responsibilities. Southern women's college faculty did not become role models for their students, as female professors did in the North. Instead, alumnae maintained contacts with the College, and current students set an example of civic activism. The Newcomb Alumnae Association, founded in 1893, allied itself with other New Orleans women's clubs to run a night school for working people. Graduates wrote a section entitled "Of Alumnae Interest" in each issue of the *Arcade,* using it as a forum to reach students and to keep in touch with each other. They frequently discussed the question of appropriate postcollege activities. Old-fashioned mothers, they warned, could no longer serve as guides for their daughters' lives. Yet the family claim continued to be strong after graduation. In the following skit, an alumna author made fun of her classmates but also expressed the conflicts between the intellectual, professional, and reform interests fostered by college attendance, and customs confining unmarried daughters to home duties.

> Yes, I'm going to stay home next year. I did want to go up north—I know
> I could *easily* get a position on *The Atlantic* or *The Century* or one of those
> magazines; Miss Stone and Mr. Butler always gave me "A" on my essays—but
> mother and father won't hear of it. Yes, after all, a woman's sphere is the
> home. No, I won't do the actual housekeeping. Mother will do that, but I'll at-
> tend to the rest. And, Jane, we *must* keep up our French and German and read
> together for a couple hours a day. And then our settlement work—I intend to
> devote *all* my time to that. And I expect I can write something.[24]

As a cure for the postgraduate blues, the Newcomb Alumnae Association recommended continuing involvement with College affairs. In two skits,

"Newcomb News at Home" and "More Newcomb News at Home," Jane's comments about her daughter Mary's student activities showed her own inability to comprehend college life. Mary's letter said, "As soon as we all get our bloomers, we will play basketball out on the court, but now we only play in the gym." Jane turned to her sister Susan, a Newcomb alumna, complaining: "That is the most improper thing I have ever heard. I shall talk seriously to Mary's father . . . about sending for her immediately. To appear outside her room in such a costume." In another letter, Mary mentioned the College chapter of Phi Beta Kappa. At first her horrified mother thought it was a "colored society." Then she decided it was a plan for all the students to wear latchkeys around their necks, to let themselves into the dormitories late at night. Finally, upon learning that it was a scholastic honor society, she sent a dollar for dues so her daughter could "sign up." Aunt Susan could not offer much help because she had never joined the Alumnae Association, kept up with College activities, or set foot on campus in twenty years. Her remarks were more laughable and inappropriate than her confused sister's.[25]

The Alumnae Association found its niche in fighting for white women's educational opportunities. Newcomb graduates became officers of the Louisiana chapter of the Southern Association of College Women and published the proceedings of each meeting in the *Arcade,* along with frequent discussions of how to raise southern academic standards. They sponsored "college days" in local high schools to interest women in attending Newcomb. Most important, perhaps, they challenged Tulane's policies on women's higher education and sought expanded privileges for Newcomb women within the University.

A campus quip accused Tulane of "marrying Newcomb for her money." In part, this joke referred to the battle between Tulane and Louisiana State University (LSU) for Morrill Act funds. Tulane's admission of women, although separately, through Newcomb College, qualified the University to receive state revenues. Responding to this pressure, LSU slowly co-educated; in 1906, it had twenty-one women students. During the legislative session of 1906, however, New Orleans women's groups argued that Tulane's greater commitment to women justified its sole possession of public funds.

After supporting Tulane in this fight, women demanded access to the University's medical school. For the next seven years, Jean Gordon and the Era Club joined the Newcomb Alumnae Association in placing their case before Tulane and the public. The University agreed to admit women to the first two years of laboratory work and to the pharmaceutical and dental programs.

Even the hiring of two female faculty in medicine, however, did not get women students into the physicians' courses. The persistence of the women's group finally paid off in 1914, when the trustees voted to allow females into all four years of medical school.[26]

Tulane was also interested in Newcomb's endowment. Under the terms of the original agreement between Josephine Newcomb and the trustees, Tulane administered Newcomb's funds. Although forbidden to use the College's money for other departments of the University, the trustees came up with several plans for diverting a few dollars. Dixon, for example, resisted the board's demand for a large "donation" to the graduate school when it agreed to admit Newcomb alumnae. The Alumnae Association sought representation on the Board of Trustees to prevent future "requests" and give themselves a voice in College policies. The board refused, citing a Louisiana statute barring women from public positions requiring voting, and subsequently denied petitions for nonvoting advisory alumnae committees.

The Alumnae Association, with student support, aired the controversy in the *Arcade*, coming perilously close to a defense of women's rights: "At Newcomb College, a college endowed by a woman in memory of her daughter, women professors of the same capacity and standing as the men professors are given much smaller salaries. We recognize that it is the custom of the time to underpay women for the same grade of work men perform, but an unjust commercial practice should not be carried into use in such a center of culture and uplift as a great twentieth century University."[27] Alumnae also satirized the board's fears about their presence at meetings:

A Meeting of the Tulane Board

Irby: If it were merely a question of having them on the Board, I'd say all right if it gave them any pleasure. But I don't propose to have any extravagant women dictating how to spend the fund. Newcomb spends quite enough money as it is. . . . Look at that budget. . . . Three dollars last month for repairing benches in the hall. If that isn't throwing away money.

Magruder: Of course, I'm new on the Board . . . but it seems only reasonable that they should have chairs to sit on.

Walmsley: The point is out of order.

Dymond: I don't believe in women in public life; they're just a nuisance. And their mothers don't do it. It seems to me that the Newcomb Alumnae are a very troublesome group of women.

Farrar: They're all suffragists, that's what's the matter with them, and there is no more objectionable class on earth.[28]

Joined by Jean Gordon and the Era Club, the Alumnae Association campaigned for a bill allowing women the vote on charitable and educational boards. They won their fight in 1916, two years before the College moved to the Broadway campus adjacent to Tulane. Alumnae felt their newly won representation would help them protect Newcomb's interests and retain its independent spirit.

Expanding Christian Social Consciousness at Agnes Scott

Loyalty to the college developed more quickly at residential Agnes Scott than at Sophie Newcomb. In spite of the religious atmosphere and strict social regulations, Agnes Scott was no Presbyterian nunnery. Young women away from home organized social and extracurricular activities to develop friendships and have a good time. In her research on the early days of Agnes Scott, Amy Friedlander found that the women faculty, who lived in the dormitories with the students, initiated and encouraged college life to develop students' attachment to the institution and to weaken ties to home and family. Professor Louise McKinney, whose career at the college spanned forty-six years, described the campus atmosphere as familial, reporting that "the girls" used to ask her to kiss them goodnight."[29]

In 1897, the first edition of the *Aurora* (the college's literary magazine and yearbook) listed four sororities, a Chafing Dish club, a Cotillion Club (members dressed like men for their yearbook picture), a Baby Club (nine girls dressed as babies and sucking their thumbs), a Bicycle Club, Art Club, Sewing Club, Deutsch Club, Choral Union, and Alumnae Club. In 1898, three new sororities, a Cooking Club, Hemstitching Club, Spooners Club, Early Risers Club, Kodak Club, Le Cercle Français, and other joined the list.

Twenty years later, students had developed more sophisticated organizations and activities. Active social calendars fostered close friendships between students and offered opportunities for taking part in the traditionally male activities of politics, debate, and athletics. Writing in the *Agnes Scott Bulletin* for 1917, Emma Jones ('18) entitled her essay "Not in the Catalogue," intending it as a description, for freshmen, of the yearly extracurricular cycle. She promised new students that "Agnes Scott will make up to you for the good times you'll miss at home." Activities began in the fall semester, with a reception given by the YWCA and each freshman signing up to join one of the two liter-ary societies, Propylean or Mnemosynean. After these initial encounters, as at other women's colleges, sophomores initiated freshmen into the campus com-munity with a series of stunts and pranks. Class concerns then gave way to a series of common holiday celebrations—Halloween, Thanksgiving, Christ-mas, Valentine's Day—and opportunities to join the Blackfriars (dramatics society), Hoasc Club (senior service honor society), debate or athletic teams, the *Agonistic* (student newspaper), the *Aurora*, or Gamma Alpha Tau (the aca-demic honor society). Toward the end of the year, "the young debutante is not so rushed as is Miss Senior." Concerts, plays, operettas, and, finally, com-mencement honored seniors and formally ushered them out of the college community.

Agnes Scott women also learned how to deal with campus regulations. In 1909–10, when they requested a holiday that the faculty refused, the stu-dents, led by the president of the student government, left the campus in a body to have a picnic in the woods. Their angry instructors took points off the students' grades, but thereafter spring holidays became an annual event.[30]

Having fun did not keep Agnes Scott students from moving toward greater self-consciousness, distance from domesticity, and activity in the public sphere. As at Sophie Newcomb, home responsibilities conflicted with stu-dents' campus lives. Although Agnes Scott was residential, the catalogue of 1896–97 found it necessary to request parents "not to interfere with the stud-ies of their daughter by withdrawing them during the session to spend a week or so at home." And in the catalogue of 1904–5, administrators urged: "It is desirable that dressmaking, dentistry and vaccination be attended to at home, that the time, strength, and thought of the student may be given to the special objects for which she has entered the Institute."[31]

Like Newcomb women, Agnes Scott students viewed the joys and duties of college life as oppositional to family responsibilities. A "Senior Sketch" from the *Aurora* of 1899 showed students disappointed because their friend Edith could not return for her senior year. As her classmates lamented, they focused on Edith's loss of the freedom to come to school rather than on her mother's illness and possible death. A telegram, however, announced the mother's recovery and Edith's imminent arrival at Agnes Scott. Similarly, in another sketch, senior Margie overheard a conversation about a college girl whose father's death was announced to her by a telegram. Thinking that they were referring to her family, Margie became hysterical until the two students talking outside her door reassured her that they were discussing a short story from a magazine in the college library. And "Aunt Mabel's" stories of college life included the tale of "Bessie, our class musician. How we all loved her and expected her to distinguish our class. . . . It was truly a sad day for the class when she was called home and had to give up graduating, but she did it so bravely that nobody would have guessed that it had been a sacrifice on her part. Even though she did not get her diploma, we always numbered her as one of our class."[32]

College life, although "homey" (as the catalogue asserted) and fun (as the students described it), created public, communal obligations. When a fictional sophomore class depended on Happy's basketball prowess to beat the juniors, she played with a painful ankle injury, against her doctor's orders, and won the game for her team. In "How Clara Got First Honor," Mattie L. Tilly ('04) told the story of best friends Clara McBride and May Rosan, who were tied for first place in their class. The faculty decided to determine the recipients of first and second honors on the basis of a final essay. May was the better writer of the two, and both women expected that she would win. May, however, knew that first honors would mean a great deal to Clara's widowed mother and to Clara herself, eager to fulfill her father's dream of seeing his child in first place. She turned in a second-rate essay, and when Clara found out, May persuaded her friend not to say anything. Although Clara graduated with first honors, her conscience bothered her, and a year later she told the story to their English professor. Without revealing the circumstances, the college announced that May Rosen had actually taken first honors at the previous commencement, and that Clara McBride, second place. In a more traditional Victorian story about women's friendships, Clara would not have discovered May's act of unselfish friendship and womanly sacrifice. Here, however, the student author gently rebuked May for well-intentioned but unethical behavior, while praising competition and merit, commonly associated with men's sphere.[33]

Students celebrated their achievements and sought meaningful ways to live as educated women. A writer for the *Mnemosynean* criticized Washington Irving's portrayal of women in his novels and stories. Although admitting that good wives and mothers were important, the student stated: "We who have seen what higher education will do for women cannot admire those who have only such accomplishments as are necessary to the education of a fine lady, and who never seem to reach any great mental height."[34] And in a valedictory to the class of 1894 from the Mnemosynean society, Mary Mel Neel warned her classmates:

> If we do not undertake our life-work with proper ideas of our duty to society and our responsibility to God, then our opportunities have been wasted, and will only bring reproach upon education; and the world will fold its sanctimonious hands and say: "What has she done with her coveted higher education?" . . . Women are often compelled by dire necessity to be the breadwinners. The nineteenth century has given her ampler opportunities and broader fields for her endeavors, but, I am sorry to say, not equal compensation for her labors.

Although women's employment opportunities were limited and salaries unjustly low, Neel considered the possibility of self-support an important and desirable option. Unlike their mothers and grandmothers, Agnes Scott graduates had choices to make. They need not marry unless the right man came along.[35]

Class prophecies depicted graduates as doctors, lawyers, opera singers, newspaperwomen, teachers, college professors, politicians, dentists, missionaries, and judges; rarely as housewives and mothers. Meant to be facetious by pointing out the individual quirks of seniors, the prophecies also demonstrated awareness of women's expanding roles and the knowledge that marriage interfered with the best-laid plans. Nellie Mandeville's intelligence and strength of character had clearly impressed her fellow students. In one prediction she was a successful New York City lawyer, while another prophet sent her to Havana to straighten out the Cuban crisis. On the other hand, Cora Strong ('97) became a humorist on the *Atlanta Constitution*, only to be dismissed for flirting with male reporters. Florida Bethel, disappointed in love, was an engineer who died in a terrible train wreck. Astronomer Midge McAden gave up stargazing for marriage. The class prophet of 1897 also reported that Ella Belle Emery, Susie May Wallace, Emma Wallace, Julia Dudley, Annie Council, and Florence Hilderth founded a "women's town" in New Mexico, "where they lived in peace and happiness until Julia, who could never find a man of good enough family to suit her, eloped with an Italian peddler, who had managed to make his way within their town walls.[36]

Additional evidence from student sources shows their interest in men but some ambivalence about giving up education, careers, or independence for marriage. In short stories, far more like Vassar writings than Newcomb fiction, women made these choices without interference from friends, family, or even the men in question, who did not actually appear on the scene. Nineteen-year-old Helen Davenport turned down a proposal from the man she loved so that she could finish college; in contrast, Marguerite gave up her singing career to marry Ted. Men were equally absent from the frequent Civil War romances in student publications. In each case they died in battle, leaving women to grieve and raise children alone.

When student authors allowed men into their stories, they usually mocked them. Jack Manning saw a beautiful girl on an Atlanta streetcar and fell in love when she smiled at him. He followed her home, learned that she was an Agnes Scott student, and arranged to go to the college's next reception. Late at night when he finally succeeded in isolating the girl from her many admirers long enough to talk to her, he found that she had smiled at him not with admiration, but out of pity because he looked so mournful. In a similar story, Harvard student John Sawyers spotted a lovely young woman at a football game. He sent her a card with his name and college written on it; she sent one back reading "Miss Elizabeth White, Wellesley." When Sawyers went to Wellesley to call on "Miss Elizabeth White," he discovered that she was not a student, but the college's cook, and he beat a hasty retreat.[37]

Through the Alumnae Association, founded in 1895, students heard of graduates' achievements and learned how to follow in their footsteps. The *Agonistic,* the *Aurora,* and the *Agnes Scott Quarterly* listed marriages and children but also noted the volunteer work, civic offices, graduate study, and jobs of alumnae. In a pamphlet published by the Alumnae Association, "wives and mothers" was only one of forty-three job categories filled by Agnes Scott graduates. Other occupations included advertising, banking, biology, bookkeeping, book reviewing, chemistry, church secretaries, educational management, home economics, industrial work, institutional work, journalism, law, library work, mechanical drawing, medicine, missions, nursing, pastor's assistants, physical education, public health service, Red Cross, secretarial work, social service, summer camp work, teaching, and YWCA jobs.

The writer of the pamphlet stressed that southern conservatism not only placed severe limits on the availability of education and training for women but also closed many occupations to them; thus, the achievements of Agnes Scott women were especially remarkable. She singled out six graduates for individual mention: Nan B. Stephens, playwright, musician, and vice president

of the National Federation of Music Clubs; Louise Davidson, theatrical manager; India Hunt, graduate of the Women's Medical College of Philadelphia
and the first women professor at the University of Virginia; Mildred Thom-
son, director of research for the schools of Arizona; Nannie Lee Winn, graduate of John Hopkins Medical School, and assistant superintendent of the New
England Hospital for Women and Children in Boston; Mary Kirkpartrick, theatrical producer. Only Hunt lived and worked in the South; Stephens listed
her residence as Atlanta, Georgia, but her career was in New York City. In
the 1920s, alumnae wrote long articles about their experiences at southern,
northern, and European graduate schools, offering advice to prospective applicants from Agnes Scott. And in June 1927 six missionary alumnae told the
Agnes Scott community about "What Happened to Us in China" during the
Chinese revolution and civil wars.[38]

President Gaines came to agree that Agnes Scott College trained women
for leadership, public service, and the professions. In the *Agnes Scott Bulletin*,
an administrative publication used to publicize the college and encourage
donations, Gaines wrote about the advantages of women's higher education.
One such article listed forty-two graduates who became teachers, including
Anna I. Young (1900, MA, Columbia) professor of mathematics at Agnes
Scott; Cora Strong (1897, BA Cornell), chair of mathematics department,
Greensboro Normal, in Greensboro, North Carolina; Lucile Alexander (1911),
adjunct professor of French, Agnes Scott; Rusha Welsey (1900), principal of
the East Atlanta School; Margaret McCallie (1909) PhB, Chicago), adjunct
professor of German, Agnes Scott; Rachel Young (1907), teacher of Latin,
Decatur High School, Decatur, Georgia; and Rose Wood (1908), teacher in
the Atlanta schools. In a special issue entitled "The Woman's College and
Women," Gaines argued that the woman's college was necessary to maintain
the advanced position of women and that women's colleges furnished and
would continue to supply leaders for all the great woman movements, such as
the Woman's Christian Temperance Union (WCTU), social settlement work,
philanthropy and charities, the Federation of Women's Clubs, suffrage, and
Christian activities. In 1918, the campus YWCA established a program to help
students select careers "open to twentieth century women."[39]

Interest in reform and politics accompanied talk of careers and service.
The *Agonistic* ("pertaining to sharp mental combat") first appeared in February
1916. In it, students discussed the world beyond Decatur, Georgia. A regular
column, "Aggie's Jollies," contained jokes about world affairs. In March 1917,

the paper reported that "all the college girls who could get off went to Atlanta to hear Taft speak." On another occasion, editors told their readers that "even if not a suffragette, you should be sorry to have missed Anna Howard Shaw's talk. The true woman is in no danger of being contaminated by society." In 1917, social feminism arrived on campus, when the college's YWCA chapter added a social service department to "educate students about the pressing needs of the present day." The *Agonistic* began discussion of industrial problems in 1921, urging students to take notice of the "industrial girls" in Atlanta department stores: "What are we going to do about the tired girl, who makes our shopping easy for us?" In 1918–19, the catalogue announced a course called "Socialism and the Social Movement," open to juniors and seniors.[40]

Agnes Scott students had no personal connections, through campus speakers, organizations (except the YWCA), or faculty to offer information and analysis of social issues. As a result, campus opinion remained naive and displayed considerable class prejudice. In response to its question about "tired" industrial girls, the *Agonistic* proposed that students join these young women for a good supper at the YWCA and attend club meetings together. As friendships between the two groups developed, students could participate in "recreational sociology," taking hikes and camping with the industrial girls, and learning "how the paper cups around chocolate are made, and how boxing is done" as they "tramped along the road munching apples together." In October 1921, Agnes Scott students presented a program of stunts on factory girls and college girls, "each thinking she is the only one who works hard." In reporting on the program, the *Agonistic* concluded: "The need is for college women to be broad enough to catch the viewpoint of the ignorant factory girl."[41]

Comments about blacks or race relations rarely appeared in student literature before the 1920s, but the following student short story reveals that in this area, too, notions of noblesse oblige prevailed. A young teacher in "a Sabbath-school for colored people" was discouraged over her pupils' slow progress. In particular, an old family nurse, Margie, never failed to attend class but did not seem to comprehend the Bible stories and their moral lessons, especially the most recent tale of Philip and the eunuch. During a social call on Margie's "mistress," the teacher asked the name of the new baby boy in the household. "Oh," said the mother, "I must tell you about what a time we had selecting a name. It will show you one of the results of your teaching on Margie." Delighted that she had made an impression on her pupil, the teacher asked for details. "Well," said the mother, "one morning we held a family consultation about the baby's name, but no two of us could agree. Even little Philip came up and stood smiling into his little brother's face. . . . Just then old Margie came towards us and stood with arms akimbo, looking at the baby. 'Is yer tryin' to git a name fur the preshus angel? Why, 'hit's jes as easy! Here's Philip and now call that un Eunik and 'hit'll jes suit fine.'" In the South of the Progressive Era, even women's higher education, itself a liberal reform, did not lead to a reexamination of racial ideology.[42]

By 1920, Sophie Newcomb and Agnes Scott Colleges had traveled a long way from the ideals of their founders. Students and alumnae of both schools would not have denied that higher education produced better wives and mothers, but they also expected their lives to include church work, social service, community leadership, and sometimes careers. As a group, these women were more politically conservative than female students elsewhere, particularly regarding suffrage, and had fewer doubts about marriage and traditional family life. Yet like other college women of this era, their education combined aspects of men's and women's culture, allowing then, as graduates, to move woman's sphere into the public arena.

NOTES

Editors' Note: Lynn Gordon's essay is reprinted by permission of Yale University Press. Copyright ©1990 Yale University Press.

1. James Ross McCain, "The Growth of Agnes Scott College, 1889–1955," *Agnes Scott College Bulletin,* ser. 53, no. 2 (April 1956): 1–6; Amy Friedlander, "Not a Veneer or a Sham: The Early Days at Agnes Scott," *Atlanta Historical Journal* (Winter 1979–80): 33–44.

2. Wallace M. Alston, "The Significance of the Life of George Washington Scott," in *Colonel George Washington Scott,* ed. Alston (Decatur, Ga.: Agnes Scott College, n.d.), 4–5.

3. McCain, "The Growth of Agnes Scott College," 2–3, 6; *Student Handbook, 1917* (Decatur, Ga.: Student Government Association, Agnes Scott College), 46ff.; "Religious Traditions at Agnes Scott," notes for chapel talk by James Ross McCain, February 23, 1952, Agnes Scott Notebooks, Agnes Scott College Archives, Agnes Scott College, Decatur, Ga. In the 1960s, Agnes Scott's reputation as a liberal arts institution conflicted with its Christian mission. The college rejected the application of Kathryn Harris, a doctoral candidate from Emory University, for a position in the Department of English because she was Jewish. President Wallace Alston told newspapers that he had taken an oath to bring "only professing Christians" onto the faculty (Gene Roberts, "Atlanta College Bars Jews on Faculty," *New York Times,* February 16, 1967). See also *Atlanta Constitution,* February 16, 1967; *Atlanta Journal,* October 17, 1968.

4. McCain, "The Growth of Agnes Scott College," 4.

5. *Catalogue of Agnes Scott Institute, 1898–99; 1903–4: 75–76; 1906–7; 1910–11; 1918–19.*

6. *Student Handbook, 1912–13,* Agnes Scott College.

7. Information on the faculty, including degrees and ranks, may be found in the *Catalogue of Agnes Scott Institute* and *Catalogue of Agnes Scott College.*

8. *New Orleans Daily Picayune,* June 14, 1894; Edwin Alderman, quoted in *New Orleans Daily Picayune,* April 28, 1903, Newcomb College Scrapbooks, Tulane University Archives, Howard-Tilton Memorial Library (hereafter cited as UAHT).

9. Right Reverend Hugh Miller Thompson, Bishop of Mississippi, speech at Newcomb College Commencement, 1892, source of clipping unknown; *World's Fair Advocate,* March 18, 1893; Judge W. W. Howe, quoted in *New Orleans Daily Picayune,* June 30, 1898; all in Newcomb College Scrapbooks.

10. Edwin Alderman, quoted in *New Orleans Daily Picayune,* April 28, 1903, Newcomb College Scrapbooks.

11. *Report of the Registrar of H. Sophie Newcomb Memorial College, 1914–1915,* UAHT, and Amelie Roman Faculty File, UAHT. Between 1890 and 1920, the College awarded 492 BA degrees; between 1893 and 1901, 29 BS degrees; between 1897 and 1920, 39 BDes (art) degrees; between 1913 and 1920, 24 BMus (music) degrees; and between 1913 and 1925, 181 BA degrees in education. Domestic science students who stayed for four years received a BA in education. Attendance figures were higher than the number of degrees warranted, indicating that many women stayed for only two years. In 1915, for example, with 66 students in the art school, the College awarded two degrees in art. Figures on degrees awarded from a statement prepared by Horace Renegar, public relations director, Tulane University, for *Mademoiselle* magazine, no date, UAHT. See also Reverend A. D. Mayo, *Southern Women in the Recent Educational Movement in the South,* Bureau of Education, Circular of Information, no. 1 (1892): 167. In *Louisiana's Art Nouveau: The Crafts of the Newcomb Style* (Gretna, La.: Pelican Press, 1976), Suzanne Ormond and Mary E. Irvine describe the art school, pottery shops, etc., at Newcomb College. In an appendix, they list art school graduates and information on their subsequent employment. It is not clear how many women needed to support themselves. Josephine Newcomb's bequest assumed an economic need, but Ormond and Irvine comment that the famous decorators came from the New Orleans gentry and were free to attend college and work at the guild after graduation because their services were not needed at home (71). See also Ellsworth Woodward, "Art in Colleges," *Newcomb Arcade* 8, no. 2 (January 1916): 26–31.

12. *Jambalaya,* 1896, 159.

13. Margaret Sterling Lea, "According to Cable," *Tulanian* (February 1905): 71–72; "The Tragedy of a Bow of Blue Ribbon," *Tulanian* 2, no. 6 (April 1906): 64–69.

14. Letter from Brandt Dixon to Newcomb parents, quoted in unknown newspaper, February 10, 1892, Newcomb College Scrapbooks.

15. Brandt V. B. Dixon, *A Brief History of the H. Sophie Newcomb College, 1887–1919* (New Orleans: Hauser Printing, 1928), 75.

16. Ibid., 32–33.

17. Delie Bancroft ('14), "The Gospel of Work," *Newcomb Arcade* 5, no. 4 (June 1913): 21–27.

18. Mildred Renshaw ('17), "To Thine Ownself Be True," *Newcomb Arcade* 8, no. 3 (March 1916): 28–31.

19. *New Orleans Daily Picayune,* April 8, 1911, and March 30, 1912; *New Orleans Times-Democrat,* March 15, 1914; *New Orleans Times Picayune,* November 11, 1914, Newcomb College Scrapbooks.

20. Dixon, *Brief History*, 33.

21. L. E. Zimmerman, "Jean Margaret Gordon," and "Kate M. Gordon," in *Notable American Women* (Cambridge: Harvard University Press, 1971), 2:64–68; Allen F. Davis, "Eleanor Laura McMain," in *Notable American Women*, 2:474–76.

22. "The Newcomb Economics Course," *Newcomb Arcade* 3, no. 4 (June 1911): 71–72.

23. Doris Kent ('17), "A History of Varsity Debating at Newcomb," *Newcomb Arcade* 9, no. 3 (April 1917): 257–61. For Agnes Scott students' version of the same event, see the account by Emma Jones Smith in Agnes Scott Notebooks, Agnes Scott College Archives: "The Newcomb girls felt that we took an unfair advantage of the judges because we wore evening dresses whereas they marched forth to battle clad in sensible white skirts and shirtwaists."

24. Elizabeth McFetridge ('12), "The Point of View: The Monologue Given by Ethel Perkins, 1893, at the Alumnae Vaudeville Show," *Newcomb Arcade* 6, no. 2 (January 1914): 40–42.

25. "'12" [author's nom de plume], "The Newcomb News at Home," *Newcomb Arcade* 7, no. 2 (February 1915): 35–40; "More Newcomb News," *Newcomb Arcade* 8, no. 3 (March 1916): 47–55.

26. See clipped articles as follows in Newcomb College Scrapbooks, UAHT *New Orleans Daily Picayune*, June 10, 1906; October 27, 1907; *Mobile Register*, September 14, 1907; a New York newspaper, November 24, 1907; *New Orleans Times-Democrat*, July 20, 1911, December 17, 1911, November 22, 1909; *New Orleans Times-Picayune*, 15 December 1914, all in Newcomb College Scrapbooks.

27. "Newcomb Rights," *Newcomb Arcade* 1, no. 2 (March 1909): 64–65.

28. "'12" [author's nom de plume], "A Meeting of the Tulane Board," *Newcomb Arcade* 7, no. 4 (August 1915): 73–79.

29. Friedlander, "Not a Veneer or a Sham," 38–39; Louise McKinney quoted in *Atlanta Constitution*, December 20, 1961; interview by Lynn Gordon with Prof. E. W. McNair, December 1980.

30. Emma Jones ('18), "Not in the Catalogue," *Agnes Scott Bulletin*, ser. 14 (April 19, 1917): no pagination; "How the Spring Holidays Came to Be," *Agonistic*, March 29, 1919.

31. *Agnes Scott Institute Catalogue, 1896–1897*: 63; ibid., *1904–1905*: 85.

32. "Senior Sketches," *Aurora*, 1899, 177–83; Mabel McKowen, "Looking Backward," *Aurora*, May 1905, 420–22.

33. Lillian Harper ('15), "Her Last Game," *Aurora*, January 1912, 115–18; Mattie L. Tilly ('04), "How Clare Got First Honor," *Aurora*, October 1902, 22–24.

34. "Washington Irving's Conception of Woman," *Mnemosynean*, 3, no. 9 (May 1894): 12–13.

35. Mary Mel Neel, "Valedictory," *Mnemosynean* 3, no. 9 (May 1894): 1–3.

36. "Mnemosynean Prophecy," *Aurora*, 1897, 137–39.

37. "Senior Decisions," *Aurora*, 1899, 143–49; Teddy ('05), "Marguerite's Success," *Aurora*, December 1904, 139–45; "A Romance," *Mnemosynean*, January 1899, 8; Mary Dillard, "Grandmother," *Aurora*, April 1907, 7–8; Laura E. Candler ('04), "The North or the South," *Aurora*, March 1903, 189–92; Lottie May Blair ('14), "Violets and a Mournful Man," *Aurora*, December 1911, 6–8; Polly, "Mistaken Identity," *Aurora*, December 1904, 173–74.

38. *The Alumnae of Agnes Scott College*; "What Happened to Us in China," *Agnes Scott Alumnae Quarterly*, June 1927, 7–8; and "The Spires of Oxford"; Vivian Little, "A Student in Paris," Leslie Gaylord, "Eternal Rome"; Carla Hinman, "Studying French in Geneva"; Marion Green, "The University of Grenoble"; "Doing Graduate Work in the South"; Isabel Ferguson, "The

Beginner in Graduate Work at Chicago"; Frances Harper, "History at Louisiana State University"; Ivylyn Girardeau, "Medicine at Tulane"; Leone Bowers Hamilton, "A Summer at an Art Academy"; Helen Lane Comfort, "Specializing in New York City"; and "What Price Graduate Work?" all in *Agnes Scott Alumnae Quarterly* (November 1927): 3–19. For a complete listing of Agnes Scott graduates, 1893–1924, see *Agnes Scott College Catalogue, 1924–1925:* 162–91. The catalogue also lists graduate degrees and married names through the class of 1921. By combining this information with career lists from the April 5, 1922, *Agonistic,* it is possible to get at least a limited picture of the postgraduate lives of Agnes Scott alumnae.

39. *Agnes Scott Bulletin,* ser. 11, no. 3 (March 27, 1914): 8–10; "The Woman's College and Women," *Agnes Scott Bulletin,* ser. 13, no. 7 (April 1916); *Student Handbook, 1918:* 10.

40. *Agonistic,* March 30, 1917 and October 25, 1921; *Agnes Scott College Catalogue, 1918–1919:* 73–74; *Student Handbook, 1917;* ibid., *1919:* 10.

41. *Agonistic,* October 25, 1921. The citizens of Atlanta did not encourage women's reform and political activities (see, for example, Taylor, "Woman's Suffrage Activities in Atlanta," 45–53; Newman, "The Role of Women in Atlanta's Churches, 1865–1906," 17–30; and Roth, "Matronage").

42. Janie Curry ('04), "What Margie Learned at Sabbath-School," *Aurora,* January 1903, 132–33.

4

WHAT MAKES A "NEWCOMB GIRL"?

Student Culture in the Progressive Era

TRENT WATTS

I n the fall of 1887, the H. Sophie Newcomb Memorial College admitted its first class of fifty-nine women. Three years later, Newcomb held its first commencement exercises, at which ten women received degrees. "You are the firstlings of our flock," declared Tulane University president Colonel William Preston Johnston in congratulating the ten women who comprised the first graduating class of the H. Sophie Newcomb Memorial College.[1] He continued: "But I prefer to think of you, shall I say, as the rare primroses in the springtime of its college existence, the first flowers of its morning." Over the past three years, he told the women, they had found in Newcomb a "sanctuary," where they learned "love of knowledge," "love of wisdom," and "love of virtue which brings with it holiness and the grace of God."[2] Johnston's remarks underscore the ambivalences surrounding the higher education of women in the New South. If, as many white southerners believed, the social order of the New South depended upon the defense of the domestic order, then attempts by upper- and middle-class white women to move beyond their traditional family roles might seem to threaten that order. The problem of reconciling the traditional icon of the Southern Lady with the end-of-the-century New Woman was particularly acute at southern women's colleges.

Defenders of women's education worked to dispel the notion that a college education would "unsex" women and to demonstrate the value for young white southern women of an education for "the practical side of life as well as . . . literary excellence."[3] The mark of an Old South upon a New South edifice is seen clearly in Newcomb's curriculum, the student body, and in the broader society's appraisals of Newcomb College. Young southern "ladies" studied physics and physiology and learned how to support themselves in careers after graduation; the College boarders lived "independently" in an intellectual cloister away from their parents, but they were "expected at all times" to maintain "quiet lady-like behavior."[4] The students received a liberal arts education, which nevertheless upheld the conservative hierarchy of the dominant white southern culture, including a traditional vision of domestic order. Yet, these ambivalences and internal contradictions are what allowed for the reciprocal and culturally productive relationship that arose between Newcomb College and southern culture.

Newcomb functioned not to disrupt white southern culture, but rather to infuse progressive energies into what the white South had long professed: that women were the loving angels of the home, that southern culture was healthy and homogeneous, and that such a social order was natural and organic—as natural as the native flora with which the Newcomb women inscribed their noted pottery. The College made numerous concessions to white southern mores and to the assumptions of its founder and its administrators, who shared many of the South's cultural assumptions about gender and sexuality, race, and social class. Johnston had been a member of President Jefferson Davis's staff and was the son of the martyred hero of Shiloh, General Albert Sidney Johnston.[5] Josephine Newcomb, a northerner by birth, nevertheless felt a deep affinity with the antebellum South, donating much of her wealth toward her own vision of its reconstruction.[6] When she made New Orleans the site of the memorial college to her daughter and, in 1899, of her own principal residence, Josephine Newcomb consciously chose a city where, as Newcomb president Brandt V. B. Dixon put it, "pre-war ideals still prevailed."[7]

Compromises between the ideals of a rigorous education and the mores of the white South were visible also in the ways Newcomb was represented in the New Orleans press. Although the *Times-Democrat*, the *Delta Journal* and the *Daily Picayune* ran pieces on Newcomb's "grand liberality" and the "equal education of the two sexes," the newspapers gave coverage increasingly to social events such as "fraternity teas" and extracurricular activities. Even the coverage of commencement exercises, dedications of new buildings, and scholarship awards were written as if they belonged on the society pages, whereas serious or "feminist" material, if present at all, was buried in long columns that reproduced commencement-day speeches or particular lectures.[8] When the Newcomb Chapel was dedicated in 1896, the *Daily Picayune* noted that the "assemblage" at the event "represented the culture and the learning of New Orleans."[9] In the same issue, a short vignette narrated the aspirations of Newcomb's most recent alumnae, the class of 1895: "Of course, we all intend to be married some day. Though we are bachelors of art and science, we don't intend to remain bachelors all our days," remarked one. "And they all shook hands, and, girl-like, sealed the pledge with a kiss all around . . . the loveliest girls that were ever dubbed masters of arts—oh, I mean of hearts!"[10]

When Mrs. Newcomb insisted that the College educate women in "the practical side of life," she presumably meant that Newcomb graduates, should they not find suitable husbands, should be able to support themselves. To this end, the College approved the development of Newcomb Pottery, founded in 1896, and, eventually, of other arts and crafts enterprises such as embroidery and bookbinding. It is no stretch to see Newcomb's fine arts program and its physical education program—both programs earning distinction for the College—as two sides of the same aesthetic vision of southern womanhood and southern culture. Both programs, as well as the short-lived School of Household Economy, aimed at producing better women for the New South. A careful look at the construction and workings of these programs serves to identity several of the ideological tensions inherent in Newcomb College.

Art was a subject believed to be especially suited to women's tastes and abilities. Newcomb embraced this belief. From the beginning, instruction in painting and drawing was offered, both as a part of the regular academic program and as a separate course of study. But the pottery program represented a departure from the early system and introduced a new objective. A "natural outgrowth of the college's efforts to educate teachers of the fine arts, and to become a centre of aesthetic culture," the Newcomb Pottery was at the same time intended as a moneymaking venture. It was "just what the South needed," wrote one observer, "in order that the prosperity of the locality should be increased, and the critical power of the public developed."[11]

Newcomb art professor Ellsworth Woodward made the cultural mission of the Newcomb Pottery clear when he called such artistic craftsmanship "a limitless field in which the world of industry ministers to the needs of refined civilization."[12] Woodward believed that the pottery program would refine the aesthetic taste of the students and create aesthetic sense in the southern public, which Woodward found sorely lacking: "During three generations a conquered people, Southerners had established a momentum of thought which did not include art. So first we must give the girls a chance to prove art a practical matter, related to the world of affairs."[13]

Newcomb's pottery gained renown quickly. By 1909, the *New Orleans Item* was suggesting that Newcomb Pottery not only aided the college's reputation, but also brought the attention of the nation to Tulane University as a whole: "The work of the young women students has done more to give the whole university a high rank in the great outer world of college life than any other branch."[14]

However, as with much that transpired at Newcomb, the pottery program was driven by conflicting concerns. Designed as a practical industry, the Pottery needed also to justify itself as part of a liberal arts curriculum, and so one sees occasional references to an "art for art's sake" ideal alongside this emphasis on pragmatism. Though the Pottery's founders were quite explicit about the enterprise providing "a real means of support for the advanced student," there were definite limits as to what the upper- and middle-class women of Newcomb could do without endangering their "respectability," or class standing.[15] For instance, it seems natural to assume that students enrolled in pottery classes learned to be *potters*—that they designed and threw pots. In fact, the College employed men to handle the "technical and physical aspect of the pottery" from preparing the clay and the glazes to throwing and firing the pots.[16] What the students learned was how to *decorate* the pottery, a practice closely related to china painting, a traditional art of ladies of leisure, which also was taught in the Newcomb Art School. The fact that the Pottery was guided by the liberal arts ideals of the College and had no need to turn a profit itself meant that aesthetics took precedence over profit. Far from worrying that industry might damage southern womanhood, then, we see in the pottery program the idea that southern womanhood was to be the salvation of industry and culture in the South.

Another of Newcomb's innovative programs, physical education, pursued an even more direct course of improving southern womanhood for the New South. According to the College catalogue: "There is a growing recognition in this as well as in foreign countries, of the need of combining physical training with mental work. Only where these are properly united can the best educational results be secured."[17] Newcomb students were required to take regular exercise, and the Physical Education Department was formed in 1891, not entirely to applause. "I received from parents and even from physicians protesting letters," recalled Dixon, "some on the grounds of a supposed tendency to render the young ladies coarse and unfeminine, others on account of health or other considerations."[18]

As physical education programs soon became part of the curriculum at all women's colleges, Newcomb found itself in the awkward position of lagging behind developments in women's education in the Northeast but of running ahead of common opinion in the South.[19] Since the mid-nineteenth century, advocates of women's education in the Northeast and in Britain had promoted regular exercise as a way to counter the debilitating effects of study, which, most physicians agreed, were particularly pronounced in the female college student. Turn-of-the-century physicians in Europe and America buttressed social prejudice against women's colleges by warning that excessive mental exertion past the onset of puberty damaged a women's fertility and thereby endangered "the race." "The New Woman," wrote G. Stanley Hall in 1904, "has taken up and utilized in her own life all that was meant for her descendants, and has so overdrawn her account with heredity that . . . she is also completely sterile."[20] These fears were tied to culturally specific forms of racism and xenophobia. In the 1875 *Sex in Education: Or a Fair Chance for Girls*, New England physician Edward Clarke asks ominously of the unsettled western territories of the United States: "Shall they be filled by our own children or by those of aliens? This is a question that our own women must answer; upon their loins depends the future destiny of the nation."[21] Regardless of region, race suicide in America was seen as "a problem in social gynaecology."[22] However, such fears for the Anglo-Saxon, Protestant "race" were particularly strong in the South, where traditional political and economic structures and cultural narratives had been threatened by Reconstruction and free people of color.

Thus, in an era when the female college student was widely associated with the neurasthenic, and white America feared degeneration and "race suicide" because its "best" women were studying rather than bearing children, women's colleges needed to develop an aggressive defense of their students' bodies. To this end, the leading northeastern women's colleges built gymnasiums or "calistheniums" and implemented required exercise regimens coupled with close medical supervision and examinations.[23] But while many physicians and educators supported at least moderate exercise for women, others remained skeptical, warning that athletics would make women crude and masculine, and even suggesting that the excitement of competition might unleash an unregulated sexual passion in the women athletes.[24] With such terrifying possibilities on either side of the exercise debate, most educators of the period took a distinctly moderate stance.

The director of the Newcomb College Physical Education Department who was to administer this physical moderation was Clara Baer. Baer was trained at the Possa Normal School of Gymnastics in Boston in what was called the "Swedish method of gymnastics." A nineteenth-century invention of the poet Peter Henrik Lang, the Lang System shunned competitive games and stressed instead graceful, deliberate movements. Along with the regular course of exercises, Baer developed a tame, refined version of basketball, which she called "basquette." In keeping with its eugenicist concerns, the Swedish system emphasized "the medical inspection and monitoring of students" along with gymnastic exercise.[25]

The reasons for bringing the Swedish system to Newcomb seem fairly clear. One proponent of Lang's ideas wrote: "In a very real sense, women have in their keeping, not alone their own lives, but those of their children after them: if the mothers are healthy and strong, the children will be beautiful with the beauty of health. The physical regeneration of the race is no Utopian dream; we can begin it here and now."[26] To this end, Baer and her staff developed a four-year course in physical education and hygiene that included instruction and practice in "aesthetic gymnastics," "voice culture" (how to breathe hygienically and gymnastically), and basketball, with lectures in such topics as diet, dress, rest, and the "mental aspect of health."[27]

The College supported the efforts of the Physical Education Department with its strict rules for resident students. "Undoubtedly," writes John Dyer, "the Newcomb girls were in the pink of health" with lights out at 10:15 and all evenings but Fridays devoted to "study and rest."[28] One aspect of well-being doctors looked for under the Swedish system was a healthy appetite and sufficient weight gain to guard against the dangers of study-induced neurasthenia.[29] In keeping with this way of thinking, the 1892 commencement speaker, Hugh Miller Thompson, the Episcopal bishop of Mississippi, asked the Newcomb graduates: "Are your appetites good and can you enjoy the good Creole cookery of your city? If you cannot feel hungry and eat plenty, your education has done you no good."[30] In 1900, Florence Dymond, president of the Alumnae Association, noted that the alumnae had opened a fund-raising lunchroom at Newcomb for the purpose of "appeasing the well-known appetite of the Newcomb girl, whose hard-working brain needs more than a pecan praline or a bottle of pickles to stimulate it to continued action throughout the afternoon."[31]

Creating utopian specimens of southern womanhood through physical fitness was no simple task at Newcomb, however. One of the difficult objections to overcome was that of the immodesty that exercise seemed to require. In the early years, Newcomb women exercised before the administrative building, in full view of Camp Street, a major route in uptown New Orleans. However, this arrangement proved unsuitable, not only because of the noise and dust but because the women drew attention from passersby, including deliverymen, who tended to stop their horses and wagons to watch.[32]

Home economics or domestic science, begun at Newcomb in 1909, like Newcomb's physical education and pottery programs, was a typical Progressive Era program for women because, at its core, it was a reaction against the chaos of modern life that so exercised progressive reformers. Home economists such as Ellen Richards promoted domestic science as "nothing less than an effort to save our social fabric from what seems inevitable disintegration."[33] Teaching Newcomb students about proper nutrition and sanitation, therefore, was not ideologically different from teaching them Swedish gymnastics or pottery decorating: in all cases, the point of this "vocations" training was explicitly aimed at perfecting the southern woman for her cultural mission.

The popularity of the domestic science course could be attributed to the belief that home economics "was both traditional and progressive at once."[34] Insofar as Newcomb's domestic science program placed its "Professional" course above the second "Homemaker's" course, it kept faith with its original "progressive" mission. Home economists used the field to extend the private-sphere concept of the "home"—and thus woman's sphere and opportunities— to the public sphere to encompass the "institutional household and the community."[35] Still, there is little doubt that the majority of domestic science students, at Newcomb as elsewhere, intended to use their educations to improve the sanitation of their own homes and the nutrition and hygiene of their husbands and children. In this sense, the home economics program was, in fact, more "practical" than a liberal arts degree for a large portion of Newcomb students.

Despite the hold of the New Orleans community and families on matters regarding daughters in attendance at Newcomb, students developed a definite identity as "Newcomb girls." Like college women everywhere, Newcomb students ordered their days around a fairly circumscribed core of classes and labs—they studied Latin and perhaps French or German, basic sciences and mathematics, English literature and history. They ate meals together, they went to chapel, they gathered on the College grounds to study and talk. In fact, what is most striking when reading about student life is how similar

Newcomb's student culture was to that of other women's colleges. In 1910, sophomore Beatrice Frye (NC 1913) expressed this sense of a shared female college culture when she wrote of the "Newcomb Ideals." "The college girl is about the same the world over; necessarily then," wrote Frye, "the same code of ideals must exist in all colleges." Even when Frye turns her attention to Newcomb's "characteristic and individual set of ideals," she has trouble imagining anything unique to Newcomb. She notes that chapel is "an important factor in the spiritual side of a college life"; but while chapel was certainly not a universal feature of Progressive Era colleges, it was common.[36] If anything, chapel was less important at Newcomb than at many schools such as Wellesley with its "Christian missionary spirit."[37] Though Mrs. Newcomb had wanted the college to have general Christian contours, she specified that it be nonsectarian, and records of faculty meetings show requests from both Catholic and Jewish students to be excused from chapel services.[38]

Frye gives cursory attention to the Newcomb student's earnest work at her studies—surely something any college student might claim—and then spends a significant amount of time discussing the ideals involved in various campus clubs: the Literary and Debating Society, the Latin Club, the Newcomb Athletic Association, the Young Women's Christian Association. Again, emphasis upon campus organizations such as these was typical of student life of the period, especially since it was through such clubs that colleges hoped to create a cohesive student body. Newcomb students were heavily invested in what were at first called "fraternities." Dixon tells how the first sororities converted rooms in the basement of the College's main building "into charming society homes," which, however, being "immediately below certain classrooms . . . did at times annoy those instructors who insisted on keeping windows open on warm days."[39] Despite this annoyance, Dixon notes that "each of these sororities came in time to assume the responsibility of some useful work in social service, such as child welfare, visiting hospitals and orphan asylums"; they even influenced "their members in the interest of conduct and good scholarship."[40]

In many respects, the social lives of Newcomb students resembled those of college women across the United States and in England. They were interested in men because many of them hoped to marry, and to this end they went on dates to dances, restaurants, the theater, and out in automobiles. But even with this interest in dating men and despite the fact that fewer students lived on campus than at most colleges, Newcomb students developed the strong homosocial and sometimes homoerotic bonds that were typical of women college students in the early twentieth century.

The Newcomb students' sense of themselves as an all-female community, self-directed and apart from the desires of men, can be seen in a skit that was performed at the Annual Alumnae Banquet in 1910.[41] The song entitled "Craigie and Dickey and Bev" concerns the opinions of three administrators—burlesques of Craighead (the University president), Dixon (Newcomb's president), and Beverley Warner (member of the Board of Administrators and rector of Trinity Episcopal Church in New Orleans)—about the proper way to educate young women. Craigie believes that coeducation is the answer—"All together we'd talk, all together we'd lark; / I'd have the girls go to school with the Boys." Dickey thinks that female students should be isolated to preserve their femininity ("I'd have girls go to school with girls; / It preserves psychological whirls"), while Bev asserts that "Woman's vocation" is to "be seen and not heard," and so "I'd give her no schooling at all; / I'd surround her with six feet of wall." The women students, however, will have none of these opinions, simply telling their elders, "Of course we must go our own way."[42] Without making it clear what "our own way" might entail, the "feminine horde" is clear in their rejection of the educational philosophies of the three men. Craigie's happy coeducation seems suspiciously designed to please male students more than women, and Bev's cloister is out of the question. Perhaps most surprising is their rejection of Dickey's segregated schooling, although the objection is his insistence that segregation will ensure traditional femininity, represented by the "psychological whirls" (which in the song rhymes with "curls") of the weaker female mind.

The scrapbook of Beatrix Fortune (NC 1906) provides evidence of both traditional heterosexual activities—flowers and candy from male suitors, attendance at dances and fraternity functions—and of unself-conscious homoerotic behavior. A photograph shows her 1905–6 dormitory room. Under the photograph, she wrote: "It would be hard to describe! so I have substituted several pictures. Two little white beds 'side by each,' *sometimes* big enough for two, though built for one."[43] Fortune's scrapbook was a prefabricated model, *The College Girls' Record, Compiled and Illustrated by Virginia Woodson Frame* (a Smith College graduate), with designated categories that imply a common college experience. The "Classmates" page contains entries for "Prettiest," "Most Hopeless," "Best Dresser," and "Most Athletic," as well as "My Upper Class Love," which Fortune altered to "Loves," though she wrote nothing beneath. Both the scrapbook's designer and publisher assume that having an upper-class love is a common feature of college life, and Fortune seems to agree. "Smashes" or "crushes" were considered part of normal female development at girls' schools and women's colleges during the nineteenth and early twentieth centuries, and were, for the most part, nonsexual. [44] Under her scrapbook's entry for "The Flowers," for instance, Fortune describes a comical picture concerning female courtship: "We were not supposed to have the pleasure of picking these [flowers], but once in a while a silly Freshman or Soph. could be seen running across the campus with roses, violets, narcissus, daffodils, or other sweet flowers for her 'lady love,' with Mr. Buehler [the much-beloved Newcomb gardener] toddling after in the dim distance."[45]

That "smashes" among Newcomb students were both common and ordinary implies that these were typical college women of their time. Intense homosocial or even homoerotic bonds among Newcomb students would not have interfered necessarily with their interest in dating, marrying, and having children. As Smith-Rosenberg points out, men and women who were "eminently respectable and socially conservative . . . considered such love [between women] both socially acceptable and fully compatible with heterosexual marriage."[46] College and even lifelong relationships of great intensity between Newcomb women would not have altered either their sense of themselves as embodiments of New Southern womanhood or compromised their larger role as a central part of the dominant, public, white southern culture.

The sort of culturally uplifting sentiment that surrounded Newcomb Pottery was rife as well in the language that Newcomb students used to describe the broader aspirations of the school and its graduates. The editor of the first issue of the *Newcomb Arcade*, for instance, explained the magazine as a way to establish a bond between Newcomb and other "great institutions of women's education," for "institutions of culture can accomplish more by concentration of interests, and . . . women's colleges are great factors in the uplift of women, and through them of civilization."[47] Student essays read at commencement show a similar attitude toward the cultural function of the educated southern woman. The appropriately named Ella B. Ernest, class essayist for 1892, read a piece entitled "Duty Is True. This Is All Ye Know on Earth and All Ye Need to Know."[48] Representing the class of 1898, Lillian Espy spoke on "the women of the world whose names have been perpetuated in history, legend and song, and distinguished among all others of their time for nobility or grandeur of character."[49] And in 1900, Mary Mitchell Young's essay reviewed the great progress made by civilization during the nineteenth century—in literature and the arts, science and technology, and finally "the growing influence of colleges and universities." Associating the Newcomb graduates with this pinnacle of progress, Young urged her class "to be faithful to its motto, 'More light, more life, more freedom, more truth and more beyond.'"[50]

This emphasis on their own superiority reaches its height in the racialist language that infuses some of the most seemingly innocent statements and behaviors of Newcomb students. For instance, the program for the 1904 "Sophomore Class Night," included a skit entitled "The Evolution of the Newcomb Girl," in which fifteen women dressed and sang the parts of various female figures from an Egyptian princess and a "barbarian" maid of China on up the perceived cultural ladder. The Native American woman is praised for having saved "the white and his noble race" from death, even though now the whites "drive her last kinsman from his resting-place." As for "Edith the Saxon," we're told that "Ages of Woman's Rights can not efface / This dainty housewife, with her simple grace." Womanhood approaches its apex with the English and French and then, in the second to last stanza, with the "Dixie girl, alike the pride / Of North and South and all the country side." Finally, though,

> The best is reached, the Newcomb Girl attained,
> Product of all the good world has gained.
> The fair, the strong, the clever, and the sweet
> Unite in her, the maid whom now you greet.[51]

It is worth noting that besides the Egyptian, who stands at the bottom of the ladder, no African woman makes Newcomb's top fifteen; and although "Southern girl" might conceivably have included African Americans, the use of the phrase "Dixie girl," with its conscious look back to the antebellum South, makes it clear that the Newcomb girl is white. One might object that a class skit is hardly high political rhetoric and that this sort of hyperbolic self-aggrandizement is to be expected from small, insular groups who are working to create a distinctive identity. Yet, it is difficult to ignore the blatant way in which the women place racialist types in a stereotypical, post-Darwinian racial hierarchy; the fact that the poem treats the stereotypes as "natural" does not make it culturally benign.

At the same time, this opinion of themselves and their mission as privileged engendered in the Newcomb students a desire to volunteer in social work activities or enter into professions such as teaching that were typical of Progressive Era women. Newcomb students were urged by professors, commencement speakers, and their own alumnae to do good works, and many heeded the call, becoming public school teachers, college professors, missionaries, lawyers, or settlement house workers.[52] Sophomore Ethel Cushman (NC 1915) contributed to the *Newcomb Arcade* a touching fictionalized sketch of a college girl who held noble "dreams of service, of using her love and her learning to brighten the lives of the poor" yet "lacked the strength to be noble."[53] The college girl meditates on the injustices of society in half-Marxist, half-religious terms as she rides the streetcar downtown to shop: "The heaping up of wealth by a few by oppression of labor . . . their deprivation not only of material things, but of a share in the free gifts of light and air and sunshine. . . . Her spirit was lost in indignation and contempt at a boasted civilization which lacked so much of the brotherhood of man. . . . She caught a vision of true service to humanity in lending influence toward the solution on an economic basis of the problems of the poor . . . and above all to the young girls of her own age whose days were spent in monotonous rounds of unending toil."[54] Despite her theoretical sophistication, however, the college girl, tired from a long day of tedious shopping, becomes indignant with a shop girl who serves a newly arrived customer ahead of her. "In dreaming of her noble future," writes Cushman, "the college girl ignores the commonplace realities of the present and thereby betrays her own ideals."[55] Clearly, Cushman intended her story as a criticism of her fellow classmates for a hypocrisy of which they might not have been conscious, and for a public-spiritedness that was nevertheless egocentric. The Newcomb girl, the story implies, was not living up to the Newcomb ideal.

There is no doubt that during the Progressive Era, the rhetoric if not the behavior of Newcomb College was often distinctly progressive. Lynn Gordon notes that Newcomb was connected to many of the most radical white women in New Orleans. Many spoke at the College: the suffragist Jean Gordon judged student debates, and the public health reformer Eleanor McMain "offered a course in social settlement work."[56] Though he explicitly denied being a "Socialist," an early commencement speaker, John Clegg, exhorted the Newcomb graduates to social action in radical terms: "The brutal slaying of a Filipino babe by the operation of your government, the growing into a life of crime and vice of a child of the slums, the giving of the fruits of labor to those who do not labor, and the starving and suffering of those who are producing wealth are results of conditions which permit not the educated American woman to be content or to remain innocent while these exist."[57]

The rhetoric of Newcomb College and its students was also typical of the rhetoric of Progressive Era southerners in its patronizing attitude toward African Americans and romanticizing of the antebellum South. If the sort of racialist and regionalist pride of "The Evolution of the Newcomb Girl" inspired these women of the New South toward public service, it also reconfirmed their feelings of racial superiority and their culture's nostalgia for the slaveholding South. One Newcomb student began her review of Mary Johnson's novel *The Long Roll*, this way: "The war is over. Why not forget it? How this is dinned into our ears morning, noon, and night. The people have sung it and the press has chorused it ad nauseam. . . . The North is unceasingly and energetically active in forever thrusting before the public in word, print, and monument its own view of the 'Salvation of the Union,' and the 'Abolition of Slavery'—a view at worst invective, at best condescending. It is hardly fair to our heroes of the war to let their memories slip by in undefending silence."[58]

Senior Natalie Scott (NC 1909) paints a more threatening picture of race relations as they were imagined by many whites in the New South in her review of George Washington Cable's novel *Kincaide's Battery*. Though she credits Cable's skill in representing "the life of New Orleans of the sixties," she criticizes the rendering of the novel's villainess, Flora, who, with her "wicked and distorted brain," is so "thoroughly malignant and depraved that she seems at first sight almost impossible." The reviewer reconciles this "almost impossible" character with reality, however, when she remembers that Flora is of mixed-race origins: "It is no uncommon thing for a fusion of races—Flora was a Spanish Creole—to bring out the vices of all."[59] This indictment of miscegenation, couched in the languages of literary criticism and racial science, exposes the same sort of fears in the educated, progressive southern "lady" that contemporary demagogues such as Thomas Dixon or Ben Tillman consistently raised in their cautionary narratives of racial violence. Here, such language is written in seemingly perfect innocence and appears on the page opposite an editorial that spoke of the mission of women's colleges to "uplift civilization."

One of the best proofs of a coherent Newcomb identity is the Alumnae Association, which, from very early on, was an active and influential group maintaining ties with the College while reaching out into the community. Gordon suggests that the Newcomb Alumnae Association served as "a cure for the postgraduate blues," especially for those alumnae who found themselves back in domestic roles after college.[60] While this was probably the case for some women, the Alumnae Association was not a garden party society. In the first two decades of the twentieth century, it made meaningful contributions not only to the cause of women's education—by founding and staffing a community "Free Night School" at the College and by fund-raising for student scholarships and loans, for instance—but also to the larger cause of women's rights, by publicizing and promoting the postgraduate careers of its members and by campaigning vigorously for broader legal rights for women.

"Of Alumnae Interest," a column appearing regularly in the *Newcomb Arcade,* kept the Newcomb community aware of alumnae-sponsored prizes and lectures, and more importantly, perhaps, reported the activities of some of the more prominent or successful alumnae, placing special emphasis upon those who had continued their studies. After noting that Caroline Richardson (NC 1895, then instructor of English at Newcomb) had spent the summer traveling in Europe, the article continues: "The alumnae contingent studying at the University of Chicago this past summer include Misses Mary and Addie Spencer, who are studying for their doctor's degrees, Lydia Frotscher, Edith Farrar, Viola Murphy, Phoebe Palfrey and Mrs. Rudolph Anderson, who is also studying for a doctor's degree."[61]

It is true that in the second column, phrases such as "was married in September" or "has a young son" appear several times, but the initial prominence of graduate students and college instructors as alumnae worth noting must have had an impact on the Newcomb undergraduates' sense of their own possibilities.

Newcomb's students, faculty, and alumnae spoke the language of their broader culture about family, and region. As white ladies, Newcomb students both benefited from and were constrained by southern and late-Victorian American notions of womanhood. As an ideal, Newcomb girls were the women white southern men claimed to defend. Within the College and in the battles over its social significance, one can see many turn-of-the century southern notions of gender, race, and progress at work. For instance, Newcomb defenders saw the College as cultured and genteel, but also as evidence of the South's participation in broader national trends. The women educated at Newcomb College took their place among their contemporaries who argued that acting as guardians of the Lost Cause, monitoring the textbooks given to southern schoolchildren, or venturing into the political arena did not compromise their standing as southern ladies.

NOTES

1. In the same year, Tulane College enrolled seventy-nine men as full-time and seven as part-time students (see John P. Dyer, *Tulane: The Biography of a University, 1834–1965* [New York: Harper and Row, 1966], 59).

2. Quoted in Brandt V. B. Dixon, *A Brief History of H. Sophie Newcomb Memorial College, 1887–1919* (New Orleans: Hauser Printing, 1928), 55.

3. Letter of donation from Josephine Newcomb to the Administrators of the Tulane Education Fund, October 11, 1886, quoted in Dixon, *Brief History,* 9–10.

4. Newcomb Announcement for 1898–99, Newcomb Archives, Newcomb College Center for Research on Women, Tulane University (hereafter cited as NA NCCROW).

5. See Arthur Marvin Shaw, *William Preston Johnston: A Transitional Figure of the Confederacy* (Baton Rouge: Louisiana State University Press, 1943).

6. Dixon, *Brief History,* 8.

7. Ibid., 58.

8. "Grand Liberality," *New Orleans Times-Democrat,* January 15, 1892; "Female Higher Education," *Delta Journal,* July 1890, in Newcomb-related newspaper clippings, University Archives, Howard-Tilton Memorial Library, Tulane University (hereafter cited as UAHT).

9. "Newcomb Dedication," *New Orleans Daily Picayune,* January 1896, in Newcomb-related newspaper clippings, UAHT.

10. "They All Want to Be Married in the Newcomb Chapel," *Unnamed newspaper clipping,* January 1896, in Newcomb-related newspaper clippings, UAHT.

11. Mary Caroline Crawford, *The College Girl of America and the Institutions Which Make Her What She Is* (Boston: L. C. Page, 1905), 229–30.

12. Allsworth [sic] Woodward, "Arts and Crafts in Newcomb College," *Newcomb Arcade* 1, no. 1 (January 1909): 27.

13. Ellsworth Woodward, "An Experiment in Applied Art in Newcomb College New Orleans," *Art Education* 6 (May 1898): 166–68.

14. "Women Gain a Point," *New Orleans Item,* November 5, 1909, Florence Dymond Scrapbook, NA NCCROW.

15. Mary G. Sheerer, "Newcomb Pottery," *Keramic Studio* 1 (1899):151.

16. Jessie Poesch with Bob Walter and Sally Main Spanola, *Newcomb Pottery: An Enterprise for Southern Women, 1895–1940* (Exton, Pa.: Schiffer, 1984), 94.

17. Quoted in Dyer, *Tulane: The Biography of a University,* 97.

18. Dixon, *Brief History,* 75–76.

19. Pamela Dean, "'Dear Sisters' and 'Hated Rivals:' Athletics and Gender at Two New South Women's Colleges, 1893–1920," *Journal of Sport History* 24 (Fall 1997): 345.

20. G. Stanley Hall, *Adolescence* (New York: D. Appleton, 1904), 2:633.

21. Quoted in Caroll Smith-Rosenberg and Charles Rosenberg, "The Female Animal: Medical and Biological Views of Women and their Role in Nineteenth-century America," in *From 'Fair Sex' to Feminism: Sport and the Socialization of Women in the Industrial and Post-Industrial Eras,* ed. J. A. Mangan and Roberta J. Park (London: Frank Cass, 1987), 27.

22. Ibid., 27.

23. Paul Atkinson, "The Feminist Physique: Physical Education and the Medicalization of Women's Education," in *From 'Fair Sex' to Feminism,* ed. Mangan and Park, 46.

24. Susan K. Cahn, *Coming on Strong: Gender and Sexuality in Twentieth-Century Women's Sport* (New York: Free Press, 1994), 21.

25. Atkinson, "The Feminist Physique," 48.

26. V. Surge, "The Physical Education of Women [1890]," in *The Education Papers: Women's Quest for Equality in Britain, 1850–1912* , ed. Dale Spender (New York: Routledge and Kegan Paul, 1987), 294.

27. *Newcomb Catalogue, 1910–11:* 76–78.

28. Dyer, *Tulane: The Biography of a University,* 155.

29. Atkinson, "The Feminist Physique," 50.

30. "Commencement Day," *New Orleans Daily Picayune,* June 15, 1892, in Newcomb-related newspaper clippings, NA NCCROW.

31. "Newcomb Graduates," *New Orleans Times-Democrat,* June 21, 1900, in Dymond Scrapbook, UAHT.

32. Dyer, *Tulane: The Biography of a University,* 91.

33. Rima D. Apple, "Liberal Arts or Vocational Training: Home Economics Education for Girls," in *Rethinking Home Economics: Women and the History of a Profession,* ed. Sarah Stage and Virginia B. Vincenti (Ithaca: Cornell University Press, 1997), 81.

34. Jane Bernard Powers, *The Girl Question in Education: Vocational Education for Young Women in the Progressive Era* (London: Falmer Press, 1992), 13.

35. Sarah Stage, "Ellen Richards and the Social Significance of the Home Economics Movement," in *Rethinking Home Economics,* ed. Stage and Vincenti, 17.

36. Beatrice Frye, "The Newcomb Ideals," *Newcomb Arcade* 3, no. 1 (November 1910): 22–24.

37. Lynn D. Gordon, *Gender and Higher Education in the Progressive Era* (New Haven: Yale University Press, 1990), 47.

38. Minutes of the Faculty Meeting, Newcomb College, October 2, 1903; November 24, 1910, NA NCCROW.

39. Dixon, *Brief History,* 133.

40. Ibid., 133–34.

41. "Have Annual Banquet," *New Orleans Times-Democrat,* May 19, 1910, NA NCCROW.

42. "Craigie and Dickey and Bev," Frotscher Scrapbook, Newcomb Scrapbook Collection, NA NCCROW.

43. Beatrix M. Fortune, Newcomb Scrapbook Collection, NA NCCROW.

44. See, for instance: Martha Vicinus, "Distance and Desire: English Boarding-School Friendships," *Signs: Journal of Women in Culture and Society* 9, no. 4 (Summer 1984): 600–622; and Carroll Smith-Rosenberg, *Disorderly Conduct: Visions of Gender in Victorian America* (New York: Oxford University Press, 1985).

45. Fortune, Newcomb Scrapbook Collection, NA NCCROW.

46. Carroll Smith-Rosenberg, "The Female World of Love and Ritual," *Signs: Journal of Women in Culture and Society* 1 (1975): 1–30.

47. "The Newcomb Arcade," editorial, *Newcomb Arcade* 1, no. 1 (January 1909): 57.

48. "Commencement Day," *New Delta,* June 23, 1892, in Newcomb-related newspaper clippings, UAHT.

49. "Newcomb College: Ninth Annual Commencement Exercises," *New Orleans Times-Democrat,* June 30, 1898, in Newcomb-related newspaper clippings, UAHT.

50. "Fair Newcomb's Commencement Day," *New Orleans Daily Picayune,* June 21, 1900, Newcomb-related newspaper clippings, UAHT.

51. "The Evolution of the Newcomb Girl" (1904), Frotscher Scrapbook.

52. *Newcomb Alumnae Pamphlet* (1907–08); Dymond Scrapbook.

53. Ethel Cushman, "The Dreaming and the Practice," *Newcomb Arcade* 4, no. 4 (June 1912): 51.

54. Ibid., 51

55. Ibid.

56. L. Gordon, *Gender and Higher Education in the Progressive Era,* 177.

57. John Clegg, "Are Not Yearnings after Things God's Way of Providing Them?" *New Orleans Times-Democrat,* June 21, 1900, NA NCCROW.

58. Review of "*The Long Roll*—Mary Johnson," *Newcomb Arcade* 4, no. 3 (March 1912): 47.

59. Natalie Scott, "Kincaide's Battery," *Newcomb Arcade* 1, no. 1 (January 1909): 56.

60. L. Gordon, *Gender and Higher Education in the Progressive Era,* 179.

61. "Of Alumnae Interest," *Newcomb Arcade* 3, no. 1 (November 1910): 33.

5

DESIGNING FOR WOMEN

The Architecture of Newcomb College (with an epilogue from 2011)

KAREN KINGSLEY

Editors' Note: Karen Kingsley's essay, published in *Louisiana History* in 1994, is reprinted here with minor revisions and an epilogue. Like Helen Horowitz's study of the Seven Sisters colleges, *Alma Mater*, Kingsley's work describes the relationship between the architectural design of Newcomb's Broadway campus and its self-conscious intentions as a college for women separate from Tulane.[1] She emphasizes the College's distinctive physical identity: "different in materials and formal qualities from Tulane, appropriate as a memorial, sufficiently Southern, and recognizably feminine." The epilogue includes a description of buildings constructed after the initial three buildings in 1918, and defines the area and buildings dedicated in perpetuity as the "Newcomb College Campus" by a resolution of the Administrators of the Tulane Educational Fund in 1987.

Only a half mile separates the Tulane University campus from that of Newcomb College, but the architectural differences between the schools create the illusion of great distance. Newcomb's neat red brick and crisp white detailing contrast sharply with Tulane's rugged buff-gray stone and sculptured Romanesque forms. Tulane's oldest buildings at its uptown New Orleans site date from 1894, while Newcomb's campus was designed in 1911 (built 1917), but this interval does not explain the great disparity in form and style. At the turn of the century, when both campuses were conceived, the prevailing public taste encompassed a broad spectrum of architectural style, but it is clear that Newcomb's architectural image was intended to contrast with that of Tulane.

Newcomb College's distinctive architectural aesthetic was shaped by the school's intended role as a southern women's college. In 1886, Josephine Louise Le Monnier Newcomb donated $100,000 to establish a women's college in the Crescent City in memory of her daughter, Harriott Sophie Newcomb, who had died in 1870. The H. Sophie Newcomb Memorial College, initially housed in a former mansion on Camp and Howard Streets, opened in October 1887.

Newcomb soon outgrew its original home, and in January 1891, the school's 174 students were moved to a larger mansion at 1220 Washington Avenue in the Garden District. Over the course of the next few years, Newcomb acquired additional structures, including an academic building, a chapel, three dormitories, and an art building and pottery.[2]

By the turn of the twentieth century, Newcomb's reputation as a progressive institution was well established. Expanding enrollments and a generous bequest from Mrs. Newcomb, who died in 1901, contributed to the school's 1908 purchase of land adjacent to Tulane University for the construction of a new campus.[3]

Tulane University's Board of Administrators envisioned several advantages to the new site, particularly the cooperative use of libraries, laboratories, and faculty. Newcomb's alumnae, on the other hand, were alarmed by the school's proximity to Tulane. Indeed, their determination to maintain a separate identity for Newcomb was to have considerable impact on the design of the College.

In 1910, the Tulane Board of Administrators appointed a Committee for the Selection of an Architect composed of four men prominent in the New Orleans business community and three academics: Edwin B. Craighead, the president of Tulane; Brandt V. B. Dixon, the president of Newcomb College; and Ellsworth Woodward, the director of the School of Art of Newcomb College.[4] In July 1911, the committee announced a competition to select an architect, and Professor Warren P. Laird, chair of the Department of Architecture at the University of Pennsylvania, was invited to act as professional advisor to the committee. Laird, along with Dixon and Woodward, would judge the entries.[5]

Architects interested in entering the Newcomb College competition were requested first to show evidence of their ability to design a college. In order to demonstrate such competence, each competitor was to submit, by September 1, 1911, a maximum of ten photographs and ten drawings of their previous work, preferably including a school or college building. The committee invited several prestigious, nationally known architectural firms to participate in this first phase of the competition. Dixon's papers include some undated notes on his recollection of the competition: "There seemed to be a great desire on the part of the building committee to limit the competition to the better known architects of the time, and to insure this, deliberate steps were taken to prevent the announcement appearing in the architectural periodicals. An announcement of the program was made through the AIA's [American Institute of Architects] chapters in the leading cities."[6] This limited circulation effectively restricted the competition to those affiliated with the professional society.

Fifty-six architects or architectural firms expressed preliminary interest in designing the Newcomb College buildings. Eight firms were admitted to the competition and received an honorarium of one thousand dollars to defray the expenses of preparing architectural drawings.[7] The remaining forty-eight applicants could enter the competition, but without financial compensation unless awarded the design contract. Only twenty-seven competitors chose to remain in the competition under these terms.[8] Designs were due on December 20, 1911.[9]

On December 30, 1911, the board appointed James Gamble Rogers of New York as architect for Newcomb College. Rogers was not one of the eight architects invited to participate in the competition, but his design was described as "the one which most nearly met all the requirements."[10] Since Rogers was not a resident of New Orleans, he was obliged, at his own expense, to maintain either a representative from his firm or a local architect to supervise construction of the buildings.[11] Rogers selected Paul Andry of the firm of Andry and Bendernagel, the designer of Tulane University's first buildings at its uptown site, to fill that position.

By the time James Gamble Rogers (1867–1947) entered the competition for Newcomb College, he had already designed about thirty buildings, mostly in the Northeast, in a variety of styles. Rogers's architectural training—first at Yale University, from which he graduated in 1889, and then at the École des Beaux-Arts in Paris (1893 to 1898)—had grounded him particularly well in the conservative neoclassicism popular in the early twentieth century. He began the practice of architecture in Chicago, working in the office of William Le Baron Jenney and afterward with the firm of Burnham and Root. Rogers opened his own practice in Chicago and then moved to New York.

In New Orleans, Rogers's 1907 design (built 1911–13) for the United States Post Office on Camp Street, now housing the Fifth Circuit Court of Appeals, is a fine example of his reinterpretation of Italian palazzos and of his predilection for multiple columns and showy effects. The post office's criterion for an architectural image modeled on classical prototypes circumscribed Rogers's designs for post offices, but he proved highly versatile within the classical language. Rogers was earning a reputation for giving a fresh look to the time-honored preferences of his clients. For example, his New Haven post office, designed 1911 (built 1913–17), differed from the one in New Orleans in its more straightforward temple-like facade. In a completely different mood is Rogers's Gothic-styled Harkness Quadrangle, 1917, at Yale University. Rogers's easy facility with all historical styles reflected his design philosophy of providing an "appropriate interpretation of traditional styles to reflect the characters of particular clients and programs."[12]

Although twelve buildings were envisioned for the campus in 1911, Newcomb could afford only four structures that were collectively estimated to cost approximately $500,000. These four structures consisted of an academic and administration building, a residence hall for two hundred students, a music instruction building, and an art instruction building. The remaining buildings—the library, a science building, a household economics building, another residence hall, a chapel, a gymnasium (with swimming pool and exercise room), and an assembly hall—were delayed until additional funds became available.[13]

Since Rogers's architectural designs were suggestive but not prescriptive, final preparation of the designs for cost estimates took some time. Bids made on the buildings in 1912 exceeded projections, and President Dixon sought ways to reduce costs through modifications to the plans. Dixon made several visits to New York between 1911 and 1913 to consult with Rogers.[14] A letter from Dixon to Tulane Committee board member Charles Janvier describes a visit taken in May 1912 to consult with Professor Laird at the University of Pennsylvania and then on to Yale, Mount Holyoke, Smith, and Vassar in order "to inspect their work and appliances in connection with the proposed arrangements for this college." Dixon's letter continued, "While in consultation with Mr. Rogers a great many sketch-plans were drawn, and I believe that the result of our work has been highly advantageous to the College."[15] Dixon reportedly spent thirty days in consultation with Rogers.[16]

Plans finally were ready for proposals from the builders in the spring of 1914.[17] Once again, bids came in above the projected amount, only to be rejected by the board. Then other events delayed progress, among them a yellow fever scare and the outbreak of World War I. The board continued to procrastinate until 1916, when the Newcomb Alumnae Association pressured it into action. In January 1917, the board authorized the construction of three buildings: Newcomb Hall, which served as both an administration and a classroom building; the art building; and a student residence.[18] The fourth structure, the music building, would have to wait. In September 1918, the new Newcomb College was ready.

When the school's relocation to a site adjacent to Tulane was first proposed, Newcomb alumnae had expressed considerable consternation over the prospect "of a closer union with Tulane."[19] In letters to the board, they demanded that "care should be taken to preserve the integrity of Newcomb, to keep their buildings distinct and separate, and not permit its architecture to be influenced in any way by that of the University. They also urged that a complete plan should be made for the sake of unity."[20] Certainly the competition program reflected these concerns in its requirement that "special care should be taken to preserve the unity and harmony of the whole. The architecture, therefore, need have no relation to other buildings of the University, which are at a considerable distance."[21]

The program also outlined more functional considerations. It stated that "in plan, form, and style it is important that the group and the several buildings should be suited to the conditions of a sub-tropical country; the material of the exterior walls should be brick of a good reserved color, an artistic quality of surface, and a minimum of expense consistent with a well studied design should be secured."[22]

The program did not dictate any particular style for Newcomb's buildings, but it is clear that the issues of function and architectural image were interwoven. As Rogers was awarded the Newcomb commission in 1912, the Selection Committee's professional advisor, Professor Laird, articulated the committee's sentiments when announcing that the "design neither sacrificed beauty nor practicality and it possessed great dignity, memorial character, a style both American and southern, and had the refinement, simplicity and charm fitting for a college for women in the South."[23]

These comments raise important issues regarding the relationship between client and architect, and between image and architecture. The competition program had outlined the conceptual disposition of the buildings, but had left the specific architectural interrelationships open-ended.[24] Although the campus-plan concept had been fundamental to the design of men's colleges since the early nineteenth century, it had only recently become an integral component of women's college designs. As the historian Helen Lefkowitz Horowitz has demonstrated, the first college buildings for women in the United States consisted of a single building housing all the school's activities.[25] Vassar (1865) and Wellesley (1875) colleges are but two examples of this concept. That pattern had been decisively broken at Smith College (1875), where a campus of separate structures had been constructed in order to group the students in smaller units. Administrators hoped in this way to avoid the subversive intellectual bonding that could occur among girls in one large building. Newcomb's campus plan belongs to what, by then, was typical for college plans for both men and women, that is, a plan of separate buildings for different activities. Yet if the scheme was no longer gender specific, the competition judges saw something in Rogers's design that, in their eyes, made it a "place for women."

Newcomb's buildings form two open-ended quadrangles, with Newcomb Hall, the academic and administrative building, in the center, linking the quads. This arrangement seems to have been proposed by Dixon as early as 1909. In September of that year, Leon Maxwell, who was interviewing for a teaching position at Newcomb, wrote to his fiancée and included a rough sketch of the school's new campus as described to him by Dixon.[26] This sketch depicts a U-shaped academic building separating two open-ended courts: the court on the Broadway side had two dormitories, a library, and a gymnasium; the art, music, and auditorium buildings flanked the other court, which featured a statue of Mrs. Newcomb.

Rogers's successful 1911 competition design, as described in the February 4, 1912, edition of the *New Orleans Daily Picayune,* was similar.[27] It consisted of two open-ended courts: the court on the Broadway side of the academic building held two dormitories and the library; the gymnasium was located in the other court, although a fountain stood in this court, not a statue of Mrs. Newcomb.[28] Another description of the plan in the June 1912 New Orleans journal *Architectural Art and Its Allies* is vague regarding the number of courts. It is clear, however, that the statue of Mrs. Newcomb existed and that the academic building, still with its two wings, was to be the most ornate of all the buildings, with a "pillared front and classic dome." [29]

Dixon apparently was unhappy with this scheme because between the summer of 1912 and that of 1917, when the campus finally was built, the plan and elevations of the building underwent several modifications; many of them were evidently influenced by Dixon. By July 1912, following Dixon's

thirty-day conference with Rogers in New York, the Newcomb plan again incorporated two quadrangles, "one central and relatively private for the Residence group, enclosed by the four buildings as shown: the other open and
materially unchanged from the plan as originally presented."[30] The foregoing
arrangement is found in a contemporary plan, drawing, and diagram. The
plan dated April 28, 1913, with revisions made on January 12, 1917, shows
the Broadway side quad completely enclosed by the administration building
(formerly called the academic building, and which was a simple rectangular
shape, not U-shaped as in Dixon's 1909 sketch), the two residence buildings, and the library facing the administration building.[31] A 1913 drawing
by Nathaniel C. Curtis affording a bird's-eye view of the Tulane campus and
the "Site of New Buildings for Newcomb College" echoes this design. The
arrangement of the buildings is identical to that in the original plan, and the
administration building sports a tall, domed structure. Neither Mrs. Newcomb's statue nor the fountain is indicated. This closed-quad scheme must
have remained intact until quite late in the design process because it also
appears in a diagram showing both the plan and the elevation of the campus
published in the 1918–19 Newcomb catalogue (figure 1).[32] Although the foregoing catalogue was prepared well in advance of the 1918–19 academic year,
it does indicate that Newcomb's design was not finalized until shortly before
the onset of construction in 1917. However, the principal building lacks a
dome in the catalogue drawings.

In January 1917, the Tulane Board of Administrators authorized construction of three buildings. An undated plan, evidently created after January 12,
1917, shows two open-ended courts. It can, therefore, be assumed to be the
last in the sequence.[33]

Whatever the intentions of either the architect or Newcomb's administrators, this open-ended quad composition, where the principal building serves
administrative purposes, is typical of college schemes in the early twentieth
century. From a practical point of view, the open-quad scheme for Newcomb,
rather than the quad enclosed on all four sides, allowed the free movement
of air for cooling and dryness, essential concerns in Louisiana. From an aesthetic point of view, the open-court plan also allowed an unimpeded view
from both Broadway and Audubon Place (now Newcomb Place) of Newcomb Hall, which was the physical as well as the symbolic center of the new
campus (figure 2). This monumentalization of the principal building and, by
extension, the whole arrangement, provided a formality and regularity that

GROUND PLAN OF PROPOSED COLLEGE BUILDINGS

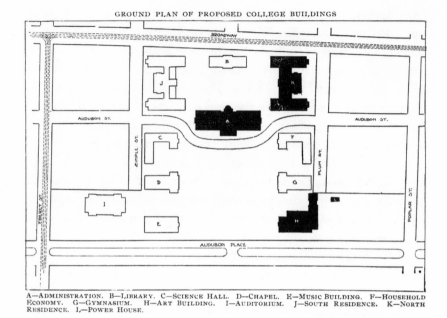

A—ADMINISTRATION. B—LIBRARY. C—SCIENCE HALL. D—CHAPEL. E—MUSIC BUILDING. F—HOUSEHOLD ECONOMY. G—GYMNASIUM. H—ART BUILDING. I—AUDITORIUM. J—SOUTH RESIDENCE. K—NORTH RESIDENCE. L—POWER HOUSE.

Figure 1. *Ground Plan of Proposed College Buildings* as published in the *1918–19 Newcomb Announcement.* The illustration shows the proposed closed-quad plan on Broadway and a campus of eleven buildings with three main buildings completed by September 1918: the Administration Building (Newcomb Hall); North Residence (Josephine Louise Residence Hall); and the Art Building. A small powerhouse (*far right*) also was constructed.

gives the campus a memorial flavor. For although Newcomb's layout in an H-formation echoes that of Tulane, the large scale and symmetry present a greater sobriety and offer vistas that the more compact arrangement and artful asymmetry of Tulane lack.

Rogers, however, avoided too rigid an overall effect at Newcomb by varying the size, massing, silhouette, and detailing of each structure. The individual buildings are similar, but not identical. And, although the buildings are spaciously separated, the colonnades of trees provide a needed unifying element to the design, as Dixon recognized in 1912 following one of his post-competition meetings with Rogers. He wrote, "The design contemplates an iron balcony or balustrade, running at practically the same level, about the entire court, thus giving a unity which seems to us highly desirable."[34] Additional unity is achieved through the use of brick for all the buildings.

Figure 2. Newcomb College, ca. 1925. *From left:* Broadway Street, Josephine Louise Residence Hall; Newcomb Hall; Newcomb Gymnasium (built in 1923); Art Building; Newcomb Place.

Although described by one source in 1912 as being of "Italian Renaissance" style, in fact, Newcomb is closer in style to the colonial or Georgian styles.[35] The brick, the simple rectangular forms of the buildings, and the white detailing conformed to the renewed interest in colonial-inspired forms in the late nineteenth and early twentieth centuries. The New York architectural firm of McKim, Mead and White was instrumental in popularizing this gentle classicism, and Newcomb's buildings show similarities with a number of educational and cultural buildings coming from their office.[36] Rogers does not copy any building directly, but his designs for Newcomb are in the same mode. Some colleges, including Harvard and Brown, adopted colonial forms for their new buildings for consistency of style with earlier structures. New campuses, such as that of Johns Hopkins, were also interested in the style because it was both fashionable and economical.[37] The plain, boxy shapes and uncomplicated rectangular plan yielded much floor area in proportion to cost of materials and labor, certainly an important consideration for Newcomb. Budgetary restrictions probably eliminated the dome and lantern on an octagonal base that existed in Rogers's first design for Newcomb Hall.

The colonial revival possessed other associations that were particularly appropriate for this women's college. Thought to represent "ethical" qualities and "chasteness and restraint in form," colonial revival buildings used simple artistic materials intended to be "expressive of the character of the people who use them."[38] More specific to a women's college, the colonial revival was often

associated with "traditional feminine qualities of delicacy and refinement" by
both architects and critics alike.[39] Indeed, the suitability of the colonial revival
for a women's college had an impeccable precedent: Mount Holyoke's first
building in 1836 was constructed of red brick with white detailing.[40]

If Newcomb's buildings are not domestic in scale, they are in detail. The
regularity of the fenestration, the light-colored columns and window mold-
ings, and the white trim to the windows are typical of residential architecture
in general. The visually unifying balconies that encircle the buildings and the
balustrade on top of Newcomb Hall's curved portico also serve to domesticate
the imagery. Other design elements also provide a homey feel, such as the
curved portico itself, the small-scale entry doors, and the sheltering extension
of the roof (figure 3). Use of the feminine Ionic order for the four-columned
pedimented facade over the main entry is to be expected, although the size of

Figure 3. A view of the Broadway quadrangle and Josephine Louise Residence Hall from the
curved sheltering portico of Newcomb Hall.

this feature, that extends almost the full height of the building, looks decidedly disproportionate.

The use of red brick for Newcomb's campus clearly distinguishes it from the large rusticated buff-gray stone of Tulane's H. H. Richardson–inspired buildings. Such a contrast happily satisfied the particular demands of Newcomb alumnae for "distinct and separate" buildings. Further, Newcomb's brick walls seem two-dimensional in quality and convey a sense of weightlessness, even without the contrast of Tulane's buildings. The restrained, almost unobtrusive patterns woven into the brick walls enhance the sense of lightness and delicacy; up close, the walls resemble a tightly stretched fabric. All in all, the differences between the two campuses invite use of the gendered terminology so popular in the nineteenth and early twentieth centuries: Tulane's buildings are "masculine" and Newcomb's "feminine." The imagery of residence must have been reassuring for students at a women's college in a time of popular resistance to women outside the domestic sphere. The residential quality takes on a particular meaning when one remembers that the first two "homes" for Newcomb were both originally family residences before they were taken over by the fledgling college. Indeed, Dixon uses the term "college home" for these buildings.[41]

But in what ways does Rogers's design achieve a southern identity? It is difficult to classify anything as significantly southern other than the open-courtyard scheme, the expansive fenestration that allows for cooling breezes, and the extension of the roof to shade the upper walls. However, possession of a two-story portico or large columns was sufficient for any building to conform to the mythology of southern colonial fixed in the public mind by the last decade of the nineteenth century.[42] The University of Virginia, with its classic porticoes, dome, formal terraces, and geometrically set trees, was considered a model for southern institutions of higher learning.[43] Newcomb was designed to be generically southern, not Louisiana southern. Perhaps that was enough.

The campus landscaping, executed by the firm of Andry and Woodward from 1918 to 1920, was a significant component of the Newcomb scheme. The competition program had stated that "No enclosing exterior walls or limits are proposed, but a well studied and pleasing arrangement of walks and garden features is desired, with trees along streets and where they will not interfere with necessary lighting of rooms."[44] The site plan shows a formal court on the Broadway side of the campus that was visually united by a series of curved paths leading to the buildings. Rogers reemployed the curve as a unifying device around the campus side of Newcomb Hall to create a terrace in front of the entrance. This sweeping effect has been lost because of the terrace's eventual use as a parking area.[45]

Dixon was convinced that the oaks of Newcomb's Washington Avenue location contributed directly to the feeling of affection held by the students toward the College. Gardens traditionally have provided an outside haven for unchaperoned women, and the gardens at Newcomb in its former location were no exception. Therefore, while still at the Washington Avenue location, Dixon planted seedling oaks and laurels that were transplanted in 1919 to the grounds of the new Newcomb, thus symbolically providing continuity by linking old with new.[46]

Rogers met the challenge presented in the design of Newcomb College. Not only is Dixon's 1909 scheme for Newcomb reflected in Rogers's plan, Rogers also skillfully accommodated the various demands of alumnae and administrators in creating the College's distinctive physical identity. Rogers designed a group of buildings that were different in materials and formal qualities from Tulane, appropriate as a memorial, sufficiently southern, and recognizably feminine. Newcomb's campus was also architecturally fashionable.

Epilogue

In the nearly one hundred years since James Gamble Rogers provided a design for Newcomb College, the school has acquired many new structures. Yet the various architects responsible for these buildings have shown a remarkable sensitivity to Rogers's initial scheme. In rough chronological order, the campus grew as follows.

In the 1920s, two dormitories were built on Newcomb Place, and both employed the red brick and white trim of Rogers's buildings. Francis J. Mac-Donnell designed the three-story Doris Hall (1925) as a cooperative dormitory where students could perform the duties of staff to pay for their room and board. Located on the corner of Willow Street, Doris Hall received an addition called "New Doris" in 1958 by Ricciuti and Associates and Joseph G. Bernard. However, the original Doris Hall and addition were torn down in 2005, and a much larger, four- and five-story, two-wing residence hall designed by Hanbury Evans Wright Vlattas + Company has been built on the site. The new building, named Weatherhead Hall, retains the red brick edifice of Doris Hall, but little of its former feminine scale.[47] Still standing is the three-story Warren House, named for Warren Newcomb, the husband of Josephine Newcomb, built in 1928 to a design by Diboll and Owen and enlarged in 1951 by Richard Koch.

Architect Emile Weil designed the music building, Dixon Hall, named for Newcomb's president, Brandt Dixon. The building was to have been one of the four original buildings in the Rogers's plan, and when finally built in 1929, it framed the south side of the open-ended Newcomb quadrangle. This structure also is faithful to the red brick and classical portico formula. A similar extension by Leake Associates in 1984, the Dixon Annex, provides a small theater and a recital hall. The patio in front of the building offers a space for outdoor performances. Adjacent to this extension is Elleonora P. McWillams Hall, completed in 1995 as the home of the Theater and Dance Department. Designed by the firm of Waggoner and Ball, the handsome structure employs red brick and extended roof eaves, but interprets the Newcomb style in a more contemporary fashion. The oak trees that frame the quadrangle on the campus side of Newcomb Hall have matured to form a magnificent and shady canopy.

An iron entrance gate designed by Richard Koch in 1934 marks the Broadway approach to Newcomb. Located on the Broadway side of Newcomb Hall and facing Josephine Louise Residence Hall is the Myra Clare Rogers Memorial Chapel, completed in 1976 by John Desmond of Desmond, Miremont, Burks. It occupies the site of a dormitory in the James Gamble Rogers plan. As well as accommodating services of all faiths, the chapel's auditorium-style interior provides an area for musical events and lectures. The red brick chapel is a frankly modern design and successfully incorporates Tiffany windows from the earlier Newcomb Chapel in the Garden District. A large rose window composed around the initials HNS (Harriott-Newcomb-Sophie) predominates in the nave.

A major renovation and expansion of the original art building was completed in 1997. The architects, Hartman-Cox of Washington, D.C., were instructed to maintain the architectural integrity of the art building and the later buildings that lie behind it and flank the quad. The Woldenberg Art Center expansion occupies the site of a swimming pool and gymnasium executed by Frank G. Churchill in 1923. The arcade that fronts the center was adapted from the 1923 structure and incorporates the remaining Tiffany windows from Newcomb's Garden District chapel. Again red brick, stucco details, and decorative diamond panels respect the original Newcomb design.

These buildings comprise the "Newcomb College Campus" along with the "Newcomb Dean's Residence" and Caroline Richardson Hall. In 1987, Newcomb and Tulane merged their faculties and administrative structure. A resolution was passed in the university senate that stated: "The historical Newcomb campus must remain an identifiable physical entity dedicated to the purposes of Newcomb College."[48] *The Resolutions of the Board of Administrators of the Tulane Educational Fund, Adopted on November 19, 1987,* dedicated "in perpetuity as the Newcomb College Campus, the area generally bounded by Broadway, Zimple Street, Newcomb Place and Plum Street, the buildings thereon, the Newcomb Dean's House, Warren House, and Caroline Richardson Hall."

The Italianate "Newcomb Dean's House" at 43 Newcomb Place was built in 1908 by the architect Paul Andry for his own use. Brandt Dixon was the first Newcomb administrator to reside in the house, which was designated as the residence of the dean of Newcomb by the Tulane Board of Administrators in 1938. The house is listed on the National Register of Historic Places and since the 2006 close of Newcomb College has gained use as the headquarters of the Newcomb College Institute.

Caroline Richardson Hall was built in 1958 to serve as the Newcomb College dining hall. Designed by the architect Robert Cummins, the two-story red brick and glass façade is fronted by a brise soleil. Since 1975, the building has been home to the Newcomb College Center for Research on Women, its central occupant.

The Newcomb alumnae's desire that their school should be architecturally "distinct and separate" from Tulane's has been honored, and despite the integration of Tulane's and Newcomb's faculties and classes, and the closure of the College, the buildings do "preserve the integrity of Newcomb" as a college designed for women. Designed as a cohesive architectural unit in the early twentieth century, it is hoped that Newcomb's campus will retain its unique character and ambience, in perpetuity.

NOTES

Editors' Note: Karen Kingsley's essay is reprinted by permission of Louisiana Historical Association. Copyright © 1994 Louisiana Historical Association.

1. Helen Lefkowitz Horowitz, *Alma Mater: Design and Experience in the Women's Colleges from Their Nineteenth Century Beginnings to the 1930s* (New York, 1984).

2. Brandt V. B. Dixon, *A Brief History of H. Sophie Newcomb Memorial College, 1887–1919* (New Orleans, 1928). Dixon's interest in architectural design is demonstrated early in his

presidency at Newcomb when in 1893 he drew plans for the Academy building because, as he claimed, the school could not afford an architect (82–88).

3. In November 1908, the board authorized the purchase of Block 2 of Audubon Place and two squares bounded by Zimple, Broadway, Plum and Audubon Streets (see Dixon, *Brief History*, 138).

4. The four nonacademic members of the committee were Charles Janvier, vice president of the Canal-Louisiana Bank and Trust Company, who was appointed chair of the Building Committee in November 1910; Charles Rosen; Alfred Raymond; and Abraham Brittin (see *Architectural Art and its Allies* 7, no. 1 [July 1911]: 19–20).

5. *Architectural Art and Its Allies* 7, no. 1 (July 1911): 19–20. The committee's scheme for a competition, and the method in which it was held, was endorsed by the Louisiana Chapter of the American Institute of Architects. At the end of the nineteenth century, architectural competitions became a common means of choosing an architect to design a college (see Paul V. Turner, *Campus: An American Planning Tradition* [New York, 1984], 177).

6. William P. Howard and J. D. Parrish, *A Report on the Competition [for the appointment of an architect for the proposed buildings of] H. Sophie Newcomb Memorial College*, 1911 (New Orleans, ca.1950).

7. These were Cram, Goodhue and Ferguson of New York, Boston, and Houston; Pell and Corbett of New York; Wilson Eyre of Philadelphia; Day Bros. and Klauder of Philadelphia; and Zantzinger, Borie and Medary of Philadelphia. Three were local firms: Andry and Bendernagel; DeBuys, Churchill and Labouisse; and Emile Weil (*Architectural Art and Its Allies* 7, no. 2 [August 1911]: 20).

8. An article in the *New Orleans Daily Picayune* on December 21, 1911, states that twenty-six sets of plans were received. However, Dixon, *Brief History*, 157, and the Minutes of the Board of Administrators of the Tulane Educational Fund state that entry no. 27 was selected unanimously. The rules of the competition preserved the anonymity of all entrants. All designs were to be accompanied by the architect's name in a sealed envelope, which would be opened only after the winning entry was selected. This process of selecting an architect by competition was common at that time. For other examples of college design competitions, see Turner, *Campus*, 177.

9. *New Orleans Times-Democrat*, July 2, 1911.

10. Dixon, *Brief History*, 157. During February, the plans were exhibited at the Delgado Art Museum (now the New Orleans Museum of Art). The submitted drawings were limited to a general plan showing the arrangement of the buildings and the treatment of the grounds; plans for each floor of the Academic and Administrative Building, a student residence and its refectory; and elevations and a section of the buildings. Also, one drawing of the main entrance to indicate the author's ability in designing brickwork. The size of the presentation drawings was limited to 24" and 30" per sheet of paper, and all drawings were to be done in a single monochrome, which should be "simple." "Elaborate rendering will be regarded with disfavor" (*Program of Competition*, 6, UAHT).

11. *Program of Competition*, 12.

12. Susan Ryan, "The Architecture of James Gamble Rogers at Yale University," *Perspecta* 18 (1982): 25–41, gives a general introduction to Rogers's work. See also Aaron Betsky, *James Gamble Rogers and the Architecture of Pragmatism* (New York, 1994).

13. *Program of Competition*, 8.

14. Dixon, *Brief History*, 158.

15. Dixon to Janvier, July 9, 1912, Newcomb Archives, Newcomb College Center for Research on Women (hereafter cited as NA NCCROW).

16. *Architectural Art and Its Allies* 7, no. 12 (June 1912): 18.

17. Dixon, *Brief History*, 158.

18. Ibid., 158–60, 169–73; John P. Dyer, *Tulane: The Biography of a University, 1834–1965* (New York, 1966), 181.

19. Dixon, *Brief History*, 139.

20. Ibid.

21. *Program of Competition*, 7.

22. Ibid.

23. Information from the Minutes of the January 18, 1912, meeting of the Board of Administrators, Newcomb Buildings Folder, UAHT.

24. For example, the two residence buildings were to be located near Broadway for access to the car lines proposed for that street; the Assembly Hall, the only building planned for use by Tulane, convenient to Freret Street; the art building "takes its place naturally near the Household Economics Building" (*Program of Competition*, 9).

25. Horowitz, *Alma Mater*. For men's colleges, see Turner, *Campus*. And basic to any study of campus architecture of the early twentieth century is Charles Z. Klauder and Herbert C. Wise, *College Architecture in America and Its Part in the Development of the Campus* (New York, 1929).

26. Letter to Miss Ruth Nottage, August 2, 1909, Maxwell Collection, 62, Correspondence 1904–1936, Box 1, Folder 1, UAHT.

27. The location of the original competition drawings is unknown, and it appears they have been destroyed.

28. *New Orleans Daily Picayune*, February 4, 1912.

29. *Architectural Art and Its Allies* 7, no. 12 (June 1912): 18.

30. Dixon to Janvier, July 9, 1912, NA NCCROW, Tulane University.

31. Paul Andry Collection, Folder 9, Southeastern Architectural Archive, Tulane University. This plan is numbered 100A.

32. Newcomb Catalogue 1918-19, Newcomb College Center for Research on Women, NA NCCROW, Tulane University.

33. This plan is numbered 108. Paul Andry Collection, Folder 9, Southeastern Architectural Archive, Tulane University.

34. Dixon to Janvier, Newcomb College Center for Research on Women, NA NCCROW, Tulane University.

35. For "Italian Renaissance," see *Architectural Art and its Allies* 7, no. 12 (June 1912): 18, and for "Greek Classic," see *New Orleans Daily Picayune*, February 4, 1912.

36. See, for example, the gymnasium at Radcliffe College (1898), Faunce Hall at Brown University (1904), and the Women's Building at the University of Illinois (1905). For the entry to Josephine Louise Residence Hall, see the entrance to McKim, Mead and White's Morgan Library, New York (1902), in Leland Roth, *The Architecture of McKim, Mead and White, 1870–1920: A Building List* (New York, 1978).

37. For a discussion of the popularity of colonial or Georgian revival for college buildings, see William B. Rhoads, *The Colonial Revival* (New York, 1977), 142–69, 198, and, for the cost factors of the style, 376.

38. Ibid., 411–14.

39. Ibid., 415. These ideas were expressed from the 1880s and into the early twentieth century by both architects and critics of architecture. For a discussion, see ibid., 422–25, and esp. 844–48 nn. 40–48. Rhoads observes that co-ed schools saw Georgian as more appropriate for women's colleges than men's in the early twentieth century (424). He cites the 1905 Georgian design of the sole building for women at the University of Illinois at Urbana, where all the other buildings were of Roman classic style. An example of the persistence of these ideas into the twentieth century is the 1924 design for the women's and men's colleges at Duke University by Horace Trumbauer (see Annabel Wharton, "Gender, Architecture, and Institutional Self-Presentation: The Case of Duke University," *South Atlantic Quarterly* 90, no. 1 [Winter 1991]: 175–217).

40. Horowitz, *Alma Mater*, 20.

41. Dixon, *Brief History*, 141.

42. Rhoads, *Colonial Revival*, 114. In a discussion of colonial revival and college campus design, Fiske Kimball, in "Recent Architecture in the South," *Architectural Record* 55, no. 3 (March 1924): 209–71, 224, describes Newcomb as following southern traditions of planning and detail.

43. Jens F. Larson and Archie M. Palmer, *Architectural Planning of the American College* (New York, 1933), 23.

44. *Program of Competition*, 7.

45. A 1920s photo in the Tulane University Archives shows its use for parking.

46. Dixon, *Brief History*, 141–43.

47. See Tulane University Uptown Campus Map http://tulane.edu/about/visiting/uptown-campus-map.cfm for more information about buildings by name; Residential College II at the Doris Site, http://tulane.edu/cpreg/rescol2.cfm.

48. Memorandum introduced into and approved by the Tulane University Senate by School of Architecture faculty Karen Kingsley and Malcolm Heard on November 6, 1987.

Josephine Louise Le Monnier Newcomb (1816–1901), the benefactress of the H. Sophie Newcomb Memorial College, the first degree-granting college for women affiliated with a university for men in the United States. Born in Baltimore, she lived with her older sister in New Orleans following the death of their mother. In 1845, she married Warren Newcomb, a prosperous partner in a family wholesale grocery firm.

Harriott Sophie Newcomb (1855–1870), known to all as "Sophie," was born in New York City, the only daughter of Josephine and Warren Newcomb. Sophie's untimely death of diphtheria at the age of fifteen inspired her widowed mother, Josephine Newcomb, to establish the college for women in her memory.

Brandt Van Blarcom Dixon (1850–1941), founding (and only) president of the H. Sophie Newcomb Memorial College, 1887–1919. The Class of 1910 commissioned this portrait by Ella Miriam Wood (NC 1908) and presented it to Newcomb College on Cap & Gown Day, 1933. Oil on canvas, 44 × 36 in., 1933. Photo by Tulane University, Judy Cooper.

The Class of 1909. The year 1909 was a pivotal one, marking the successful close of a lengthy lawsuit challenging Mrs. Newcomb's will leaving $2,668,307 to the College, and the beginning of many student-initiated College traditions including publication of the literary magazine, the *Newcomb Arcade,* and the introduction of the prestigious 1909 Prize.

Illustration by Caroline Wogan Durieux (NC 1916) for the April 1915 issue of the *Newcomb Arcade*, the literary magazine published by Newcomb students from 1909 to 1934.

A domestic science class on the Washington Avenue campus, ca. 1910. The study of chemistry, especially in relation to foods and dietetics, was a requirement of Newcomb's brief but popular Domestic Science Program, 1909–20.

The 1919 Newcomb faculty on the steps of Newcomb Hall, their new home on the Broadway campus. More than two-thirds of Newcomb's fifty-nine-member faculty was female compared to less than one-third nationally.

Newcomb deans commemorate the retirement of Anna Many, ca. 1953. The five deans who followed Brandt Dixon as college leaders are pictured here. *Top row (left to right):* John R. Hubbard (1953–65), Pierce Butler (1919–38), Logan Wilson (1943–51); *bottom:* Frederick Hard (1938–43), Anna Many (1951–53).

Students in their physical education uniforms, ca. 1910. Brown wool bloomers and white middy blouses replaced the long shirtwaist dress (and corset underneath) in 1894 as the appropriate attire for physical exercise in Newcomb's nationally recognized physical education program.

Students learning the finer points of teeing off, 1953. Instruction in golf was one of many physical education courses Newcomb students could take to fulfill their physical education requirement.

The Barracudas, ca. 1950s. Members of Newcomb's synchronized swimming club enjoy a practice session in the Newcomb swimming pool. For some Newcomb students, however, wearing College-supplied wool bathing suits and passing the swimming test required for graduation were anything but joyful.

The Tulane Lady Wave Basketball team, ca. 1980s. Tulane's first athletic scholarships in women's team sports (1975) followed the passage of Title IX and led to Tulane's nationally ranked basketball team.

Junior Year Abroad students begin their studies with a trip to Stonehenge, Wiltshire, United Kingdom, ca. 1980s.

Newcomb Nursery School director Pat Schindler, the three-year-old class, and a visiting limbo dancer, 1983. From its founding as the New Orleans Nursery School in 1926, the Newcomb Nursery School (1939–2005) offered Newcomb students opportunities for observation and teaching in early childhood education and set the standard for preschool education in the community.

II

DISTINCTIONS

T
he 'Coordinate Plan' which the University had adopted," wrote Newcomb College president Brandt V. B. Dixon, "provided for a separate
president and faculty, to whom should be given the power to determine its own policy, and course of study, as though the two institutions
were entirely distinct."[1] This arrangement between Tulane University and the
H. Sophie Newcomb Memorial College would be the College's defining mark
of distinction: its founding in 1886 as the first degree-granting college for
women affiliated with a university for men in the United States.

The coordinate college plan originated in the British school system with
Queen's College, London (chartered 1853), and Girton College of Cambridge
University (founded 1869).[2] Regardless of locale, the coordinate plan everywhere arose as a protest against the separate women's college and, more
often than not, as a concession to women's demands for an education equal
to that offered to men.[3] Proponents of women's education perceived the
women's colleges of the time to be little more than finishing schools and
sought women's full access to institutions for men. However, the all-male
institutions feared the enrollment of women would damage the prestige of
their institutions, that current students would be so disheartened by the
presence of women they would leave in protest, and that alumni opposition
would greatly reduce donations to their alma maters. The founding of Radcliffe College of Harvard University, for example, was described by twenty-
first-century Harvard president Drew Faust as a "compromise between what
women wanted and what Harvard would give them, as an alternative to the
two prevailing models of coeducation and separate women's institutions."[4]
As late as the 1960s, the coordinate college structure was seen as a viable
alternative to the admission of women to men's colleges. The founding of
Kirkland College (1968–78) as the women's affiliate of Hamilton College is

an example of this later manifestation; similar arguments opposing coeducation and arguing for a women's college within a male university were made
in studies that preceded the admission of women to Yale College (1969) and
Princeton University (1969).[5]

The status of coordinate colleges as "neither women's college nor coeducational institution" often led to the belief that the coordinate arrangement
represented a transitory phase, a "temporary expedient" in the progression
toward the preferred coeducation.[6] This conception of the coordinate college
as "neither-nor" rather than "best of both" also may have contributed to the
lack of scholarly attention given to the coordinate arrangement. As a result,
the histories of the coordinate colleges, and knowledge of the coordinate plan
as an institutional arrangement of women's higher education, often have been
neglected, marginalized, or misconstrued.

The history of Newcomb College presents a good example. Newcomb's
designation as the "first coordinate college" frequently has been over-
shadowed by the prominence of Radcliffe College of Harvard University (organized as the Harvard "Annex" in 1879 and chartered as Radcliffe College in
1894) and Barnard College of Columbia University (founded 1889). Radcliffe
and Barnard's affiliation as members of the Seven Sisters colleges, situated
parallel to northeastern, elite male Ivy League institutions, made them more
visible prototypes of the coordinate college.[7] Similarly, their founding in a
region of the country supportive of higher education contrasted with Newcomb's emergence in a region that only in the early twentieth century felt
"the faint stirrings of a need for the education of women."[8] Moreover, while
the Seven Sisters colleges formed each other's reference group and presented
a collective voice for educating women, southern women's colleges never created comparable alliances.[9]

Newcomb's ranking as the first U.S. coordinate college for women is
qualified by the words "degree-granting." Radcliffe's precursor, the Harvard
"Annex," had no degree-granting powers, and the students who completed
the four-year course of study were awarded certificates stating they had
completed work equal to that of Harvard men.[10] The 1894 charter establishing Radcliffe College authorized the awarding of degrees, which were to be
countersigned by the president of Harvard. In contrast, Newcomb students,
from the first graduating class in 1890 onward, received the diploma of the
University signed by both College and University officials. Until 2007, diplomas awarded by Tulane University differed only in the name of the college

from which the student was graduating. The Newcomb diploma was countersigned by the dean, the University president, and the chair of the Administrators and read:

> TULANE UNIVERSITY,
> On the recommendation of the Faculty of the
> H. Sophie Newcomb Memorial College,
> The Administrators of the Tulane Educational Fund
> have this day conferred upon
> [name of graduate]
> The degree of
> Bachelor of [Arts, Fine Arts, or Science],
> With all the rights, honors, and privileges appertaining thereto.[11]

The Coordinate College Plan

By the early 1900s, the coordinate college represented a third type of higher education open to women in the United States. Unlike the independent women's college or coeducational institution, however, the exact parameters of the coordinate college remained loosely constructed and defined largely by local needs and resources. The adaptability of the arrangement to local conditions is evident in the 1904 *Encyclopedia Americana* definition of "coordinate colleges" as those that are connected "more or less closely with an older college for men" whose "standards of entrance and graduation are the same as in the men's colleges with which they are affiliated" and whose instructors are usually the same as those at the men's colleges.[12]

The coordinate arrangement between Newcomb and Tulane, as defined by Dixon, was born in some measure to reassure Josephine Louise Newcomb that her money would not be appropriated for overall University use. Newcomb's financial independence, degree-conferring authority, administrative structure, and its right to hire faculty and determine curriculum made the early College more similar in structure to independent women's colleges than to most other coordinate colleges. In fact, most Newcomb College and Tulane University administrators throughout the nineteenth and twentieth centuries looked to the women's colleges of the Northeast as models of women's education, yet at the same time adjusted the model to account for the South's more traditional ideas of women's roles.

In 1891, Dixon visited Vassar, Wellesley, Smith, and Bryn Mawr, stating that he found much to observe as "I had never before been inside a sure-enough women's college."[13] When, in 1909, Dixon again visited the region, he included Barnard among the colleges he visited but skipped Radcliffe altogether.[14] Barnard's founders had traveled to New Orleans to study the Newcomb plan, and in Dixon's reciprocal visit is some indication that he, along with other administrators, sought to mold Newcomb on the model of the most separate of the coordinate colleges, one that functioned nearly the same as an independent women's college.[15] There was one central distinction, however, of which Dixon and other coordinate college administrators were acutely aware: although they were "president" in title, the hierarchy of authority within the coordinate system placed them in a position subordinate to the university administration. Dixon mentioned frequently that he was required to contact first the president of the University, who would then carry his concerns or requests before the board or appropriate authority.[16] He also mentioned moving outside this realm of authority to achieve his objectives.[17]

Besides degree-conferring powers, Newcomb's coordinate arrangement gave the College the right to hire and maintain its own faculty. By contrast, the faculty of Columbia University appointed the faculty of Barnard, while Radcliffe contracted with individual Harvard professors to offer instruction at Radcliffe. Faust explained that "one of the peculiar results of the [coordinate] arrangement" was that Radcliffe "would never have a faculty." As a consequence, Radcliffe students were denied the opportunity of studying with a female professor until 1948, when the first woman was hired on the faculty of Harvard College.[18] Ruth Hubbard, the distinguished scientist, Radcliffe alumna, and the first woman to receive a tenured biology professorship (1974) at Harvard, reflected: "From the beginning, Radcliffe apparently failed to recognize that, by proudly offering its students the privilege to sit at the feet of Harvard's Great Men, it failed to awaken in us the expectation that we might someday be Great Women."[19]

Newcomb's practices of hiring faculty situated the College in a more favorable position, somewhat in the middle of academic undertakings with fewer women on the faculty than at women's colleges, but greater numbers than on the faculties of coeducational institutions. In the first year of Newcomb's founding, 60 percent of the faculty was female. When Newcomb moved to the Broadway campus for the 1918–19 academic year, more than two-thirds of the fifty-nine-member faculty was female compared to less than one-third nationally.[20] That same year, 55 percent of Bryn Mawr's faculty was female, 80 percent of Vassar's, 82 percent of Wellesley's, and just 29 and 30 percent, respectively, at coed Oberlin and Swarthmore. Astonishingly, 100 percent of Barnard's faculty was female.[21] Jane Miller's essay on Newcomb's scientists shows how preferences by the women's and coordinate colleges for hiring female scholars created an employment network among the institutions that would benefit both women academics and students.

Women scholars hired for academic positions held qualifications similar to those of their male counterparts. On Newcomb's 1918–19 faculty, 40 percent of the women held a master's degree or doctorate compared to 47 percent of the men.[22] These women held doctorates in Greek, Latin, psychology, physics, biology, geology, and English. Taking into account the number of women on the Newcomb faculty who were instructors in art or music, for which only a bachelor's degree was necessary, Newcomb's women faculty had academic credentials as impressive as those of the male faculty. Thus, early Newcomb students had the opportunity of studying with female professors who, by their presence alone, encouraged their students to greater ambition.

However, in the late 1930s, just as women were making slow gains as a percentage of the faculties in postsecondary institutions nationwide, College and University administrators began to redefine Newcomb's predominantly female faculty as a detriment to the overall academic mission.[23] Clarence Mohr's essay explains how Tulane's movement to become nationally recognized for research and graduate education placed Newcomb's emphasis on undergraduate teaching in jeopardy. Logan Wilson, dean of Newcomb from 1944 to 1951, saw the women faculty as "local" and, though "excellent classroom teachers," not sufficiently committed to scholarly production. He "tried to recruit" what he called "a somewhat broader-based faculty than Newcomb had" because "the women out-numbered the men" and he "wanted it about one-half and one-half." He recalled: "None of the women ever dressed me down for that but I think there was some resistance to the idea."[24]

John "Jack" Hubbard, dean from 1953 to 1965, concurred with Wilson's position, though his desire to nationally recruit male faculty (not "magnolia-scented") who would pursue "genuine scholarship" was framed more subtly:

> The objective really was to try to change, what some people perceived to
> be . . . a kind of magnolia-scented extension of New Orleans society into
> a genuine liberal arts operation that would take the young girl's mind and

stretch it and bend it and shape it and develop it as well as any boy's mind. . . .
[A]nd here were some talented young ladies and what was needed, it seemed
to me, was a faculty that would challenge them and a library with the requisite
resources to support genuine scholarship. And happily, [Tulane University
president] Mr. Harris saw this in exactly the same way as I did and he gave
me all the support one could have wanted, and we set about trying to make
Newcomb College recognized throughout the land as a serious, genuine, intellectual operation.[25]

Newcomb and Tulane's preference for hiring male faculty has had lasting
consequences. In 1989–90, faculty on the uptown campus (which excludes
Tulane Medical School and School of Public Health) numbered 444, of which
just 89, or 20 percent, were women.[26] Nearly twenty years later, for the
2009–10 academic year, full-time faculty on the uptown campus numbered
557, of which 36 percent were female.[27] Thus, although there was a separate
Newcomb faculty until 1987, long before this time and long after, the plenti-
ful models of capable women scholars available to students at most women's
colleges ceased to be prevalent at Newcomb. This was one disadvantage of
Newcomb's ever-evolving coordinate college structure that it shared with coeducational institutions and some coordinate colleges, though never to the
extreme of Radcliffe.

Programs of the College

The power to choose a faculty member of a particular sex was but one reason why authority over hiring was important for Newcomb. Another was the
power to choose faculty with particular expertise. Newcomb's "power to determine its own policy and course of study" allowed educators to keep in the
forefront of their minds the purpose of an education for women. Initially, this
power was directed toward designing a curriculum that addressed the educational needs of young women of the South and encompassed Mrs. Newcomb's
mandate that education look to "the practical" as well as "the literary." This
focus led to the development of curriculum in the arts, physical education,
and science—three areas that became hallmark programs of the College.

The first of these, the art program, came about as Ellsworth and William
Woodward attempted to create a path for women's employment in an impoverished South. The Woodward brothers were two of the seven faculty

members employed by the College at its opening, and Ellsworth especially was central to the founding of the art program. Educated at the Rhode Island School of Design, he envisioned a working community of trained artists that would extend into the city and beyond.

In 1894, Ellsworth worked with Dixon to hire Mary Given Sheerer, who was trained at the Art Academy of Cincinnati, to begin Newcomb's pottery program.[28] The Newcomb Pottery enterprise (1895–1940) grew under his direction. In her essay, Jessie Poesch describes these early art faculty and their work to develop a program that would bring national and international recognition to the College.[29] For Dixon, the pottery program combined the liberal arts with the curriculum of such universities as Drexel and Pratt. Here was an experiment, or model industry, to provide employment for women in a milieu where few opportunities existed. As an early brochure noted: "Most students expect their years of school training to bring them more than cultural value. They wish to prepare themselves for self-support."[30]

The art program was enlarged in the years between 1895 and 1939, and as Poesch describes, other crafts came to be included. By 1941, more than seventy thousand pieces of pottery had been produced with Newcomb College registration numbers and an unknown quantity of other crafts.[31] Those items judged to meet the standards of the faculty jury were sold by Newcomb students, arts craftsmen, and faculty, often from the school's showroom. Although pottery remains the most collectable of the crafts, today the embroidery, though more rare, has almost equal appeal.[32]

Newcomb was ahead of its time in the development of its art program. It was not until the 1930s that an art curriculum would be offered in most women's colleges or that "art and music" would be "considered as intellectually important as the humanities, social sciences, and the physical and biological sciences."[33] In contrast, all early Newcomb students studied art, regardless of their major or track. The University catalogues stated that the study of art offers advantages "in the cultivation of correct taste, at the same time that it offers a desirable relaxation from the more exacting work of the class room."[34] This might have been a covert assurance for parents that academic work would not ruin the body of women for childbearing, something feared and written about into the late nineteenth and early twentieth centuries, but it also reflected a very real desire to make Newcomb a community focused upon art. To many art students and community members, Newcomb College and the art school were synonymous.[35] The success of women artists educated at Newcomb, such as Caroline Wogan Durieux (NC 1916), Angela Gregory (NC 1925), Ida Kohlmeyer (NC 1933), Mignon Faget (NC 1955), Lynda Benglis (NC 1964), Julie Dermansky (NC 1987), and Phoebe Washburn (NC 1996), attests to the continuing excellence of the College's art program. The more recent period of the art program, with an outstanding curriculum in ceramics and a world-class hot-glass facility, is an area deserving of more scholarly work; the Newcomb Music Department, not discussed in this volume at all, is also a program that deserves further attention.

In another early area of curricular achievement, Clara Baer, a pioneer of the physical health movement, began the first physical education certification program in the South, which, by 1907, had developed into the first four-year program in physical education leading to a bachelor's degree. As Joan Paul relates in her essay, these were the first of many "firsts" that earned Baer recognition in the Basketball Hall of Fame. Baer published the first basketball rules for women in 1895 and invented the popular game "Newcomb ball." The daughter of a New Orleans flour merchant, Baer was educated in Boston. She returned home and remade the culture of southern education into a place where young women could partake in physical activity, something unheard of until she invented games specifically for women.[36]

Baer—who held the titles of professor of anatomy and physiology and director of pedagogical gymnastics—along with her successors in the Newcomb Physical Education Department, sent well-qualified students across the South to teach physical education. One of their protégées was Mary Douglas Ayres Ewell (NC 1917), who had earned a bachelor of arts degree and a teacher certificate in physical education. In 1919, she was named coach for the University of Tennessee (UT) girls' basketball team. In 1920, UT women students, with Ayres's approval, requested "equal rights and privileges" with male athletes including team travel to other colleges for athletic events, increased funding for the women's program, and representation on the Athletic Council.[37] As a Newcomb student, Ayers had learned the importance of physical activity for women, and as a professional, she encouraged her students to question assumptions about the gendered nature of sports decades before Title IX of the Education Amendments to the Civil Rights Act was enacted in 1972.

Baer's influence on the curriculum of the College continued for nearly a century. Beginning in 1891, when she joined the Newcomb faculty, "physical training" was required of all students, and by 1909, the *College Bulletin* clearly stated that all Newcomb students were required each year to take "two hours, each week, of regular gymnastic exercise." In 1924, a swimming pool was built as part of the Physical Education Building, and in 1927, successful completion of a swimming test was added to the graduation requirements.[38] "The swimming test," along with the myths surrounding it, continues today in the memories of hundreds of alumnae. One myth attributes the compulsory swimming test to the demise of Sophie by accidental drowning. In fact, completion of a swimming test was required by numerous elite schools, including Radcliffe (from 1920 to 1936) and Cornell University, Dixon's alma mater.[39] In the 1980s, the requirement that Newcomb students complete four semesters of physical education remained the only graduation requirement that differed between Newcomb and A&S. The requirement was abolished in 1987.

The enthusiasm enjoyed by early Newcomb students for participating in intramural sports and athletic competitions waned in the 1940s.[40] In the 1970s, the tennis champion Linda Tuero (NC 1971) sparked renewed interest in women's athletics at Newcomb, and then the passage of Title IX opened opportunities for women in sports previously unimaginable.[41] Newcomb became a charter member of the Association for Intercollegiate Athletics for Women, but as at other institutions where the men's National Collegiate Athletic Association lobbied against equal funding for women's teams, Newcomb's athletes at first received no funding. As important as it was for women to gain entry into college athletics for the opportunity to play competitively, it was even more important for women to be able to attend college on athletic scholarships. In 1976–77, federal legislation enabled the creation of nine scholarships that were awarded to women on the volleyball and basketball teams.[42] Women athletes gained distinction in team sports, as evidenced by Tulane's championship women's basketball teams in the 1990s. By the 2010–11 basketball season, coach Lisa Stockton had posted more than four hundred wins and coached teams to regional and national championships and her student athletes to All-American honors and positions in the Women's National Basketball Association.[43] In the 2010–11 academic year, fifty-eight women received full scholarship awards and twenty-five received partial awards in six different sports.[44]

The third program to establish Newcomb's curricular success was located in the scientific branch of the three-pronged mission—"language, art, science"—that is inscribed in the Newcomb seal. Among some of the first science graduates were the Spencer sisters, Adelin (NC 1890) and Mary Cass (NC 1892), who became geology and math professors, respectively; the Loeber sisters, Maud (NC 1893) and Edith (NC 1894), who became a pediatrician and a gynecologist; and the much-published Willey Glover Denis (NC 1899). Denis's 1920 appointment as assistant professor in the Department of Physiology of Tulane Medical School is considered to be the first appointment of a woman to a major medical school; her later appointment, in 1925, as chair of the Department of Biological Chemistry at Tulane, made her the first woman to chair a medical school department.[45]

The career of Adelin Spencer (1870–1937) is especially interesting given her standing as a member of Newcomb's first graduating class. Spencer earned her bachelor's degree in 1890, her master's degree from Tulane in 1894, and her PhD from Cornell in 1896. She then returned to teach chemistry and geology at Newcomb. Her obituary noted that she had discovered a new genus and species of sea urchin in the form of a minute fossil on display at the Peabody Museum at Yale.[46]

Like Spencer, other science graduates earned advanced degrees from Cornell, an institution Dixon felt provided a suitable environment for his serious scholars. The graduate programs at Bryn Mawr, the University of California, and the University of Chicago also were well attended by early Newcomb graduates. Later Newcomb alumnae attended Tulane Medical School and other graduate programs that allowed them to prepare for careers in science. Many scientific "stars" of the College could be added to the list of chemists Miller discusses. A few of the Newcomb women who could be studied include Margherita Cotonio Bourne (NC 1919), the first American woman admitted to Britain's Royal Academy of Medicine; Selma DeBakey (NC 1937) and Lois DeBakey (NC 1940), science writers; Melessa Phillips (NC 1969), winner of the Kellogg National Fellow Award in 1990; and Cheryl Nickerson (NC 1983), an astrobiologist whose work earned her a 2001 Presidential Early Career Award for Scientists and Engineers.[47]

Neither Women's College nor Coeducational Institution, but the Best of Both Worlds

Besides Newcomb's early curricular success, the College gained support because the coordinate arrangement itself offered the benefits of both a coeducational university and a women's college. A 1930s College brochure promoted this idea, announcing that "Newcomb is especially fortunate in combining the advantages of both types of institutions, without suffering from the disadvantages of either."[48]

Newcomb, the brochure noted, was "well-equipped to provide each student with every opportunity to develop her greatest individual potentiality."[49] As with women's colleges, these advantages included frequent contacts between students and faculty, a supportive environment for studying male-dominated fields in science and math, and leadership opportunities in the classroom and in student organizations.[50] The disadvantages of the women's colleges, according to the brochure's authors, rested on the enrollment of a single sex. "There are educators," the Newcomb brochure pronounced, "who do not consider the complete segregation of girls during the college years as entirely wise."[51] Many "girls" agreed with the educators regarding this disadvantage of the single-sex women's colleges and, thus, by extension, the advantage of the coordinate system. By the 1920s Flapper era, the separation of women and men was often seen as "inhibiting healthy relations between the sexes," and female students increasingly chose not to "waste" themselves in a world without men.[52] A 1934 editorial in the *Newcomb Arcade*, written as if to assuage parents' fears that their daughter's attendance at a women's college would limit her marital prospects, posited that Newcomb had become "a convenient place to send your daughters between seventeen and twenty-one, a place where she will learn to make herself more attractive."[53]

Contrary to the brochure's pronouncements, the coordinate system held some of the same disadvantages as coeducation. As already noted, coordinate and coeducational colleges had fewer women on their faculties than did women's colleges. Moreover, the coordinate arrangement, like coeducational institutions, established a standard of academic excellence and leadership that was defined as male. Newcomb would not have its first woman dean until 1951, and even after Newcomb's students and women faculty had proven themselves academically, as the scientific "stars" of the College had done, they would not be taken quite as seriously as their male counterparts in A&S. Newcomb students would remain valued not for their own education, but for the education of the men they could attract as husbands. They would not take center stage as leaders, no clear sisterhood or feminist leadership would be promoted, and learning by women would not be valued on its own terms as it was in the women's colleges.

On the other hand, the advantages of being "a part of Tulane University" were greater for students than was indicated by the brochure's acknowledgment that Newcomb "also shares the varied interests of the large institution."[54] Students quickly took advantage of the benefits of the coordinate plan such as the ability to cross-register between colleges and the availability of graduate work offered through Tulane's graduate and professional schools. The enrollment of Newcomb graduates in Tulane's Graduate School was nearly immediate. By the 1900–1901 academic year, Newcomb alumnae accounted for twenty-two of the thirty-four graduate students enrolled, while graduates of A&S numbered just three.[55] This trend continued for a number of years. The 1909–10 *Catalogue of Students* lists twenty-two of the forty-three students enrolled in the Graduate Department as Newcomb alumnae, five A&S alumni, and sixteen other students from undergraduate programs at schools such as the universities of Michigan, Missouri, and Cincinnati, and the University of the South (Sewanee).[56]

While most people think of cross-registration as women being allowed to cross into male-dominated classrooms, cross-registration at Tulane began first when Tulane allowed men to take art and music at Newcomb in the second decade of the twentieth century; and then in the professional schools, which allowed a limited number of A&S and Newcomb students to combine the liberal arts curriculum with a course of study in law or medicine.[57] Bessie Margolin (NC 1929; Law 1930) was an early beneficiary of the cross-registration between colleges that was promoted particularly in the interwar years. Margolin matriculated through Newcomb but took courses at both Newcomb and the Tulane University School of Law. In accepting the 1975 Tulane Distinguished Alumni Award, Margolin praised the structure that allowed her this education: "Tulane held something very special to me as a woman . . . the fullest opportunity and encouragement to fulfill myself as a human being intellectually, culturally, socially, and as a citizen with rights and responsibilities equal to those of men. As a student interested in a professional career, as well as a serious liberal arts education, I was uniquely fortunate that my home town university was one of the few in the nation at that time, which not only had a tradition of serious higher education for women . . . exemplified by the excellent standards of Newcomb . . . but which welcomed women into its graduate and professional schools."[58] In short, the strength of Newcomb's coordinate relationship rested in offering the benefits of both a coeducational institution and a women's college, as well as the benefits of a research university. Jack Hubbard spoke of these advantages in 1986: "Here was Newcomb College, a coordinate college, that is to say, a women's college, but a part of a major university with all the resources of a major university. I considered this arrangement to really to be the best of all possible worlds. I still do."[59]

Changes in the Coordinate Plan

Newcomb's standing as an institution "entirely distinct" from Tulane visibly began to unravel with the move to the Broadway campus in 1918. Dixon was to be Newcomb's only president, and his successor in 1919, Pierce Butler, was named dean—conforming to the title given to the heads of other colleges of the University.[60] Butler had been groomed to assume leadership of the College, having been appointed professor of history in 1902, head of English in 1907, and often being placed in charge of College matters when Dixon was away.[61] Butler's administration, which would last until 1938, was emblematic of the duality of the coordinate plan, marking both the ongoing reinterpretation of the educational experience offered to women at Tulane and the tensions surrounding the erosion of Newcomb's semi-autonomous administrative structure within the University, particularly with regard to finances.

Butler was a prolific scholar, the editor of the *Southern Review*, and the author of a number of publications including a biography of Judah P. Benjamin and *Women of Medieval France*. He was especially interested in Newcomb's academic standards and its standing in the Southern Association of College Women. The head of that organization, Elizabeth Avery Colton, had visited 142 institutions of higher education for women in the South between 1910 and 1917. Her findings showed that many institutions took on nonacademic goals more appropriately left to "preparatory schools, finishing schools, and [normal] colleges." This judgment went straight to the heart of what had been one of the hallmarks of early Newcomb: its special students and numerous special programs offering certificates rather than degrees.[62] Although leaving untouched the popular and prestigious art and music schools (which, nevertheless had many special students), Butler otherwise acted quickly. He ended the High School in 1920 and thwarted the continuation of the programs in domestic science (1909–20) and education (1909–21). His opposition to the founding of the Newcomb Nursery school was unequivocal, as Susan Tucker's essay illuminates. Alumnae remember him saying: "It took me long enough to get rid of home economics at Newcomb and I'm not going to take more of this silly stuff on."[63]

With the elimination of programs traditionally defined as fields of study for women, the balancing act for Butler during the interwar years was to keep Newcomb's enrollment up (i.e., continuing to appeal to local women who might not want a full four-year course of study and degree in liberal arts) while building a demanding curriculum, comparable to those of the northeastern women's colleges. Yet, to the modern eye, Butler's tenure made Newcomb more, rather than less, insular. Unlike Dixon, Butler was an insider, a member of the social and educated elite of the South.[64] Many of his decisions reflect a background that at once glorified the race relations of the past and established a standard of academic excellence for the women's college that was defined by masculine values. He wrote icily of the intentions of the YWCA to bring integration to local chapters. When asked by one prospective student "if Creoles would be welcomed at Newcomb," he responded firmly that she probably had "misunderstood the definition of Creole. If she thought of any definition other than that of a white descendant, she should know that indeed such a person could not be found at the College."[65] This statement alone gives future scholars reason to undertake a demographic comparison between the population of New Orleans and Newcomb students over time. Overall, however, it is safe to conclude that for Butler, as for Mrs. Newcomb earlier, Newcomb was intended to provide an education for southern elite white girls, some of whom should be pushed to excel and others who should be seen as future wives and mothers. The two usually would not be intertwined.

The 1936–37 Semi-Centennial Celebration of Newcomb's founding was symbolic of this schism. In his desire to promote women in the sciences during this celebration, Butler invited Dr. Alice Hamilton, the founder of occupational medicine and the first female professor at Harvard Medical School. Butler also invited the well-known art critic Thomas Craven to speak, a nod to the prominence of the Art School. Other events included an art exhibit and a historical pageant focused on the education of girls in Louisiana, staged with the help of local schoolchildren. Written by the alumnae and inspired by an idea of Caroline Richardson (NC 1895 and first counselor to women),[66] the pageant was meant to evoke "a record of the struggle that women of this state made against great odds to bring their children learning and culture." The pageant began with a depiction of the Ursuline nuns in 1728, and the final episode, called "Newcomb's Daughters," reflected on the continuing educational advancement of women. One episode included dramatic performances of the role some Newcomb students would play before marriage as teachers in the rural countryside of the twentieth century and as community volunteers.[67]

While Butler's scholarly work aligned him with the Tulane professoriate, his deanship echoed Dixon's in challenging the University's assumptions that

Newcomb's money could be used for purposes other than the women's college. As Butler began his administrative tenure, the University reconfigured funds left by Mrs. Newcomb, calling them the "1920 endowment." Only the vigilance of the Newcomb administration and faculty on behalf of the women's college kept Newcomb's budget "separate" as the University pressed for more centralized administration. Butler's interactions with Tulane University president Albert Bledsoe Dinwiddie (1918–35), as described in the essay by Tucker, often revolved around issues of who would have the last say about Newcomb's curriculum offerings and how Newcomb funds would be spent.

Butler's power struggle with Dinwiddie over Newcomb's money and philosophy of women's education continued with the University presidency of Rufus C. Harris (1937–59). In an early correspondence with Harris, Butler wrote of the necessity of recognizing that Newcomb was "far more 'spread out' than the College of Arts and Sciences, with our fully equipped and costly special schools." At the same time, Butler wanted to make sure that Harris considered that "the relation of the finances of Newcomb to the finances of the University" was in need of "clarifying." He was not opposed to Newcomb's contribution to the University budget, but he also wanted Newcomb's share of bequests to the University not specifically designated for other units. Butler felt "that no clear statement on these matters has ever been made."[68]

Not everyone on the Newcomb campus saw integration with the University as an advantage. By 1937, according to Mohr, an anachronistic "spirit of separation" divided Newcomb from other colleges of the University, and Butler from many on the Newcomb faculty. Butler, more so than other Newcomb faculty members, was willing to accept the reasoning that his replacement as dean would best come from outside the College. Hoping to deter such an appointment, eleven prominent faculty members wrote to Harris on October 20, 1937, urging the appointment of Anna E. Many (NC 1909; counselor to women and assistant professor of math, 1922–51; acting dean, 1944; dean 1951–53) as Butler's replacement. Many, they noted, was a "person of vision and judgment" who had experience in the past as acting dean and, moreover, had familiarity with "policies and problems of the college and of similar co-ordinated colleges for women."[69] By June 8, they and a number of alumnae were very disappointed when Tulane A&S English professor Charles Frederick Hard (1938–43) was chosen. They issued a "Statement" entering a "protest" about the lack of "voice in the choice of . . . administrators."[70] At least one alumna, Carmelite Janvier (NC 1911), also wrote in protest to Harris, asserting not only her own comments but also evoking the memory of her father, a former Tulane board member who had "belief in the sacredness of Mrs. Newcomb's confidence in entrusting to the Tulane board the funds for establishing and maintaining a college for women in New Orleans." By implication, she then underscored her own thoughts on the violation of this trust. "Why," she asked, "was it as necessary to place as Dean someone who . . . has not had any experience either as a member of the faculty of a women's college or as the head of a department of a men's college or as chairman of an important committee in the University? Was there no one in this country with such experience who could have been secured?"[71] Hard's associations with Newcomb—his wife (a Wellesley College graduate) taught English at Newcomb, her grandmother had been the first librarian of Newcomb's library, and her mother and aunt among the first generation of Newcomb graduates—apparently meant little to Janvier.

Entering into the discussion to ward off such disruptions to Harris's plans, Butler asked for cooperation and a spirit of "pull-together-ness."[72] Hard, like Butler, had an impressive list of publications, and one can see in retrospect that Butler and Harris (and soon Hard) were interpreting the strength of a women's college based on national standards of scholarly productivity. However, they were overlooking the contributions that women scholars as administrators might make in creating and building upon existing programs for women. In April 1938, Hard had been asked by Harris to set down his "general observations . . . relative to Newcomb College." In his memo, Hard mainly recounted the need for more research among the Newcomb faculty, for making Newcomb part of the effort to push Tulane's status as a research university. Point one concerned "individual productivity in scholarship among the faculty members" and their making a "substantial contribution to graduate teaching." Three other points concerned making Newcomb more connected to the University—adjustments of salary so that Newcomb faculty were not "at a disadvantage," more sharing of faculty among the colleges, and the creation of a joint library. Another point noted the contributions Newcomb had made, particularly in art and music, but the need, too, for "special literary and historical studies of the cultural backgrounds of Louisiana and the south . . . Latin-American relationships."[73] All these were worthy but ambitious building projects, and after 1941, adjustment to wartime became the central focus of Hard's tenure. Whereas Butler oversaw the establishment of the coordinate college as the neighbor of Tulane and cautiously allowed the integration of Newcomb students into some coeducational activities of the University throughout the interwar years, Hard supervised changes to the geographic insularity of the women's side of campus. He assisted in the construction of the University's first student center (on the location of present-day Stern Hall), and on the north side of Freret Street, the "Newcomb side" of campus, McAlister Auditorium, and the Cunningham Observatory.[74] He witnessed the installation of Navy men on the Newcomb side of campus, albeit closer to the old Sugar Bowl stadium. He celebrated the dedication of the joint library he recommended to Harris in his memo of 1938, when in 1940 the Newcomb Library was joined with Tulane's Tilton Library and that of Howard Library, a private city library, on the Newcomb side of campus.[75] Although the new library held a gloriously engraved memorial stone commemorating the joining of the three libraries, it was named after just two of the libraries and called simply Howard-Tilton.

Newcomb students recalled that the new library meant that letters from the University would no longer notify them that University library books were first for the use of men. But the new library also ended the communities of women browsing the stacks of their own library. It is significant that of the remaining coordinate colleges, only Barnard maintains its own library. While the opportunity for women to study in an environment predominantly shaped by and for women has been re-created at Tulane through the Nadine Robbert Vorhoff Library (founded in 1975) of the Newcomb Center for Research on Women, and at Harvard University through the Schlesinger Library (founded 1943) of the Radcliffe Institute for Advanced Study.

Hard departed in 1944 to become president of Scripps College, the women's college of the Claremont Colleges, where he would be its longest-serving president, from 1944 to 1964.[76] Interestingly, he had learned enough as dean of Newcomb to impress others, more so than he had initially impressed Carmelite Janvier and the Newcomb faculty, with his ability to oversee the education of college women.

While the growth of the University to the Newcomb side of campus eroded Newcomb's physical separateness, World War II encouraged greater integration among males and females in student activities. At the same time, the departure of many men for war created leadership roles for women as officers in University student government and editors of University publications. Gloria Monninger (NC 1943) became the first woman to edit the student newspaper, the *Hullabaloo*.

From the viewpoint of the administration and faculty, the war years and the years immediately following further complicated the crafting of a curriculum that gave ample attention to the need for women graduates to work, at least at some point in their lives, while acknowledging the preferred role of alumnae as volunteer community leaders, wives, and mothers. Some graduates found great satisfaction as part of the workforce, only to be forced to retreat into the home in the face of massive public sentiment after the war. Arriving in 1944, Dean Logan Wilson (1944–51) harnessed older concerns that educated women would not make suitable wives, or might not even want marriage, and newer wartime fears about the shortage of men available as mates. A sociologist, Wilson noted that women students had two main concerns in life: finding a mate and finding an occupation. The first usually governed the second since when she found a mate, she would become a housewife. He sought to enlighten Newcomb students through his teaching and taught a course open to juniors and seniors called "The Family" but which the press dubbed, "Marriage or How to Find a Husband." Students were required to write on the marriages of selected Newcomb alumnae.[77] While this could be the beginnings of an intellectual pursuit that asked how women might combine their academic, professional, and sexual lives, Wilson was quick to build upon the rhetoric of the time, stating: "Women not only have the main responsibility in home-making and in the upbringing of the young but also (perhaps by default on the part of men) are the main workers in our religious, cultural, and civic organizations. Seeing to it that deserving young women have the best possible educational advantages should be a matter of vital concern to all public-spirited citizens."[78]

Wilson's view that higher education should prepare women for roles in the family and community existed alongside his goal to raise College standards by requiring the College Entrance Exam for Newcomb admission beginning in 1948. Reflecting on the purpose of women's education some thirty-five years after his tenure as Newcomb dean, Wilson reiterated the relationship between family roles and women's education: "The fact remains, that even now [1987], the role of women is more important in terms of the future development of upcoming youth than it is of men because men just don't give as much attention to it. And that's part of the role, and this needs to be taken into account in the education of women."[79]

Wilson's philosophy of education represented one side in the debate concerning the function of women's education. A similar view expressed by

Harold Lee, professor in the Department of Philosophy from 1943 to 1965, held that "the purposes of higher education for women are not . . . exactly the same as the purposes for men's higher education" and therefore "the requirements for graduation . . . don't need to be the same for women as they do for men." To Lee, professional study made sense for men but not for women.[80] His view evidently was shared by students for, as Mohr reports in his essay, by the early 1960s only 25 percent of Newcomb students, as opposed to 80 percent of Tulane students, saw graduate school as the next step in their education.

Yet opposition to a curriculum intended to educate women for domestic roles was evident among the faculty. Mildred Christian, professor in the Department of English from 1948 to 1967, recalled: "I remember that at the last meeting of the faculty that I attended, I was alarmed to hear, mainly male faculty. . . . I listened to the conversation that was going on, the propaganda really, and it was all toward making women study women's subjects. There was a certain condescension in women's subjects. The tone was such that you knew that women were being relegated to the unimportant future. And I personally wanted to fight that instantly."[81]

Heated debates among Newcomb faculty over curricular decisions and the purpose of higher education for women continued even as a separate Newcomb curriculum, officially maintained until 1987, was substantially modified in the years 1940 to 1960. As more Newcomb and A&S students cross-registered for classes between the colleges and shared instruction increased, the "power" of the Newcomb faculty "to determine its own policy, and course of study" weakened substantially.[82]

One of Dean Hubbard's efforts to address this problem and to make "Newcomb College recognized throughout the land" led to the creation of Newcomb's Junior Year Abroad Program, described by Alice Gail Bier in her essay. This would be one of the first study-abroad programs in the nation, and one quickly made available to male students in the University.

Hubbard's efforts did not slow the rising sentiment among University administrators that Newcomb was becoming an administrative burden. A revolving cycle of deans with short tenures brought its own series of problems for Newcomb's status within the University. Deans Charles Hounshell (1966–69), James F. Davidson (1969–79), and acting deans Francis Lawrence (1976–78), and William Smither (1978–79) oversaw a student body split between activities available in the larger University and the activities available only to Newcomb students. Tulane's growing national reputation meant that by the 1970s, for college aspirants unfamiliar with Newcomb's history or the term "coordinate college," the name "Tulane" held greater appeal than did "Newcomb." The national movement for women's rights played a part in this as students and their families struggled with what an education long denied women should mean. Enrollment at Newcomb appeared to place them as second-class citizens within the University, a place that in previous times had been unquestioned.[83] Yet Newcomb's enrollment fluctuated with demographic trends and remained strong even as the number of women's colleges shrank from more than 200 in 1960, to 83 in 1993, and to fewer than 50 in 2011.[84] The closing of women's colleges along with the admission of women to previously all-male institutions created a different sort of anomaly: the single-sex college for men. Whereas the advantages of the coordinate college for women as both women's college and coeducational institution continued to have resonance, men's colleges, including the all-male coordinate colleges, struggled to preserve a relevant mission. For those at Tulane willing to enter into discussion, the problem with the coordinate system was not Newcomb College, but the declining relevance of A&S.

To Newcomb dean James Davidson, the creation of a women's center was one way of addressing women's changing work and family roles and ensuring Newcomb's position as a college for the education of both alumnae and students.[85] Beth Willinger's essay tells of the founding of the Newcomb Women's Center in 1975 for this purpose and its subsequent evolution as the Newcomb College Center for Research on Women. In 1986, the Women's Center would help host the Newcomb centennial celebration, which included a symposium on women's higher education and a ceremony recognizing fifteen accomplished Newcomb alumnae. However, soon after Newcomb celebrated its one-hundred-year history, a proposal to merge the faculties of Newcomb and A&S in 1987 brought a fight to reestablish Newcomb as a separate and distinct college within the University. A similar struggle had been fought successfully by Barnard to maintain its independence from Columbia when Columbia College went coed in 1983. Few at Newcomb viewed the complete legal and financial independence that Barnard achieved as a viable outcome for Newcomb. The alternative, to merge fully with A&S as Radcliffe would with Harvard, was also viewed unfavorably. While the stated goal of Radcliffe had been for women to gain a Harvard education, Newcomb faculty, students, and alumnae historically had argued for a continuing, though changing, coordinate college structure. In the debate over the merger of the Newcomb and A&S faculties, organized efforts by the Newcomb alumnae failed to persuade the Tulane Administrators to maintain a separate Newcomb faculty. Yet their persistence in arguing their position led to some success as the Administrators voted to establish the Newcomb Foundation with a start-up fund of $2 million. Through this endowment, the Office of Newcomb Student Programs was created to advise student groups such as the Newcomb Senate, honor societies, class officers, and to promote leadership among Newcomb students. The Newcomb Fellows Program also was created as part of the effort to bring a diverse but committed group of faculty back to the College, and then to make funds available competitively to these faculty for projects involving Newcomb students.[86] An increased budget was recommended for the Newcomb College Center for Research on Women. And the departments of music and art were renamed the *Newcomb* Art Department and *Newcomb* Music Department. In 1989, Ann Die was hired as dean of Newcomb College to develop the ideas outlined in the Resolutions and to oversee Newcomb's five remaining units: the offices of Newcomb Alumnae, Newcomb Student Advising, Newcomb Student Programs, the Newcomb College Center for Research on Women, and the Newcomb Nursery School and Child Care Center. Subsequent deans leading up to 2005 worked to develop programming to prepare Newcomb women for their futures and to continue Newcomb's traditions such as Daisy Chain, the Big–Little Sis program and pinning ceremony, graduation, and Newcomb academic and service awards. These programs and activities succeeded in providing a select number of students with the leadership opportunities, faculty mentoring, academic advising, and high intellectual expectations they would experience at a women's college, or, rather, at the ever-evolving coordinate college that was Newcomb.

Lessons Learned

The period 1919–2006 allowed women at Tulane, in varying degrees, the experiences of both a women's college and a coeducational institution. Tulane offered women, with some exceptions, increasing parity with men at Tulane, as well as the opportunity to gain considerable respect as scholars and artists in the national arena. The study of Kirkland's brief experience in the last quarter of the twentieth century suggests that the coordinate structure as an intermediary step brought "more equitable coeducation than most other colleges achieved by adding women directly into a historically men's college."[87]

Throughout all these changes, Newcomb College excelled over the College of Arts and Sciences in the achievements of its administration, faculty, and students, and the quality of its teaching and programming. Yet this excellence was not always viewed favorably by the University administration, who devoted attention to the practicality of maintaining two separate liberal arts colleges. Newcomb's distinctions often were born of an adaptability required of being not only a college for women, but also an appendage of the University. The University's efforts to create a unified public presence under the name and reputation of Tulane University were frustrated when "Newcomb College" was given as the affiliation of a student, faculty member, or alumna recognized for achievement. There was, by necessity, friction. Mrs. Newcomb entrusted the Administrators of the Tulane Educational Fund with oversight of the memorial college. Hence, the Administrators always had the power of the purse, and Newcomb's leaders were forced to negotiate with the Tulane administration as to how those funds would be used and how the College would function.

Not until 1987, with the merger of the undergraduate faculties, did Newcomb have an endowment of its own, and then only a modest one. The student-alumnae protests following the 2005 announcement of the closing of the College led the Administrators to "return" to Newcomb—in the form of the Newcomb College Institute—funds functioning as Newcomb-endowed funds as well as Newcomb's true endowment, approximately $40 million. Ironically, this would be the first time Newcomb funds would largely be in the control of the Newcomb administration.[88]

More than a few voices in the 2005–6 restructuring suggested that the proposed combined undergraduate college should at least be renamed for Sophie Newcomb in recognition of the fact that Josephine Newcomb had made a greater financial contribution to the University than had Paul Tulane. The undergraduate college is now named Newcomb-Tulane College, another distinction—some might say fatality—born of the advantages and disadvantages of an evolving coordinate college system in the twenty-first century.[89]

NOTES

1. Brandt V. B. Dixon, *A Brief History of the H. Sophie Newcomb Memorial College, 1887–1919* (New Orleans: Hauser Printing, 1928), 37.

2. Thomas Woody, *A History of Women's Education in the United States* (Lancaster, Pa.: Science Press, 1929), 304.

3. Ibid.

4. Drew Gilpin Faust, "Mingling Promiscuously: A History of Women and Men at Harvard," lecture delivered to the Harvard class of 2005, http://nrs.harvard.edu/urn-3:HUL .InstRepos:4677615.

5. Marcia Synnott, "A Friendly Rivalry: Yale and Princeton Pursue Parallel Paths to Coeducation," in *Going Coed: Women's Experiences in Formerly Men's Colleges and Universities, 1950–2000*, ed. Leslie Miller-Bernal and Susan L Poulson (Nashville: Vanderbilt University Press, 2004), 111–14.

6. Faust, "Mingling Promiscuously."

7. Helen Lefkowitz Horowitz, *Alma Mater: Design and Experience in the Women's Colleges from Their Nineteenth-Century Beginnings to the 1930s* (New York: Knopf, 1984), 6, 95; "The Seven Sisters," Mount Holyoke College, www.mtholyoke.edu/cic/about/history.shtml. The only entry on Newcomb in the entire 1998 *Historical Dictionary of Women's Education in the United States*, ed. Linda Eisenmann [Westport, Ct.: Greenwood Press]) is under "coordinate colleges."

8. Emilie M. McVea, "Women's Colleges and the Southern Association," in *Proceedings of the Association of Colleges and Secondary Schools of the Southern States* (New Orleans: 1922), 108.

9. Horowitz, *Alma Mater*, xvi.

10. Woody, *A History of Women's Education in the United States*, 308.

11. When in 1987 the faculties of Newcomb and A&S were merged as the Faculty of Liberal Arts and Sciences, the text of the Newcomb diploma remained unchanged.

12. Other coordinate colleges founded prior to 1910 include Evelyn College of Princeton (1887, closed 1897); Pembroke College of Brown University (1891, closed 1971); Margaret Morrison Carnegie College of Carnegie Mellon (1903, closed 1973); William Smith of Hobart-William Smith (1908); Jackson College for Women of Tufts (1910, closed 1980) ("Timeline of Women's Colleges in the United States," Wikipedia).

13. Dixon, *Brief History*, 85.

14. Ibid., 144, 147–48.

15. John P. Dyer, *Tulane: The Biography of a University, 1834–1965* (New York: Harper and Row, 1966), 53n.

16. Dixon, *Brief History*, 37, 42, 43, 46–47, 67, 101,127.

17. Ibid., 129–30.

18. Faust, "Mingling Promiscuously."

19. Quoted ibid.

20. *Bulletin of the Tulane University of Louisiana, The H. Sophie Newcomb Memorial College for Women: Announcement for 1918–1919* 19, no. 4 (New Orleans: Tulane University Press, 1918): 12–15 (hereafter cited as *Newcomb Announcement*), NA NCCROW.

21. Faust, "Mingling Promiscuously."

22. *Newcomb Announcement, 1918–19*: 12–15.

23. U.S. Department of Education, National Center for Education Statistics, "Historical Summary of Faculty, Students, Degrees, and Finance in Degree-Granting Institutions: 1869–70 to 2000–01," http://nces.ed.gov/programs/digest/d02/dt171.asp.

24. Logan Wilson, Oral History interview by Constance Walker, January 24, 1987, tape recording, NA NCCROW.

25. John Hubbard, Oral History interview by Jill Jackson, March 6, 1986, tape recording, NA NCCROW.

26. *Gender-Based Pay Equity Report: Update with 1989–90 Data,* Tulane University–Uptown Campus, Report to the Senate Committee on Affirmative Action, May 7, 1990, NA NCCROW.

27. Lisa Martin, Tulane University Workforce Management Organization, Reporting Specialist, Correspondence, October 13, 2009. If part-time faculty are included in the 2009–10 uptown faculty roster, the percentage of female faculty increases to 38.7, still far below the percentage of females on the pre–World War II Newcomb faculty.

28. Jessie Poesch, *Newcomb Pottery: An Enterprise for Southern Women, 1895–1940,* with Walter Bob and Sally Main Spanola (Eaton, Pa.: Schiffer, 1984), 17.

29. For awards, see Jessie Poesch, *Newcomb Pottery & Crafts: An Educational Enterprise for Women 1895–1940,* with Sally Main (Atglen, Pa: Schiffer, 2003), 157.

30. "A Special Word to Those Who Wish to Study Art: Art School for Women, Newcomb College," Art Reference Files, NA NCCROW.

31. Walter Bob, "Marks and Makers," in *Newcomb Pottery,* by Poesch, 89–93.

32. See Poesch, *Newcomb Pottery,* 37, 77–78; Suzanne Ormond and Mary E. Irvine, *Louisiana's Art Nouveau: The Crafts of the Newcomb Style* (Gretna, La.: Pelican, 1976), 79–82, 88, 91, 104; and Jean Moore Bragg and Susan Saward, *The Newcomb Style: Newcomb College Arts & Crafts and Art Pottery, Collector's Guide* (New Orleans: Jean Bragg Gallery, 2002), 123–90.

33. Mariam K. Chamberlain, ed., *Women in Academe: Progress and Prospects* (New York: Russell Sage Foundation, 1988), 113.

34. Tulane University of Louisiana, *Catalogue, 1890–91: Announcement for 1891–92* (New Orleans: Tulane University Press, 1891), 80, NA NCCROW.

35. See Poesch, *Newcomb Pottery,* 94–106; Poesch, *Newcomb Pottery & Crafts,* 281–97; Ormond and Irvine, *Louisiana's Art Nouveau,* 149–73; Bragg and Saward, *The Newcomb Style,* 119–46; Judith H. Bonner, *Newcomb Centennial 1886–1986, An Exhibition of Art by the Art Faculty at the New Orleans Museum of Art: Exhibition and Catalogue* (New Orleans: Newcomb College, 1986); Patricia Brady, *Encyclopedia of New Orleans Artists, 1718–1918* (New Orleans: Historic New Orleans Collection, 1987); and Newcomb Alumnae Clippings Scrapbook, NA NCCROW.

36. See also Joan Paul, "Clara Gregory Baer: Catalyst for Women's Basketball," in *A Century of Women's Basketball: From Frailty to Final Four,* ed. Joan S. Hult and Marianna Trekell (Reston, Va.: American Alliance for Health, Physical Education, Recreation and Dance, 1991), 37–51.

37. Mary Douglas Ayres Ewell, Biographical Files, NA NCCROW; University of Tennessee, Women's Studies Program, *Mary Douglas Ayres Ewell: 1998 Notable UT Woman Award Recipient,* http://web.utk.edu/~wstudy/history/eminent/ewell.php .

38. *Tulane University of Louisiana: Catalogue, 1891–92, Announcement for 1892–93* (New Orleans: Tulane University Press, 1892), 88, 102; *Newcomb Announcement, 1909–10:* 37; *1925–26:* 10; *1927–28:* 80, NA NCCROW.

39. Christine Lagoria, "The Life Acquatic," *New York Times,* December 29, 2009; Radcliffe College, Dept. of Physical Education Records, 1901–73; Inventory: Historical Note, RG XV, Radcliffe College Archives, Schlesinger Library, Radcliffe Institute, Harvard University, http://oasis.lib.harvard.edu.

40. Ked Dixon, "Study of Newcomb Student Organizations," 1918–1987, thesis file, NA NCCROW.

41. Linda Tuero, Biographical Files, Athletics Department Collection, NA NCCROW. Title IX of the Education Amendments of 1972.

42. Athletics Department Collection, NA NCCROW; *Tulane Hullabaloo,* September 17, 1976, 18.

43. TulaneTalk-L@tulane.edu, "Ms. 400 Lisa Stockton," January 7, 2011; "Women's Basketball," Tulane Green Wave Athletics, http://tulanegreenwave.cstv.com/sports/w-baskbl/tul-w -baskbl-body.html.

44. Scott Connors, Assistant Provost for Athletic Compliance, Tulane Athletics, to Beth Willinger, March 9, 2011.

45. See Biographical Files under individual names, as well as Women in Medicine Files, Collective Biographical Files, NA NCCROW.

46. Adelin Spencer, Biographical Files, NA NCCROW; Class of 1890 files, NA NCCROW; Student Records, NA NCCROW.

47. "Noted Woman Anesthetist Tells Why: Maude Loeber, A Noted Expert on Babies, Talks of Dr. Dixon," *New Orleans Item,* January 1, 1930; Women in Medicine Files, Collective Biographical Files, NA NCCROW; Biographical Files under individual names, NA NCCROW.

48. Newcomb College, Tulane University: Pictures and Practical Information, May 1930 (hereafter cited as 1930 College brochure).

49. Ibid.

50. Jillian Kinzie, Paul D. Umbach et al., "Women Students at Coeducational and Women's Colleges: How Do Their Experiences Compare?" *Journal of College Student Development* 48, no. 2 (March–April 2007): 145–65; M. Elizabeth Tidball, "Women's Colleges and Achievers Revisited," *Signs: Journal of Women in Culture and Society* 5, no. 3 (January 1980): 504–17; E. A. Langdon, "Women's Colleges Then and Now: Access Then, Equity Now," *Peabody Journal of Education* 76, no. 1 (2001): 5–30.

51. 1930 College brochure.

52. Horowitz, *Alma Mater,* 282, 284, 285.

53. *Newcomb Arcade* 26, no. 2 (February 1934): 3–4.

54. 1930 College brochure.

55. *Register of Tulane University of Louisiana, 1900–1901* (New Orleans: Tulane University, 1901), 108–9, NA NCCROW.

56. *Bulletin of Tulane University of Louisiana, The Register 1909–1910, ser. 11 (May 1910)* (New Orleans: Tulane University Press, 1910), 370–71, NA NCCROW.

57. Ibid., 14. About 1909, the bulletins of A&S contained policy information for students who wished to combine the academic and law course (six years) or academic and medical course (seven years). Not until the 1960s does this arrangement receive attention in the Newcomb bulletins (*Tulane University Bulletin: The H. Sophie Newcomb Memorial College for Women, 1963–1964* (New Orleans, 1962), 40, NA NCCROW.

58. Bessie Margolin, Biographical Files, NA NCCROW.

59. Hubbard interview.

60. Tulane Board of Administrators, Minutes for April 14, 1919, Minute Book fourteen, UAHT.

61. Pierce Butler, Biographical Files, NA NCCROW; Dixon, *Brief History*, 147.

62. Elizabeth Avery Colton, *The Various Types of Southern Colleges for Women* (Raleigh, N.C.: Mitchell Printing, 1917); Amy Thompson McCandless, "Progressivism and the Higher Education of Southern Women," *North Carolina Historical Review* 70, no. 3 (July 1993): 321.

63. Quoted by Dorothy Seago, transcribed interview with Adele Salzer, 1976, Friends of the Cabildo Tape, Oral History Collection, NA NCCROW.

64. His memoir, *The Unhurried Years and Laurel Hill: The record of a Teacher* (New Orleans: R. L. Crager, 1954) tells of a longing for the plantation South.

65. Newcomb College Faculty Minutes, May 22, 1928, NA NCCROW; Pierce Butler to Edith Baumberger, July 13, 1910, Student Records, NA NCCROW.

66. Caroline Richardson (NC 1895; PhD, Columbia; and professor of English at Newcomb) died in 1932. The building housing the Newcomb College Center for Research on Women is named after her.

67. Newcomb College Faculty Minutes, September 25, 1936; Newcomb Alumnae, Program for the Semi-Centennial Celebration: *Education of Women in Louisiana*, June 7, 1937; Newcomb 50th-Year Anniversary, Printed Matter File, NA NCCROW.

68. Pierce Butler to Rufus C. Harris, October 4, 1937, Vertical Files, Harris, UAHT.

69. Susan D. Tew, Lionel C. Durel, Clara de Milt, and others to Rufus C. Harris, October 20, 1937, Butler Vertical Files, UAHT.

70. "A Statement to President Harris from the Newcomb Faculty," June 2, 1938, Butler Vertical Files, UAHT.

71. Carmelite Janvier to Rufus C. Harris, May 29, 1938, Butler Vertical Files, UAHT.

72. Pierce Butler to Rufus C. Harris, June 3, 1938, Harris Vertical Files, UAHT.

73. Frederick Hard to Rufus C. Harris, April 30, 1938, Vertical Files, Harris, UAHT.

74. Dyer, *Tulane: The Biography of a University*, 267.

75. Ibid., 259–62. Now Jones Hall.

76. Frederick Hard (1944–1964), in A History of Scripps Presidents. http://www.scripps college.edu/offices/president/inauguration/frederick-hard.php.

77. Frances Bryson, "How to Make Marriage Work," *New Orleans States-Item,* November 20, 1945.

78. Logan Wilson, "Newcomb in Balance: The Need and the Opportunity at the 'Start the Dorm' Dinner," Josephine Louise House, April 24, 1950, typewritten speech, Dean's Records, NA NCCROW.

79. L. Wilson interview.

80. Harold Lee, Oral History interview by Florence Bass, February 18, 1986, NA NCCROW.

81. Mildred Christian, Oral History interview by Florence Bass, April 21, 1986. NA NCCROW.

82. The 1940s saw the first efforts to list degree requirements in a standard fashion. See, for example, the curricula for both Newcomb and A&S in Tulane University of Louisiana, *Bulletin* 48, no. 1 (January 1947).

83. The admissions offices were joined in 1986. After this time, any number of students arrived at the University not knowing that they were Newcomb students (Allison Raynor, e-mail to Susan Tucker, July 11, 2007; Leslie Franklin, e-mail to Susan Tucker, July 11, 2007).

84. Lisa E. Wolf-Wendel, "Women's Colleges," in *Women in Higher Education: An Encyclopedia*, ed. Ana M. Martinez Aleman and Kirsten A. Renn (Santa Barbara: ABC-CLIO, 2002),

61–65. The Women's College Coalition website lists forty-eight women's colleges in the United States, and does not include the Newcomb College Institute (www.womenscolleges.org/).

85. James Davidson, Oral History by Beth Willinger, July 25, 1986, NA NCCROW.

86. Newcomb Dean's Records, NA NCCROW. See also *The Resolutions of the Board of Administrators of the Tulane Educational Fund Adopted on November 19, 1987, Regarding the Reorganization of Newcomb College and the College of Arts and Sciences* (hereafter cited as Resolutions of 1987).

87. Leslie Miller-Bernal, "Coeducation after a Decade of Coordination: The Case of Hamilton College," in *Going Coed*, ed. Miller-Bernal and Poulson, 256.

88. Dyer, *Tulane: The Biography of a University*, 57. The board dedicated "Two Million Dollars of University funds functioning as endowment to Newcomb College as an anchor for a restricted endowment fund which shall be dedicated to the purposes of the Newcomb Foundation" (Resolutions of 1987, Dean's Records); Newcomb Foundation Files, 1996; Newcomb Foundation, Reference Files, NA NCCROW; "Complete Recommendations of the Newcomb-Tulane Task Force Approved by the Board on March 16, 2006," http://renewal.tulane.edu/traditions_031606_board.shtml).

89. For a discussion of the names set forth, see Save Newcomb College Files, NA NCCROW.

6

COMING TOGETHER
Newcomb and Tulane in the Postwar Decades

CLARENCE L. MOHR

I n 2005–6, the Administrators of the Tulane Educational Fund voted to restructure the University. Newcomb College and Paul Tulane College, as separate and distinct liberal arts colleges for women and men, were united as the single undergraduate college, Newcomb-Tulane College, and the H. Sophie Newcomb Memorial College Institute was created.[1] The origins of this "coming together" may be traced back to the years following World War II, when Tulane University began a dramatic ascent from regional respectability to national stature. The relationship between Newcomb College and Tulane College (previously the College of Arts and Sciences) was often at the core of arguments for and against this ascent.

Described in the 1950s as an attempt at "*coordination,* not *integration* or *unification*," the initial efforts of Tulane University president Rufus Carrollton Harris to reconfigure departmental operations across college lines became an important first step toward the eventual merging of the A&S and Newcomb faculties into a single entity in 1987 and the closing of the colleges in 2006. Requiring six decades to complete, the unification process was attended by controversy at its inception as well as in its final stages. From beginning to end, arguments over a variety of curricular, jurisdictional, and procedural matters bearing on Newcomb's autonomy were rooted in unresolved (and often unacknowledged) contradictions surrounding women's education during an era when the principles of individual merit were often compromised by tacit concessions to traditional views concerning male prerogative and feminine domesticity.[2]

Josephine Louise Newcomb's bequest to establish a college "in the Tulane University of Louisiana, for the higher education of white girls and young women" had commingled racial and gender stipulations in Newcomb's founding document. In a single phrase, she affirmed the importance of equal education for some women and the need to stop short of the more complete equality that racial integration and coeducation would have implied. In the segregationist and patriarchal culture of the late nineteenth century, both blacks and women had a recognized "place" that was separate from and subordinate to that of white men. With some modifications, this basic value system would remain intact until well after World War II. Throughout most of its history, therefore, Newcomb College faced the challenge of enlarging the scope of female opportunity within a framework of externally imposed limits.[3]

From the beginning, Tulane's Board of Administrators controlled the Newcomb endowment (valued at more than $3.5 million in 1923). In 1918, when the College relocated to a site contiguous to the rest of Tulane's campus, the administration had begun the first efforts to exert greater administrative control over the University's semi-independent professional schools, a fact that caused Newcomb loyalists to guard their prerogatives all the more jealously. Brandt V. B. Dixon—Newcomb's chief administrative officer from 1887 to 1919—tended to regard closer identification with Tulane as dangerous, and his outlook signaled the beginning of a chronic anxiety over the College's future.[4]

Earlier events had fueled concern that the goals of Tulane University might be pursued at Newcomb's expense. Graduate education was an early and serious bone of contention. In 1901, for example, the Administrators assessed Newcomb $100 for each female student taking graduate work, followed the next year by a levy of $2,500 to support the graduate program. In 1910, Tulane president Edwin B. Craighead petitioned the Administrators for a transfer of $20,000 annually from Newcomb Funds for support of the Graduate School. A storm of protest erupted, and the request was shelved, but not before the University faculty attempted to censure Dixon for making derogatory remarks about the quality of graduate education at the University.[5] A generation later, as Rufus Harris assumed Tulane's presidency, his newly appointed graduate dean, Roger P. McCutcheon, outlined a detailed plan in which graduate education would unify Tulane's intellectual resources by giving common purpose to what had become "a collection of separate and separatist schools and colleges." McCutcheon stressed, however, that "I am assuming that part of the program for [graduate school] development will be the fixing of the College of Arts and Sciences as a major foundation of our educational edifice."[6] Supporters of the University's female coordinate college could scarcely have been encouraged by this line of reasoning.

The approach of World War II forced Tulane to postpone the expansion of graduate education, and by the time peace returned, Harris had given considerable thought to Newcomb's place within the framework of an emerging research university. Harris saw Newcomb's persistent "spirit of separation" as a historical anachronism.[7] Whereas the geographic boundaries between Newcomb and the larger University had grown indistinct, an ingrained tradition of collegiate prerogatives was sustained by the administrative jurisdiction of separate deans, the existence of separate alumni and admissions offices for Newcomb, and the practice of housing the "A&S" and "Newcomb" components of each department in separate buildings or, occasionally, on different floors of the same building. Both the physical and the bureaucratic aspects of the collegiate division posed problems for mobilizing Tulane's limited resources for maximum effect. In 1954, after obtaining board approval to redesignate Newcomb's art and music programs as "departments" rather than "schools," Harris began to consolidate lines of authority through the appointment of special department heads called "University chairs." In effect, the University chairs exercised joint authority over both the A&S and the Newcomb components of their departments.[8]

On the face of it, Newcomb had much to gain from identifying its mission with the larger University goals. While searching for a candidate to fill the Newcomb deanship during the early 1950s, Harris visited the South's leading private women's colleges and concluded that "in the total picture," Newcomb substantially excelled vis-à-vis its regional counterparts. When compared to "small, isolated boarding schools" like Hollins, Sweet Briar, Randolph Macon, and Agnes Scott, Newcomb could claim many advantages, including the resources of a major research library and the "inspiration of graduate teaching." Newcomb, Harris believed, "should be the outstanding college for women in the South." In essence, Newcomb was being put on notice that its mission must conform to the University's larger graduate-level agenda.[9]

The subtleties of Harris's argument were not lost upon John R. Hubbard, who assumed the post of Newcomb dean in 1953. In his first annual report, Hubbard echoed the sentiments expressed two years earlier by a special Committee on University Planning and Development, which had cited three impediments to progress: inadequate fund-raising, a "preoccupation with local loyalty," and the fact that each individual college had "worked primarily to further its own program" while paying little attention to the "development of the University as a whole." Hubbard agreed that relations between Newcomb and other colleges should be governed by the "primary aim of building a university of the first rank." Tulane's limited resources made "two separate and distinct ventures in the liberal arts manifestly indefensible."[10]

For the remainder of the decade, Hubbard worked to achieve curricular uniformity and departmental symmetry between Newcomb and A&S. After "spirited" discussions, Newcomb's biology department was split into separate departments of botany and zoology. More lengthy negotiations resulted in the approval of a bachelor of fine arts degree for men and, somewhat later, of the bachelor of sciences for women. The issue of excessive localism was addressed through Newcomb's adoption of a junior year abroad program in 1954–55, and by Hubbard's campaign to broaden the geographical base of female undergraduate admissions.[11]

Although Hubbard had the temerity to go on record with blunt assertions that Newcomb should recognize its unfavorable competitive position when compared to the elite women's colleges of the Northeast and Far West, he was less clear about the goals of intra-university cooperation and the possible loss of collegiate identity. He coupled his announcement with a Winston Churchill–like declaration that he had not become dean of the College "to preside over the liquidation of its institutional integrity." But the meaning of any new relationship of Newcomb to A&S remained unclear. When the list of university department chairs was drawn up in 1955, only six out of the twenty posts went to Newcomb faculty, and that number soon shrank to five. The Department of Sociology and Anthropology furnished the most truculent display of intercollege antagonisms when A&S professor Forrest E. LaViolette denounced the "Machiavellian" appointment of a Newcomb professor to be University chair. What distinguished the A&S faculty, it seemed, was a combination of "greater teaching strength," vastly superior "actual and potential research and publishing strength," a deeper "sensitivity to contemporary currents of thought," and even a "greater feeling of interpersonal stimulation. . . . [O]ur educational aims are clearer and less confused because we are not on the staff of a young woman's college," LaViolette observed with a concluding flourish.[12]

In 1953, Newcomb itself had helped clarify the underlying issues by staging a symposium entitled "Trends in Liberal Arts Education for Women." The most flamboyant speaker was Mills College president Lynn White, whose rather self-serving brand of "feminine education" included a deemphasis on graduate training and assertions that girls would profit from instruction in "the theory and preparation of a Basque Paella, or a well-marinated shish kabob."[13] In New Orleans, however, White argued that women's colleges, with "women scholars of the first quality," provided the "chief means by which a girl may discover self-respect and explore her potentialities." Probably the most nuanced presentation of the Newcomb symposium came from Dean Nancy Lewis of Brown University's Pembroke College. Turning contemporary wisdom on its head, Lewis opened her talk with a half-serious critique of higher education for failing to prepare the typical male "to function adequately in his role as a family member." After developing her remarks into a parody of fashionable Freudian claims about female anxieties, Lewis turned her attention to women, stressing their gross underrepresentation at the PhD level, and called for an undergraduate curriculum that would foster the "fullest possible development" of the female student's "intellectual and spiritual powers." Dean Lewis was the only speaker whose remarks were not reported in the local press.[14]

By linking Newcomb's future to the development of graduate education, Tulane appeared to emphasize the primacy of intellect in undergraduate women. But not everyone was persuaded. In 1955, the university mathematics chair, William L. Duren Jr., himself an A&S professor, noted just how unclear Newcomb's mission within the larger university seemed. "I think we ought to understand how we are proposing to educate young women and not presume that the education of young women at Newcomb will be well served as an adjunct to the big graduate school," he admonished.[15]

The basis of Duren's concern rested on a perception that the Newcomb faculty's "former isolationism" had been replaced by a "sharp demand for equality in the graduate program" and an unpromising framework for undergraduate educational strategies. Many of Duren's concerns were echoed by Hubbard as he struggled to reconcile the priorities of a small female liberal arts college with the demands of graduate research. Having promised in 1954 to effect change without compromising Newcomb's "unique character," Hubbard first had to adjust rising enrollment to keeping a "genuine rapport between teacher and student." Hubbard worried that the expansion of graduate offerings had created a false sense of priorities in some departments. Providing the "finest undergraduate program in this region" was Newcomb's raison d'être, and all faculty thus shared a responsibility for undergraduate teaching. Newcomb students had a right to expect the "best talents" the faculty could provide. What Hubbard did not say—but what most Newcomb faculty undoubtedly realized—was that undergraduate teaching pursued in isolation from original scholarship would be tantamount to professional suicide.

At Newcomb these issues were complicated by contradictory attitudes toward women both within and outside the academic world. Theoretically, women of the 1950s were free to pursue advanced study and enter professions on the same basis as men. Some actually did so. In 1957, for example, Tulane enrolled a total of 218 full-time women students in divisions other than Newcomb College. Most were registered in the School of Social Work (71) and the Graduate School (60), but an additional 51 women had established beachheads in such traditionally male professions as business administration (26), medicine (12), architecture (6), engineering (4), and law (3).[16] As the decade wore on, a significant minority of Tulane's female undergraduates elected to pursue advanced studies. A poll of 1961 A&S graduates—virtually all male—revealed that some 81 percent planned to attend graduate or professional school, while during the same period Hubbard estimated that 25 percent of Newcomb graduates, including 40 percent of those who had participated in the junior year abroad program, would seek higher degrees. The experiences of Tulane's graduate and professional women during the 1950s, together with the example of Newcomb graduates like Diane Fournet Davis, who received a PhD in physics from MIT in 1957, lent a certain credence to the gender-neutral, individualist rationale for subsuming women's education into a larger, research-oriented academic mission.[17]

Proponents of women's colleges frequently pointed out that their schools offered female faculty and administrators more opportunities for leadership than were available in coeducational settings. Lynn White had expounded this theme at considerable length during the 1953 Newcomb symposium, but Harris took virtually the opposite stance when stressing the competitive advantages arising from Newcomb's overwhelmingly male faculty and administration. At several southern women's colleges, Harris believed, female presidents had proved "unable or unwilling to get strong men on the faculty." In the absence of male professors, the schools allegedly lost "vitality" and became "too much of a convent."[18]

During the 1950s and for some time thereafter, Tulane had few women faculty at the upper ranks and no female deans outside the School of Social Work. If anything, the era saw a retreat from the modest advances of the World War II years when Professor Clara de Milt had served as chair of Tulane's chemistry department and the physicist Rose Mooney of the

Newcomb faculty became one of the highest-ranking female scientists on the Manhattan Project, serving as associate chief of the X-ray structure section of the Manhattan District's Metallurgical Laboratory in Chicago.[19] The 1950s, on the other hand, witnessed a renewed emphasis on feminine domesticity. At Tulane this outlook was apparent in the search for new deans. In addition to scholarly credentials, administrative ability, and a pleasing personality, the well-qualified (always male) applicant for a Tulane deanship also needed a "charming wife," or, more precisely, the kind of woman who "may be a social asset . . . with the faculty of the college as well as in the city." An awareness of this larger social reality formed the backdrop for all discussions of Newcomb College, subtly overriding the asexual logic of liberal individualism.[20]

An attentive listener to Harris's comments on the importance of male faculty and the subordinate role of academic wives would have detected clear echoes of the gender anxiety expressed by college modernizers during the late nineteenth and early twentieth centuries, when America's first modern universities took shape.[21] Like the educational orators of this earlier era, Harris seemed bent upon eradicating all effete or effeminizing connotations from the image of Tulane as a research university. Women's education within this new Tulane was inherently ambiguous. Depending upon a professor's individual outlook, the new relationship could be seen as representing either a threat to the sequestered tranquility of the feminine liberal arts ideal or a promise to bring women's education into the academic mainstream.

Hubbard took the latter view and was quick to emphasize those areas in which Newcomb's practices reinforced larger University aims. On the critically important subject of undergraduate admissions, Newcomb provided a model that A&S would eventually emulate. Tulane's first real step toward restricted undergraduate admissions came with Newcomb College's decision to adopt the College Entrance Examination Board's Scholastic Aptitude Test (SAT) as a requirement for all applicants beginning with the 1948–49 academic year. Fully a decade would elapse before A&S would follow.[22]

Yet Hubbard faced a number of problems. Initially Newcomb's declining enrollments precluded any serious attempt to turn away students with low test scores.[23] By the mid-1950s, applications were again increasing, but average SAT scores of 954 were "nothing to brag about." Attrition rates also were unacceptably high. Worse still, the College's annual pool of applicants remained considerably smaller than those of the fourteen women's colleges "with which we like to compare ourselves," a list that included all of the elite "Seven Sisters" schools of the Northeast but only three southern institutions. Judged against this national yardstick, Newcomb was forced to confront the chilling realization that "we have been too provincial for too long."[24]

Conspicuously absent from Hubbard's agenda for change was any mention of the College's traditional approach to the monitoring and supervision of student life. Generally speaking, the regulatory noose became tighter as the number of nonlocal students increased and residential facilities expanded. During the mid-1950s, more than three hundred Newcomb students from New Orleans lived beyond the reach of the dorm council authority, and for a time the same was true of the sizable contingent of out-of-town students who stayed in local "approved boarding houses" because dormitory space was unavailable. Numbering sixty students in 1955, the group swelled to more than one hundred by 1956–57. With the opening of William Preston Johnston House in 1958, however, nearly all non–New Orleans students were housed on campus and brought under effective day-to-day scrutiny.[25]

By the end of the decade, Newcomb freshmen faced an intricate web of rules governing curfew hours, procedures for signing in and out, chaperone requirements, dining room etiquette, and innumerable other details, all subject to a graduated scale of punishments that began with a simple "report," escalated to a more serious "call-down," and culminated with a "campus" that prohibited the recipient from leaving the Tulane-Newcomb grounds or "having dates, social association, or communications with men." Filling seventeen closely printed pages, the conduct rules embodied social and moral premises that would have been familiar to most Newcomb students, particularly those from Louisiana and other southern states. Only the occasional concession to the festival culture of the surrounding environment offered a hint of New Orleans's forbidden fruit. Carnival balls, for example, merited special curfew arrangements as did the "approved clubs in which there is dancing and a late floor show."[26]

The early 1960s witnessed a growing challenge to conventional ideas about collegiate supervision of student conduct. During the 1963–64 academic year, requests from the University's various dormitory House Councils and the Newcomb and A&S student-government organizations led the University Senate Committee on Student Affairs to authorize open-house periods, including visits to individual student rooms, in men's and women's residences on Sunday afternoons between 2:00 p.m. and 6:00 p.m. The concession was a relatively modest one that might have gone largely unnoticed by outsiders had not a *Newsweek* article announcing the "Morals Revolution" on university campuses appeared shortly after the policy took effect. This alarmist piece sent tremors through the Newcomb Alumnae Association and prompted an organized letter-writing campaign by the ad hoc group "Citizens for Student Welfare," whose supporters—alumni and concerned parents—deluged the Board of Administrators with protests. Virtually all those writing resorted to explicit analogies between the college dormitory and the family home and insisted that Tulane prohibit opposite-sex visitations to "bedrooms."[27]

Coming barely a year after the admission of Tulane's first black students, the campaign against "bedroom" visitations revealed the growing uneasiness with which at least some traditionalist parents viewed the future. Like segregation itself, the ideal of the southern lady formed part of a larger complex of cultural values rooted in the acceptance of patriarchal authority and the concomitant need to protect white female virtue—a priority given tangible form in the differing conduct rules for men and women. As a southern women's college, Newcomb had embodied quite self-consciously the governing axioms of regional culture. But with segregation discredited, other cardinal tenets of the southern way of life seemed suddenly open to challenge. Ultimately, the University refused to assume the mantle of surrogate parent.

It was the underlying connection between housing regulations and other aspects of student life that gave significance to what was otherwise little more than an expedient institutional withdrawal from the enforcement of legally problematic and culturally outmoded restrictions on personal conduct. An early demonstration of the manner in which disputes over housing rules might be linked to larger external issues took place during the 1965–66 academic year, when three Newcomb freshmen attacked the existing House Council system in a mimeographed flyer entitled *Women Strike for Rights*. The protofeminist vocabulary of the document, with its emphasis on the "Lie of Custodianism" and the "Lie of Immaturity," breathed the spirit of the emerging student Left. And while the authors' allegations that House Council officers exercised power illegally were easily brushed aside, other issues raised by the freshmen critics—including the double standard surrounding curfews and conduct rules for women and men, as well as the requirement of self-accusation in disciplinary proceedings—struck at the weaknesses of a social policing system that would soon find itself under siege. As on prior occasions, moreover, civil rights became linked to the attack on in loco parentis when

Susan Jennings, one of the dissenting freshmen, received a racist postcard after participating in the initial stage of sorority rush in company with two black students from New Orleans.[28]

During the second half of the 1960s, competing ideological pressures complicated the debate over women's education at Tulane, giving discussions about Newcomb's future an oftentimes contradictory quality. On the one hand, arguments for consolidation in the name of efficiency continued to be heard, and at the same time, the nominally egalitarian logic of coeducation in a manner was voiced in a way that did not auger well for Newcomb's autonomy. For example, in 1964, when applying for a $6 million capital grant from the Ford Foundation, Tulane officials argued that the presence of separately administered male and female undergraduate units had "limited the total development of the University." Tulane's grant writers found "little reason for continuing two distinct colleges" and concluded that a Newcomb–A&S merger could be accomplished "without affecting the traditions and life of either college."[29]

The rise of student activism called many aspects of collegiate tradition into question. Prior to the late 1960s, those undergraduates with the talent and inclination to become student leaders were drawn almost inexorably into the most tradition-bound segments of undergraduate life, from Greek organizations to football and student government. In a self-evaluation during the mid-1960s, the Newcomb Panhellenic Council stressed that "sororities encourage their members to run for office, to attend student body meetings, [and] to vote in campus elections." This claim was supported by statistics showing that all thirteen members of the Newcomb Inter-House Council were sorority members as were all four cheerleaders, ten of eleven Mortar Board members, and thirteen of fourteen members of the *Jambalaya* staff.[30]

In the wake of desegregation, however, Tulane's Greek system came under growing criticism for policies of ethnic exclusion. Sometime around the mid-1960s, Tulane sororities abandoned the long-standing practice of holding what were, in effect, two separate rushes—one for Jewish girls and the other for gentiles. The old practice, which had involved assigning high pledge quotas to the two Jewish sororities and sending out forms during the summer asking female freshmen to return photographs and select Jewish or non-Jewish rush, may have been abandoned as unnecessary in light of the universal requirement that female pledges have letters of recommendation from sorority alumnae. Black students, however, posed difficulties that were less easily resolved. Rebuffs experienced by black rushees in 1965 were repeated two years later, causing widespread negative reaction. In 1967, no black women participated in sorority rush.

Fraternity membership declined, and although no comparable statistics on sorority membership are available, it seems likely that fewer Newcomb women pledged sororities in the late 1960s than in 1961, when membership rates hovered near 70 percent.[31] A new style of leadership emerged, and indeed the rise of student activism at Tulane can be dated from the 1967 student senate elections, when Newcomb student body president Sylvia Dreyfus sent a letter to all women undergraduates endorsing the candidacy of a fraternity member who vocally condemned racial discrimination in Greek letter societies. He won the election handily, receiving particularly strong support from Newcomb College.[32] The issues that would preoccupy campus politics for the next three years—student conduct regulations, university governance, press censorship, civil liberties, ROTC, U.S. foreign policy in Asia and Latin America—were new in a double sense. What held the student movement together was not so much a program as an outlook—a basic orientation that was youth-centered, anti-authoritarian, and vaguely existentialist in its emphasis upon individual autonomy and free choice. This shared consciousness also provided fertile ground for the questioning of old orthodoxies about women's proper role in an egalitarian society. Only a small minority of Newcomb students participated in the cycle of protests and mass demonstrations that swept Tulane's campus in the late 1960s. But all who were present during years of upheaval felt the winds of change blowing around them, and many sensed that Newcomb would be called upon to redefine its aims and values if it hoped to survive in a new era of rising female expectations.

Organized feminism made its campus debut at Tulane in 1969 with the creation of a short-lived group called "Tulane Women's Liberation." An additional boost came the next year with the organization of the New Orleans chapter of the National Organization for Women, and, in 1971, the University Senate gave official recognition to "Tulane Women for Change," apparently the successor organization to the 1969 Women's Liberation group. According to one of the founders of Tulane Women for Change, the group aimed to provide a forum in which women might "come to grips with the socialization that impedes their progress." In what may have been a bureaucratic coincidence, 1971 was also the year when Tulane's revised affirmative action plan began to address the issue of salary inequities involving female faculty members.

Tension between tradition and change became a hallmark of the 1970s. Although male students at Tulane remained overwhelmingly traditional in their attitudes toward women (a scientifically selected sample of 119 male undergraduates in 1975 found only 9.3 percent who were "positively willing" to marry a feminist), dissent over sex stereotyping became more vocal among men and women. In 1972, for example, unsuccessful efforts to make individual accomplishment rather than beauty the basis for selection to the homecoming court drew strong support from the *Hullabaloo,* which editorialized against the "sexist beauty court" and urged alumni to end the practice of "treating women as prize cattle to be paraded and inspected and evaluated on appearance."[33]

Nationally, the 1970s also witnessed a steady national decline in the popularity (and number) of women's colleges as a smaller group of female freshmen faced a larger array of educational choices. In an effort to enlarge its entering classes, Newcomb at times all but abandoned selectivity. From 1970 to 1980, the combined freshman SAT scores at Newcomb lagged behind those of A&S, Engineering, and Architecture. Although Newcomb retained a strong sense of community throughout the period, disillusioned feminists within the Newcomb student body warned that "a revolution in the minds and hearts of those who run the Newcomb system" would be necessary if the College were to remain able to justify its existence in a new era of women's activism. In a 1971 valedictory to the school, a graduating Newcomb senior summarized a line of criticism that was steadily gathering momentum: "Sororities and the Newcomb Student Senate together form a reactionary block which discourages independence, free thinking, feminine aggressiveness, intellectuality, self-expression, and creativity within the [C]ollege—all the things that any women's college should stand for. The emphasis should be on encouraging every effort at self-sufficiency [that] any student puts forth—especially since Newcomb is in the South, a region not noted for its hordes of liberated women. . . . We defenders-to-the-death of Newcomb autonomy are fighting what presently seems to be a losing battle against creeping co-education, state university style."[34]

Uncertainty about Newcomb's future intensified after the arrival of President F. Sheldon Hackney in 1975. While denying any wish "to change Newcomb or alter its role in the University or its relationship to the rest of the University," Hackney moved swiftly to secure the resignation of Dean James F. Davidson, making it clear that he wished to see the College reorient its outlook in the face of new realities.[35] From 1976 to 1979, Hackney served on the American Council on Education's Commission on Women in Higher Education, and during the first year of his presidency, in addition to hiring the University's first woman dean of students, Tulane adopted a comprehensive report looking toward greater equity in women's athletics as required under Title IX of the 1972 amendments to the Higher Education Act of 1965. In March 1976, the anthropologist Margaret Mead spoke at the official dedication of the Newcomb Women's Center, and the following month the *Tulanian* published a thematic issue entitled "Spotlight on Women," which opened with the observation that "every time we liberate a woman we liberate a man," a phrase quoted from Mead's Women's Center address.[36] While there is little evidence that Hackney directly admonished deans or academic departments to appoint more women, it is clear that those participating in the two-year search for a new dean of Newcomb College attached importance to identifying strong female candidates. Their efforts resulted in the appointment of Dr. Susan Wittig, who took office on July 1, 1979.[37]

The changes Hackney instituted, while important in both a symbolic and a substantive sense, served primarily to postpone basic decisions about Newcomb's place in the University. In 1980, it fell to his successor, Eamon Kelly, to seek a middle ground between advocates of collegiate autonomy and proponents of greater assimilation. The context of the 1980s debate over the meaning of Newcomb's coordinate college status had little if any connection with the arguments in support of single-sex education advanced nationally in organizations such as the American Association of University Women. Indeed, it seems doubtful that the majority of those who sought to defend Newcomb's independence would have described themselves as feminists. Traditionalists might be a more accurate label for Friends for Newcomb, who, in July 1986, began an intensive lobbying campaign with the president and Board of Administrators in opposition to various changes. Alarmed over what they regarded as a diminution in Newcomb's separate identity and a loss of what had been distinctive elements in an older Newcomb experience, the Friends coalition objected to the elimination of the music department's role in scheduling space in Dixon Hall; the relocation of certain academic departments, including women's physical education, to sites outside Newcomb Hall; the shift from some all-female to coed dormitories; and the high turnover rate in Newcomb deans. (There were a total of four "acting" and two "permanent" deans in the decade after 1976.)

In 1985, the University Senate, over strong objections from Newcomb delegates, adopted a single code of conduct for male and female undergraduates. In 1986, the previously separate "Tulane" and "Newcomb" admissions staffs were consolidated into a single centralized organization. The unified conduct code was perceived by its opponents as a blow to the Newcomb system of student self-government, while the consolidated admissions office assumed the character of a symbolic threat to the autonomy or identity of Newcomb College. For traditionalists, both actions seemed to chip away at important boundaries between Newcomb and the all-male College of Arts and Sciences. By contrast, those favoring the changes tended to regard the new conduct code as a long-overdue step toward the elimination of an outmoded sexual double standard, and to look upon centralized admissions as a more cost-effective approach to undergraduate recruiting for both Newcomb and A&S. The decision to consolidate admissions had, in fact, been prompted by a 1983 shortfall of some one hundred students in the Newcomb freshman class.

The controversy that grew out of these and various ancillary issues prompted a general reexamination of the Newcomb–A&S relationship. Both the board and the University Senate appointed special committees on collegiate organization. The Newcomb Friends organization and then the University administration engaged legal counsel, and the inevitable team of outside consultants weighed in with independent recommendations. Eventually, the University Senate and the board were asked to choose between three alternate models of collegiate organization. The University Senate's Special Committee on the Future of Collegial Education at Tulane advanced plans "A" and "B." Plan "A," the "Barnard model," offered the choice of making Newcomb a more "separate college" and allowing A&S to admit women as well as men. Plan "B" followed the Harvard/Radcliffe example by merging the two college faculties into a single body with one dean. Under this arrangement, students would continue to enroll in Newcomb or Arts and Sciences as before, and each college, but not the united faculty, would be administered by a separate dean. Academic requirements would be identical, and there would be one Honor Board, one Committee on Promotions and Tenure, one Curriculum Committee, and one admissions operation. Plan "B" was widely perceived to be favored by President Kelly and others in higher administration. The Newcomb Faculty, the Newcomb Alumnae Association Board, and the Friends for Newcomb introduced Plan "C," which would have reestablished the collegiate structures as they existed prior to 1979, when a single curriculum was adopted for Newcomb and A&S. Newcomb would have a separate director of admissions, and its curriculum would be allowed to differ from that of A&S. The Newcomb endowment would be separated from that of the University as a whole, and the faculty would be allowed to grow to the size of the A&S faculty.

Midway through these deliberations, Newcomb College hosted a Symposium on Higher Education for Women featuring six invited speakers, including former Newcomb dean James Davidson and education professor Patricia Palmieri, whose 1981 Harvard dissertation had provided an insightful portrait of women faculty at Wellesley College during the early twentieth century.[38] Palmieri's historical reappraisal of women's colleges opened the program. Despite a closing paper entitled "The New Life Patterns of Educated Women," the focus of the symposium was on Newcomb itself, with four out of six presentations given by Newcomb faculty, administrators, or alumnae.

Besides these unpublished presentations, what is remarkable in the surviving record of committee proceedings is the seeming preoccupation of all parties with bureaucratic and organizational matters (or what might be called "turf" disputes) and the corresponding neglect of underlying questions concerning the relative merits of single-sex versus coeducational learning environments. Several factors help explain the focus on organizational issues. In part, it reflected a weariness with the bureaucratic duplication inherent in dual committee structures for promotion and tenure decisions, honor code enforcement, and a host of other time-consuming matters. Thus, while the University Senate's Special Committee on the Future of Collegial Education had been charged to find "new and positive ways . . . [for the colleges] to carry out their traditional missions of providing support to men and to women for their special needs," the group's actual meetings focused on identifying "the structure and levels at which unified action by the colleges is necessary and those at which separate procedures and services may be effective."[39]

What resulted was a classic political compromise. In November 1987, the Board of Administrators adopted a lengthy policy statement ratifying plan "B," which the outside consultants and the University Senate had previously endorsed. Henceforth Newcomb College and A&S would have a single faculty of Liberal Arts and Sciences, common academic and honor code requirements, and a single promotion and tenure process presided over by a single administrator—the dean of Liberal Arts and Sciences (LAS). Both colleges would continue to be administered by separate deans exercising oversight of routine operations. The campus area bounded by Broadway, Zimple Street, Newcomb Place, and Plum Street was officially designated the Newcomb College campus, and the board declared that the University departments of art and music would henceforth be known officially as the Newcomb Art Department and the Newcomb Music Department. Finally, $2 million of University funds were dedicated to a Newcomb Foundation to demonstrate the board's commitment to the special goals of Newcomb College and to encourage their support by other constituencies.

But what was the larger meaning? The question yields more readily to a negative than a positive answer. In the wake of the 1987 agreements, Tulane was left with two undergraduate colleges served by one faculty. (All courses had become coeducational by 1972.) If the new scheme was intended to rectify the administrative instability that had plagued Newcomb in the 1970s and 1980s, it must be judged a categorical failure. Between 1987 and 2006, Newcomb College had a total of nine deans. All were female, and all but two served in an "acting" capacity. The average tenure in office was two years. If the goal of faculty unification was to reduce or eliminate intradepartmental factionalism, the outcome was disappointing at best. Departmental rancor was at least as common during the 1990s and the first decade of the twenty-first century as during any previous period.

In truth, the rationale for a "one faculty–two college" plan had more to do with history and budgetary economy than with any clearly defined administrative principles or educational objectives. After 1987, each college developed a system of faculty fellows and claimed to have a distinct mission related in some fashion to the gender of its students. In the real world of administrative power relations, however, effective control of budgetary decisions had passed from the dean of Newcomb to the newly created dean of Liberal Arts and Sciences—a shift that was only partially offset by the Tulane board's 1996 reinstatement of $11.9 million to the Newcomb endowment.[40] Within the university at large, those academic activities given a "Newcomb" designation—the music department, the art gallery, the nursery and child care center—served as reminders of Newcomb's origins during a time when women's education had been closely linked to the Victorian notion of separate spheres.[41] By contrast, the Newcomb Center for Research on Women, with its program of seminars, outreach activities, guest speakers, visiting scholars, research projects, and library and archival services, embodied the activism of the feminist revolution.

On the positive side of the ledger, it seems fair to conclude that the new arrangements allowed Newcomb to accommodate itself more readily to the aspirations of college women who entered undergraduate school with the intention of pursuing postgraduate and professional programs once reserved for men. Leadership training gained in a predominantly female setting (such as the Newcomb Senate) now paved the way for involvement in larger undertakings. In 1993, for example, the Associated Student Body (ASB), Tulane's university-wide student-government organization, had an all-female executive cabinet, something that would have been unimaginable in 1977, when the ASB elected its first female president. Undergraduate research became a priority for colleges across America during the 1990s, and the Newcomb Foundation, created in the 1987 settlement, played an important role in funding a new program of grants for the purpose of encouraging faculty/female student interaction and collaboration.

When Hurricane Katrina struck in 2005, there were growing indications that Newcomb's collegiate self-awareness no longer partook of a defensive or separatist spirit. A prospective applicant consulting the Tulane catalogue (or the Newcomb website) in 2004 would have encountered, with slight variations in wording, the following statement: "Vital to Newcomb's identity as a coordinate college for women within a major research university is the participation of students, in collaboration with faculty and staff, in the production of new knowledge and research on women and the integration of this research into the undergraduate curriculum in all fields."[42] Like a maxim above the entrance of some freshly renovated temple, the sentiment behind these words embodied the substance of Newcomb's postwar history.

Or so it seemed until the summer of 2005, when Hurricane Katrina laid waste to New Orleans and plunged Tulane into a state of suspended animation that would be ended only with the University's belated reopening in January 2006. Faced with extensive and costly flood damage, loss of tuition revenue, and a burgeoning debt that had soared to $100 million over a four-month span, Tulane president Scott Cowen struggled to devise a plan that would ensure the school's survival. The result was a sweeping plan of reorganization that cut the number of doctoral programs from forty-five to eighteen, stripped the University of some 230 faculty (including many with tenure), and abolished the Graduate School, the College of Engineering, Paul Tulane College, and the H. Sophie Newcomb Memorial College. Henceforth male and female freshman students would enroll in a single undergraduate college, and later transfer to one of the University's remaining colleges or professional schools.[43] A newly created Newcomb College Institute would seek to enrich women's educational experiences in the wake of Newcomb College's demise. More than fifty years after President Harris started down the rocky road of collegiate coordination, the journey seemed destined to continue as unhappy alumnae and their supporters in "The Future of Newcomb College, Inc." pursued legal action seeking a restoration of Newcomb's separate collegiate status. In 2011, all that can be said with certainty is that consensus on the meaning of women's education at Tulane remains elusive.

NOTES

In a somewhat different form, most of the material in this essay appeared in "Coming Together (and Falling Apart): Tulane University and H. Sophie Newcomb Memorial College in the Postwar Decades," *Louisiana History* 49 (Winter 2008): 53–92.

1. Complete Recommendations of the Newcomb-Tulane Task Force Approved by the Board on March 16, 2006, http://renewal.tulane.edu/traditions_031606_board.shtml.

2. "A Proposal to Further Coordination between Departments in Newcomb College and the College of Arts and Sciences," 1 (quotation), Box 30, Rufus Carrollton Harris Papers, Tulane University Archives (hereafter cited as RCH); Clarence L. Mohr and Joseph E. Gordon, *Tulane: The Emergence of a Modern University* (Baton Rouge: Louisiana State University Press, 2001), chap. 1; Barbara M. Solomon, *In the Company of Educated Women* (New Haven: Yale University Press, 1985), chap. 12.

3. Amy Thompson McCandless, *The Past in the Present: Women's Higher Education in the Twentieth-Century American South* (Tuscaloosa: University of Alabama Press, 1999), esp. chaps. 3 and 7; Glenda Elizabeth Gilmore, *Gender and Jim Crow: Women and the Politics of White Supremacy in North Carolina, 1896–1920* (Chapel Hill: University of North Carolina Press, 1996), 36–44.

4. John Dyer, *Tulane: A Biography of a University, 1834–1965* (New York: Harper and Row, 1966), 52–56 (quotation on 52), 180–81, 250–51; [Logan Wilson], *Some Plain Facts about Newcomb College Finances,* printed leaflet, 1950, 3, Box 32, RCH; Brandt V. B. Dixon, *A Brief History of H. Sophie Newcomb Memorial College, 1887–1919: A Personal Reminiscence* (New Orleans: Hauser Printing, 1928), 150–51.

5. Dyer, *Tulane: A Biography of a University,* 116–17, 127–28; Dixon, *Brief History,* 126–28, 150–54.

6. Roger P. McCutcheon, "Suggested Developments in the Graduate School," typescript accompanying December 8, 1937, memorandum to Rufus C. Harris, Box 28, RCH (all quotations).

7. Rufus C. Harris to Joseph M. Jones, July 24, 1953, Box 23, RCH; F. Sheldon Hackney Papers, Tulane University Archives (hereafter cited as FSH).

8. Dyer, *Tulane: A Biography of a University,* 250–52; BOA Minutes, January 14, 1952. See also Dean Logan Wilson's portion of the February 1951 "Committee on University Planning and

Development Progress Report," 31, Box 30, RCH; "A Proposal to Further Coordination between Departments in Newcomb College and the College of Arts and Sciences," November 9, 1954, Box 30, RCH.

9. BOA Minutes, February 18, 1952.

10. "Progress Report, Committee on University Planning and Development," 11, Box 30, RCH (first–fourth quotations); "Report of the Dean of the H. Sophie Newcomb Memorial College, Session 1953–1954," 26, Box 32, RCH (fifth–sixth quotations) (hereafter cited as "Newcomb Dean's Report").

11. *Newcomb Dean's Report . . . 1953–54,* 4, 5 (quotation); *Newcomb Dean's Report . . . 1955–56,* 10; "The Bachelor of Fine Arts Degree for Men" and "The Bachelor of Science Degree for Women," extracts from a December 2, 1957, letter of Arts and Science Dean William W. Peery, in Senate Committee on University Educational Policy, Minutes, January 8, 1958, Box 30, RCH. On the origins of the Junior Year Abroad, see *Newcomb Dean's Report . . . 1953–54,* 9–13. On the quest for geographic diversity, see *Newcomb Dean's Report . . . 1956–57,* 1–8.

12. *Newcomb Dean's Report . . . 1953–54,* 27 (first quotation); "University Chairmen, 1955–56 Session, 1956–57 Session," Box 39, RCH; Forrest E. LaViolette to Rufus C. Harris, February 10, 1955, Box 39, RCH (all subsequent quotations).

13. Lynn White, *Educating Our Daughters: A Challenge to the Colleges* (New York: Harper and Brothers, 1950), 78; Solomon, *In the Company of Educated Women,* 191–200 (Lynn White quotations on 191, 192); BOA Minutes, May 12, 1952, October 14, 1953.

14. *Trends in Liberal Arts Education for Women* (New Orleans: Newcomb College, 1954), 107, 114, 123 (quotations); *New Orleans States,* November 5, 1953; *New Orleans Item,* November 6, 1953; BOA Minutes, November 11, 1953.

15. William L. Duren Jr. to Rufus C. Harris, February 7, 1955, Box 39, RCH.

16. F[lorence] W. Tappino to Clarence Scheps, September 16, 1957; Clarence Scheps to Rufus C. Harris, October 10, 1957, Box 24, RCH.

17. Herbert E. Longenecker to Nils Y. Wessel, June 26, 1962, Box 24, RCH; *New Orleans Times-Picayune,* June 26, 1957 (Tulane clipping scrapbooks).

18. BOA Minutes, February 18, 1952.

19. Margaret W. Rossiter, *Women Scientists in America: Before Affirmative Action, 1940–1972* (Baltimore: Johns Hopkins University Press, 1995), 5, 9. According to the listing in Dyer, *Tulane: A Biography of a University,* appendix VII, only thirteen of Newcomb's thirty-six full professors between 1948 and 1965 were female. No studies comparing research accomplishment, faculty rank, and compensation for men and women were undertaken during the 1950s. Strictly speaking, Newcomb College did have one female dean, Anna Many, the longtime counselor to women who was promoted to "dean" in 1951, two years before her retirement in 1953.

20. BOA Minutes, April 17, 1952, Item #4 of President's Monthly Report (first and second quotations); BOA Minutes, May 18, 1955 (third quotation).

21. Geraldine Joncich Clifford, "'Shaking Dangerous Questions from the Crease': Gender and American Higher Education," *Feminist Issues* 3 (Fall 1983): 3–62, esp. 48–53.

22. Roger L. Geiger, *To Advance Knowledge: The Growth of American Research Universities, 1900–1940* (New York: Oxford University Press, 1986), 129–39, 221; John Duffy, *The Tulane University Medical Center: One Hundred and Fifty Years of Medical Education* (Baton Rouge: Louisiana State University Press, 1984), 155; Report of the Dean of the Graduate School, Session 1945–46,

in *Tulane Bulletin*, ser. 48, no. 3 (March 1947), 40; *Report of the Senate Committee on Educational Policy, l946–47*, 2 (summary of meeting on March 5, l947), RCH, Box 30.

23. *Newcomb Dean's Report . . . 1953–54*, 3, Box 30, RCH.

24. *Newcomb Dean's Report . . . 1957–58*, 3–4, Box 32, RCH.

25. *The Newcomber, 1959–60*, 93 (first quotation), Newcomb Archives, Newcomb College Center for Research on Women, Tulane University (hereafter cited as NA NCCROW); *Newcomb Dean's Report . . . 1953–54*, 1; *Newcomb Dean's Report . . .1956–57*, 3, Box 32, RCH; "Report on Needs of Newcomb College for the Three Years Beginning with 1955–56," 2, Box 30, RCH (second quotation).

26. *Newcomber 1959–1960*, l05–7 (first four quotations), 99 (fifth quotation).

27. University Senate Committee on Student Affairs, Report to the University Senate, 1963–64, Box 99, HEL; Harriet Bobo and Tucker Couvillon, "Tulane-Newcomb Open Houses," [undated, 1964], Box 61, HEL; "The Morals Revolution on the U. S. Campus," *Newsweek*, April 6, 1964, 52–59; John H. Stibbs, "Twenty-Five Years of Student Life at Tulane University [1949–75]," 28, typescript, Box 64, HEL.

28. Tulane *Hullabaloo*, January 13, 1966, 1 (quotations), 5; ibid., December 9, 1965, 1.

29. "A Supplement to a Proposal Submitted to the Ford Foundation from Tulane University, September, 1963" [January 1964], bound volume in Tulane University Archives.

30. Stibbs, "Twenty-Five Years of Student Life at Tulane University, "24 (first quotation); "Panhellenic Evaluation Submitted by Newcomb Panhellenic Council," Box 61, HEL (second quotation).

31. Tulane *Hullabaloo*, November 10, 1967, 1; Eli N. Evans, *The Provincials: A Personal History of Jews in the South* (New York: Atheneum, 1973), 244–45; Tulane *Hullabaloo*, September 22, 1967, 1–2; ibid., November 10, 1967, 1; ibid., September 20, 1968, 8 (quotations); ibid., September 27, 1968, 1; Minutes of the Tulane Student Senate, November 18, 1969, ASB, 1954–92; Stibbs, "Twenty-Five Years of Student Life at Tulane University," 24; Mohr and Gordon, *Tulane: The Emergence of a Modern University*, 41 n. 71.

32. Tulane *Hullabaloo*, March 6, 1967, 2; ibid., March 10, 1967, 1, 8; undated *Crisis* flyers and *STRIKE Student Demands in Policy and Planning*, separate leaflets, Box 67, HEL.

33. *The Place of Women*, flyer announcing meeting of Tulane Women's Liberation, November 13, 1969, Box 27–28, HEL; Minutes of the Tulane University Senate, November 1, 1971; Tulane *Hullabaloo*, November 12, 1971, 4 (first quotation); Celest M. Newbrough to Dear Friend, undated form letter announcing formation of New Orleans affiliate of the National Organization for Women, Box 27–28, HEL; J. Valenti to Herbert E. Longenecker, memo, "Subject: Discrimination against Women," January 15, 1971, Box 27–28, HEL; Jane N. Kohlmann, "The Male Perception of Females' Changing Roles: A Study of Tulane Male Undergraduates" (senior honors thesis, Tulane University, 1975), 63 (second quotation); Tulane *Hullabaloo*, September 29, 1972, 10 (third and fourth quotations). On the history of women's consciousness-raising experiences in New Orleans and their relation to prefeminist involvement in social activism, see Cathy Cade, *A Lesbian Photo Album: The Lives of Seven Lesbian Feminists* (Oakland, Calif.: Waterwomen Books, 1987), 85. Cf. Sara Evans, *Personal Politics: The Roots of Women's Liberation in the Civil Rights Movement and the New Left* (New York: Vintage, 1980), 35, 38, 183.

34. Solomon, *In the Company of Educated Women*, 44, 203; Francis L. Lawrence, "Tulane Freshmen Enrollment, 1958–1980[;] Twenty Years of Challenge, 1980–2000," Box 2, Eamon M.

Kelly Papers, Tulane University Archives (hereafter cited as EMK), 24; Margaret Blain, "Toward Co-Education," Tulane *Hullabaloo,* May 7, 1971, 8 (all quotations). During the early 1970s, venerable male bastions such as Yale, Princeton, and the University of Virginia admitted women undergraduates while equally prominent women's colleges such as Vassar admitted men. By 1976, only 5 percent of American colleges and universities restricted their enrollment to women. Two decades earlier, the figure had been 13 percent.

35. F. Sheldon Hackney, "Memo to the Newcomb College Faculty," May 11, 1976, 1, Box 23, FSH. For a representative sampling of the ongoing debate, see Judy Mofitt, "Forum Discusses Newcomb's Autonomy and Visitation," Tulane *Hullabaloo,* March 26, 1971; Alan Loeb, "Newcomb: Can It Keep Its Identity?" Tulane *Hullabaloo,* March 17, 1972, 9; Kay Kahler, "Unliberated Newcomb," Tulane *Hullabaloo,* February 9, 1973, 10; and Louisa Rogers, "Slipping Newcomb Noose," Tulane *Hullabaloo,* February 9, 1973, 14.

36. *Tulanian* 47 (April 1976): 3 (quotation), 5, 8.

37. Newcomb Dean Search Committee to Members of the Faculties of Newcomb College and the College of Arts and Sciences, September 17, 1976, Raymond A. Esthus to F. Sheldon Hackney and Robert Stevens, May 11, 1976, F. Sheldon Hackney to Raymond A. Esthus, December 20, 1976, M. Y. Darensbourg to F. Sheldon Hackney and Robert Stevens, March 2, 1977, Weber D. Donaldson Jr. to F. Sheldon Hackney and Robert Stevens, March 4, 1977, John William Corrington to F. Sheldon Hackney, April 20, 1977, F. Sheldon Hackney to John William Corrington, April 29, 1976, Stuart S. Bamforth to Michael Mislove, September 11, 1978, Michael Mislove to F. Sheldon Hackney, December 17, 1978, Box 23, FSH; Presidents Annual Report, 1978–79, Box 10, FSH; BOA Minutes July, 5, 1979.

38. A copy of the 1987 symposium program is preserved in NA NCCROW. Patricia Palmieri, "In Adamless Eden: A Social Portrait of the Academic Community at Wellesley College, 1875–1920" (PhD diss., Harvard University, 1981). Palmieri's article "Here Was Fellowship: A Social Portrait of Academic Women at Wellesley, 1895–1920," *History of Education Quarterly* 23(Summer 1983): 195–214, painted a picture of life in a single-sex environment that appealed to many latter-day supporters of women's colleges.

39. Jefferson L. Sulzer, "Memo on Appointment of Special Committee in Collegiate Education," November 14, 1986, 3, Box 42, EMK.

40. Jeanie Watson to Martha Gilliland, February 20, 1997 (first quotation); attachment B to same memo (second quotation), NA NCCROW.

41. Lynn D. Gordon, *Gender and Higher Education in the Progressive Era* (New Haven: Yale University Press, 1990), chap, 5.

42. *Tulane University Bulletin* 2003–5,115–16; cf. 2004 website language concerning Newcomb Fellows (www.tulane.edu/ percent7Enewcomb/new_fell.html).

43. "Tulane University: A Plan for Renewal," December 22, 2005, http://renewal.tulane .edu/renewalplan.pdf

7

THE ART PROGRAM AT NEWCOMB COLLEGE AND THE NEWCOMB POTTERY, 1886-1940

JESSIE POESCH

Editors' Note: This essay by Jessie Poesch was first published in *Southern Arts and Crafts: 1890–1940* in conjunction with exhibitions held at the Mint Museum of Art (Charlotte, North Carolina), the Morris Museum of Art (Augusta, Georgia), and the Birmingham Museum of Art (Birmingham, Alabama) in 1996–97. Poesch describes Newcomb's art program beginning with its philosophical roots in the Arts and Crafts tradition, with the employment of the Woodward brothers, William and Ellsworth, and Gertrude Roberts Smith; and the development of the art curriculum to include not only the award-winning pottery, but also metalwork, jewelry design, silversmithing, and bookbinding. Newcomb's broadly focused art program with its emphasis on art education was intended to inform the aesthetic sensibilities of all Newcomb students as much as to prepare students for careers as artists and teachers. For those interested in collecting Newcomb crafts, Jessie Poesch's *Newcomb Pottery & Crafts: An Educational Enterprise for Women, 1895–1940* (2003) will be of particular interest.

When the H. Sophie Newcomb Memorial College was established in 1886–87 as a coordinate college for women at Tulane University in New Orleans, courses in art were included.[1] The founder and donor, Josephine Louise Newcomb, wanted this institution, dedicated to the memory of her daughter, to provide young women with opportunities for solid learning and for "practical" and industrial subjects. Remarkably for an institution of higher learning, the small original faculty of twelve included two instructors in drawing and painting, Ellsworth Woodward and Gertrude Roberts Smith. In the curriculum outlined in the 1888–89 catalogue, all freshmen took "Industrial Drawing," deemed a practical skill, and all sophomores took "Drawing and Design." In this way, the College began to fulfill Mrs. Newcomb's wish that the new institution unite the "educational ideas of Vassar and Smith on one side and Pratt and Drexel on the other."[2]

The discipline and awareness of creative art was seen as fundamental to a liberal arts education from the beginning. Though requirements have varied through the years, studio art and art history, or music and theater, have been integral parts of the College curriculum. For its first four decades or so, if it wasn't the only liberal arts institution in the Deep South with a professional art program and excellent equipment, it was certainly one of the very few.

Two years before the founding of the College, in 1884, Tulane University had sought out William Woodward (1859–1939) to join the faculty. He later recalled, writing in the third person, the beginnings of his interest in art, his training, and that of his brother, and how they were recruited:

Visited the Centennial Exposition at Philadelphia in 1876 with his father and brother Ellsworth and there received the inspiration which led him to join the classes at the [Rhode Island] School at Providence one month after they were organized as the direct result of the potent awakening impulse given by the Exposition. Joined one year after by his brother Ellsworth. They attended several years the full course and were appointed instructors in the School. . . . When President William Johnston took charge of the organization of Tulane University . . . he looked to the Massachusetts Normal Art School, Boston [where Woodward had next taken courses], as the place to secure a member of the faculty who would be rounded in Art expression—mechanical and architectural as well as artist. . . . [I] accepted the position and arrived at the end of 1884.[3]

As indicated, both William Woodward and his younger brother Ellsworth (1861–1939), who was invited to join the faculty shortly after, received their initial artistic training at the fledgling Rhode Island School of Design. Rhode Island was at the time a center for the manufacture of silverware, jewelry, textiles, and tools, and the school's aim was to train skilled artists-craftsmen. It saw its role as more than a technical school. Rather, it was to be a transforming one for the nation, one that would "train the taste and skill of American workmen, and should change our vast resources of stone and clay and wood and metal into forms of beauty and usefulness that would increase the nation's wealth as well as make more beautiful its social life."[4]

William Woodward had followed his study at Rhode Island with classes at the Massachusetts Normal Art School. The decision of Tulane's president to select someone who had trained at the Rhode Island School of Design and the Massachusetts Normal Art School, which stressed training teachers, was significant, as both were leaders of a new emphasis in art education. The latter had opened in 1873 and was described as "the first institution of the kind established in this country" with a program stressing "the arts of design."[5] Its first director was Walter Smith, who had come from the South Kensington School in England, one of the new art schools there that had been established after the Great Exhibition of 1851 and that represented a movement to reform and improve the level of design of manufactured objects such as silver, furniture, and ceramics. In fact, one of the successes of that school was an arrangement with the Minton pottery works at which a number of women students found employment as designers.[6] Thus Smith's presence in Boston represented a direct link with the design reform movement gaining currency in England, the ideas of which were soon intermingled with those of the Arts and Crafts movement. Smith was an energetic advocate of art education in secondary and professional schools. He and other optimistic nineteenth-century reformers saw artistic, moral, and "civilized" values as intertwined. In 1878, the Massachusetts School's *Report* stated that the training it offered represented "instruction which underlies all handicrafts as the alphabet underlies all literature." Such training was seen as benefiting society in a broad way, contributing to "the development of skill, the improvement of popular taste, and the enhancement of general well being, all [of which] conspire to the refinement of the sensibilities, the enlargement of the capacity for enjoyment, and the deepening of the river of life."[7]

It was just such a broadly focused approach to art, as part of a liberal arts program, that Tulane's president hoped to establish at Newcomb. (William Woodward soon became involved with the development of the School of Architecture, Ellsworth with Newcomb's program.) In 1894–95, Newcomb College's listing of courses stated, "A well rounded art education demands a sympathetic understanding and appreciation of all the ways by which art finds expression." Fine arts and "industrial" or craft arts were seen as intimately interrelated.

In the first year after Newcomb's beginnings, the founders once again looked to the Massachusetts Normal Art School. On October 1, 1887, Gertrude Roberts (1868–1962), soon Gertrude Roberts Smith, was appointed to the faculty of the new institution. She would become a vital and influential teacher until her retirement in 1934. The direct link with new ideas in art education, and the training and connections with New England, became important as the program developed.

It was not until 1893 that Ellsworth Woodward had the idea of introducing a pottery program. He worried that the young women he taught had few opportunities for employment. The new project was to be a practical outgrowth of their instruction. From the beginning, the enterprise that was known as Newcomb Pottery had a dual purpose—to create pottery (and soon some other handcrafted objects) of high artistic quality, and to provide young women who had received education in art at the College an opportunity to earn money. It was to be a "model industry." It was to become the most conspicuous and best-known aspect of the College's art program—evidence, for the public, of the validity of instruction in art.

During its entire existence, 1895 to 1940, the quasi-commercial enterprise known as Newcomb Pottery remained under the umbrella of the College's art program; it probably was never a fully self-supporting "industry." Nonetheless it flourished, undoubtedly because of the foresight of a small group of enlightened instructors and their connections.

In the early years of the twentieth century, the distinctive blue and greenish wares of the Newcomb Pottery became well known. Each piece was different, with decoration based on the luxuriant natural environment of the Deep South. The wares were sold in the showrooms of Arts and Crafts societies in various parts of the country and in other specialty shops from Maine to California. Between 1900 and 1915, the pottery was awarded prizes in eight international expositions. Examples of the pottery were illustrated in a surprising number of magazines and journals in the United States and in several published abroad.[8] Newcomb was regularly discussed alongside the other major art potteries of the time, such as Rookwood, Grueby, and Dedham, among others. It was like these in that it was an enterprise dedicated to producing artistic wares of the highest standard. It differed from most of the other art potteries of the time, however, in two ways: It was intimately connected with the educational program of a college, and it was located in the Deep South. During its early and most creative years, it was the only well-known art pottery of the region. (George Ohr's pottery in Biloxi, Mississippi, was a highly individual endeavor. Though he had a limited popularity and notoriety in his lifetime, he sold few of his wares. It is only in relatively recent years that his work has received the acclaim and attention it deserves.)

In 1894, Mary Given Sheerer (1865–1954) was asked to join the faculty. Her first title was instructor in china decoration, soon modified to assistant professor of pottery. She came to Newcomb from the Cincinnati School of Design (now the Art Academy of Cincinnati). This was another important connection, as the Cincinnati School also was strongly influenced by progressive English ideas associated with the Arts and Crafts movement. Benn Pitman, an Englishman, had become associated with the school in 1873 and inspired a whole generation of women woodcarvers, metalworkers, and china painters in that city, creating one of the beginnings of what might be called the women's art movement in America.[9] There is no evidence that Mary Sheerer was ever directly involved with the Rookwood Pottery in Cincinnati, but she was familiar with it. (Rookwood was established by a woman in 1880. It had both men and women designers.) She had had a summer course in china painting, but her primary training was in drawing, painting, and sculpture.[10] She also had studied at the Art Students League in New York and, according to an article in the *New Orleans Times-Democrat* of November 2, 1896, had had "the advantage of personal inspection of most of the celebrated potteries of Europe."

On June 8, 1896, the *New Orleans Daily Picayune* carried a front-page story, "Practical Art Education for Women," announcing the first exhibition of the new art enterprise at the College. "Yesterday morning the first exhibit of home work made entirely at the Newcomb College Pottery was thrown open to the public." The writer proudly noted that it had been a little over a year since the College had set out on its new venture, "appreciating the benefits that would accrue to the women of Louisiana by opening a new field in which talent and effort might strive for recognition and working women have an opportunity of branching out into new lives." The writer further explained:

> Art design and decorative work are fully in the reach of the gentler sex, and well adapted to the strength and condition of females. . . . Designing . . . is . . . taught, so as to prepare the graduates in the art industries for earning a livelihood in the prosecution of the work they have learned. Believing that the practice of art as a mere accomplishment is of no avail, the college from its inception has taught the relations of art to industry. . . . [It has] recently established a department of ceramics, the first products of which are now on

exhibition at the school. . . . [This shows] a healthful and vigorous beginning of an industry which is in every way adapted to be carried on profitably in the community.

The article makes all too clear how opportunities for "the gentler sex" were deemed limited because of their "strength and condition." Woodward shared something of this belief, and a professional potter, first Jules Gabry and then Joseph Meyer (1848–1931), was employed to turn the pottery and fire the kilns. Meyer was to be with the Pottery from 1896 to 1927. A gifted thrower, he could apparently throw any shape drawn by one of the women.

The women conceived and executed the designs. Though they were not initially allowed to do the heavy "man's work" of preparing, throwing, and firing the clay, graduate and undergraduates alike were made aware of the entire process. They became familiar with local clays, techniques of relief ornamentation, and under- and over-glaze painting, and they observed the uses of the kiln. In 1910, Paul Cox, the second graduate of the professional ceramics program under Charles Fergus Binns at the New York State School of Claymaking and Ceramics (Alfred University), joined the staff as ceramic technician, staying until 1918. He created the formula for the blue matte glaze that characterized the pottery after 1910. In 1914–15, for the first time, the courses in pottery making were designed "to acquaint the pupil with processes of pottery making [and to] prepare her to conduct a studio pottery as well as to teach the subject." From this date onward, the students could, if they wished, have a hands-on involvement with the entire process of pottery making. In succeeding years, several other ceramists and technicians joined the faculty.

The three main faculty members, however, who were most responsible for teaching the College art classes and guiding the pottery enterprise until they each retired in the 1930s were Ellsworth Woodward, Gertrude Roberts Smith, and Mary Given Sheerer.

Ellsworth Woodward was the articulate head of the art department who supervised and guided the overall art curriculum and the pottery enterprise. (He retired in 1931 after directing the art program for forty-six years.) Every piece that was offered for sale was reviewed; if it did not meet artistic and technical standards, the official stamp, adopted in 1897, had to be effaced with an emery wheel. Woodward apparently headed this jury or faculty committee. He carried on the correspondence with people and organizations with similar interests and with places where the wares were sold.[11]

We know that from 1898 onward, Newcomb Pottery began sending collections to be exhibited and sold at the annual shows of the various Arts and Crafts societies, which had only recently formed, such as those in Boston, Chicago, and Minneapolis. In 1900, Susan Frackleton, a talented art potter who was part of a group based in Milwaukee and Chicago, the National League of Mineral Painters, invited Newcomb to send some pieces, together with the League's, to the International Exposition in Paris. To their surprise and joy, the Newcomb Pottery group was awarded a bronze medal. This was one of the nine medals given to five American pottery entrants, the first significant recognition that American art potteries received in Europe. From this time on, there was a growing network of contacts with shops, agents, and exhibiting societies. As early as 1902, Newcomb pottery was being consigned to "a leading California firm," probably that of Paul Elder and Co. of San Francisco.[12]

Most of Woodward's correspondence has been lost, but a fragmentary collection written from 1916 to 1930 has recently come to light.[13] Not only did the work have to meet Woodward's standards, but he autocratically demanded that the vendors provide proper settings. In writing to a potential agent in McPherson, Kansas, on May 18, 1916, he inquired about the "population and character of your city. Newcomb pottery is an art pottery of an exclusive type and requires an educated point of view for its appreciation. Its display must be sympathetic, and the one who cares for it must care for it. When these conditions are assured it is an excellent seller." The respondent quickly replied, vowing that he "personally" cared for the pottery and noted that his shop handled prints by Zorn, Whistler, Brangwyn, Millet, Pennell, and others. On November 11, 1920, the secretary for the Society of Arts and Crafts of Boston assured Woodward, "We are showing the pottery against a blue background, so don't be afraid of our red cases!" Both Woodward and Sheerer visited the Boston Society's premises when they were in that city, maintaining a personal contact.[14]

Gertrude Roberts Smith taught various drawing, painting, and design courses from 1889–90 until her retirement in August 1934—forty-five years. She was no doubt one of the faculty jury who reviewed the craft work. In the early years of the Pottery, she executed designs on several pieces, perhaps as demonstrations or experiments. In 1902–3, a course in needlework was offered as another "opportunity for the practical application of art." She taught this, and by the 1907–8 *Bulletin*, she is listed as professor of watercolor painting and decoration of textiles. She supervised the design and making of the embroideries that became another of the crafts of the Newcomb enterprise. Heavy linen crash served as a base, and much of the thread was Persian silk, carefully selected and colored with Oriental dyes that would not easily fade. Relatively simple basic stitches were used. Flat patterns, clearly defined forms, and conventionalized motifs, such as advocated by the Arts and Crafts aesthetic of the time, were used.[15] While in New Orleans, she established a reputation as an excellent watercolorist. At her retirement in 1934, a local newspaper article praised her work and her excellence as a teacher but said she was too modest, consistently shunning publicity. Her roof studio in the art building was described as filled with "textiles, wondrous weaves," "baskets and pottery from far-away lands," and "sketches thumb-tacked all about the walls." She was described as "not only well informed, but keenly interested in subjects that are in no way related to her own particular work as a teacher of design and a painter."[16]

Weaving and textiles were a long-term interest of hers. A few years before her retirement, Smith began to spend summers in or near Valley Town in the mountains of North Carolina. This was at the height of the Great Depression. While there, she and a colleague became interested in the tradition of weaving that had once existed in the area. Various churches, fraternities, and schools had already begun to encourage "gift shop" weaving among the poor but proud mountain people, and these luxury items were not selling well. Smith, instead, was interested in the tradition of creating utilitarian fabrics and coverlets of wool and, working with local people, she inspired "a renaissance in utilitarian weaving in Water Valley."[17] She settled in Andrews, North Carolina, after her retirement and apparently continued her interest in mountain crafts. Gertrude Roberts Smith in her teaching at Newcomb put into practice the principles of the English-rooted Arts and Crafts movement and, in her later years, helped to launch the 1930s movement to revive traditional American arts and crafts. In 1952, she moved to Asheville, where she died in 1962.

Ellsworth Woodward and Gertrude Roberts Smith shaped the art curriculum and made vital contributions to the Pottery. But it was Mary Sheerer who was responsible for shaping the standards and guiding the day-to-day production of the pottery. Her initial appointment as instructor in china decoration makes her work sound, by today's standards, like a dilettantish pursuit. In the late nineteenth century, however, this was one of the avenues opening up for women who wished to pursue a career in the arts. Students in these early years painted designs on porcelain blank plates. Once the Pottery got under way, these classes were gradually abandoned. Under any circumstances, Sheerer was no dilettante. Throughout her career, she took opportunities for further study, such as at Harvard Summer School, classes with Arthur Dow in New York (Pratt or Columbia), and at Dow's summer school in Ipswich, Massachusetts.

During the first experimental years of the Pottery, the undergraduate women in the Normal Art Course, under the direction of Sheerer, created the designs. During the first decade, she decorated a number of pieces herself, demonstrating techniques such as sgraffito, and creating designs based on clearly defined incised lines done with blue and green underglazes and a glossy final glaze.

A small pool of new designers emerged each year from the undergraduate courses in design. Some of these remained and were designated as "art craftsmen," earning money (albeit minimal) from their work. Early Newcomb pottery became known for the clarity and elegance of the designs, all based on close observation of nature, but skillfully transformed by simplification into flat, graphic designs. There is little doubt that Mary Sheerer deserves the credit for this reputation and for her roles in teaching the undergraduates and directing and encouraging the graduate designers. She helped to formulate some of the basic design guidelines for the pottery, which she described in an article in 1899:

> It was decided that the decorator should be given full rein to his [sic] fancy—provided he did not overstep the bounds of pottery decoration—and that no special style should be followed, but rather that each should follow his own style, making the decoration in this way more spontaneous—less conventional. . . . The qualities and limitations of the southern clays were to be studied and used, if possible, and in addition southern flora and fauna were hoped to become the main spring of the decorations.[18]

In teaching, judicious use was made of recent publications on design, such as the 1902 edition of A. E. Lilley and W. Midgley's *A Book of Studies in Plant Form and Design* (London), in which a series of plates illustrated ways that photographs and realistic drawings of plants could then be visually analyzed, in profile, frontal, and in cross-section, on the basis of which simplified or

Cherokee rose design pottery vase, ca. 1930. Low-relief carving, underglaze painting with matt glaze, height: 6 in., Anna Frances Simpson, decorator; Jonathan Hunt, potter.

"conventionalized" designs were created. Many of these books are still on the shelves of the main library at Tulane University.[19] In 1900, either through the contacts of the Woodwards or through Mary Sheerer, two scholarships to Arthur Dow's Ipswich summer school in Massachusetts were awarded to young pottery decorators from Newcomb. Between 1900 and 1906, eight students, as well as Sheerer, attended one or more sessions there. Dow was the author of the influential book *Composition*, which encouraged sensitivity to formal and abstract qualities, such as the use of line, the relationships of lights and darks (tonal concepts), and analysis of structure, rather than the "time-honored approach through imitation." Dow's book was regularly used in Newcomb's art classes. (Georgia O'Keeffe was probably Dow's most famous pupil). The young designers were encouraged to broaden their experience and training. Henrietta Bailey, who graduated in 1903, was one of those attending Dow's classes. She was to become one of the longtime pottery designers and later taught pottery decoration when Sheerer was on leave. Sadie Irvine, who graduated in 1906, was another of the longtime pottery designers and studied at the Art Students League in 1910.

Mary Sheerer, through her work, teaching, and occasional articles, gradually became known in the world of ceramics. In 1924, 1925, and 1926, she chaired the art division at the annual conventions of the American Ceramic Society, an organization, as Newcomb's dean noted, "which has a membership of over two thousand, composed largely of scientific men and practical manufacturers connected with pottery making and kindred industries, but within the past few years the society has realized the indispensable value of Art in its product, and has established an Art Division."[20] In the summer of 1925, Sheerer was one of the delegates from the United States sent to attend the Exposition of Decorative Arts (the famous "Art-Deco" exposition); the United States did not send any objects, but the delegation reported back. She remarked on the way the new art expressed the "mechanical, scientific age as shown in right-angled, triangled, straightened lines of our new architecture in New York and Paris."[21] In the period 1910–18, when the Arts and Crafts movement was losing its impetus, and while Paul Cox was on the staff, the designers adopted naturalistic, low-relief designs. After about 1922, more angular, semi-abstract forms were introduced.

Sheerer's sensitivity to excellence in a wide range of crafts is indicated by a lecture she gave entitled "Local and Foreign Crafts" to a local club. Among others, she identified George Ohr as "one of the first American potters." This was at a time when his work was receiving little recognition.[22]

On March 19, 1930, the New Orleans Item carried an article, "Distinguished Ceramicist Recognized All over America as Authority," which reported Sheerer's being listed in Who's Who in America and described her as one who "has never . . . rested on her laurels; . . . she is constantly feeling out for new things, turning fresh soil." She was quoted: "Through the use of clay, my philosophy of living . . . has been developed. . . . To hold its shape, clay must be plastic. So the mind."

In 1931, Sheerer was named a fellow of the American Ceramic Society.[23] She retired in that year and returned to Cincinnati. There she taught life-drawing classes for the Art Work Shop, a program designed to provide free art training for the unemployed. Like Gertrude Roberts Smith, she helped others during the crisis of the Depression.[24]

Sheerer made several gifts to the Cincinnati Art Museum—an etching by Matisse, a piece of Austrian glass acquired at the Paris Exposition of 1925, a Swedish Orrefors glass bowl, and some Japanese prints—all further evidence of her discriminating taste.[25]

Pottery was the major product of the Newcomb enterprise. The creation of other craft objects, however, was also encouraged. Mention already has been made of the embroidery. Woodblock prints and calendars were made by the students from at least 1900 onward. Sadie Irvine, for example, did linocuts, prints, bookplates, and book and magazine illustration through the years. Calligraphy was incorporated into the course work fairly early. The best-known specialist was the 1919 graduate Ruth Bultmann, who was given a special exhibit of her work by the Alumnae Association in 1926.

Metalwork was experimented with as early as 1901, when a perforated brass lamp shade was made to go with a pottery base.[26] Mary Williams Butler was a pottery designer who became expert in metalwork. Upon receiving her diploma in 1901, she was employed as an assistant teacher and remained on the faculty until her death in 1937.[27] In 1908, she spent the summer studying in Boston with Denman Ross, one of the founders of the Society of Arts and Crafts of Boston and a lecturer in the theory of design at Harvard. She was responsible for adding courses in metalwork in 1908–9.[28] Initially students worked in copper; advanced students worked in silver. Jewelry and stone setting also was taught. In 1934, Mary Butler studied at the Rhode Island School of Design and also did professional work at the Kalo Shop in Chicago.[29] Courses in the history of painting and sculpture had been offered from the beginning, probably taught by Woodward. In time, Mary Butler took these over. Following her death, Newcomb's dean [Pierce Butler] wrote: "Through her fine intellectual background and her wide reading she became a competent lecturer in the History of European Art. She was a teacher of real power, . . . capable of influencing her pupils in real development."[30] Butler's classes were among the first in the art department to which young men, especially from the School of Architecture, came across the campus to take.

Silversmithing became the specialty of Juanita Mauras. She completed her course work in 1906, then did two years of graduate work, after which she was listed as one of the professional art craftsmen through 1929, when she served as an assistant in the art department until her 1945 retirement. A May 12, 1930, article in the *New Orleans Item* lauded her and identified her as a "pioneer in the profession of making hand-wrought silverware" in the South; it reported that her work was so well-liked that "she is fairly swamped with orders from every part of the United States." Unfortunately, few works by her hand are known to the College today. Surviving photographs show angular "moderne" silver objects on display.

Ellsworth Woodward and graduate art student Elsie Marice examine an array of hand-wrought silver in the Art School salesroom, ca. 1927–28. Pottery works are on display in the background. (Newcomb Art Department Scrapbook, UAHT)

In the fall of 1913, the College introduced a course in bookbinding, fostered by Lota Lee Troy, who joined the faculty in 1909. She received a diploma in art from Greensboro College in North Carolina in 1902 and subsequently studied at Teachers College of Columbia University, where her mentors included two famous English bookbinders.[31] Bookbinding became her craft specialty, though she also taught drawing, watercolor, art education, and design at various levels. In 1928, she was elected to the Guild of Book Work, with headquarters in New York, an important professional honor.[32] Eunice Baccich, one of Troy's students, received her degree in 1919. Following World War I, she worked as an occupational therapist in a military hospital. From 1919 to 1929, she was an art craftsman, after which she became an assistant in bookbinding. As did a number of former students for whom art became a career, she honed her skills by further study, in 1937 at the Rhode Island

School of Design, and in the summer of 1938 at the Academy of Applied Art in Munich, Germany.

Though metalwork and jewelry design were introduced into the curriculum in 1908–9, the work especially flourished in the 1920s and 1930s, when a number of young women who were art craftsmen were active. One of these, Miriam Levy, subsequently joined a New Orleans firm, Hausmann Jewelers, as a special designer.

As touched upon here, a number of the students and graduate designers had productive careers in the world of Arts and Crafts. Several became teachers in public schools in New Orleans and elsewhere. Harriet Joor, a member of the very first pottery class in 1895, taught first at Chicago University, published articles on art and design, and then taught for many years at Southwestern Louisiana University in Lafayette, Louisiana. Maude Robinson, a student in 1903–4, was teaching a ceramics course in New York in 1929. The majority married and raised families, still the preferred career. Some became involved in community and artistic activities.

Newcomb Pottery, as a quasi-commercial enterprise, was terminated in 1940. The wave of enthusiasm for Arts and Crafts subsided during World War I; the program was further diminished by the economic effects of the Great Depression. Moreover, from the time of World War I, many of those who had training in art were finding other outlets for their talents. In truth, the enterprise had never expanded beyond a "model industry" as Woodward had first defined it, partly because he preferred keeping it under the aegis of the College. (Classes in studio art and art history are still an important part of the Newcomb/Tulane curriculum.) In the period between 1895 and 1940, between ninety-one and ninety-five women were active in the formal enterprise. A larger number participated in and received degrees in the regular art curriculum.

Though difficult to measure, the program had a far-reaching effect, certainly on those who were involved and those who bought the Newcomb Pottery products. The "model" of an art program, not necessarily only the Arts and Crafts aspects, probably influenced the development of similar ones elsewhere in the South. In 1915, when Newcomb exhibited at the Panama-Pacific International Exposition in San Francisco, it was one of only eight schools in the nation invited to have a "model room." Needless to say, virtually all universities and colleges, North and South, now have active art programs.

NOTES

Editors' Note: Jesse Poesch's essay is reprinted by permission of The Mint Museum, Charlotte, North Carolina. Copyright © 1996 The Mint Museum, Charlotte North Carolina.

1. Throughout this essay, I have relied in part upon my own previous research as found in Jessie Poesch, *Newcomb Pottery: An Enterprise for Southern Women 1895–1940* (Exton, Pa.: Schiffer, 1984); and Jessie Poesch, *100 Years of Ceramics at Newcomb 1894–1994: A Faculty Retrospective* (New Orleans: Newcomb Art Department, 1994). On occasion, I have plagiarized myself. I have also made extensive use of the various college catalogues and bulletins.

2. "President Dixon Talks of Newcomb," *New Orleans Picayune*, April 10, 1901.

3. William Woodward manuscript notes; former faculty records, Tulane University Archives, Howard-Tilton Memorial Library (hereafter cited as UAHT).

4. *The Rhode Island School of Design 1878–1888* (Providence: J. A. and R. A. Reid, 1888), 12.

5. *Annual Report, Massachusetts State Board of Education, 1872–73*, 41.

6. "Improvements in Minor British Industries: Minton's Art-Pottery Studio, South Kensington." *Art Journal* 34 (1872): 100.

7. *Annual Report, Massachusetts State Board of Education, 1872–73*, 41.

8. Poesch, *Newcomb*, 150–54.

9. Carol Macht, introduction to *The Ladies, God Bless 'Em: The Women's Art Movement in the Nineteenth Century* (Cincinnati: Cincinnati Art Museum, 1976), 7.

10. In 1983, Kenneth Trapp, then with the Cincinnati Art Museum, provided me with information about her course work and associations in Cincinnati.

11. UAHT. Editors' note: The nomenclature of the art department changed over the years. The name was Department of Art, 1887–1909; School of Art, 1909–45; Department of Art, 1945–87; and Newcomb Art Department, 1987 to present.

12. Poesch, *Newcomb*, 45; "Newcomb Notes," *New Orleans Picayune*, March 15, 1902.

13. UAHT.

14. Letters from Macomber of the Society of Arts and Crafts of Boston. A visit of Woodward in 1921 is mentioned in a June 21, 1922, letter; Sheerer visited on June 27, 1922, and is also mentioned as having been there on October 12, 1923, UAHT.

15. Poesch, *Newcomb*, 40.

16. "Exotic Chaos of Beauty Forms Background for Gertrude Roberts Smith in Her Roof Studio," *New Orleans Item-Tribune*, June 10, 1934.

17. "Hand Weaving Revived in Hills of Carolina," *New Orleans States*, "Society" section, September 25, 1932.

18. Mary G. Sheerer, "Newcomb Pottery," *Keramic Studio* 1 (1899): 151.

19. For a list, see Poesch, *Newcomb*, 154–55.

20. Note, Dean of Newcomb, February 15, 1924, in Mary Sheerer folder, UAHT.

21. Mary Sheerer, "A 'Reaction' to a Visit to the Ceramics Section at Paris, 1925," *Bulletin of the American Ceramic Society* 5 (March 1926): 182–85.

22. *New Orleans Times-Picayune*, April 11, 1928.

23. *New Orleans Item*, March 11, 1931.

24. *Cincinnati Enquirer*, May 5, 1935, 8.

25. Trapp (see note 10 above).

26. *New Orleans Picayune,* December 9, 1901; Poesch, *Newcomb,* plates 14, 39.

27. Former faculty records, UAHT; *New Orleans Item,* October 1, 1937.

28. *New Orleans Times-Democrat,* May 8, 1909.

29. "Christmas Rush on in Class at Newcomb," *New Orleans Times-Picayune,* December 12, 1934.

30. Former faculty files, UAHT, October 25, 1937.

31. Former faculty files, UAHT.

32. *New Orleans States,* February 2, 1928.

8

CLARA GREGORY BAER
Catalyst for Women's Basketball

JOAN PAUL

Editors' Note: Joan Paul's essay was originally published in *A Century of Women's Basketball: From Frailty to Final Four*, edited by Joan S. Hult and Marianna Trekell (Reston, Va.: National Association for Girls and Women in Sport, 1991). Paul's essay describes Baer's pioneering work in the field of physical education including the development of the game of basketball for women and "Newcomb ball." Baer was ahead of her time in emphasizing structured physical activity as integral to the education and well-being of the whole woman. Her long history at Newcomb, from 1891 to 1929, placed Newcomb at the forefront in the development of a physical education curriculum for women.

On the evening of March 13, 1895, 560 of the most fashionable women of the city gathered at the Southern Athletic Club in New Orleans to witness the first publicly played basketball game in the South. Sixty young women belonging to the ladies' physical culture classes, initiated and taught by Clara Gregory Baer of H. Sophie Newcomb Memorial College, marched out before their audience dressed in blue bloomers and blue with white-trimmed blouses, the colors of the Southern Athletic Club. Baer had them perform synchronized Swedish gymnastic routines to begin the evening's festivities. Then, two teams of eleven players each took positions on the floor divided into a court of eleven squares, with a player from each team occupying one of the spaces. This was the main event of the evening, a demonstration of the new game "basket ball." Each player had a white or blue sash "artistically draped" around the waist of her gymnasium costume for team identity.

This strange game probably appeared even stranger to the all-female audience, which had no prior knowledge of the game of basketball or its rules and was seeing its first team sport played between women contestants. When the game ended, hair pins and handkerchiefs littered the floor. Because the rules disallowed a player leaving her "base," one viewer later described the game as "something like baseball." With 560 out of 600 invited women attending the performance and the reception that followed, the newspapers reported the occasion as representative of the most fashionable social element in New Orleans, and the night was termed a huge success.[1]

For basketball to first be played and viewed by women rather than men in a geographic area as conservative as the South is surprising. The woman who was responsible for this notable event was diminutive in stature, but gargantuan in her accomplishments for women in sport and physical education. Many of her pioneer achievements have been overlooked by sport and physical education historians, including the facts that she wrote and published the first rules of basketball for women, and that she was responsible for the game's introduction to the South and for continuing to promote the sport for decades. Clara Gregory Baer was educated primarily in the Upper South and the Northeast, and perhaps because of this she was less acculturated to the smothering domesticity that permeated the lives of most middle- and upper-class southern women, keeping them away from the playing fields. She was the quintessential champion of the southern woman in sport and exercise from the early 1890s until her death in 1938.[2]

Baer's Early Life

Clara Baer was born on August 27, 1863, in Algiers, Louisiana, to Hamilton John Baer, a broker/flour merchant, and his wife, Ellen Douglas Riley, the daughter of a well-known antebellum steamboat captain.[3] A number of factors probably influenced John Baer's decision to send his daughter Clara to Louisville, Kentucky, to attend high school. Algiers was an isolated island in the nineteenth century, lying just across the Mississippi River from New Orleans, where access to the city could only be gained by boat as there were no bridges. When Clara was born, New Orleans lay under Union siege and had since April 28, 1862.[4] Baer's mother died when Clara was only four years old, so her maternal grandmother, Margaret Riley, moved from Woodville, Mississippi, to Algiers to live with John Baer and his family to care for Clara, her sister, and two brothers.[5]

The era from 1865 to 1877, generally referred to as Reconstruction, was a difficult time for the South politically, economically, and educationally.

Reconstruction was not a very accurate title for this time as little rebuilding was occurring; the term simply denotes the period of military occupation of the South by federal troops. The state and local governments were unstable, most crops in this agricultural land could not be sold, banks had no money to lend, and educational opportunities were limited as well as poor in quality. Only 21 percent of New Orleans children attended school in 1870, and as late as 1877 only 20 percent of the children in the entire state of Louisiana were enrolled in schools. Although the state legislature passed a compulsory school attendance law that year, it was never enforced, and there were no public high schools in Louisiana until the 1880s.[6]

Education

Because of these circumstances, Clara Baer was sent to live with relatives and attend high school in Louisville, Kentucky.[7] After high school, Baer went to Boston in the late 1880s to further her education. She studied under S. S. Curry at the Boston School of Expression, under Charles Emerson of the Emerson School of Oratory, and then in 1890 she became a student of Nils Posse.[8] Posse had directed the Boston Normal School of Gymnastics the year before beginning his own school, and it was with Posse that Baer specifically found her life's calling. Baer had planned to be a teacher of expression, but after reading an advertisement about the Posse School, the new subject of "physical education" became her total focus for the next thirty-eight years.[9]

Physical Education Career

Turning down a regular faculty appointment to teach Swedish gymnastics at the Boston School of Oratory where she had taught in the summer of 1891, Baer opted to return to New Orleans and the challenge of creating a department of physical culture at the newly established H. Sophie Newcomb Memorial College.[10] Newcomb College, opened in 1887, was an affiliate of Tulane University and the first degree-granting coordinate college in the country.[11]

On October 1, 1891, Clara Baer became instructor of physical culture at Newcomb at a yearly salary of $1,600. By her second year, she was given the title of director of physical education, and her salary was increased to $2,400.[12] Baer began the first certification programs in physical education in Louisiana and the South in 1893–94 and instituted the first four-year program in physical education leading to a bachelor's degree in 1909.[13] This program began fourteen years prior to the physical education major created by Alfred D. Browne at Peabody College in Nashville, Tennessee, which is often credited with being the first major program in the South.[14]

Physical education was not only a novelty in the South in the 1890s, but controversial, as many students and their parents felt that strenuous exercise for women was neither socially appropriate nor healthy. Clara Baer had to have great tact and courage to develop a department of physical education for women in the New Orleans of 1891.[15] The young women who attended Newcomb College in the 1890s were often driven to the college in carriages and accompanied by their "mammy nurses," who waited outside while they attended classes.[16]

When Baer introduced the bloomer suit as required gymnastic class attire in 1894, the young women who came to class in long dresses, bustles, hats, gloves, and heels balked at this perceived immodesty. For three years, Baer had led her students in gymnastic drills and had them play games in their long voluminous skirts and shirtwaists with tight, form-fitting corsets worn beneath. It was only after the students were exercised more strenuously in the warm and humid climate of New Orleans that Baer was able to "sweat off" the corsets from beneath the bloomers.[17]

Baer was an energetic crusader for physical education. Besides teaching at Newcomb College, she spent her winter evenings and her summer vacations during the 1890s in the promotion of physical education. She taught gymnastics to the more elite women of New Orleans at the exclusive, all-male Southern Athletic Club, which allowed the wives, sisters, and daughters of its members to attend Baer's classes there one evening a week.[18] Two other nights a week Baer taught her gymnastics and games at the Newcomb gymnasium to the city's working women, primarily stenographers, store clerks, and public school teachers.[19] Baer taught three summers in the Louisiana Chautauqua at Ruston,[20] one summer at the Summer School of Methods in Waynesville, North Carolina,[21] and for several weeks during seven summers she taught in educational institutes in small towns throughout the state.[22] From 1898 through 1910, Baer taught in and directed the Monteagle Summer School for Higher Physical Culture in the Cumberland Mountains of Tennessee. Teachers throughout the South as well as from other geographic regions attended this school in the summers, and this extended Baer's sphere of influence.[23]

Professional Contributions

Clara Baer was active in professional physical education organizations, served as officer and filled responsible committee roles, gave lectures at state and national conventions, published in professional journals, and was a force in shaping physical education at the local, state, regional, and national levels. She was instrumental in getting a compulsory physical education law passed in 1894, making Louisiana the second state in the nation behind Ohio (1892) to have such a law.[24] Baer was the first southern physical educator known to apply the science of anthropometry to education, the first to gain the rank of full professor (1899), the first to teach adapted or remedial exercises,[25] the first to write a physical education text,[26] the first and perhaps only one to invent a popular game and revolutionize another to make it appropriate for women, and the first to develop certification and a major degree program in physical education. These accomplishments are of the magnitude to give her permanent stature as a truly outstanding leader in the early development of physical education.[27]

Basketball at Newcomb College

Basketball, the only major sport to develop from a physical education need, was invented by James Naismith at Springfield College in December 1891. By the fall of 1892, the women at Smith College had begun playing the game under the leadership of Senda Berenson.[28] In 1893, basketball was introduced to Newcomb College and to the South by Clara Gregory Baer.[29] The Newcomb version of basketball quickly spread throughout Louisiana.

Baer published the first basketball rules for women in 1895,[30] the same year she publicly introduced the game of basketball to New Orleans. Before publishing her rules, Baer contacted Naismith, inventor of the original game, to solicit his approval and permission for the many changes she had made. Naismith thought her modifications were so numerous that he suggested she consider having them printed with a different title. Baer did publish her game under the name "Basquette,"[31] appropriate because of southern Louisiana's French culture and the feminine connotation of the name.

For almost a decade, Baer's students in the outdoor classes at Newcomb College played basketball in their long skirts. Baer favored the outdoors for her "girls," but it was considered daring to wear the bloomer suit indoors, much less out in public. It was around 1902 before the girls were taken outside for games or exercises in their bloomers.[32] Basketball and Newcomb ball

were probably most responsible for the Newcomb women accepting bloomers as soon as they did. These games could be played and enjoyed so much
more freely and comfortably in the bloomers than in their long-skirted, high-
necked, and long-sleeved shirtwaists, with corsets worn underneath.

Baer's strong advocacy for physical education focused on hygienic objectives, but she saw health in the broadest sense as including mental, spiritual,
and emotional aspects as well as physical. She believed exercise was important for women as well as men, and that it was necessary in achieving total
well-being. Baer also believed that exercise was much more effective when it
was experienced in an enjoyable manner.

Nineteenth-century physical education was primarily composed of formal Swedish and German gymnastics; synchronized wand, dumbbell, and
Indian club drills; marching; calisthenics; and the taking of anthropometric
measurements. Sports and games, although played by school boys and college
men since early in the century, were looked upon more as extracurricular
activities than as academic endeavors. The women physical educators were
the first to make sport a regular part of their education curriculum. More of
the male physical educators emphasized varsity sports, but they were slower
to merge them with class work.

Perhaps Baer saw basketball as a sport that would help entice the young
upper-class women students of Newcomb College, who generally showed
an aversion to exercise, into becoming more willing participants of physical
education activities. When she first introduced the game to her students in
1893, she found that the rules were too strenuous and allowed for entirely
too much roughness for women. After a few trials with the men's rules and
when objections from parents and physicians became more numerous, she
decided the game would have to be modified or abandoned. Most of her
students were delicate, unaccustomed to exercise, and found any type of
strenuous activity distasteful.[33] In spite of the game's early failure, Baer saw
possibilities in basketball if it could be modified to more readily meet the
needs of women. She decided this could and should be done, and in January
1894, she modified the game.[34]

"Victorianizing the Game"

The first elements that Baer removed from the game were features that
caused overexertion or led to what she called "nervous fatigue."[35] To prevent
too much running, Baer divided the court into many sections. Although

Naismith, John Betts, and others credit Baer with the three-division court, she never used fewer than seven divisions in her regulation games.[36] She did suggest in 1911 that practice games could be played on a court with five divisions if there were no more than ten players involved. In Baer's first modification of basketball, she divided the court into eight and eleven squares, and the floor divisions used depended upon whether sixteen or twenty-two girls played at once.[37] One player per team occupied each square, and this limited running to no more than a few steps. Jay Seaver, when president of the New York Chautauqua School of Physical Education, wrote Baer to express his approval of her rules for women's basketball. He stated that her use of the multiple-sectioned court was "rational and helpful in developing the game for girls." He went on to mention that allowing girls to move only when the ball was in the air cultivated rapid thinking and made passing more important than continual running.[38]

To further ensure that the young women were not overactive within their limited playing area, which at the largest in 1895 was no more than a 23' × 25' space and could be as small as 8' × 12', Baer disallowed any running except when the ball was in the air. When she went to the seven division court in 1908, the centers' area was expanded to 16' × 46', the forward and backward guard spaces to 30' × 23', and the goal area to 12' × 12'. She also instituted a rule that gave a player six seconds, later reduced to four, to aim at the goal without interference from anywhere on the court before shooting.[39]

The second objective in Baer's modification of basketball was to change all rules that resulted in rough play. To do this she eliminated dribbling, disallowed all guarding or attempts to interfere with an opponent's pass or shot for the goal, and made falling down a foul. By limiting the floor space and allowing no more than two players to occupy an area, collisions were practically eliminated.

Next Baer felt she should introduce features into the game that were uniquely suitable for women and would reinforce values held dear by women and men. When Baer had gone to Newcomb in 1891 to create the department of physical education, the college president, Brandt V. B. Dixon, received many letters of protest from parents supported by physicians that claimed young ladies would be made coarse and unfeminine or their health could be harmed by unladylike exercise.[40] Baer was well aware of the potential upheaval the game could cause if it did not conform to the Victorian concepts of femininity revered by southerners. Women were expected to be nonaggressive, gentle, poised, quiet rather than boisterous, and always mannerly and ladylike. They

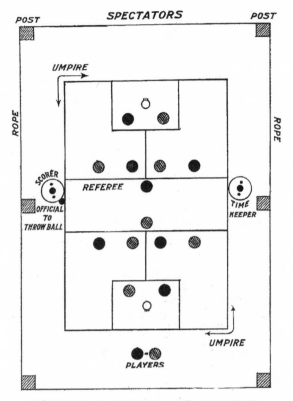

POSITIONS OF PLAYERS AND OFFICIALS

Clara Baer's diagram *Positions of Players and Officials* illustrates the positions of players and officials on the seven-division court, and the location of spectators. From the *Newcomb College Basketball Guide for Women* (n.d.).

were never expected to be too competitive, act proud or haughty, or glory in physical prowess at the expense of more gentle qualities.

For these special needs, Baer put in rules that called for goals to be changed after every score, which reversed the offensive and defensive duties of the players, countering the possibility that one player could become a "star." Baer used "running" centers rather than "jumping" centers so height would not be a factor in the game.[41] She disallowed any yelling or talking by players during a game, and even made audible signals a foul. If a player aimed for the goal and then did not shoot, this also constituted a foul. One wonders if Baer was trying to cultivate decisiveness on the part of the players with this rule since women had the reputation of being fickle and changeable and were thought to find it difficult if not impossible to make up their minds.

Two decades after Baer published the first basketball rules for women, she stated that her rules developed along original lines because Newcomb College was so far from other women's colleges.[42] Certainly her rules published in 1895 under the name "Basquette" were distinctive, and many of the more unusual aspects of her game remained intact through their final revision in 1914.

Invention of Newcomb Ball

The introduction of basketball to the Newcomb College students provided the stimulus for Baer to invent a game of her own. While waiting for goals to be delivered so basketball could be played with standard equipment, Clara Baer devised a lead-up or practice game for basketball which she called "Newcomb ball," or simply "Newcomb." It was a game that could be played in a smaller area than basketball, could accommodate almost any number of students, and required only a rope, a ball, and three division lines marked on the floor.[43] The purpose of the game was to teach throwing and catching, which were the most basic skills used in Baer's game of basketball. Points were scored by throwing the ball in the opponent's court, where it could not be caught by an opponent. The game of Newcomb provided for a change of routine, was recreational, was lively enough to provide exercise, and was pleasurable to the students.

Newcomb ball was so simple and fun that it quickly spread to schools and playgrounds. It even became a varsity sport for males and females in the public schools and colleges of Louisiana, and then spread to all parts of the country by the end of the first decade of the twentieth century. Some of the states fielding varsity teams between 1900 and 1914 besides Louisiana were Oklahoma, Ohio, Michigan, Texas, Massachusetts, Tennessee, New York, Mississippi, and Missouri.[44] When Baer published her first set of basketball rules in 1895, she patented and published rules for Newcomb ball at the same time. This game continues to be described in modern elementary physical educations texts and game books and is still played by children in America's parks and playgrounds.

Values of Basketball: 1895–1922

Basketball was being played by women in almost every part of the country by 1895. The rules used were dependent upon the school or college where it was played, and the games ranged from using men's regulation rules to extreme modification.[45] Wherever the game was introduced, it seems to have quickly gained popularity with the students. The women's colleges were the leaders in the promotion of the game, and most of the schools in the South and East appeared to hold similar philosophical views regarding the game's purpose and significance. Where western colleges were more inclined to accept intercollegiate play, the eastern and southern women's schools were opposed to highly competitive contests.[46] The schools in these more conservative areas saw basketball as a means to an end rather than as an end in itself. The leading women's colleges playing basketball in the 1890s were Smith, Vassar, Wellesley, Bryn Mawr, and Newcomb.

Some of the major views of the game as seen by the early physical education directors in these elite schools were that basketball was a worthwhile game because (1) it combined pleasure with exercise;[47] (2) it was important to women's symmetrical development rather than for training athletes;[48] (3) it helped to develop better physiques and greater strength and endurance;[49] (4) it promoted cooperation among players; (5) it had educational and health related benefits; and (6) it was thought to teach personal aesthetics to the players.[50] Women who played basketball were said to develop "quick perception and judgment" and "physical and moral courage, self-reliance and self-control, that ability to meet success and defeat with dignity."[51] Baer thought the game caused women to think while helping them develop gracefulness.[52]

There was also some concern about possible negative outcomes to women who played basketball. Berenson warned that women should always be on guard to not allow the excitement of the game coupled with the desire to win make them "do sadly unwomanly things."[53] Baer was attentive to these things, but another of her worries was for a player to appear concerned with "star" status. To prevent such undesirable attitudes, Baer made her rules to counteract this problem and specifically had this thought in mind as she formulated her rules.[54]

The Distinctiveness of Newcomb College "Basket Ball"

Clara Baer published revisions of her rules in 1908, 1911, and 1914 under the title *Newcomb College Basket Ball Rules*, dropping the title "Basquette" with the second publishing. The rules now advocated only seven court divisions rather than the eight to eleven used in 1895. Her court divisions always matched the number of players per team. From 1908 until 1922, when Newcomb College moved to Spalding rules, Baer advocated seven players per team. Other than a change in court divisions, her rules remained fairly consistent throughout the quarter of a century of their use.

The distinctive features of Baer's rules contrasted with other rules used for women around the country were (1) the running centers; (2) changing baskets after each goal; (3) not stopping the game for fouls; (4) the elimination of "guarding" and "dribbling"; (5) using no backboards on the baskets; (6) allowing only one-handed shooting and passing;[55] (7) the manner of scoring;[56] (8) allowing no movement on the court except when the ball was in the air; (9) declaring falling down a foul; (10) allowing no talking or audible signals during the game; and (11) the many divisions of the court.[57]

Baer believed that her rules calling for a seven-division court provided near equal opportunities for both strong and weak players. The strongest players were centers, and the weakest were put at "goal." Since the game was not stopped for fouls, the scorers marked all fouls as they occurred. At the end of each half, the fouls were canceled out with the team having the fewer fouls receiving one point for each of the opponent's excessive fouls.

The one-handed push shot required by Baer's rules introduced this major shooting technique years before it became popular and was recognized as the most scientifically accepted method.[58] The mandatory one-hand push shot, except from center, was to secure "a more upright and graceful position, put the ball in line of vision," and secure freer respiration.[59] The two-handed pass or throw was made a foul because it was said to cause the shoulders to be forwardly inclined, with "consequent flattening of the chest."[60]

Women's basketball grew rapidly in the South, but it followed a pattern consistent with the social and cultural mores of the region. Sport for women in the South was looked upon more favorably when it was viewed as contributing to good health or as reinforcing social expectations. Clara Baer, as well as most other southern leaders prior to the mid-1920s, never advocated interscholastic or intercollegiate sport for women. The major basketball contests for the year at Newcomb College were games between the freshman and the sophomore classes and the alumnae game each spring between the graduates and the "varsity" basketball team. The "varsity" team, or what later was called the "all-star" team, was composed of the best players in the College.

These special basketball games were turned into gala affairs at Newcomb College and became classic events. The alumnae game was considered the height of the athletic season. Hundreds of the alumnae, who were now society matrons, debutantes, teachers, and young businesswomen, returned to either play or spectate and cheer. It was claimed that the Louisiana State University–Tulane football squads had nothing on the Newcomb cheers, as the society matrons dropped their dignity in the heat of the struggle to join in the boisterous rooting.[61] Although the women students and graduates of Newcomb College loudly and enthusiastically cheered their teams, Baer's rules always disallowed verbal signals or talking by players during the game. J. E. Lombard, who became Louisiana's first state director of physical education in 1918,[62] wrote in 1910 that he, too, believed there should be no talking during a game between members of a team unless it was a quiet conversation during time-out. He also felt that clapping by players made the game less scientific than when silent signals were used.[63]

By the second decade of the twentieth century, most of the southern schools, both secondary schools and colleges even in Baer's state of Louisiana, had adopted the "official" Spalding rules for basketball. However, Baer was still recognized and credited with blazing the path for the spread of basketball among women in the South and Southwest.[64]

Conclusion

In the spring of 1929, Clara Gregory Baer retired from Newcomb College with the title of professor emeritus, after spending thirty-eight years as head of the Physical Education Department, which she had created.[65] Clara Baer had made a significant impact on the growth of physical education and women's basketball in the South that also had repercussions across the country.

Only recently has Baer received the historical credit for publishing the first rules on women's basketball.[66] By introducing the game of basketball to every little hamlet across Louisiana in the state's Chautauqua and institute programs; teaching the game to all of the teachers attending the Monteagle, Tennessee, Summer School of Physical Culture for twelve years; spreading the game through her major students and gymnastic clubs; and publishing rules for women several years before any others were in print, Baer was a prime catalyst, perhaps second to none, in the sport's early growth and development. Certainly Clara Gregory Baer deserves much recognition and belated accolades for the important pioneering role she played in the promotion and acceptance of basketball for girls and women.

NOTES

Editors' Note: Joan Paul's essay is reprinted by permission of National Association for Girls and Women in Sport. Copyright © 1991 National Association for Girls and Women in Sport.

1. "Fair Women Make Fair Athletes," *New Orleans Daily Picayune,* March 14, 1895, 3.

2. As a child, Baer was thought to be tubercular, so she was encouraged to play "tomboyish" games in the outdoors (see Charles L. Richards, "Likes Short Skirts and Bobbed Hair," unidentified newspaper clipping from 1929, in Sophie Newcomb Physical Education Department Scrapbook Newcomb Archives, Newcomb College Center for Research on Women [hereafter cited as NA NCCROW]). On January 19, 1938, at seventy-five, Clara Baer died of an apparent heart attack. For accounts of her death, see "Pay Tribute to Gym Founder," *New Orleans Item,* January 20, 1938, in Louisiana Collection, Tulane University Library; "Retired Newcomb College Teacher Fatally Stricken: Miss Clara G. Baer, Physical Education Pioneer Succumbs," *New Orleans Times-Picayune,* January 20,1938, 2, supplied by New Orleans Public Library.

3. Jane Hemenway (Bolingbrook, Ill.) to author, November 4, 1983; "Interesting Career of Late Mrs. Margaret A. Riley," *New Orleans Times-Democrat,* August 11, 1904.

4. Edwin Adams Davis, *Louisiana: The Pelican State,* 4th ed. (Baton Rouge: Louisiana State University Press, 1975). In the Hemenway letter, it was stated that H. J. Baer had nicknamed his daughter "Dixie." This may have been in defiance of the situation into which she had been born. Baer's nieces and nephews called her "Aunt Dixie" all of their lives.

5. "Interesting Career of Late Mrs. Margaret A. Riley." Two children, a boy and a girl, had died in childhood (see Hemenway letter, 1983).

6. Even in the 1890s, most often it was only the well-to-do children in Louisiana who received a secondary education (Davis, *Louisiana: The Pelican State;* "Biennial Report of the State Superintendent of Public Education to the General Assembly, 1892-1893," *Advocate: Official Journal of the State of Louisiana* [Baton Rouge, 1894]: 41–45; C. A. Ives, "As I Remember," in *Bureau of Educational Materials and Research* [Baton Rouge, 1964]: 105–8, Louisiana Department of Educational Research Library).

7. Clara G. Baer to Robert Sharp, president of Tulane University, February 5, 1916; "Retired Newcomb College Teacher Fatally Stricken."

8. Ruth Marshall, reference librarian, Boston Public Library, to author, October 29, 1983.

9. For a more definitive review of Baer's work in physical education, see Joan Paul, "Clara Gregory Baer: Harbinger of Southern Physical Education," *Research Quarterly for Exercise & Sport,* centennial issue (April 1985): 46–55.

10. Baer to Sharp, February 5, 1916.

11. Radcliffe was founded in 1879, eight years prior to Newcomb, but was not chartered and empowered to grant degrees until 1894 (see John P. Dyer, *Tulane: The Biography of a University, 1834–1965* [New York: Harper and Row, 1966]). See also *Tulane University Catalogue: 1888–89* for a complete history of Newcomb's founding.

12. "Information Card," Baer File, Tulane Archives.

13. This was the first such program in physical education in the South until after World War I.

14. Anna Ley Ingraham, professor, Department of Teaching and Learning, George Peabody College/Vanderbilt University, to author, September 9, 1983.

15. Dean Pierce Butler to the Carnegie Foundations, January 27, 1938, Baer File, Tulane University Archives.

16. Marie Louise Tobin, "Newcomb Reviews Half a Century," *New Orleans Times-Picayune*, October 11, 1936, Louisiana State University Archives, Baton Rouge.

17. "Newcomb Athletics," unidentified newspaper clipping, 1922, in Florence Ambrose Smith Scrapbook, NA NCCROW.

18. The New Orleans Southern Athletic Club purchased a complete Swedish gymnastics outfit consisting of ladders, oblique ropes, vaulting boxes, stall bars, benches, and vertical ladders so that Baer could instruct the members' wives, sisters, mothers, and daughters in gymnastics (see "Ladies' Gymnasium," *New Orleans Times-Picayune*, October 28, 1891, 3).

19. "The Stenographers Class in Physical Culture," *New Orleans Daily Picayune*, February 4, 1895, 3; "A 'Women Workers' Physical Culture Class," *New Orleans Daily Picayune*, March 21, 1895, 3; "Woman's World and Work-Ladies Evening Gymnastics Club," *New Orleans Daily Picayune*, May 31, 1895, 3.

20. "The Louisiana Chautauqua—Faculty and Lecturers," *New Orleans Daily Picayune*, April 12, 1895, 21.

21. Baer to Sharp, February 5, 1916.

22. By 1896, only a small percentage of Louisiana teachers had attended college; it was suggested that no more than one high school teacher per parish had a bachelor's degree (see Ives, "As I Remember").

23. At its peak, Monteagle had nineteen schools in which teachers could receive credit toward degrees and certification. Physical education became a part of the Summer School in 1890. In 1895, Vanderbilt University accredited graduates of the Monteagle Summer School of Higher Physical Culture (see Katherine Strobel, "The Monteagle Summer School," *Journal of Physical Education and Recreation* 50 [April 1979]: 80–84; and *Monteagle Summer School Programs, 1899–1910*, Monteagle Archives, Tennessee).

24. The law approved on July 7, 1894, stated that the laws of health and physical education should be taught in every district of the state (Act #78, 1894 Legislature, Archives and Records Service, State of Louisiana, 90). "A Talk with Miss Clara G. Baer," *New Orleans Daily Picayune*, October 4, 1895, 8.

25. Clara Gregory Baer, "The Health of College Women," *National Education Association* (1916): 690–93; Clara Gregory Baer, "Therapeutic Gymnastics as an Aid in College Work," *American Physical Education Review* 21 (December 1916): 513–21.

26. See Clara G. Baer, *Progressive Lessons in Physical Education* (New Orleans: School Board of New Orleans, 1896).

27. It appears remarkable that Baer's accomplishments would have been so obscure as to continue to escape the notice of physical education and sport historians. The only references to Baer in history texts are brief mentions of her in connection with basketball, most often identifying her as the one responsible for the three-division court, which is absolutely in error.

28. See Senda Berenson, "Basket Ball for Women," *Physical Education* 3 (September 1894): 106–9.

29. Clara Gregory Baer, "History of the Development of Physical Education at Newcomb College," *National Education Association* (1914): 701–4; Clara Gregory Baer, *Newcomb College Basket Ball Rules for Girls and Women* (New Orleans: Tulane Press, 1908).

30. The history books always give credit to Senda Berenson because she chaired the committee that wrote the first "official" rules for women in 1901. Note should be made that Baer published her rules six years prior to the publication of Berenson's.

31. Clara Gregory Baer, *Basquette* (New Orleans: L. Graham and Sons, 1895); Baer, *Newcomb College Basket Ball Rules*.

32. "Dancing and Athletics Making N.O. College Girls into Athletes Who Rival Best Country Can Produce," unidentified newspaper clipping, probably ca. 1920s, Newcomb Scrapbook, NA NCCROW. Although most references designate 1903 as the first year Newcomb women played outdoors in bloomer suits, a picture in the February 22, 1902, *Harper's Weekly* shows the Newcomb women outdoors in their bloomers.

33. Baer, *Basquette*.

34. Clara Gregory Baer, *Newcomb College Basket Ball Guide for Women* (New Orleans: Tulane Press, 1914), in Tulane Archives.

35. Baer, *Basquette*.

36. See John Rickards Betts, *America's Sporting Heritage: 1850–1950* (Reading, Mass.: Addison-Wesley, 1974). There are two possible explanations for Baer being credited with the three-division basketball court. James Naismith claimed in his 1941 *Basketball: Its Origins and Development* (New York: Associated Press) that Baer mistakenly thought he had intended for the court to be marked into three divisions because she had misread his directions. Since the book was written fifty years after the fact, Naismith may have mistakenly identified the person who first used the three divisions, and other writers simply repeated what he had said. The other possible solution to the mystery is that writers, as well as Naismith himself, confused "Newcomb ball" with "Newcomb basket ball." The Newcomb ball rules called for the three-division court and were first published the same year as Baer's basketball rules (*Basquette*); her revisions to Newcomb ball were also made in the same years as her basketball revisions.

37. Baer, *Basquette*.

38. Parts of Seaver's letter are quoted in Baer's 1911 *Basket Ball Rules*. This gives credence to the probability that the use of Baer's rules went beyond southern boundaries.

39. A shot from center would be thirty feet or more and thus it was given a value of four points.

40. Dale A. Somers, *The Rise of Sport in New Orleans, 1850–1900* (Baton Rouge: Louisiana State University Press, 1972).

41. The ball was put into play by an out-of-bounds official, who threw the ball chest-high between the two centers, who tried to capture the ball. The centers also had the largest division on the court to cover and had the greatest distance to shoot at the goal.

42. Baer, "History of the Development of Physical Education."

43. Clara Gregory Baer, *Newcomb Ball: A Game for the Gymnasium and Playground* (New Orleans: L. Graham & Sons, Ltd., 1895).

44. Baer's Newcomb ball rule books contain pictures of playground and school teams of ages from across the country. They also show Newcomb ball varsity college teams for men as well as women (see Baer, *Newcomb Ball*).

45. Senda Berenson, ed., "Editorial," *Basket Ball for Women* (New York: American Sports, 1903).

46. Sophia Foster Richardson, "Tendencies in Athletics for Women in Colleges and Universities," *Popular Science Monthly* 50 (February 1897): 517–26.

47. "College Girls and Basket-Ball," *Harper's Weekly* 46 (February 22, 1902): 234–35.

48. Richardson, "Tendencies in Athletics."

49. Senda Berenson, "The Significance of Basket Ball for Women," *Basket Ball for Women* (New York: American Sports, 1901), 20–27.

50. Baer suggested that her rules demanded attention to aesthetic issues such as how women stand, walk, run, and throw plus their neat appearance (see Baer, *Newcomb College Basket Ball Guide*).

51. Berenson, "The Significance of Basket Ball for Women."

52. Baer, *Newcomb College Basket Ball Guide*.

53. Berenson is primarily warning against rough play (see Berenson, "The Significance of Basketball for Women").

54. The reason Baer had the team change goals after each basket was to ensure that players spent equal time on offense and on defense. She believed that the glory would go to those who made the most points, and by changing goals, players would have a more equal opportunity to score.

55. Baer appeared to be influenced by Nils Posse, her teacher, who believed that no exercise should be taught that "compressed the chest," and Baer felt two-handed passes or shots would do this (see Baron Nils Posse, *Swedish System of Education Gymnastics*, 2nd ed. [Boston: Lee and Shepard, 1896]).

56. A basket from center counted four points, from guard three, and from goal two.

57. In Baer's 1895 rules, she included a choice of two courts, depending on the number of players per team. One court was divided into eight sections with goals at diagonal corners of the gymnasium, and the other had eleven divisions with the goals at the middle ends of the court. Her 1908, 1911, and 1914 rules all called for the seven-division court, although she suggested that practice games with only ten players might be played on a five-division court.

58. Hank Lusetti from Stanford is credited with initiating the one-handed push shot in the 1930s, but Baer's "girls" were using it three decades earlier.

59. Baer, *Newcomb College Basket Ball Rules*, 1911.

60. Ibid.; Paul, "Clara Gregory Baer."

61. "Frantic Yells Help Varsity to Big Victory over Alumnae," unidentified newspaper clipping (April 10, 1920), in Newcomb Scrapbook, NA NCCROW.

62. Joan Paul, "Fifty Years of LAHPERD," presentation at the Louisiana Association for Health, Physical Education, Recreation and Dance Convention, March 9, 1984.

63. J. E. Lombard, "Basket Ball for Women in the South," *Spalding's Official Women's Basket Ball Guide, 1910–1911* (New York: American Sports Publishing, 1910), 59–61.

64. Ibid.

65. A. B. Dinwiddie, "President's Statement: Commencement," *Tulane News Bulletin* 9 (June 1929); "Information Card," Baer File, Tulane Archives.

66. As early as 1914, Clara Baer realized that she was not being given credit for her pioneering work in the development of women's basketball or for the publication of the first rules. In the 1914 edition of her rules, she pointed out this fact and said it was not meant to reflect on the work of others, just to be historically correct. For the other works on Baer, see Joan Paul, "Clara Gregory Baer: An Early Role Model for Southern Women in Physical Education," paper presented at the NASPE History Academy, AAHPERD Convention, April 8, 1983; and Joan Paul, "Clara G. Baer: Pioneer in Sport for Southern Women," paper presented at the NASSH Convention, May 19, 1984; Paul, "Clara Gregory Baer," *Research Quarterly* (1985).

9

A FEMALE-DOMINATED FIELD

Chemistry at Newcomb College, 1887–1970s

JANE MILLER

W hen William Preston Johnston and Brandt Dixon set out to hire the first faculty of the H. Sophie Newcomb Memorial College, they chose first from a pool of local teachers, most of whom did not have college or university degrees. Yet, among this 1887 faculty of thirteen, three of the five faculty members who held degrees had science backgrounds.[1] Thus, from the College's first beginnings, the "Scientific" field was one of four areas of concentration (Classical, Literary, and Industrial were the other three), and throughout Newcomb's history, science was an overlooked star, graduating small generations of successful scientists.

Among the graduates of Newcomb College were the mathematicians Mary Cass Spencer (NC 1892) and Anna Many (NC 1907); the physicians Maud Loeber (NC 1903) and Florence Gilpin Boatner (NC 1923); the physicists Eleanor Reams (NC 1905) and Rose LeDieu Mooney (NC 1926), the highest-ranking female member of the Manhattan Project; the psychologist Charlotte Harriet Boatner (NC 1929); and the biochemist and first woman dean of a U.S. medical school—the Woman's Medical College of Pennsylvania—Marion Spencer Fay (NC 1915). These and other early Newcomb-educated scientists rarely achieved the acclaim of the astronomers and physicists of Vassar, the mathematicians and geologists of Bryn Mawr, the botanists and psychologists of Wellesley, or the zoologists and chemists of Mount Holyoke.[2] Yet following in the lead of these elite women's colleges, Newcomb's early science graduates went on to earn advanced degrees at Bryn Mawr, Cornell, and the universities of Chicago, Michigan and Pennsylvania. In their educational choices, they stood firmly within a privileged cadre of American women: their graduate schools trained the majority of the 228 female scientists who earned doctoral degrees before 1900, as well as the 1,591 women included in the *American*

Men of Science (AMS) who held doctorates in 1938.[3] Moreover, the women's colleges, including Newcomb, offered one of the few places of employment for women science graduates.[4] Thus, the study of Newcomb's science faculty and students illustrates both the particular features that distinguished Newcomb College from other women's colleges in the South, and the tradition of promoting careers in science through generations of women.

The history of chemistry at Newcomb College tells an especially rich tale. The first Newcomb catalogue (1887–88) listed Evelyn Walton Ordway as a professor of chemistry and physics.[5] Ordway, who had earned her BS from the Massachusetts Institute of Technology, was "one of the few women of her day who could be classified unmistakably as a scientist."[6] Even before Newcomb's opening, she and her husband, John M. Ordway, chair of the Department of Applied Chemistry at Tulane, gave public lectures on alchemy, crystals, and sanitary science to stimulate interest in chemistry.[7] Ordway's presence on the faculty as a married woman was itself unusual. For example, in 1906, Barnard College refused to allow the continued employment of Harriet Brooks, a talented instructor of physics, after she announced her engagement. Instead of supporting her professional ambitions, Barnard dean Laura Gill wrote to Brooks: "The trustees expected a married woman 'to dignify her home-making into a profession, and not assume that she can carry on two full professions at a time.'"[8] Whereas women faculty members were to give up employment upon marriage, male faculty members at women's colleges were expected to be married.[9]

The Ordways were unusual also among faculty at southern women's colleges for their belief that chemistry should be considered as a central science—a bridge and support for physics, biology, geology, and medicine—and as an academic field of study that would lead to employment in the scientific professions. In the second year after Newcomb's opening, the catalogue description for course work in physics and chemistry specified that "each student here cultivates the ability to conduct the various experiments, determinations and analyses, and acquires that practical knowledge which finds its use and application in Pharmacy, Medicine and Industrial Arts."[10] In the late nineteenth and early twentieth centuries, many southern schools, particularly land-grant state institutions, deemed chemistry useful in understanding the subjects that were then referred to as "women's studies"—nutrition, sanitation, and home economics. These programs were intended to train women to be thrifty and efficient homemakers, home extension agents, settlement workers, or domestic science instructors.[11] In neighboring states, both Mississippi State College for Women and the Texas College of Industrial Arts for Women emphasized a science curriculum particularly suited to home economics. For example, the College of Industrial Arts for Women (now Texas Women's University) took great pains to state that chemistry had a connection to the practicalities of life: "The method used in teaching these branches are intended to ground the pupil in the great principles of nature and at the same time familiarize her with the Physics and Chemistry of every-day life. The work is designed to lead the pupil into a realization of fundamental principles rather than to burden the mind with a mass of disconnected facts. . . . We desire to humanize these subjects by emphasizing those parts that pertain to household duties and industrial pursuits."[12]

In contrast, Newcomb College, while recognizing the usefulness of chemistry for the household, gave priority to its use in "the more important industrial operations."[13] University catalogues also reveal that the scientific course of study for Newcomb students was quite similar to that for the men of Tulane College. In their four years of study, students at both colleges were required to take biology, physics, astronomy, psychology, chemistry, geology, three years of mathematics, and four years of French or German. The main difference appears to be in the laboratory work required: only chemistry laboratory was required of Newcomb students, whereas Tulane College students were required, or provided the opportunity, to take in addition to chemistry laboratory, biology laboratory, and physical laboratory.[14] The course descriptions also provide evidence that texts assigned to Newcomb students were the same or similar to those assigned to Tulane College students.[15] Thus, differences that did exist in the scientific program for male and female students point not to the ability of the students to perform the exacting work required, but rather to the resources available to them. Tulane men had a greater range and greater number of advanced-level courses, and likely better-equipped laboratories from which to learn.

The curriculum designed to provide Newcomb students with a science education comparable to that offered to men resembled the one taught at more geographically distant Randolph-Macon, Goucher College, and the other four schools that, along with Newcomb, would be the only southern colleges to meet the criteria for accreditation established by the Association of Colleges in 1917.[16] Goucher, then the Woman's College of Baltimore, in particular, served as a model. As early as 1893, Goucher's chemistry curriculum and laboratories had been approved by members of the Johns Hopkins faculty, and Goucher students were admitted to the Johns Hopkins University School of Medicine.[17]

Ordway had a similar long-term goal for her students at Newcomb.[18] With her urging, and that of her husband, Dixon had enlisted the help of Stanford E. Chaillé of the Tulane Medical Department. Dr. Chaillé is listed in the 1887 *Bulletin* as a professor of physiology and hygiene, though it does not appear that he actually taught at Newcomb.[19] Regardless, Ordway built the curriculum in the sciences such that, by 1889, when the College began planning the move to its Washington Avenue campus, a science building was planned as part of the complex.[20] Although a separate science building was not built—the proposed building becoming instead the Academy, or the high school—Ordway's laboratories were given a full floor. The 1890–91 *Bulletin* describes how the better facilities of the Washington Avenue campus promoted Ordway's goal of developing a first-rate "chemical department": "The well-equipped laboratory has accommodations for forty-eight students, and a table being assigned to each that she may conduct experiments and record observations separately."[21] By 1893, two of the College's first eight graduates (1890) were studying for master's degrees in chemistry at Tulane: Maggie Powers and Adelin E. Spencer, each of whom, before returning to Tulane, had earned a master's degree in philosophy from Cornell.[22]

From Newcomb's very first decade, then, Ordway could see that her teaching inspired serious scholars. The emphasis on chemistry, a course required of all Newcomb students regardless of course of study, would continue even as other areas of study were added to the curriculum.[23] Over time, specialized chemistry courses—such as "Ceramic Chemistry" for those interested in pottery and "The Teaching of Chemistry" for future teachers—were developed in response to varied student interests.[24]

The Progressive Era brought a short lived (1909–23) household economy program that urged the adoption of a scientific approach to everyday issues as well as to a variety of economic, political, and social problems. General chemistry was required of all students enrolled in the School of Household Economy and was "designed to give a thorough knowledge of chemical principles and their application in the chemistry of daily life." Within this program, the teaching of chemistry focused on food and its properties in the same way that chemistry courses offered at the state schools did. Yet in the Newcomb tradition, the instruction appears to have encouraged both a practical and highly technical knowledge of chemistry.[25]

The rigorous teaching of chemistry at Newcomb served a function in the lives of the faculty as well as the students. The school became part of a network of eastern and southern women's colleges that provided employment for women chemistry graduates. Prior to the passage of the Equal Employment Opportunity Act of 1972, the "old boys' network" denied women access to most academic positions. Graduate school faculties were reluctant to take on women students because they felt they could not place the women in academic positions after graduation. Women's colleges were often the only institutions to hire women.[26] As with other women's colleges, Newcomb recognized the value of hiring women chemists both as role models for students and to provide a place of employment for women professionals.

The practice of choosing women as teaching assistants and appointing women to the faculty, beginning with Ordway, continued through the 1970s and encouraged the blossoming of many outstanding chemists. One can trace in these professors and students the creation of ladders of opportunities in which the older women guided the careers of the young female chemists.

As an example, Willey Glover Denis (NC1899) was encouraged by Evelyn Ordway to pursue graduate work at Bryn Mawr in the sciences rather than in her undergraduate major field of linguistics. Ordway's involvement in the struggle to have women admitted to the Tulane Medical Department, an idea unalterably opposed by the medical department dean Stanford E. Chaillé, had made her sensitive to the fact that Bryn Mawr was one of the few women's colleges offering graduate work in the sciences.[27] At Bryn Mawr, Denis studied chemistry and geology, which, as Ordway had known might happen, convinced the younger woman to return to Tulane to take a degree in chemistry.[28] She then went to the University of Chicago (1907), where her doctoral work involved the oxidation of aldehydes, ketones, and alcohols. Denis continued her research, and by 1909, she had published a number of papers. In one, she discussed the effect of calcium, magnesium, potassium, and sodium ions on nerve impulse transmissions.[29] This study, in particular, attracted the attention of the scientific community and was instrumental in steering Denis toward biochemistry and medicine. She entered Tulane Medical School as a special student in 1909, withdrew in 1910, reentered, and shortly thereafter withdrew again. Given that women were admitted only to the first two years of laboratory work, her doctoral work gave her no particular advantage in the medical program, which was closed to women until 1914. Denis then began work at Harvard Medical School in the biochemical laboratory of Otto Folin.[30]

Although Harvard was even later in admitting women to medical school than Tulane, Folin, who had worked with other women at the University of Chicago, supported Denis's work. Denis returned to study at the University of Chicago in 1911, but continued working with Folin and also Ann Stone Minot (1898–1980), another pioneering woman in biochemistry. In an ironic twist, in 1920, Denis returned to the Tulane College of Medicine as an assistant professor in the Department of Physiology and Physiological Chemistry. In 1925, she was made head of the new Department of Biological Chemistry.[31] Today, the medical school announces this appointment with pride, stating that "Dr. Denis became the first woman to chair a major department of any major medical school in the United States."[32] In addition to her academic achievements, Dr. Denis's ninety-nine papers offered significant advances in biochemical analytical methods.[33]

Another person influenced by Evelyn Ordway was Ann Hero Northrup, a New Orleanian who had graduated from Vassar in 1896. Northrup was appointed acting professor of chemistry at Newcomb College in 1903, and full professor one year later, largely because Ordway thought her the best candidate to succeed her.[34] Northrup was reportedly a woman who had "great energy and a forceful personality." She was a charter member of the Louisiana Section of the American Chemical Society (ACS) and president of the local chapter of the American Association of University Professors (AAUP). She built a rigorous undergraduate program, adding to the course offerings and raising standards, and oversaw the move of Newcomb's chemistry department to the Broadway campus in 1918. The new classroom building contained lecture rooms, modern student laboratories, balance rooms, and research space for the faculty.[35]

In 1914, Northrup, like Ordway, married a Tulane University professor, but there is no indication that she was asked to leave her position because of this marriage. She retired in 1926 to live and study in Europe and California. In her retirement, she translated from German three books concerned with chemistry—an activity that would later influence the work of another Newcomb chemist. One of these works was Emil Fischer's autobiography, *Aus meinem Leben*.[36]

A student of Northrup's, Clara de Milt (NC 1911), continued to build upon the work of her Newcomb predecessors. De Milt taught in local high schools before returning to Newcomb in 1919 to teach chemistry and biology while pursuing graduate work at Tulane (MS, 1921). She completed her doctoral work in organic chemistry at the University of Chicago (1925), and was appointed assistant professor in charge of the Newcomb Department of Chemistry in 1926; she was promoted to associate professor and department head in 1928, and full professor in 1930. In 1941, she assumed the chair of the graduate program at Tulane, and in 1946, she was appointed chair of the Tulane Department of Chemistry.[37] Even after many years of teaching, de Milt remained inspired by Northrup's teaching methods, and in 1933, she published *A Laboratory Outline of General Chemistry*, a manual originally designed by Northrup.[38]

Like Northrup, de Milt inspired not only those she taught, but others who came long after her. Students remembered her classes on the history and philosophy of science and of chemistry as lively and spirited. She insisted on excellence, adding "Qualitative Organic Chemistry," a course not offered at Tulane College, as a requirement for Newcomb chemistry majors. Students responded to both her enthusiasm and her insistence on excellence. For example, during the middle years of her Newcomb career, of the nine or so students who earned a bachelor of science degree annually, seven had majored in chemistry.[39] During her tenure as chair of the graduate program at Tulane, there was an expansion of graduate work and the first PhD in organic chemistry was awarded.[40]

De Milt took great interest in the students and faculty, shepherding their careers and strongly urging postgraduate work and publication. She often said, "I don't want you girls to be somebody who was sent for and didn't come."[41] She encouraged collaborative student and faculty research, as demonstrated by a 1935 program of the Academy of Sciences that included four papers written jointly by Newcomb faculty and students. Articles written under her guidance by her students appeared in some fourteen peer-reviewed journals in the years 1936–53.[42] Whenever possible, de Milt hired Newcomb graduates as laboratory instructors and faculty. Ruth Rogan Benerito (NC 1935), Virginia Fenner McConnell (NC 1926), and Katharine Douglas King (NC 1946) were among the faculty she hired.

De Milt's pedagogy involved both an emphasis on exactitude in experiments and a vivacious rendition of history.[43] Writing on the instruction of science, de Milt stressed the "elegance of science" and the belief that "chemistry courses must show . . . a dynamic quality . . . must bring out the distinction between science and technology . . . [and] offer the student an opportunity to think deductively . . . and yield permanent gratification to the esthetic judgment. . . . Conspicuous among the qualities of elegance are: brevity, conciseness, originality, economy of materials, imaginative power, intuitive penetration, perfect adaptation of a means to an end."[44]

Under de Milt's tutelage, the Newcomb class of 1935 shone especially bright, with three outstanding chemistry graduates: Edith Lucile Smith, who went on to earn a PhD in chemistry at the University of Rochester; Margaret Strange Klapper, a MD from Tulane; and Ruth Rogan Benerito, a PhD from the University of Chicago. In 1938, Smith began working at the Tulane School of Medicine. She also worked at the University of Pennsylvania before accepting an appointment at Dartmouth, a pioneering position for a woman chemist at an Ivy League school. Klapper received her medical degree in 1939, and became a member of the faculty of the Tulane medical school in 1942. In 1946, she moved to the University of Alabama School of Medicine in Birmingham, where she later served as professor and dean.[45]

Ruth Rogan Benerito's career offers another impressive record, and her journey to and from the College seems particularly telling of the path of women chemists in the 1940s and 1950s. During the Depression, there was little work for women, and Benerito taught school and worked in laboratories while earning a MS from Tulane, studying under Dr. Rose Mooney (NC 1926). Benerito then taught for three years at Randolph-Macon Woman's College, returning to Newcomb in 1943 to teach physical chemistry. During summers and a leave of absence, she studied at the University of Chicago and received a PhD in physical chemistry in 1948. After de Milt's death in 1953, Benerito, then an assistant professor, was asked to head the Department of Chemistry. As the administration was unwilling to promote Benerito to associate professor or increase her salary in compensation for the increased responsibility, she resigned her position at Newcomb and accepted a position at the Southern Regional Research Laboratory of the United States Department of Agriculture (USDA).[46]

At the Southern Regional Research Laboratory, Benerito conducted research in the physical chemistry of surfaces and colloids. She was primarily responsible for elucidating the chemistry of permanent-press coatings for fabrics and for the ability of cotton fabrics to resist stains and become flame-retardant. She is the author of legions of papers and has been granted more than fifty patents, placing her second among women with the largest number of patents in the United States. She has won many awards, including the Garvan Medal, the Southern Chemist and Southwest Chemist Awards of the

American Chemical Society, the Federal Woman's award, the USDA Distinguished Service Award (twice), an honorary DSc from Tulane, and in 2002,
the prestigious Lemelson-MIT Lifetime Achievement Award. In 1971, she was
named by a national panel of judges as one of the seventy-five most important
women in the country and featured in an article in *Ladies' Home Journal*.[47]

De Milt's encouragement of women chemists also benefited women in
the wider academic community. When de Milt was allowed to hire a physical
chemist, she appointed Anna Jane Harrison (PhD, University of Missouri)
to her first teaching position. Dr. Harrison later went on to Mount Holyoke,
where she had a brilliant career in research and teaching, becoming the first
woman elected president of the American Chemical Society and president of
the American Association for the Advancement of Science (AAAS).[48] Almost
forty years after her death, de Milt's work was the subject of an academic
presentation by Margaret Rossiter, whose volume on women in American
science is a classic in the field.[49]

According to student reports of de Milt's tenure as chair of the Newcomb
chemistry department, comprehensive exams required a thorough knowledge
of chemistry, and to receive an A grade, a student was required to obtain
a score of 90 or above. There were many laboratory assignments, but the
modus operandi was cooperation, not competition, as it was at Tulane College, where students sabotaged or stole lab preparations. A great camaraderie
existed among the chemistry majors, and the faculty was judged supportive
and helpful.[50]

The faculty also was known for their eccentricities. Anna Many, a math-
ematician, a counselor to women for many years, and the first woman to
hold the Newcomb deanship, remained single throughout her life. Yet Many,
revealing the importance of dating and marriage customs even to serious scientists, insisted that her nephew have at least one date with each of the unmarried teaching assistants.[51]

Among the "annual traditions" was the yearly preparation of cold cream
and deodorant for Dr. de Milt's personal use. The manufacture of these con-
coctions was required of the undergraduate students in the laboratories. De
Milt also insisted that any of the chemistry faculty who enrolled in the Tulane
Graduate School do their research under her supervision.[52]

There is also the puzzle surrounding the payment of salaries. The generosity that Newcomb College extended in allowing female professors—that
is, Ordway and Northrup—to continue their appointments after marriage

becomes suspect if one turns to other archival collections. No record exists to indicate that Evelyn Ordway was paid by the College. In the collection of Agnes Riley, instructor of chemistry from 1932 to 1938, one finds a note about her marriage in 1937. The following year, her reappointment letter states that she will be employed "without salary." A handwritten note at the bottom of this letter reads: "At that time a faculty wife could not be in a paid position in most universities including Tulane."[53]

Certainly, this record reflects the tenuous nature of women's roles as chemists and academicians even though outstanding work was being done at the College and by its graduates. Rossiter's documentation of the double standard for women and men, the underrecognition of women's achievements, and the discrimination against women reveals that women chemists fared worse than all other women scientists, save physicists.[54] As an employer, Newcomb College was no exception. Rather, women's salaries—or lack thereof—conformed to widely held beliefs about the value of women's work and the role of the male as the primary (sole) breadwinner. Tenure and employment contracts did not exist, and women were less likely to be promoted. During de Milt's term as chair of the chemistry department, the salaries of Newcomb faculty and female staff were lower than those at Tulane.[55] Many women, de Milt among them, felt these practices were justified because most women did not have families to support.[56]

The years after de Milt's death saw many changes, but not so many that the pattern of female leadership within the department ceased. Although Benerito chose not to succeed de Milt as head of Newcomb's chemistry department, the College chose Dr. Phyllida Mave Willis, who came from Wellesley College, to serve as chair from 1954 to 1959. When Willis resigned, June Zimmerman Fullmer arrived. Fullmer's work was in physical biochemistry, and her publications on Humphrey Davy remain important to an understanding of nineteenth-century chemistry.[57]

When Fullmer received a Guggenheim Fellowship in 1963, Virginia McConnell became acting chair, and from the next year until 1970, chair. McConnell, a member of the faculty since 1942, was a New Orleanian and Newcomb graduate who had earned a MS from Tulane in organic chemistry. Like de Milt and Fullmer, McConnell was considered an authority on the history of chemistry. And like the person one might consider her "grandmother in science"—that is, the teacher of her teacher, Ann Hero Northrup— McConnell became an expert on the life and work of Emil Fischer and his study of organic substances such as sugars, enzymes, and proteins. Recall that Ann Hero Northrup, in her retirement, translated Fischer's autobiography.[58]

During McConnell's tenure as chair, the Department of Chemistry continued to produce notable graduates. Among them is Linda Smith Wilson (NC 1957), who received a PhD from the University of Wisconsin in inorganic chemistry. A nationally recognized expert on science policy, Wilson was unable to find a position in chemistry when she moved to St. Louis with her husband. She therefore entered academic administration and became the last president of Radcliffe College of Harvard University in 1989. Another notable graduate was Janina R. Galler (NC 1969), who finished Newcomb in two years, majoring in chemistry and philosophy. She entered Albert Einstein School of Medicine, receiving an MD, summa cum laude, in one year. Trained in child psychiatry at Massachusetts General Hospital, she is currently a senior scientist at Judge Baker Children's Center in Boston, and a professor of psychiatry at Harvard Medical School.[59]

The 1960s and 1970s brought major changes for Newcomb's Department of Chemistry. During these years, there was a push to merge the Tulane and Newcomb departments, and the ten faculty members of the Tulane department and the five members of the Newcomb department worked closely together. When McConnell retired in 1970, she was followed as chair by Adam Aguiar, who, in 1963, had been the first male hired by the Newcomb Department of Chemistry. He oversaw the merging of the Tulane and Newcomb chemistry departments in 1971, after which time most classes were taught on the Tulane campus. Marietta Darensbourg was titular head of the Newcomb chemistry department from 1971 to 1972.[60]

The merger of the Newcomb and Tulane chemistry departments had a negative effect on the number of women graduating with a major in chemistry—something that occurred in other sciences as well.[61] Newcomb chemistry majors numbered on the average four or five between 1967 and 1970, but only one or two from 1971 to 1978.[62] The departmental merger also had a negative effect on the number of women faculty in the chemistry department. After Darensbourg left Tulane in 1983, there were few or no women faculty for many years. In 2002, just one of the seventeen members of the Department of Chemistry was a woman; in 2005, there were no permanent women faculty members in this department of thirteen.[63] Yet, Newcomb students often earned top grades and awards within the chemistry department. Erin Bowers, Class of 2006, won the Ann Hero Northrup Award—set aside for women students in honor of this early Newcomb teacher—but she also won a prestigious Goldwater Scholarship, a national award to encourage students to pursue careers in the sciences, engineering, and mathematics.[64]

The legacy of Newcomb's women chemists, then, is a mixed one. The College's early development of strong role models and encouragement of continued study in chemistry propelled women along a nontraditional path. The College itself functioned as part of a network of women's colleges that employed women scientists at a time when few other opportunities existed. Together, Newcomb chemistry students and faculty pushed the standards of excellence so that their ability attracted more attention than their gender. The history of chemistry emerged as an area of particular expertise spanning more than three generations of Newcomb teachers and seven decades of Newcomb students. Today, chemistry remains one of the majors seemingly most avoided by women students. The statistics that Rossiter found for those "starred" men and women of science, the leaders identified in *American Men of Science, 1921–43*, revealed chemistry to be one of the most male-dominated scientific fields.[65] Sadly, this is more true for Tulane women in the early years of the twenty-first century than it was for Newcomb women in the early years of the twentieth century.

NOTES

1. These included Florian Cajöri, professor of mathematics, and John M. Ordway, professor of biology, both of whom are listed as holding an AM degree; and Evelyn Ordway professor of chemistry and physics, whose degree designation is not given until the next year, though she had obtained a bachelor of science degree in 1881. Announcement for 1887–88" (New Orleans, 1887), 84 (hereafter cited as *Newcomb Announcement*, followed by year).

2. Margaret W. Rossiter, *Women Scientists in America: Struggles and Strategies to 1940* (Baltimore: Johns Hopkins University Press, 1982), 19, 24, 145.

3. Ibid., 36, 150.

4. Ibid., 1–28.

5. *Tulane University of Louisiana, Catalogue, 1886–87*; "H. Sophie Newcomb Memorial College. *Newcomb Announcement*, 1887–88.

6. John P. Dyer, *Tulane: The Biography of a University, 1834–1965* (New York: Harper and Row, 1966), 99.

7. *New Orleans Daily Picayune*, July 6, 1909, 6, 5; *New Orleans Times-Picayune*, March 15, 1928, 2, 8. Evelyn Ordway, for example, spoke to the ladies' Quarante Club (see Quarante Papers, Collection 401, Box 1, Special Collections, Howard-Tilton Memorial Library, Tulane University, New Orleans; hereafter cited as SCHT).

8. Rossiter, *Women Scientists in America*, 16.

9. Ibid.

10. *Newcomb Announcement, 1889–90*: 80.

11. Rossiter, *Women Scientists in America*, 170–71, 299–300; Melissa Walker, "Home Economics," in *Historical Dictionary of Women's Education in the United States*, ed. Linda Eisemann (Westport, Ct.: Greenwood Press,1998), 206–7.

12. College of Industrial Arts for Women, *College Bulletin* 14 (June 1906): 36.

13. *Newcomb Announcement, 1890–91*: 79.

14. *Catalogue, 1889–90*, "College Announcement for 1890–91," 22; *Newcomb Announcement for 1890–91*: 77.

15. *Bulletin of the Tulane University of Louisiana*, ser. 6 (May 1906), *The Register 1905–1906*: "Chemistry," College of Arts and Sciences, 68–69; "Chemistry," H. Sophie Newcomb College, 126.

16. Amy T. McCandless, *The Past in the Present: Women's Higher Education in the Twentieth-Century American South* (Tuscaloosa: University of Alabama Press, 1999), 35. The other four colleges were Agnes Scott, Converse, Florida State, and Westhampton.

17. Anna Knipp and Thaddeus P. Thomas, *The History of Goucher College* (Baltimore: Goucher College, 1938), 108–9.

18. Dyer, "Education in New Orleans," in *The Past as Prelude*, ed. Hodding Carter (New Orleans: Tulane University, 1968), 116–45; Collective Biographical Files: Physicians, Newcomb Archives, Newcomb College Center for Research on Women, Tulane University (hereafter cited as NA NCCROW).

19. *Tulane Bulletin, 1887–88* (New Orleans, 1888), 84.

20. *Self-Study of the Department of Chemistry of Newcomb College*, ca. 1965; Collective Biographical Files, Virginia McConnell, NA NCCROW.

21. *Tulane Bulletin, 1889–90, Newcomb Announcement, 1890–91*: 79.

22. "Catalogue of Students," *Tulane Bulletin, 1893–94*: 118; *Newcomb College Graduates: 1890–1950*, NA NCCROW. Also by this time, Adelin's sister Mary Cass Spencer (NC 1892) had returned to teach physics and mathematics at the College and the High School after receiving a master's degree at Cornell.

23. *Tulane Bulletin, 1889–90*: 68.

24. *Tulane Bulletin, 1921–22, Newcomb Announcement, 1922–23*, ser. 23, no. 4: 44; *Tulane Bulletin, 1936–37, Newcomb Announcement, 1937–38*, ser. 38, no. 2: 52.

25. Nancy A. Rogers, "Household Economy at Newcomb College" (honors thesis, Tulane University, 1990), Reference Files, NA NCCROW; *Tulane Bulletin, 1911–12*: 58; Newcomb College, Office of the Dean, Policy Files, NA NCCROW.

26. Rossiter, *Women Scientists in America*, 1–28, esp. 9–22.

27. Dyer, "Education in New Orleans," 77. The Medical Department was renamed the College of Medicine in 1915.

28. Collective Biographical Files: Physicians, NA NCCROW.

29. Marelene Rayner-Canham and Geoffrey Rayner-Canham, *Women in Chemistry: Their Changing Roles from Alchemical Times to the Mid-Twentieth Century* (Washington, D.C.: American Chemical Society: Chemical Heritage Foundation, 1998), 144–46; Willey Denis, "The Rate of Diffusion of the Inorganic Salts of the Blood into Solutions of Non-Electrolytes and Its Bearing

on the Theories of the Immediate Stimulus to the Heart Rhythm," *American Journal of Physiology* 17 (1906–7): 35–41.

30. Rayner-Canham and Rayner-Canham, *Women in Chemistry,* 144–46; Collective Biographical Files: Physicians, NA NCCROW.

31. Rayner-Canham, *Women in Chemistry,* 144–46.

32. Rudolph Matas Library, Tulane Contributions to Medical Science and Education, www .tulane.edu/~matas/historical/medschool/doctors/denis.htm, paper copy in Collective Biographical Files, NA NCCROW. Denis died of cancer in 1929.

33. Rayner-Canham and Rayner-Canham, *Women in Chemistry,* 144–46.

34. *Tulane Bulletin, 1904–5,* ser. 5, no. 3: 5; *Tulane Bulletin, 1905–6,* ser. 6, no. 4: 5; Newcomb College Dean's Office, Faculty Minutes, NA NCCROW.

35. *"Self-Study Report of the Department of Chemistry of Newcomb College";* Collective Biographical Files: Clara de Milt and Ann Hero Northrup, NA NCCROW.

36. Collective Biographical Files: Ann Hero Northrup, NA NCCROW. Emil Fischer was the 1902 Nobel laureate in chemistry. The book's title can be loosely translated "Out of My Life."

37. Collective Biographical Files: Clara de Milt, NA NCCROW.

38. Clara de Milt and Ann Hero Northrup, *A Laboratory Outline of General Chemistry* (Ann Arbor, Mich.: Edwards Brothers, 1933).

39. Collective Biographical Files: Clara de Milt; *Newcomb College Graduates: 1890–1950,* NA NCCROW.

40. Ibid.

41. Ruth Rogan Benerito taped and transcribed interview, February 2, 1987, 5, NA NCCROW.

42. A listing of some of these papers appears in Virginia Fenner McConnell, "Clara de Milt, Historian of Science," *Chymia* (1964): 201–15.

43. Ibid.

44. Clara de Milt, "Carl Weltzein and the Congress of Karlshrue," *Chymia: Studies in the History of Chemistry,* ed. Tenney L. Davis (Philadelphia: University of Pennsylvania Press, 1947).

45. Collective Biographical Files: Edith Lucile Smith and Margaret Strange Klapper, NA NCCROW.

46. Collective Biographical Files: Ruth Rogan Benerito, NA NCCROW.

47. Ibid.; "America's 75 Most Important Women," *Ladies' Home Journal,* January 1971, NA NCCROW.

48. Collective Biographical Files: Anna Jane Harrison, NA NCCROW.

49. Margaret Rossiter, "Where the Women Were: Clara de Milt of Tulane University and Virginia Bartow of the University of Illinois," paper presented at the American Chemical Society conference, Boston, April 24, 1990.

50. Jane Miller. The author was a member of the Newcomb Department of Chemistry as a teaching assistant from 1948 to 1950 and as an instructor from 1950 to 1952. Descriptions of chemistry at Newcomb during the de Milt years come from my personal recollections as well as my biographical files. See also Agnes Riley, NA NCCROW; and the footnotes to Virginia McConnell's article on her teacher (NA NCCROW).

51. Ibid.

52. Ibid.

53. Marten ten Hoor to Agnes Sanders Riley, July 6, 1937 (postscript added ca. 1989), Riley Collection, NA NCCROW.

54. Rossiter, *Women Scientists in America*, 291.

55. The discrepancies between Newcomb and Tulane faculty salaries are well documented. See Brandt V. B. Dixon, *A Brief History of H. Sophie Newcomb Memorial College 1887–1919* (New Orleans: Hauser Printing, 1928) 151, 169–70, 193–94; Dyer, *Tulane: The Biography of a University*, 98–99; Newcomb College, office of the Dean, Faculty Minutes, 1905, NAC 019, NA NACCROW.

56. Rossiter, "Where the Women Were."

57. Collective Biographical Files, NA NCCROW; Faculty Listings, Reference Files, NA NCCROW.

58. Emil Fischer Papers, Bancroft Library, University of California, Berkeley; personal conversation with Mary McConnell, October 21, 2004.

59. Collective Biographical Files: Linda Smith Wilson and Janina Galler, NA NCCROW.

60. Faculty Listings, Reference Files, NA NCCROW.

61. In 1990, when psychology was not included, Newcomb women took home about half as many science degrees as did Tulane College men.

62. Newcomb Dean's Office, Departmental Records, NA NCCROW.

63. In 2002, this was Assistant Professor Pernilla Wittung-Stafshede, PhD (*Tulane Bulletin, 1999–2001* [New Orleans, 1999], 154).

64. Commencement Files, NA NCCROW; www.act.org/goldwater/.

65. Rossiter, *Women Scientists in America*, 290–96.

10

POLITICS OF PLAY

*Elite New Orleans Women and the Origins
of the Newcomb College Nursery School, 1924–1940*

SUSAN TUCKER

I n the summer of 1927, a group of young, well-to do New Orleans mothers
worked with contractors and carpenters to erect a small L-shaped building on the corner of Plum and Audubon Streets.[1] The property was owned
by Tulane University, but the building was financed by Edith Rosenwald
Stern,[2] a Sears heiress who had become a New Orleanian upon marriage.
Combining features of a typical New Orleans raised-shotgun house with
largely British standards about open spaces for children, and earlier German
theories on a peaceful learning environment, Stern and the other women
supervised painters whose work yielded walls of a uniform cream color with
highly glossed brown trim and wooden coatracks in this same shiny brown.
Painters also remade the small tables, chairs, and shelves into islands of blue,
dark red, jade green, and yellow. The building had the simplicity of a house
without a hallway and enabled viewing from one screen porch across to another. There was also an office, an equipment room, and screened porches
connecting three classrooms, each with its own "dressing room," a place with
child-sized toilets and sinks.[3] Outside, painted hollow blocks, swings, slides,
and a jungle gym completed the grounds, just behind Josephine Louise Residence Hall at Newcomb College. This essay tells of this school's history in the
period 1924–40, and of the mothers' creation of one of the first ten cooperative nursery schools for young children in the United States.[4] The story of the
mothers and their interactions with Tulane University and Newcomb College
raises a number of important questions about change in the city, and about
the place of elite women in creating change. How did the power of money
and social prestige influence the formation of academic studies? Could an
academic institution accommodate the education of women such that one or

two courses were taught with the future of motherhood in mind? Could an academic institution concerned with the liberal arts and sciences also educate the teachers of young children? Could the learning of young children enlighten the study of psychology, sociology, and education by older students? More central to what we know of Newcomb College, how did a coordinate college for women set within a university for men answer these questions? These questions themselves form a great legacy of a distinctive program created by educated women.

Beginning the Nursery School

As they worked to prepare the building in this summer of 1927, nineteen mothers already had devoted at least three years in planning their nursery school—a design that always included the location of the school on the Tulane University campus. In 1924, six of them had pooled money for the initial work to be accomplished. Blanche Sternberger Benjamin, a Wellesley College alumna who had completed psychology courses at Newcomb College, dedicated one thousand dollars to the project, and Stern, five thousand dollars.[5] Lillian Godchaux Feibleman (NC 1920), Irma Samson Barnett (NC 1916), Madeline Bourne Hackett, and Helen Watson Bradburn (NC 1920) also contributed their personal funds and time to the creation of the School.[6] They soon were joined by thirteen others.[7]

As a group, these women were among the few women in America who had had the privilege of education and, especially, the privilege of knowing their roles would be ones of power and change. Stern, though not a college graduate, had had a varied education as a high school student at the University of Chicago Lab School and as a member of a widely traveled family. Among the others, twelve had graduated from Newcomb, and one, from Vassar. The records of both colleges show them as active alumnae whose civic and personal activities were covered in newsletters and other correspondence. A few had trained for careers in music, social work, and journalism, and all of the women would become known for their work, whether as professionals themselves or as supporters of various civic efforts.[8] By 1937, at least fourteen already had experience as community leaders; they had been key players in the World War I Women's Volunteer Ambulance Corps, the National Council of Jewish Women, the Travelers Aid Society, and the Junior League. In comparison to Stern's wealth, the other women's lifestyles appear only comfortable and some even modest, but they were all upper-middle-class women, professional women, or the wives of Tulane faculty members or liberal clergymen. Of the nineteen, ten were from Jewish families whose influence on the city was well established. Perhaps most important to the founding of the Newcomb Nursery School, all of these women sought to use their influence for improving the lives of children, and also felt compelled to question the way Newcomb College educated its young adult women.[9] In these goals, they were not unlike their contemporaries with similar educational and economic backgrounds across the United States. They sought change that allowed them to draw upon research, particularly research concerned with the so-called "normal child" and America's middle class. And, unlike an earlier generation of reformers, who had emerged somewhat guardedly from the world of the private home, these younger women saw themselves as equal partners with teachers and other professionals.[10]

One aspect of the national goals for preschools focused on the idea that the education of young children would assist in breaking down some of the class, ethnic, and racial biases haunting democracy in America. In racially segregated New Orleans, the mothers confined such efforts to creating a school for white children from different religious and economic groups, the latter to be achieved by the inclusion of the children of Tulane employees.[11] Stern held a particular vision that was based, in part, on her own elementary school, the University of Chicago Lab School. Established in 1896, this school was governed by principles centered on the education of citizens. Professors planned the curriculum, setting aside time for teachers and undergraduates to observe the children. A preschool had been introduced there in 1916.[12] In addition, Stern had collected information on nursery schools in England, New York City, and Detroit.[13]

Using similar materials, in 1924 Vassar graduate Madeline Bourne Hackett directed local efforts for the study of early childhood education, choosing research articles, features from the *Ladies' Home Journal,* and newspaper articles on childhood education.[14] This prepared the mothers for the summer of 1925, when one of them, Helen Watson Bradburn (both a Newcomb alumna and an instructor in the Newcomb Department of Sociology), approached Tulane president Albert Dinwiddie about their proposed school and a research bureau alongside it. The following summer, in 1926, she wrote a formal letter indicating that the School would open in October. In her letter to Dinwiddie, Bradburn wrote of funding that was already in place; benefits the University would receive through affiliation; and similar programs at Vassar, Columbia, Iowa, Harvard, Chicago, Kansas, Michigan, and Yale. Julia Kirkwood, a Newcomb graduate of 1921 who had received her doctorate at the State University of Iowa and had worked in the preschool there, would serve as director of the mothers' school. This venture, Bradburn said, could be of particular benefit to Newcomb students. "Since the majority of Newcomb's graduates have to face problems of teaching or child rearing, we feel that such experience would be invaluable in preparing them either as preschool teachers for whom there is a demand, or as mothers," she wrote.[15] It is noteworthy that here she raised a question about the curriculum of the College, one that would require, of course, the agreement of Newcomb dean Pierce Butler. It is likely that she did not mention Butler by name since she knew he was opposed to programs that made scholarly endeavors for women at all different from the prescribed liberal arts and sciences curriculum of various standardizing bodies. Recall that in the early 1920s, as noted elsewhere in this volume, such efforts for standardization had meant the closing of the Newcomb High School and the discontinuation of the Domestic Science program. Whatever her motivations in going over Butler's head, Bradburn must have been pleased to hear from Dinwiddie that he was "favorably inclined," although he noted that he had to refer such work to the Tulane Administrators and also "look over our facilities."[16]

As Bradburn was discussing the proposed work, Stern was attending Columbia University's Institute for Child Welfare. There she met Patty Smith Hill, national leader of the American kindergarten and nursery school movement. Acting upon the advice of Hill, Stern hired two Columbia-educated teachers to assist Julia Kirkwood in the New Orleans school.[17] Thus, though they had no formal agreement to affiliate the Nursery School with Tulane, and had some idea that the Newcomb administration would be opposed to the project, the mothers moved ahead with their plans. If Tulane would not aid them, they would situate the School in two rooms and the yard of Blanche Benjamin's house at 514 Walnut Street. They also discussed an affiliation with Isidore Newman School, a private elementary and secondary school.[18]

Although Stern acted as guarantor of the project, the mothers elected Lillian Godchaux Feibleman as chairperson. A Newcomb graduate, Feibleman resembled her fellow alumna Bradburn in an optimistic and confident style.[19] She had met with President Dinwiddie and Newcomb dean Pierce Butler, as well as G. P. Wycoff (sociology professor at Newcomb and Tulane). Wycoff noted that Feibleman presented "the serious interest of the group with reference to the three-year child study program." Both he and Butler told them that Newcomb College had no interest in accommodating a nursery school. Yet the mothers continued to seek Dinwiddie's approval and to ask him for space at Newcomb, thus asking him to override Butler.[20]

Wycoff soon became uncomfortable with this approach. He especially objected to their assumption of a role in the proposed research bureau. Although Stern had formulated this idea at the latest during the time of her summer course work in 1926, and Bradburn (a professional as well as a mother) had spoken of the research bureau in 1925, Wycoff presented the idea as his own when he wrote of the proposed nursery school. For example, in mid-October 1926, he told Dinwiddie that the mothers "finally accepted the idea that the University is interested in the long time research idea rather than in the immediate nursery school," noting that this concession came only after "a long talk" with him.[21]

Soon after that, Wycoff began to understand that not only did the mothers think the immediate start-up of the school essential, but they also imagined their role in the proposed research bureau as equal to his own and those of the other faculty members. "Mrs. Feibleman and Mrs. Stern went farther into the matter of organization than I had in talking with them," he noted. He then offered this advice to Dinwiddie, "If their proposal of a Board composed of equal numbers from the University and their group seems unwise I think they can be persuaded to agree to an advisory board of that composition."[22]

Throughout these two and a half months, the mothers kept up a busy schedule, meeting with or writing often to Wycoff, Butler, and Dinwiddie. Despite the reservations he expressed to Dinwiddie, Wycoff was their only Tulane inside supporter; he believed that the school would find the support of the Spelman Foundation, and more importantly he had faith in Stern's connections. She had been told about sources for outside funding when she was studying at Columbia.[23]

Dinwiddie was diplomatic but not truly interested. Butler's reaction, however, was consistently one of a flat denial. Unlike Dinwiddie, whose positive responses were perhaps more decorous than real, Butler did not temper his refusal. Asked about the availability of some rooms in Newcomb Hall, the main classroom building, Butler proved "decidedly against the use of that space on account of interference with student activities . . . and possible noise on the grounds under the recitation room windows." Other Newcomb buildings were suggested, but Butler told the mothers that absolutely nothing was available.[24]

His refusal had been expected, however, and the mothers had earlier considered how to continue without Newcomb's support. One way they accomplished this was by enlisting the support of national contacts and continuing with their rush of information to Dinwiddie. Wycoff apprised Dinwiddie that "it might be well to assure the group of women interested that we will make provision at some future time."[25] Wycoff then both kept efforts in progress and offered a way for optimism.

After the October notification of Butler's refusal, the mothers rerouted their request to Dinwiddie and the Tulane Board of Administrators. They said nothing of Butler at all, but instead outlined seven specific arrangements and emphasized their own role as joint contributors to both the nursery school and the research bureau.[26]

The idea of a research bureau, in other correspondence as well as in this most formal presentation, was uniformly mentioned.[27] The mothers always recognized that to complete this part of their goals, they would need additional funding and an affiliation with Tulane University because it had both undergraduate and graduate programs. The Spelman Foundation required the involvement of both programs. However, neither the mothers, Wycoff, Dinwiddie, nor Butler ever considered that Tulane's male undergraduate college might be home for the nursery school. In other words, the mothers lobbied for Dinwiddie's support because he could, as president, request that Butler change his mind, and because Tulane's support, which guaranteed both the inclusion of the male undergraduate College of Arts and Sciences as well as graduate programs, would be actually all that was needed for a beginning.[28]

After the mothers' formal letter to the board, neither Dinwiddie nor Wycoff offered the same cordiality as they had in earlier correspondence. Dinwiddie at first had his secretary reply for him.[29] Wycoff voiced displeasure and concern, noting that he had advised them to arrange for financing before approaching the Board of Administrators.[30]

The mothers were impatient because the projected opening date for the school was six weeks behind schedule. The Tulane board met on November 10, and voted not to assist in founding a preschool. Dinwiddie did not inform the mothers of this vote for more than two weeks. Finally, in a letter dated November 26, he apologized for his delay, attributing it to illness, travel, the suicide of a board member, and the death of a colleague. The board,

Dinwiddie wrote, "was not willing to undertake a project of this kind as a part of the University programs. I am sorry to have to give this unfavorable report but the action of the Board was very positive and seems to be final."[31]

Contingent Plans and a School Both within and outside Tulane

Certainly, the mothers knew about the unfavorable response within hours after the board meeting. They had a contingency plan, and true to their spirited nature, they proceeded. On the day after the board met, that is, on November 11, 1926, the New Orleans Nursery School opened its doors to twenty children in the rented back cottage of a grocery store on the corner of Zimpel and Broadway Streets, some seven blocks closer to Newcomb College than the earlier alternative location, Blanche Benjamin's house. This location was within one block of the main building at Newcomb and so afforded easy access to a playground in the yard of a faculty house that they had also arranged to use.

Despite the refusal of the Tulane board, the mothers had some success. Within two weeks, Newcomb College agreed to pay two hundred dollars so that its undergraduates could observe in the Nursery School.[32] Wycoff, Bradburn, and Irene Conrad (the latter two both mothers and faculty members) had apparently prevailed over Butler in this matter, at least. In this, they acted like other young faculty members within the most prestigious women's colleges. Whereas they understood the need to make sure female students learned the same curriculum as male students, they also understood that many new courses could be introduced.[33]

To fund the School, each family enrolling a child bought a one-hundred-dollar bond, which was, in fact, an entrance fee that they could later sell upon leaving. One parent from each family served as a member on the Nursery School's board.[34] The two teachers hired from Columbia were Myrtle Lester and Mary Price, who each received $2,100 per year. Director Julia Kirkwood received $2,500 per year. A French teacher and a nurse also were hired. By the end of the first month, the total budget for the year was projected to be $9,709—a lean budget, given that all but $1,000 of it was devoted to salaries.[35]

While this budget exceeded the mothers' first estimate of $7,500, they proved right in their decision to proceed on their own. They continued to seek the support of Newcomb and Tulane, and just three months later, they achieved a victory that cemented their connection with the College and

University. By February 1927, the committee overseeing Newcomb College as part of the Tulane board reported its selection of the rear of the Luria property (just behind Josephine Louise Residence Hall) as being "the most available for the use of this Nursery School."[36]

In late spring 1927, the mothers planned for a sign about their Nursery School on this University-owned lot.[37] This, their beloved "temporary" home, was never mentioned in any official minutes or correspondence by Newcomb dean Pierce Butler. And while the Tulane board decided to grant use of the property in March 1927, Dinwiddie also reiterated that "the Tulane Board does not feel prepared to take over the school." He noted that they did not wish to ask the Spelman Foundation for help with the Nursery School because Tulane was "already corresponding with this Foundation in regard to another matter."[38]

Still, the mothers did not stop in their own plans and in their determination that Tulane affiliation would come. To appreciate their resolve, consider that Stern had not heard formally of the board's recommendation until after April 20. Using the fact that she had not been informed in writing about the decision, she wrote to Dinwiddie to ask that they might better lay the groundwork for future communication. She asked for an agreement that the mothers might make improvements to the property without always contacting the University.[39] Apparently this was granted because before late September, the mothers had overseen the building of the raised, ten-room cottage with three porches at a cost of $7,979.41.[40]

National and Local Responses

The building itself was clearly designed for a nursery school. Its New Orleans–style screened porches and connecting rooms imitated the focus on open-air promoted by the English nursery school leader Margaret McMillan, whose book the mothers used as a reference in their planning.[41] The children were divided into three groups, and each group occupied its own playroom, dressing room, and porch. (In winter, gas stoves, with pipes that had to be drained each night by the teachers, provided heat.) A mulberry tree and milkweed plants formed another part of the landscape and served as a home for cocoons and the chance to learn about the life cycle of butterflies. A fence was erected with imported wood from England and a memorable tree house was built.[42]

In 1928, the mothers again asked for affiliation with Tulane and New-comb, and the University board again declined. The board minutes recorded that Tulane was "entirely without funds for the operation of such a school . . . and for this reason alone we would not be able to consider a proposal to take over the School."[43]

The refusal by Newcomb, and then by Tulane, to bring the Nursery School into the College and University actually fell right in line with the history of preschools all over the United States. Most apparent are the similarities between Newcomb and other women's colleges. No women's college, save Mills, agreed to outside funding, even from the Spelman Foundation, as part of a nursery school. Administrators were wary of such funding and how it would disrupt the liberal arts and sciences. And, although Vassar and Smith established nursery schools during 1925 and 1926, administrators within the women's colleges in general were adamant that preschools might detract young women from other more rigorous study—study just won in the late nineteenth century.[44] Such objections were exactly those of Newcomb dean Pierce Butler. He saw in the Nursery School an educational venture glorifying motherhood, and he reasoned that any course of study that diverged from the education offered men would make women seem less suited for an equivalent academic life. His goals concerned the education of women as scholars, something he saw as very different from their education as mothers. He did not want to be accused of managing a school that taught what might be considered frivolous courses.[45] Dorothy Seago, a Newcomb alumna and young PhD in psychology on leave from Hollins College in 1926, remembered that Butler's response was, "It took me long enough to get rid of Home Economics in Newcomb and I'm not going to take more of this silly stuff on."[46]

In all likelihood, he was responding also to the fact that Dinwiddie acted for Tulane, but encouraged the offering of space only at Newcomb. Wycoff's desire "to connect this work with Tulane at once by giving them some space at Newcomb" suggests that Newcomb was the only college or division within the University that could work with young children.[47] Surely this tactic by Wycoff and Dinwiddie angered Butler, compounding worries about the encroachment of Tulane into Newcomb's funds and also onto Newcomb's new campus, then only eight years old.[48] Butler continued to be wary of the School, never allowing it to become officially a part of the College during his tenure as dean, which lasted until 1939.

Dinwiddie's response can also be seen as both a part of a national pattern and a uniquely local one. For him, a nursery school with a research bureau (whether located within the fields of education, psychology, social work, sociology, or medicine) was a new, interdisciplinary, and little-tested concern that complicated traditional views of scholarship. Even within coeducational institutions, such innovative approaches were not received with wholehearted enthusiasm.[49] Instead, various administrative configurations were arranged so that nursery schools were not located within prestigious units. For example, Columbia's Institute for Child Welfare (where Stern had studied in the summer of 1926) was created outside the more established Teachers College.[50]

Almost everywhere, child study was approached with some guardedness, reflecting its novelty and also a suspicion of all careers, and especially all volunteer efforts, dominated by women. Nursery schools and their link to wealthy women angered people with traditional ideas on the place of mothers and children in the home. Marten ten Hoor, the head of the Tulane Department of Philosophy, noted in a public statement that the "Nursery School offers assistance to mothers who wish to park their babies while they play golf, play bridge."[51] Other educators similarly drew upon popular discussions of the "whims" of the mothers so inclined to put their faith in nursery schools. A child's place, various articles cautioned, was at home, not within a schoolroom. Only at home could a mother best win her child's confidence and friendship. Nursery school would "over stimulate a child unnecessarily" and place him or her "in danger of epidemic diseases." Whereas day care centers offered an alternative for working-class mothers, the very idea that middle-class mothers, let alone wealthy women, needed such schools for their own young children seemed wasteful.[52]

In addition, Tulane's response was complicated by the fact that the mothers wanted to involve the Spelman Foundation. Dinwiddie was counting on this foundation for the newly proposed School of Social Work. This was his priority, one on which he and Wycoff had begun work as early as 1920. They were successful, for the Spelman Foundation donated $93,000 in 1927. But Dinwiddie declined to believe other funding would be forthcoming for a nursery school.[53]

The nationally known educator Patty Smith Hill tried to convince him otherwise. Informed by the mothers of the problems in gaining any sort of affiliation with the College and University, Hill wrote to Dinwiddie about her continued belief in the New Orleans school. In a three-page letter, she noted that the mothers had displayed "unusual cooperation" and were both "intelligent and faithful" in regards to their plans. She wanted the School to prosper and she wanted the University as partner.[54]

Her choice of wording offers some clue to her own judgment concerning Dinwiddie's reluctance to affiliate with the preschool. She appealed to him as "a Southern woman," therefore, marking her kinship to the Tulane board and perhaps attempting to alleviate potential concerns about the vision of the mothers as too disruptive for New Orleans, as too northern. Edith Stern was, after all, from Chicago and was often too progressive for traditional New Orleans. Certainly, too, the Spelman Foundation was known for its liberal causes. Hill tried to alleviate such concerns, appealing to him that it was important for "the South to keep in the forefront of education with little children."[55]

Though her words did not convince him, persistent and very wealthy Edith Stern was not easily deterred. Linked with well-connected and prominent women like Lillian Feibleman, professional women such as Helen Bradburn and Mabel Clarke Simmons, and faculty wives, Stern built a formidable and unstoppable network. The outside world eventually came to their side. Whereas parents in previous times relied upon the advice of their families, new learning in the 1920s guided parents to the advice of growing numbers of psychiatrists, pediatricians, psychologists, social workers, and teachers.[56]

The Newcomb mothers promoted this type of thinking. Not only did the first newspaper article describing the school tell of the physical aspects, but the unnamed journalist also hailed the mothers' efforts for creating a place for "child to meet child" and where the "biggest lesson in life is taught in learning to live with" others.[57] The mothers kept their ideas in the spotlight. For example, in 1929, Stern and Tess Mayer Crager represented those in favor of childhood education before a National Council of Jewish Women debate.[58] In that same year, Crager also wrote in the Newcomb College literary magazine of new ways of raising children in which educated women learned from professional caregivers and the work of nursery schools in the United States and Europe.[59]

The mothers also made sure that Dinwiddie and the Tulane board were aware of a study on nursery schools at the University of Minnesota, Yale University, the State University of Iowa, and other institutions.[60] In her letter about the study, Stern noted the similarities she found in the New Orleans school and that of the University of Chicago Nursery School.[61]

Unquestionably, the mothers convinced many that their School was a useful response that drew upon the latest thinking about children and society.

Certainly, they made sure that neither Tulane University nor Newcomb College forgot the potential of attaching the Nursery School to the social sciences, education, and medicine. They were successful because of Stern's money and their collectively strong network of diverse interests and backgrounds.

The School and Its Network, 1928 and Beyond

The Nursery School grew steadily. Appealing to elite families and to young faculty, the School enrolled students from white Jewish, Catholic, and Protestant middle-class and upper-class homes. The waiting lists became legendary; even in 2011, parents in New Orleans recalled phoning the Nursery School hours after a child's birth to secure a coveted place. The early class rosters show four to fifteen children from Tulane faculty and staff families in classes of twenty to thirty-five students.[62] Within the School, Stern and others began plans for another private school to accommodate older children. During one year, the Nursery School shared its address with the New Orleans School of Progressive Education and accommodated kindergartners and first-graders.[63] The latter school would become Metairie Park Country Day School.

Just as the mothers had planned, the move adjacent to Newcomb College stimulated increasing interest among faculty members. The little school added additional resources for college students who wanted to learn about young children and for faculty and administrators who wanted the chance to enhance the study of education, psychology, sociology, and other subjects.[64] In 1929, the Child Guidance Center was established at Newcomb and housed within what is now the home of the Newcomb College Institute on Newcomb Place. The Center's staff, funded by the Commonwealth Association, welcomed the chance to work with the Nursery School students.[65]

The founding of other nursery schools in the city followed the graduation of some of the Newcomb student observers. At least thirteen of the Newcomb undergraduates involved in the Nursery School in its first decades were instrumental in starting early childhood classes around the city.[66]

Among these teachers in this new field was a bright, young woman named Rena Wilson (NC 1929), who would head the Newcomb Nursery School, as it came to be called, from 1933 to 1970. Wilson carried the dream of the mothers forward even when the Depression put an end to the cooperative nature of the venture. She oversaw the transition of the School to a recognized part of the College, to become the Newcomb College Nursery School, in 1940.

At this time, the desirability of having the school become part of the College was very much on the minds of both the new dean, Frederick Hard, and the still relatively new Tulane president, Rufus Harris. Hard remembered that "some years ago" the University had "the opportunity of establishing this relationship" and that Stern had "offered substantial financial support." Although he felt "some hesitancy" since she had been rejected earlier, he nevertheless wrote to her, and she replied that she would be willing "to continue a small degree of financial support." Hard then placed the School under the auspices of the Newcomb College Department of Psychology.[67]

In 1957, when the School was rebuilt, it was again Edith Stern who partially funded construction. In the photograph that is most often used today in exhibits about the School, Stern and Wilson are pictured together, seriously considering the children around them. In this image, they stand cutting a decorated sheet cake that holds, of course, a miniature school building. In such fanciful and real environments, they and their students were indeed quite successful. Both school buildings hold important places in the memories of countless students—both those who had not yet entered kindergarten and those who were in college and university.

From the School grew not only the other preschool education programs in the city but also the Newcomb Child Care Center, founded in 1980 as a response to the women's movement and other social changes. The Center— designed for the full-time child-care needs of faculty and staff—and the older half-day program of the former Nursery School were incorporated under the title of the Newcomb Children's Center. Rena Wilson (director, 1933–70) became a legendary figure in the city. Mary Anne Marshall Bendler (director, 1970–79), Pat Schindler (director, 1980–96), and others after them continued to forge a powerful alliance with influential parents from whom the College and the University could draw support. Often their young children would later attend the elite colleges of the Northeast, but just as often their biographies, at least in New Orleans announcements of various sorts, would mention their attendance at Newcomb Nursery School.

Conclusion

Such allegiances remain an odd sort of recognition for the College and the University, an ironic one, which still does not often ask about the meaning of educating either men or women to understand the development of young children.

For now, recall that the record of the School's founders—all elite women—is one of spirited determination, tactful correspondence, and diplomatic sidestepping of any refusals, and there were many, from the College and the University. Their story, then, concerns the politics involved in considering the education of women who might one day be mothers and the politics of the work of privileged mothers in the community of the College. It is a classic "town and gown" story cloaked in both the frisson of discord that has always existed between Newcomb College and Tulane University, and another story of these two institutions as one unit working with, and also against, women from the city.

Collectively this group of women who founded the Newcomb Nursery School proved astute political players. Almost as persistent were College and University administrators who did not see the value of the proposed school's affiliation with them for reasons such as space limitations; prejudice against preschool education in a college or university setting; and fear that women students would be tainted by an education that considered motherhood alongside traditional disciplines in the arts and sciences.

The Nursery School would be abolished after Hurricane Katrina and the failure of the New Orleans levees in 2005. In 2011, the Newcomb Children's Center exists solely as a child-care facility for faculty and staff and comes under the management of Tulane University Administrative Services. The continuing history, though, represents both new and old questions that could be studied further in the history of women's education. And, as the mothers planned, from 1927 onward, there have been the daily comings and goings of little children on Tulane University's campus, and especially on the Newcomb side of campus—itself still geographically marked by the efforts of women.

NOTES

1. All materials here noted from the Nursery School Papers can be found in the Newcomb Archives, Newcomb College Center for Research on Women, Tulane University, New Orleans (hereafter cited as NSP). This building faced Audubon Street and was demolished to make way for the 1957 building, which is still standing in 2011.

2. Copy of S. B. Keane's notation dated February 23, 1927; Resolutions of the Board concerned with Newcomb, Compilation, Papers of the Dean, Newcomb Archives, Newcomb College Center for Research on Women, Tulane University, New Orleans, Louisiana (hereafter cited as NA NCCROW).

3. "When School Begins as Play," *New Orleans Times-Picayune*, September 1927, Clippings file, NSP.

4. Dorothy Hewes, "Some of the Earliest Cooperative Nursery Schools," unpublished listing dated August 24, 1996, NSP.

5. The purchase power of $1,000 in 1924 is equivalent to $12,800 in 2011.

6. Budget file, NSP.

7. Ethel Bauer, "Tots 2 to 4 Go to Nursery School in New Orleans," *New Orleans Times-Picayune,* November 22, 1926, Clippings file, NSP. Some of the others were Helen Stern Seiferth, Helene Goldsmith Godchaux, Tess Mayer Crager, Marion Odenheimer Saal Moor, Ethel Landau Jacobs, Mabel Clarke Simmons, Gladys Howcott Monrose, Pauline Mendelson Bloch, Consuelo Abaunza Faust, Elaine Pujo Reily, and Irene Conrad. Still others involved in the project, identified only by their married names, were Mrs. J. B. Teagarden (the wife of the Unitarian minister) and Mrs. Arthur Shuey.

8. Gerda Weissmann Klein, *A Passion for Sharing: The Life of Edith Rosenwald Stern* (Chappaqua, N.Y.: Rosell, 1984); Obituary files, NSP; Vassar Club of Louisiana, Special Collections, Vassar College Libraries, Poughkeepsie, N.Y. In later life, the mothers would establish civic groups such as the auxiliaries for Touro Infirmary and the Lighthouse for the Blind. A good number would serve as "first women" on the boards of other charitable organizations, hitherto all male boards

9. Correspondence, Obituary, and Mothers files, NSP.

10. Hamilton Cravens, "Child-Saving in the Age of Professionalism, 1915–1930," in *American Childhood: A Research Guide and Historical Handbook,* ed. Joseph M. Hawes and N. Ray Hiner (Westport, Ct.: Greenwood Press, 1985), 419.

11. Violet Knight Harris to Rena Wilson, n.d. 1990, General Correspondence file, NSP.

12. Klein, *A Passion for Sharing,* 14; "University of Chicago Laboratory School," *The New Encyclopaedia Britannica,* 15th ed. (Chicago: Encyclopaedia Britannica, 1987), 12:186.

13. Edgar B. Stern collection, Scrapbook Number 5. Louisiana Research Collection, Howard-Tilton Memorial Library, Tulane University; Rena Wilson, transcribed interview, January 19, 1987, NSP.

14. Clippings file, NSP. Few of the clippings are dated.

15. Helen Watson Bradburn to A. B. Dinwiddie, August 4, 1926, Correspondence file, NSP.

16. A. B. Dinwiddie to Mrs. Muir Bradburn, August 10, 1926, Correspondence file, NSP.

17. Bauer, "Tots 2 to 4 Go to Nursery School in New Orleans"; Patty Smith Hill to A. B. Dinwiddie, March 24, 1927, Papers of the President, University Archives, Howard-Tilton Memorial Library, Tulane University (hereafter cited as UAHT).

18. G. P. Wycoff to A. B. Dinwiddie, October 7 and October 10, 1926, Papers of the President, UAHT.

19. Lillian Godchaux Feibleman to A. B. Dinwiddie, November 4, 1926, Correspondence file, NSP.

20. G. P. Wycoff to A. B. Dinwiddie, October 7, October 10, October 15, and November 2, 1926; Wycoff to Mrs. Muir Bradburn, October 16, 1926, Papers of the President, UAHT.

21. G. P. Wycoff to A. B. Dinwiddie, October 7 and 15, 1926, Papers of the President, UAHT.

22. G. P. Wycoff to A. B. Dinwiddie, November 9, 1926, Papers of the President, UAHT.

23. G. P. Wycoff to A. B. Dinwiddie, October 15, 1926, Papers of the President, UAHT.

24. G. P. Wycoff to Mrs. Muir Bradburn, October 26, 1926, Correspondence file, NSP.

25. G. P. Wycoff to A. B. Dinwiddie, October 10, 1926, Papers of the President, UAHT.

26. Mrs. T. Jeff Feibleman to A. B. Dinwiddie, November 4, 1926, Papers of the President, UAHT.

27. The first letter from Bradburn, August 4, 1926, makes clear an interest in a research bureau.

28. A. B. Dinwiddie to G. P. Wycoff, November 2, 1926; Patty Smith Hill to A. B. Dinwiddie, March 24, 1927, Papers of the President, UAHT.

29. Secretary to Mrs. R. Jeff Feibleman, November 9, 1926, Papers of the President, UAHT.

30. G. P. Wycoff to A. B. Dinwiddie, November 9, 1926, Papers of the President, UAHT.

31. A. B. Dinwiddie to Mrs. T. Jeff Feibleman, November 26, 1926, Papers of the President, UAHT.

32. Pierce Butler to A. B. Dinwiddie, correspondence file, NSP.

33. Patricia Palmieri, *In Adamless Eden: The Community of Women Faculty at Wellesley* (New Haven: Yale University Press, 1995), 161–62, 178–80; Newcomb College, Bulletins, 1926–40, NA NCCROW.

34. Rena Wilson, Oral History Interview, January 1996, Oral History Collection, NA NCCROW.

35. Budget files, NSP.

36. Copy of S. B. Keane's notation dated February 23, 1927, Resolutions of the Board Concerned with Newcomb, Compilation, Papers of the Dean, NA NCCROW.

37. Edith Stern to A. B. Dinwiddie, April 20, 1927, Papers of the President, UAHT.

38. A. B. Dinwiddie to Patty Smith Hill, March 29, 1927, Papers of the President, UAHT.

39. Edith Stern to A. B. Dinwiddie, April 20, 1927, Papers of the President, UAHT.

40. Budget files, NSP; "When School Begins as Play," *New Orleans Times-Picayune,* September [?], 1927, Clippings file, NSP.

41. Margaret McMillan, *The Nursery School* (New York: Dutton, 1921).

42. Wilson interview.

43. A. B. Dinwiddie to Edith Stern, June 16, 1928, Papers of the President, UAHT.

44. Cravens, "Child-Saving in the Age of Professionalism," 449–50.

45. A similar approach (to avoid all courses except those that offered the same intellectual training to men) is discussed in Amy Thompson McCandless, *The Past in the Present: Women's Higher Education in the Twentieth-Century American South* (Tuscaloosa: University of Alabama Press, 1999), 51–82; and Barbara Miller Solomon, *In the Company of Educated Women: A History of Women in Higher Education in America* (New Haven: Yale University Press, 1985), 80.

46. Dorothy Seago, transcribed interview by Adele Salzer, 1976, Friends of the Cabildo Tape, Oral History Collection, NA NCCROW.

47. G. P. Wycoff to A.B. Dinwiddie, October 7, 1926, Papers of the President, UAHT.

48. Brandt V. B. Dixon, *A Brief History of H. Sophie Newcomb Memorial College 1887–1919* (New Orleans: Hauser Printing, 1928), 110; John P. Dyer, *Tulane: The Biography of a University, 1834–1965* (New York: Harper and Row, 1966), 56–57, 104, 116–17.

49. Cravens, "Child-Saving in the Age of Professionalism," 441–43.

50. Ibid., 442.

51. Klein, *A Passion for Sharing,* 80.

52. See Nanette Whitbread, *The Evolution of the Nursery Infant School: A History of Infant and Nursery Education in Britain, 1800–1970* (London: Routledge and Kegan Paul, 1972); and

Emily D. Cahan, *Past Caring: A History of U.S. Preschool Care and Education for the Poor, 1820–1965* (New York: Columbia University, 1989).

53. Dyer, *Tulane: The Biography of a University,*197; A. B. Dinwiddie to Patty Smith Hill, March 29, 1927, Papers of the President, UAHT.

54. Patty Smith Hill to A. B. Dinwiddie, March 24, 1927, Papers of the President, UAHT.

55. Ibid.

56. Christina Hardyment, *Dream Babies: Three Centuries of Good Advice on Child Care* (New York: Harper and Row, 1983), 157–214.

57. "When School Begins as Play," *New Orleans Times-Picayune,* September [?], 1927, Clippings file, NSP.

58. "Women Debate Nursery School," *New Orleans Times-Picayune,* January 15, 1929, Clippings file, NSP.

59. Tess Mayer Crager, "Work and the Maternal MA," *Newcomb Arcade,* February 1925, 117–19; "The Nursery School," *Newcomb Arcade,* February 1929, 114–18.

60. Questionnaire and Answers to a Survey, 1927, Miscellaneous file, NSP.

61. Edith Stern to A. B. Dinwiddie, May 14, 1928, Papers of the President, UAHT.

62. Registration files, NSP.

63. Stern collection.

64. Miscellaneous file, NSP.

65. Ibid. For example, Ruth Dreyfous (who was a Newcomb alumna, the aunt of one of the first nursery school students, and also a counselor with the Child Guidance Center) continued over a ten-year period to test some of these students, following them through high school.

66. Rena Wilson interview: Belle Watson Hunter, Grace Ellington, Amelie Chalaron Yeargain, Dorothy Gamble Favrot, Fernande Katz, Pamela Robinson Plater, Pocahontas Smith, Delphine Caron Lawson, Rose Feingold, Bessie Fitzenreiter Hiern, Beulah Johnson, Florence Swan, Shirley Hardy—to name a few—graduated from Newcomb in the 1920s, 1930s, and 1940s and entered preschool teaching after student work at the Newcomb Nursery School. Some of them would found the preschools and kindergartens at such New Orleans private schools as McGehee's, Academy of the Sacred Heart, Newman School, St. Martin's Episcopal, and a number of other private and public schools.

67. Frederick Hard to Rufus C. Harris, March 13, 1940; Edith R. Stern to Frederick Hard, March 12, 1940; Rufus C. Harris to Frederick Hard, March 20, 1940, Frederick Hard Vertical Files, UAHT.

11

FROM SOUTHERN BELLES TO CITIZENS OF THE WORLD

Newcomb's Junior Year Abroad Program

ALICE GAIL BIER

In the fall of 1954, an ocean liner weighed anchor in New York City carrying two excited Newcomb students to England for a year of study at the University of Birmingham. They would be the first of more than 3,100 Tulane students to study abroad on the program that began as the Newcomb College Junior Year Abroad (JYA) Program.[1] In the early 1950s, Newcomb's JYA was one of only a handful of programs that provided an intensive educational experience and immersion into a foreign culture. It expanded quickly in that decade to include France, Spain, Germany, and Italy. In later years, Israel, Malta, Brazil, and Argentina were added. JYA also broadened its scope to include qualified students from the colleges of Arts and Sciences (A&S, later Tulane College), Architecture, Engineering and University College.

The JYA Program was shaped by the cultural context of Newcomb College, Tulane University, and the South, as well as by national and international sociopolitical events. Similarly, JYA students experienced and remembered their year of study in the context of their own biographies. Reminiscences written in celebration of JYA's thirty-third anniversary and first reunion recount the JYA experience as "the central experience of my educational development"; "a pivotal year"; "the most meaningful, exciting, scary, exhilarating time of my life."[2]

Few students returned unchanged from their JYA experience. Recalling her 1957–58 experience at the University of Birmingham, Roberta Atkinson Guillory remembered the year as "really magic," as "a year when education was taking place on many levels of my life: a year of broadening perspectives, of exchanging a small-town provincial worldview for a deeper understanding of what it means to be a citizen of the world community. I would certainly say it permanently affected my life, and I wouldn't trade it for anything. The JYA friends I traveled with have remained some of the best friends of my life. Ever the romantic, I remember being in London in love, walking hand in hand through the park in a misty rain, and wondering if life would ever be so perfect again."[3]

The Founding of an Uncommon Program

In the early 1950s, Newcomb "girls" were, for the most part, segregated from the "boys" at A&S. Sixty-five percent of the freshman class came from Louisiana and another 10 percent from other southern states. However, Tulane had begun to convert itself from a local institution to a national graduate research university. Additionally, international interests were expanding on campus as Tulane established or expanded educational assistance and research programs in Central and South America;[4] and faculty, particularly in the language departments, promoted study in Europe. Nightly headlines focused on the Korean War and Senator Joseph McCarthy's attacks on "un-American activities." Cold War interests began permeating politics, the arts, and education, including research priorities in the natural and social sciences. International education was seen by some as a means of fighting communism; although more than one Tulane faculty member viewed this notion as simplistic.[5] The Marshall Plan was presenting American ways to West Germans, and the United States provided economic and educational aid to Spain in exchange for placement of U.S. military bases in that country. Locally, desegregation in education was gaining momentum. These events and prospects served as the backdrop for the creation of Newcomb College's Junior Year Abroad Program.

In 1953, a smoky New York City bar provided the venue of a discussion between John Hubbard, newly appointed dean of Newcomb College, and Peter Hansen, a potential music professor, that led to the beginning of Newcomb's JYA Program. Hansen, who had worked with a study abroad program in Germany, had attended a conference where he learned about Sweet Briar College's program in Paris. While many justifications for establishing a study abroad program had been made over the years, Hansen introduced the idea to Hubbard because he thought it was "simply a good idea."[6] Hubbard concurred, later stating: "[Sweet Briar's program] had been very successful for young Southern belles and here Newcomb was situated in New Orleans with heavy French and Spanish overtones and it seemed perfectly natural that

Newcomb should have a European experience for its students."[7] The study abroad program also presented Hubbard with a means of addressing what he considered to be the "excessive localism" of the Newcomb student body and faculty.[8]

At his first press conference as dean, Hubbard spoke of his plan for what would become the JYA Program. However, the lofty purposes and academic goals he outlined were presented differently the next morning, when a local newspaper, the *New Orleans States*, began the story: "If the new dean of the Sophie Newcomb College has his way, he'd have no students in his classrooms next fall. They'd all be in Europe."[9]

Despite the whimsical headline, the underlying characteristics of JYA programs were well established. Hubbard held a firm belief that the United States owed it to our European colleagues to send them only our best students, and therefore Newcomb's program was designed as a year-long honors program with participating students demonstrating high academic qualifications and seriousness of purpose.[10] Since the goal was immersion, Newcomb students would enroll in the same courses as host country students with no more than two Newcomb students permitted to attend the same institution, and those two students would not be allowed to room together.[11] The overall objective was an in-depth cultural experience by which Newcomb students would be exposed to alternative ways of thinking, experience great personal growth, and expand their knowledge of the world. From all accounts, these policies had the desired effect.

Dorene Abramson and Judith L. Billings, students in the departments of English and history respectively, were the excited Newcomb students selected to set sail as the first to study abroad. They were aided by two members of the University of Birmingham faculty who had been visiting professors at Tulane. While Abramson and Billings studied in England, Hubbard and William S. Woods, chair of the French department, traveled through Europe "armed with letters of introduction from New Orleans and New York friends and from the French Consulate."[12] By the end of the 1954–55 academic year, the second program, JYA France, was in place and Madame Andrée Alvernhe had been hired as a resident director to help students adjust to the social and academic life in Paris.

After the first two JYA students returned from England, Woods commented on the success of the JYA Program in providing a transformative experience for Newcomb students:

If they are typical of what is going to happen, then I am certain that the whole project is definitely worthwhile. From being charming and lovely, but rather provincial girls whose interests were bounded naturally by their limited experience, they have suddenly become citizens of the world. They consider themselves ambassadors of America. They have been called on to explain America's position, American customs, and in order to do that, they have had to begin to question their own practices, they have had to begin to justify our positions, to be informed. They have had to begin to realize that there are other peoples in the world with their own points of view, meet our prejudices, their own strengths and weaknesses. And they have begun to see that in mutual understanding lies mutual trust and respect.[13]

Building a Successful Program

In early September 1955, nineteen more Newcomb students set sail on the *Ile de France* from New York. Six students were to study at the universities of Birmingham and Reading in the United Kingdom and seventeen in Paris, primarily at the Sorbonne.[14] Depending on their major, the Paris students might also have enrolled in courses at the Institute d'études politiques (Sciences po), the École du Louvre, the Institut Britanique, or the Musée de l'homme.[15]

The JYA France program was organized somewhat differently than JYA England. Newcomb students in Britain attended different universities and depended on the support of local faculty and staff. In contrast, students in Paris were accompanied by a Tulane faculty member, the Professor-in-Charge (PIC) for the continent, and aided by Madame Alvernhe. This additional support was deemed necessary because of the differences between the French and American educational systems. JYA France began with intensive language study after which the students spent the academic year living in a women's residence, the Maison des Étudiants, or with French families. The students were enrolled in a special Sorbonne program for foreigners where they studied language, literature, history, art, music, theater, and the history of ideas.[16] In addition, specially created French classes ensured that Newcomb students would satisfy degree requirements needed at home. Woods became the first PIC for the continent, whose job it was to monitor the students' work and class attendance, oversee compliance with accrediting standards, and visit the British universities to observe the progress of students studying there.

In the late 1950s, JYA programs were established in Madrid, Tübingen, and Rome and extended throughout England, Scotland, and Wales. Ultimately, students enrolled in more than thirty universities in the United Kingdom. At the same time, the success of the JYA program brought about several administrative changes at home. First, as part of the continual administrative move toward greater coordination between Newcomb College and A&S, the JYA programs were opened to male students. Second, a University steering committee on the program was established with membership consisting of the director of the JYA Program, two faculty representatives each from Newcomb and A&S, and one representative each from Engineering and Architecture. The program became officially known henceforth as the Tulane-Newcomb Junior Year Abroad Program.[17] Despite this name change, the JYA Program was always closely identified as a Newcomb program: Budgets and financing remained under the Newcomb dean; the JYA office retained its location in Newcomb Hall; the director served as a member of the Newcomb executive committee; and Newcomb students participated in greater number than students from other Tulane colleges.

JYA France served as the model for the programs in Spain, Germany, and Italy and thereby solidified the characteristics of the JYA Program—especially its selectivity and emphasis on cultural and scholarly immersion.[18] In order to be selected for non-English-speaking countries, students were required to pass a language proficiency test as well as an interview conducted by a faculty member of the appropriate foreign-language department. The year-long program then began with a four- to six-week intensive language and cultural immersion program. Students usually were assigned to live with host families in towns far from the city, where they were to spend the year so as to have an experience of more than one region of the country. For example, students planning to study in Paris first went to Dijon (and later, Angers); JYA Madrid participants studied Spanish in Burgos (and later, Léon). For many JYA participants, the experience of living with a family formed the beginning of lifelong international friendships. As one recalled: "A prominent association has been my attachment to my host family in Dijon. In the twenty intervening years since I first met them, we have maintained close ties and visited one another often on both sides of the Atlantic. Only weeks ago, the younger generation of the family returned to France after spending the summer with mine."[19] As with the Paris program, a local resident director was hired to guide students in their academic choices, advise them on cultural issues, arrange housing, negotiate the bureaucracy, and serve as the link between the foreign program and Newcomb's JYA office.

The JYA Experience

Every September during the 1950s and 1960s, one would find in the society section of the New Orleans newspapers a group photo of Newcomb students bound for study in Europe. The predominantly southern co-eds would be primly posed, carefully coiffed, and stylishly outfitted. In later years, a few male students would also appear alongside the Newcomb women. Some of these JYA participants, the papers noted, would miss the fall social season in New Orleans, Carnival events, and the socially important debutante balls for their year of study in Europe. One JYA alumna recalled: "I spent my Junior Year Abroad the same year most of my friends were making their debuts. . . . My debut wasn't to New Orleans society but to life itself."[20]

Although New Orleans is a city rich with historical influences from Spain, France, the Caribbean, and Africa, in the early and mid-1950s, life took place within socially prescribed boundaries that were changing with glacial slowness. Desegregation and its consequences were part of the ongoing discourse at the University. Plans to admit African American students at the graduate level were deliberated by the Tulane board for nearly a decade before the first African American students were admitted to the School of Social Work in 1963.[21] In New Orleans, the *Brown v. Board of Education* decision propelled a strong reaction against public school integration. In contrast, however, more than half of Tulane students in the 1950s supported desegregation in some form, and faculty were often vocally and publicly supportive of integration.[22] Still, socializing between African American and white students was uncommon, and, for some of the southern students who went abroad, mixing socially with others of a different race or ethnicity was distasteful. In the words of one committee member: "In the fifties, the U.K. and France were integrated, or at least not legally segregated like the U.S. Meeting blacks or persons of color was normal in British and French universities due to the colonial influence. When early JYA students returned from the U.K. complaining about racial mixing in the foreign universities, the JYA committee decided that during the interview process of future participants it would ask how they would react if a person of color asked them to dance."[23]

In other ways also, JYA students moved far from the comfort zone of their social and cultural circles. Many students had never before traveled extensively, and the experience was profound. Both Mignon Faget and Charlotte Barkerding Travieso describe the kinds of changes in cultural view that Hubbard hoped would come about:

> Being from a very strict Creole family, I had never seen anything outside of the region [southern United States]. JYA opened my eyes to my personal heritage, i.e., France, as well as to the cultural heritage in the cities and great museums of Europe.[24]

> Not a day goes by that I am not reminded, in some way, of my JYA year in Paris. Being a town student at Newcomb, and the graduate of an all-girls' high school in New Orleans, I was very sheltered, and *very* unworldly. . . . However, I went *everywhere,* turned that extra corner, walked that extra mile, hitchhiked alone through many countries and created an unforgettable year for myself. . . . One of the lasting benefits is the trust and wisdom that I can do anything I want to do, that life is always presenting me with choice levels.[25]

JYA students found themselves in situations where their accustomed social discourse and ideas were challenged or not useful. One student commented, "Conversations between students are generally on a much higher level [than among U.S. students]." Or, as another remarked: "Good looks and clothes are considered secondary to intelligence and character. Instead of asking, *Is she good looking?* A boy asks, *Is she clever?*"[26] Once abroad, placement in the home of a host family with a very different income level or rooming with a student with few material possessions often proved unsettling. More typically, JYA students remembered learning from such experiences. For Virginia Niehaus Roddy, her year at the University of Birmingham in 1958–59 was "the loneliest of my life": "However, I learned from the family in whose house I was living how to cope with tragedy (an autistic child) and how to enjoy life and retain pride and dignity with very little money. As a consequence, my 'values,' which had previously been superficial at best, changed drastically."[27]

Emily Clark's experience at the same university sixteen years later highlights the JYA multicultural experience even for students in English-speaking countries: "I nearly didn't stay. I got mono my second week at the University of Birmingham and was taken to a grim hospital where dour nurses gave me warm orangeade and the 20-odd relatives of the Pakistani man next door camped out all day in the hall outside my glass-walled isolation room, chewing cardamom seeds and staring at me. I wanted home and Coke on ice. But I stayed and it was wonderful. I grew to love warm beer and curry and fulfilled a childhood dream when I went to the Palace of Knossos on Crete. Perhaps most important of all, I learned to appreciate the difference between Rambo and Rabelais—a good first step for all who wish for world peace."[28]

Newcomb students studied in public institutions, and, as they began to have more contact with the local students, they frequently found that the conversations in the hallways and bars were about social and political issues. Campus life, many Newcomb students found, proved a rich environment for reflection: "I think the one thing that made a lasting impression on me was that Americans are far too materialistic. British students simply did not have the money nor material things (stereos, cars, clothes, etc.) at the universities that I was used to seeing on American campuses—and it was *nice* not to have all that stuff around. It was a nicer, simpler existence."[29]

Tumultuous Times at Home and Abroad

In the 1960s, Tulane was marked by changing moral codes, conflicts over desegregation and race relations, and growing protests over the Vietnam War. Strict gender separation of residence halls came under attack, and criticism was made of the double standard surrounding curfews and conduct rules for women and men. The once primarily local student body began to take on a national character with increasing enrollments of students from outside the Southeast. Yet, 85 percent of JYA participants came from southern states.[30]

Protests and strikes at British, French, Spanish and other institutions were increasingly frequent in the 1960s as students worldwide criticized social policies, educational elitism, treatment of minorities, and the U.S. war in Vietnam. Frequently, classes were canceled or transportation strikes made it difficult to get to class. Although JYA-ers in France and Spain often took classes organized specifically for them, these too often were canceled or inaccessible. At the Sorbonne, French protesters allowed classes for foreigners to continue, but in both France and Spain, professors hired at the host institutions to teach Newcomb students had a difficult choice between supporting a strike or earning some income on the side. Students opened their minds to critically evaluate the policies of both the host country and their own. One student remembered: "Franco's declaring a state of emergency, the Guardia Civiles, guards with guns outside our classrooms, walking through Madrid alone at midnight and feeling safe . . . doing without heat, hot water, and lights frequently. . . . What did I gain from all this? Among other things: an appreciation for all freedoms in the U.S.A.; a distaste for American opulence and over-stuffed luxury; learning to live a simpler, less materialistic lifestyle; appreciating another perspective and other customs."[31]

Regardless of the turmoil, the students applied their academic skills learned at home to their studies abroad. Their foreign professors and fellow students in the host country often were, for the first time, coming in direct contact with an American and finding their own assumptions challenged. A University of Southampton administrator wrote, "Your students have confirmed and strengthened Tulane's reputation in these parts, and we look forward to their successors coming to us."[32] A resident advisor in Spain reflected on the JYA students' impact on their hosts: "[The JYA] Program has made enormous steps toward improved international understanding—not only from an American's standpoint but from that of the Europeans who are surprised at Tulane-Newcomb's serious, academically minded students and their efforts to become well-acquainted with each group's country."[33]

Students abroad at the end of the 1960s returned to a country vastly transformed by the events that had happened during their study abroad—the assassinations of Martin Luther King and Robert Kennedy, the 1968 summer of city riots, the landing of three men on the moon, the trial of the Chicago Eight, Woodstock, and increasing protests of America's involvement in Southeast Asia. In the mid-1970s, JYA students watched foreign news broadcasts covering U.S. events with a mixture of detachment, frustration, and commitment to new values. They were challenged by host country students to explain Watergate, Nixon's resignation, and the continued bombing of North Vietnam. One student recalled: "We all learned a different way of thinking about ourselves as Americans. It was during Vietnam, which was especially difficult as we represented a cause we couldn't explain very well."[34] Yet, many memories in later years were of the personal challenges they overcame and how they grew as people and citizens: "For the first time I began to look at the rest of the world and other peoples from other than an isolated and insular 'American' perspective. At the same time I found that I understood more AND doubted or questioned more beliefs than ever before in my life. I am still coming to grips with some of these personal revelations. Upon returning to the States, I found I had another cultural adjustment—as if seeing 'home' through new eyes. It had never looked so good and yet I saw so much more that needed to be changed."[35]

The JYA Program underwent significant changes during the 1970s. As the European economy entered into a period of stagnation, universities reexamined their budgets and considered measures to lessen the financial burden of foreign students on public systems of higher education. The devaluation of the dollar in the world market significantly increased Tulane's overseas JYA Program administrative costs, and participating students found the programs more expensive. At home, the JYA Program again came under scrutiny as a part of fiscal reform and a reevaluation of university structures that were perceived as exclusive. Critics noted that JYA was not academically or financially accessible to the larger student body. Semester-length programs that would keep more tuition dollars at home and be less expensive for participating students were suggested as an alternative. The position of PIC was also challenged as the living and travel costs associated with those positions were balanced against the utility of the PIC.[36]

Meanwhile, Franco's death in 1975 brought uncertainty to the political future of Spain and resulted in JYA Program changes. The national police reacted violently to demonstrations for democracy, and university closures were frequent. Joyce Crespo, resident director of JYA Madrid, together with the six other American programs, formed a consortium, the Universidades Norteamericanas Reunidas, to sustain the program during the political upheaval. According to the plan, the "Reunidas" classes would operate even when strikes closed down the university. Furthermore, the classes would better conform to home campus expectations. Two less desirable components of the solution were that fewer courses would be offered and students would study exclusively with other American students. In an effort to compensate for the latter and maximize the contact between American and Spanish students, the program administrators placed only one or two Reunidas students in each of a number of Spanish residence halls.[37]

In the late 1970s, personnel changes heralded some new directions for JYA. In New Orleans, Marcelle d'Aquin Saussy (NC 1961), herself a 1959–60 JYA participant, was named the director of the Tulane-Newcomb JYA Program, replacing Barry P. Becnel, who had directed the program for twelve years. Meanwhile, in Germany, the program was consolidated at the Universität Hamburg and declared a Senatsprogramm. This official recognition, gained through the efforts of Dr. Hedwig Bock in Hamburg's Department of English, endowed the Newcomb program with special rights at the university. In France, Madame Alvernhe retired and was replaced by Elizabeth Hare. Additionally, the first student exchanges were put in place. Exchange agreements were signed with the Universität Hamburg and the Sorbonne. In each case, Tulane would provide to each institution a one-year graduate assistantship at Tulane in exchange for the foreign institution's reception and oversight of JYA. In 1983–84, Israel was added as a JYA destination.[38]

The Legacy

The history of Newcomb's Junior Year Abroad Program is about its effect on the lives of its participants, the intellectual challenge and engagement of a year of study and life abroad, and the transformation of the Newcomb student. It is a story of how Newcomb women returned with a different concept of citizenship in their own country and in the world. In the words of Michael Zimmerman, PIC in Great Britain in 1979–80: "JYA students discover the larger world and, hence, often become far more cosmopolitan than do students remaining back in the United States. To some extent, they become 'citizens' of the world."[39]

However, the return from a year of living and studying abroad was not always easy. For many, the culture shock of returning home was nearly as great as the adjustment to a foreign culture. Newcomb acting dean Smithers noted the "accelerated maturity" of the JYA students, and their often expressed feelings of isolation and distance from previous friends who seemed stuck in time and place.[40] One student wrote, "I was pledge trainer for my sorority the year I came back, and that was one of the hardest things I ever had to do because I had grown away from so much."[41] Despite the difficult readjustment, JYA students earned an impressive number of awards including Rhodes, Truman, Luce, and Marshall Scholarships, Watson, Fulbright, and International Telephone and Telegraph Fellowships, along with numerous awards for graduate education. JYA alumnae have gone on to all walks of life: university professor, jewelry designer, art museum administrator, doctor, military personnel, lawyer, accountant, executive, business owner. Many have made use of their language skills in their occupations, some teaching French, German, or Spanish at the high school level, while others pursued their language interests to earn master's degrees and PhDs. Some have spent their lives in the country where they initially went with the JYA Program.

Postscript

While the late 1970s represented a turning point for JYA and a time in which some feared that the program might end, the Tulane-Newcomb Junior Year Abroad Program continued. The number of participants rose and fell with national and international economic fluctuations, wars and threats of wars, and the ebb and flow of financial and administration program support. Between seventy and ninety students went JYA in any given year. In the mid-1990s, Tulane faced yet another fiscal crisis resulting in the termination of the PIC position in the United Kingdom. Former participants, Tulane faculty, past PICs and the JYA director, Marcelle Saussy, rose to defend the program and successfully fought for its continuation, although with significantly reduced resources. In 1998, after drifting for two years, the Tulane-Newcomb Junior Year Abroad program was brought under the administration of the newly created Center for International Studies (CIS). Under the first director of the CIS, JYA Program destinations were expanded beyond the traditional western European countries, and innovative programs developed in Senegal, South Africa, Argentina, Malta, and Brazil.

When Hurricane Katrina hit New Orleans in 2005, 66 students were in the JYA Program, members of an elite student group of more than 3,200 students in its fifty-one-year history, including some 2,500 Newcomb students. However, Katrina was not the only element to bring change to the organization of JYA programs or the administrative structure of international study programs. Students participating in the JYA program in the United Kingdom (England, Northern Ireland, Scotland, and Wales) and the Republic of Ireland now apply simultaneously to the Office of Study Abroad and a university in the United Kingdom or Ireland. They may choose among any of the public universities in the United Kingdom and Ireland, and once approved, they enroll directly at the university as a visiting student with responsibility for arranging their own housing and course of study. In 2008–9, the former JYA Paris program joined the EDUCO program, a consortium of Emory, Duke, and Cornell universities. In 2010, the long-lived JYA program in Madrid became part of the WIPT consortium (Wisconsin, Indiana, Purdue, and Tulane).

As part of the rotation of these consortia, Tulane will send a professor to be resident advisor every four years, the first to be in 2012.[42]

In the fall of 2007, international programs were restructured as the Center for Global Education to harmonize the activities of inbound international students and scholars through the Office of International Students and Scholars and with outbound study abroad students through the Office of Study Abroad. Associated with this reorganization has been a steady increase in Tulane study abroad programs, the majority of them semester-long or summer programs, coupled with an increasing interest among students in opportunities for study abroad. The relative decrease in students in year-long study abroad programs has meant that little remains of the JYA Program as a separate entity.

More than four hundred students are expected to participate in some 120 programs in forty countries in the 2011–12 academic year, about sixty will enroll in year-long study programs. As with the first two students to study abroad, the vast majority (about 66 percent) of Newcomb-Tulane study abroad students will be women.[43]

NOTES

1. The number includes students between the fall of 1954 and fall of the 2002–3 academic year. On figures for JYA, Crystal A. Vicknair, Office of Study Abroad, e-mail September 3, 2009.

2. Karen Oser Edmunds, Jane Hanemann Nalty, and Marcelle D'Aquin Saussy, *Tulane-Newcomb Junior Year Abroad Reunion,* October 31, 1986, manuscript copy, JYA Reunion files, folder 1, Newcomb Archives, Newcomb College Center for Research on Women, Tulane University (hereafter cited as NA NCCROW).

3. Roberta Atkinson Guillory, 1957–58, University of Reading, in Edmunds, Nalty, and Saussy, *Tulane-Newcomb Junior Year Abroad Reunion.*

4. Clarence L. Mohr and Joseph E. Gordon, *Tulane: The Emergence of a Modern University, 1945–1980* (Baton Rouge: Louisiana State University Press, 2001), 124.

5. Ibid., 121–27.

6. Peter Hansen, conversation with the author, May 2001; see also Marcelle d'Aquin Saussy, "Tulane-Newcomb JYA: Around Europe in 25 Years," *Tulanian* (Fall 1978): 18.

7. John Hubbard, Oral History interview by Jill Jackson, 1986, NA NCCROW. Twenty-five years later, Hubbard, then president of the University of Southern California, wrote, "Founding the JYA program at Newcomb College was one of the best ideas I ever had in my life" (Saussy, "Tulane-Newcomb JYA," 1978).

8. Mohr and Gordon, *Tulane: The Emergence of a Modern University,* 17.

9. Iris Turner, "Newcomb Dean Believes in Education by Travel," *New Orleans States,* July 18, 1953.

10. Hubbard interview.

11. Turner, "Newcomb Dean Believes in Education by Travel."

12. Hubbard interview.

13. William Woods quoted in "Bon Voyage, or Don't You Wish You Were Going?" *Newcomb Alumnae Newsletter,* Summer 1955, 2, NA NCCROW.

14. "Europe Is Their Camp," *Tulanian* 30, no. 3 (February 1957): 5; Marcelle d'Aquin Saussy, "Around Europe in 25 Years," *Tulanian* (Fall 1978): 18; William S. Woods to Dean Lumiansky, August 23, 1962, History of JYA File, JYA Office Files, 1955–1994, NA NCCROW.

15. Memorandum to the Newcomb Student Body: Proposed Establishment of a Program of Study in France, September 29, 1954, History of JYA File, NA NCCROW.

16. Saussy, "Around Europe in 25 Years."

17. Haley F. Thomas to Mrs. A. Brown Moore, February 9, 1959, History of JYA File; "Undergraduate Study Abroad," Tulane University Parents' Council, October 17, 1997, 2, JYA Report Notebooks. The first A&S students, Charles B. Hillebrandt, Dale Grundfest, and Charles Levy Jr., studied at King's College, the University of Birmingham, and University College London respectively in 1957–58. The School of Engineering began their participation in 1961–62; the schools of Architecture and Business began their JYA participation in 1963–64.

18. A GPA of 3.2 was required (A = 4; B = 3; etc.).

19. Susan Friedlander Keith, 1966–67, University of Paris, in Edmunds, Nalty, and Saussy, *Tulane-Newcomb Junior Year Abroad Reunion.*

20. Elsa Gruen Dobson, 1966–67, University of Glasgow, in Edmunds, Nalty, and Saussy, *Tulane-Newcomb Junior Year Abroad Reunion.*

21. Mohr and Gordon, *Tulane: The Emergence of a Modern University,* 131–54, 233–34.

22. Ibid., 154–55.

23. Donald Pizer, interview by Alice Gail Bier, 2003.

24. Mignon Faget, 1955–56, University of Paris, in Edmunds, Nalty, and Saussy, *Tulane-Newcomb Junior Year Abroad Reunion.*

25. Charlotte Barkerding Travieso, 1962–63, University of Paris, in Edmunds, Nalty, and Saussy, *Tulane-Newcomb Junior Year Abroad Reunion.*

26. "Homecoming Students Tell Memories of Year Abroad," *Tulane Hullabaloo,* October 23, 1959.

27. Virginia Niehaus Roddy, 1958–59, University of Birmingham, in Edmunds, Nalty, and Saussy, *Tulane-Newcomb Junior Year Abroad Reunion.*

28. Emily Clark, 1974–75, University of Birmingham, in Edmunds, Nalty, and Saussy, *Tulane-Newcomb Junior Year Abroad Reunion.*

29. Emily Stevens Leonard, 1972–73, University of Aberystwyth, in Edmunds, Nalty, and Saussy, *Tulane-Newcomb Junior Year Abroad Reunion.*

30. Mohr and Gordon, *Tulane: The Emergence of a Modern University,* 296–97.

31. Nancy Greene Havera, 1968–69, University of Madrid, in Edmunds, Nalty, and Saussy, *Tulane-Newcomb Junior Year Abroad Reunion.*

32. Marcelle Saussy, Orientation talk, n.d., JYA Report Notebooks.

33. Diane Bucy de Fernandez, 1966–67, University of Madrid, in Edmunds, Nalty, and Saussy, *Tulane-Newcomb Junior Year Abroad Reunion.*

34. Livvy Kazer Lipson, 1966–67, University of Reading, in Edmunds, Nalty, and Saussy, *Tulane-Newcomb Junior Year Abroad Reunion.*

35. Beth Gaddy Miles, 1972–73, University of Cardiff, in Edmunds, Nalty, and Saussy, *Tulane-Newcomb Junior Year Abroad Reunion*.

36. Stuart S. Bamforth to Karl H. Hofmann, memorandum, February 2, 1979, JYA Miscellaneous series, NA NCCROW.

37. At that time, Spanish university courses were a full academic year in length, attendance was optional, and there was one final exam. Reunidas courses would be semester-long; midterms, written papers, and course attendance would be required; and a letter grading system would be used.

38. Faculty Advisory Committee Meeting Minutes (February 15, June 7, September 28, October 14, 1982), JYA Report Notebooks.

39. Michael Zimmerman, quoted in Edmunds, Nalty, and Saussy, *Tulane-Newcomb Junior Year Abroad Reunion*.

40. Saussy, "Around Europe in 25 Years."

41. Lynn Chapman Rencher, 1959–60, University of Birmingham, in Edmunds, Nalty and Saussy, *Tulane-Newcomb Junior Year Abroad Reunion*.

42. Molly Travis, associate dean for international programs, and executive director, Center for Global Education, to Beth Willinger, February 2, 2011; "Office of Study Abroad, Center for Global Education, 2009–10 Abridged Report," n.d.

43. Ibid.

12

"CHANGING NEWCOMB INTO A COLLEGE FOR THE EDUCATION OF WOMEN"

Centering Women's Lives

BETH WILLINGER

The social and political movements sweeping the nation in the late 1960s and early 1970s provided the backdrop for a familiar tug-of-war between Newcomb College and Tulane University over issues of autonomy verses absorption. On one hand stood the vacant second floor of Caroline Richardson Dining Hall, a "Newcomb building," with numerous University units clamoring for the needed space. On the other hand was the emerging women's movement, focusing on equal rights for women in education, employment, and public office. This essay tells a story of how these two forces came together, resulting in the creation of the Newcomb Women's Center, which exists today as the Newcomb College Center for Research on Women.

In 1972, the philosophy of in loco parentis was no longer a viable justification for protective policies concerning student life. Newcomb eliminated the mandatory meal plan, and with insufficient student contracts to operate the dining facility, it was closed.[1] Food services continued on the first floor of Caroline Richardson Dining Hall, but the second floor of the building became vacant. Newcomb administrators, fearful of losing possession of the building, acted quickly. Dean James Davidson proposed to reconfigure the space into a multipurpose facility consisting of a "closed lounge" for Newcomb students living off campus; a women's center, consisting of career planning materials and seminars; an art gallery–study area; an office; and a mezzanine.[2]

The proposal did not receive warm support. The University Center Governing Council, a committee composed of faculty, students, and University administrators, believed the proposed Newcomb Student Lounge would "separate the Newcomb town students from the rest of the University community" and "would infringe on the functions of this [University] Center, and deprive not only the town students but the student body as a whole of the interaction that is the heart of the function of a student union."[3] The vote by the Governing Council against creation of the town students' lounge put Davidson on the defensive. His views on the separation between Newcomb College and Tulane University were quoted in the *Tulane Hullabaloo:* "It is not just simple ownership on one hand or completely votable use of the University on the other. It is not an 'either/or' proposition. Newcomb was established as a separate college, and the responsibility was given to the Tulane Board of Administrators, but that responsibility includes recognizing Newcomb's separateness as well as its inclusiveness. They have an obligation to maintain Newcomb as a distinctive college, and its concerns should be recognized."[4]

However, Davidson recognized the need for flexibility. He had been lobbying the University administration for a career counselor for women, and his subsequent proposal reflected this interest by placing greater emphasis on the career and professional development functions of the women's center, while downplaying the student lounge.[5]

While the need for a Newcomb Student Lounge was challenged, no one at this time appears to have asked why Newcomb, a college founded for the education of women, had need of a women's center. In part this was because the women's center would serve a new constituency, the older woman. Newcomb associate dean Joseph Cohen, writing poignantly about women's traditional life-cycle experiences as the premise for the establishment of a center, identified the angst of the sixties generation. His 1973 "Proposal for A Newcomb College Educational Center for Women" began with the following descriptive paragraph.

> Beginning in the early 1960s, impressive numbers of adult women have consistently sought information and counseling from my office in an effort to determine and implement through the educational process new life goals in search of human fulfillment. In the past year alone [1972–73], more than 200 women, many of them former Newcomb students, have come to the office to explore the possibilities of their returning to complete their education and prepare themselves for gainful employment. Ranging in age from twenty-five to forty-five, the majority of these women fall into one dominant pattern: they began college after secondary school, were moderately successful in their studies, dropped out to be married, have two or more children, performed

volunteer civic service while their children were pre-schoolers, and now feel the need, with time and energy on their hands, to do something personally meaningful with their lives.[6]

After great negotiating efforts on the part of Davidson, in November 1973, his revised plan for the renovation of Caroline Richardson Hall for use as a women's center was approved by the Committee on Physical Facilities and fund-raising efforts were begun.[7] In the summer of 1974, Newcomb Alumnae Association president Nadine Robbert Vorhoff (NC 1941) announced that Nell Winston Saussy (NC 1949) was heading a $50,000 fund-raising drive to provide for the renovation of Caroline Richardson Hall and the furnishings of the Women's Center.[8]

The Committee on Caroline Richardson Hall became the "Newcomb Women's Center Committee" and added two student members and nine alumnae to the roster in January 1975. The chief mandate to the committee was to secure "funding for undergraduate career counseling." Cohen was committee chair, and his proposal served as a starting point.[9]

The National Context

Nationally, thousands of women were expressing the same frustrations as the women who sought Dean Cohen's counsel and were considering a return to college. In 1960, women received approximately one-third of all postsecondary degrees, and in 1970, approximately 40 percent of all degrees awarded nationally were earned by women.[10] The President's Task Force on Higher Education, charged by Richard Nixon with investigating barriers to women's full participation in higher education, identified three in their report: "overt discrimination" by those acting in official capacities; "institutional barriers" that make participation in higher education incompatible with many of women's other interests and activities; and "ingrained assumptions" on the part of both men and women that "deny the talents and aspirations of the latter."[11]

One approach to removing the institutional barriers to women's educational advancement was launched through the continuing education movement. During the 1950s and 1960s, an extensive network of continuing education programs developed, and by 1971, approximately 375 institutions were credited with establishing some sort of program directed to adult women.[12] In this way, the "women's continuing education" movement opened opportunities for women to obtain a postsecondary degree much like the GI Bill had done for men.[13] Unlike the GI Bill, however, the cost of continuing education was borne largely by the women themselves. Moreover, the re-entry of mature women did not change the structure of the institutions or the content of the curriculum. At Tulane, for example, Newcomb students were required to enroll full-time; child-care services were unavailable; numerous buildings lacked proper bathroom facilities for women; and the curriculum centered on male experiences and societal contributions, not yet asking, "What about the women?"

The creation of campus-based women's centers was a more specific response to women's appeals for continuing education, but these would vary widely in approach. The Radcliffe Institute for Independent Study was founded in 1960 by Radcliffe president Mary Ingraham Bunting, who sought to change what she described as a "climate of unexpectation" for women struggling to resume intellectual or artistic work after raising families.[14] The institute gave women a place to work, financial assistance, and a supportive community of peers, but it did not reintroduce them into Harvard's degree-granting structure. In contrast, beginning in 1970, the [University of] Michigan Center for the Education of Women (founded in 1964) encouraged women's full academic re-entry by providing scholarships at the undergraduate, graduate, and professional levels.[15]

However, the majority of the early women's centers were not designed as centers for women's continuing education. For example, the Arthur and Elizabeth Schlesinger Library on the History of Women at Radcliffe (established 1967) had begun as the Women's Archives in 1943. The library was concerned not so much with the education of women, or scholarship by women, but scholarship about women.[16] Other centers forming in the 1970s addressed the barriers to women's participation in education and employment by initiating the study of women's lives. Mariam Chamberlain explains that the motivation of campus women's centers "went beyond that [the education of women] to include some of the radical ideas of the growing women's movement . . . women's centers raised and examined new and more fundamental questions about women's lives, roles, and expectations."[17] For example, the Center for the American Woman and Politics at Rutgers was founded in 1971 to compile information and monitor the status of women in government and politics. The Wellesley Center for Research on Women (now the Wellesley Centers for Women) was founded in 1974 and began the study of gender-equitable education.[18]

Simultaneous with the establishment of campus-based women's centers was the development of curriculum focused on women's lives.[19] Assuming the mantle as the academic arm of the women's movement, women's studies programs and women's research centers sought to make the study of women a serious and legitimate academic endeavor. Women's studies scholars put forth the ambitious goal of transforming the curriculum in all disciplines to reflect women's current and historical position as half the world's population. "Balancing" the curriculum by including knowledge about women's lives and experiences was viewed as a critical step in efforts to end sex discrimination at all educational levels.

The Design of the Newcomb Women's Center

Dean Cohen's proposal calling for an "Educational Center for Women" at Newcomb fit firmly within the national continuing education movement while also reinforcing Newcomb's historical mission to educate women by including "re-entry women," women who were entering or returning to college later in life. Cohen suggested the responsibilities of the Center would include counseling, curriculum planning, and a "Clearinghouse."[20] Thus, Cohen's plan was a way for Newcomb to address the life-cycle patterns of women as they differed from those of men.

The curriculum-planning component of Cohen's proposal was the most ambitious but largely targeted an alumnae constituency. The proposal called for an exploration of the educational needs of current undergraduates and the proposed re-entry students, and suggested noncredit seminars and workshops on topics such as the lifestyles of educated women and programs featuring alumnae who had achieved some prominence. He recommended that the duties of a director include responsibility for organizing and teaching the "Colloquium on Women" (a team-taught course first offered at Newcomb in 1972) and one additional credit course of "major interest to women."[21]

Members of the Newcomb Women's Center Committee criticized Cohen's proposal for its neglect of curriculum development and its emphasis on the needs of re-entry women rather than those of the undergraduate population of eighteen- to twenty-two-year-old women that Newcomb traditionally served. Dr. Jean Danielson, then a Newcomb College assistant professor of political science, wrote in response: "Your proposal is fine—as far as it goes—but it just doesn't go far enough. . . . Unless we are capable of changing

Newcomb into a college for the education of women; then, minimally, at least, so as to provide options, we need a center for women, all women. Continuing education would be a significant part of this center, but so would the education of our undergraduate women."[22]

Danielson went on to note her preference for having more women's studies "courses available and available to more" and raised the possibility of "a degree in women's studies," which she posited "might be discussed, debated I suspect." Danielson, who was the only member of the committee to position the proposed center within the framework of Newcomb' mission, concluded: "Ultimately the future of a woman's college must rest on its meaningfulness to women. I should think that a women's center concerned with the whole woman and her relationship to the society in which she lives should be a significant step towards this end."[23]

The "revised draft of the revised draft of the draft" incorporated Danielson's suggestion regarding curriculum offerings focusing on women. These courses were not designated as "women's studies" or "feminist studies" courses, however, and the introduction of a major or minor in women's studies was not mentioned. The preamble also signaled an expanded mission for the College suggested by Danielson:

> For nearly one century Newcomb College has provided quality liberal arts education to thousands of women, and it reaffirms that commitment in the 1970s. In addition to developing intellectually and aesthetically, women today are demanding the opportunity to explore new career and personal options.
>
> In response to these new needs, faculty, students, and administrators, in a concerted effort, have developed courses and a colloquium, in an effort to create awareness of women's past accomplishments and new opportunities for the future. Newcomb College has now responded by formally establishing a Women's Center to facilitate the total development of women.[24]

Notably, this revision reaffirmed Newcomb's traditional-age student body as the "most important single component of the Women's Center." The Center's mission was envisioned as one that would supplement undergraduate education by providing information, counseling, and programs essential for career planning and development—resources that also were to be made available to alumnae. This document also suggested that a future proposal seek funding "to stimulate and support research about women in the Gulf

South," noting that "an important component of centers developing in other regions is research detailing the position, attitudes, and problems of women." Finally, the proposal listed several curriculum changes already under way including the development of "academic courses related to women's accomplishments."[25]

Thus, the discussion concerning the goals of the Newcomb Center in the 1970s reflected both the national movement of the 1960s to make possible the continuing education of women and the movement of the 1970s to bring about change in the structure and curriculum of academic institutions to address women's life experiences and new life goals. Significantly, the revised proposal suggested a means of expanding Newcomb's mission to include education *for* and *about* women.[26]

Despite disagreements among committee members concerning the mission of the Center, there was an underlying accord. The committee was comprised of Newcomb administrators, alumnae, faculty, and students appointed by the Newcomb administration. Thus, in contrast to campus-based women's centers that had "bottom-up" beginnings rooted in student protest and aimed at transforming a bureaucratic-patriarchal academic institution, and society more generally, the Newcomb Center had a "top-down" origin aimed at retaining the physical boundaries of the Newcomb campus and helping women to achieve their educational and employment objectives.[27]

The historical and social context in which this committee worked was influenced as much by race and class as by gender. Tulane University had been legally desegregated just ten years before plans for the Center began. Cohen's proposal outlined the barriers primarily experienced by white women and explicitly stated that the Center would serve the women "from the socioeconomic brackets from which we draw our current enrollment and from which our alumnae have come." By and large, the University attracted and served predominantly white middle- and upper-middle-class students, faculty, and administrators. Thus, it was logically consistent for the envisioned Center to address the discrimination experienced by women born of privilege. Programmatic emphasis was placed on helping students to develop the personal skills and resources that would enable them to work around the barriers to educational and career mobility, such as gaining entrance into professional schools and nontraditional professional careers, working for equal pay and career advancement, and in providing "role models" as well as advice on managing family and career. Guided by a philosophy of liberal feminism, the Center's founding committee sought to eliminate gender discrimination by working within the existing system and by giving primacy to individual strategies for advancement.

In the fall of 1975, the Newcomb Women's Center of Tulane University opened its doors on the second floor of Caroline Richardson Hall. Newcomb alumnae had exceeded their campaign goal of $50,000 and tastefully renovated and furnished the Center. Although Davidson's proposal to the Carnegie Foundation in 1974 had not been funded, he allocated College funds for the support of the Center.[28]

The Center staff consisted of a part-time coordinator and an administrative assistant. Dr. Shirley Scritchfield, a newly minted PhD, accepted the joint appointment as coordinator of the Center and assistant professor of sociology. In the first year alone, the Center sponsored career-planning workshops and academic programming; offered courses focusing on the new scholarship on women; provided individual career counseling; cohosted a major film festival; published a biannual newsletter; sponsored rotating art exhibits; and began a resource library.

The first edition of the Center's newsletter, *Womantalk*, published in November 1975, carried the bold headline "Newcomb Women's Center Now a Reality." The article's author, Meneve Dunham, assistant dean of Newcomb College and chairperson of the Center's Advisory Committee, boasted that "the center comes complete with a director, a career-planning/women's studies library, and several non-credit courses."[29] Dunham's emphasis underscores the Center's orientation toward career-planning. In its first year, the Center offered some fifteen noncredit adult continuing education seminars directed primarily to Newcomb alumnae. The courses featured day classes such as "Discovery of Self," "Managing Your Money," and "Child Management," and evening classes such as "Planning a Career," "Tennis," and the "Legal Rights of Women."

Dunham's focus on the noncredit courses *for* women, rather than on the four College-approved credit courses *on and about* women's lives, suggests the newsletter itself was directed to an alumnae and not a student audience. Her focus illuminates the interests and concerns of re-entry women in the mid-1970s, yet obscures the administrative and political obstacles associated with introducing knowledge about women into the curriculum. Courses offered for credit required the approval first of the Newcomb College Curriculum Committee and then the Newcomb faculty, a process that could take months. Noncredit courses required no such approvals. Moreover, materials for noncredit courses could be adapted from University College's noncredit courses to highlight women's—rather than men's—interests and experiences. In contrast, the scholarship on women was only then being written. Further, whereas noncredit courses emerged from a liberal feminist position that sought to gain for women the same advantages as those held by men, women's studies courses emerged from a feminist position that sought to rewrite the curriculum. Many women's colleges, particularly those located in the South, were known to be conservative supporters of traditional roles for women, and it was considered "radical" just to make the study of women a subject for academic discourse. Skepticism about the development of women's studies courses at Tulane continued well into the 1980s. To illustrate, in the January 1977 issue of the *Tulane Hullabaloo,* Elaine Spurlin (Tomlinson), the Center's second director, was quoted as saying, "A lot of the political issues (e.g., making contraceptives available at the student health center) haven't surfaced here that have in other places . . . for instance, there is no demand for a Women's Studies curriculum."[30]

Elaine Spurlin (Tomlinson) had been hired as the director in 1976. When Scritchfield's one-year appointment ended, the administration created a full-time position and sought a career counselor with responsibilities for "counseling underclassmen, seniors, and alumnae in exploring career options and goals."[31] Tomlinson's administration (1976–80) was marked by exceptional programming in support of women's career planning and development. Workshops focused on resume writing, dressing for success, career assessment, promoting careers in science and math, and successful interviewing. The resource library acquired books pertaining to nontraditional careers for women, and a part-time, preprofessional advisor was hired to assist students seeking admission to nontraditional programs such as medicine and law. Less attention, however, was given to the new scholarship on women than under Scritchfield. When Tomlinson resigned, Alice Maxwell (1980–82), who had been hired as assistant director and career counselor, took over as acting director of the Center. Maxwell continued the career development workshops begun by Tomlinson, established an alumni network to assist students with internship opportunities, and brought some organizational structure to women's studies courses then being offered by several departments throughout the University.

The success of these programming efforts gained the attention of faculty and administrators who began to see the possibilities of a more formal integration of the Center into the research and teaching mission of the College and University. In 1978, Newcomb conducted its first deliberate search for a female dean and hired Dr. Susan Wittig.[32] Dean Wittig's vision for the Center emphasized the new scholarship on women and placed the Center within the emerging network of research centers as having a unique focus on the history of southern women, particularly women in the Gulf South. These ideas, while representing a departure from the Center's career-focused programming and the qualifications of the existing staff, conveyed a growing belief among the faculty that the Center should take a leadership role in promoting feminist scholarship. More women were joining the Tulane faculty, and those whose research and teaching included the study of women felt the Center's work should give credibility to the developing field of women's studies and to the scholarship they were engaged in producing. At the same time, there was a growing sense among other departments of the University that the Center had served its purpose as a career counseling center and that the building could be used to better advantage. Thus, despite the Women's Center's successful programming and outreach to alumnae, the question over the use of the building, and the mission of the Center, was coming full circle.

In the spring of 1982, both Maxwell and Wittig resigned their posts. It was in this climate of uncertainty that Beth Willinger, encouraged by faculty members who knew of her interest in the sociology of gender, applied for the position of acting director of the Center. During her interview with Ray Esthus, then Newcomb interim dean, Esthus outlined a proposal whereby the Center would be moved to much smaller quarters and the second floor of Caroline Richardson Hall assigned to an academic department. Attempting to counter the proposed move, Willinger outlined her ideas for establishing a women's studies program to be coordinated out of the Center that would model the existing Jewish Studies program. His response, reflective of the overall lack of support held by administrators for women's studies at the time, was an unenthusiastic, "Yes, well, one-third of our students are Jewish." To which Willinger replied, "Yes, but all of them are women."[33]

Willinger was offered a one-year visiting appointment. Given the gloomy forecast for the Center's future, it appeared unlikely there would be a Newcomb Women's Center to direct after the 1982–83 academic year. With a new PhD in sociology from Tulane, Willinger's qualifications were more similar to Scritchfield's than to her immediate predecessors. Willinger continued the

Center's career services while adding new programmatic activities to further the research and teaching aims of the Center. Her first public program—a lecture series similar to the team-taught "Colloquium on Women" course—featured faculty from various disciplines who discussed how the recent scholarship on women was influencing their field. The Center's emphasis on feminist scholarship, however, created a very different sort of program, and its outreach to faculty and students targeted a very different audience than it had previously.

Willinger's efforts to engage a much larger audience in the intellectual excitement surrounding the new scholarship were influenced both by faculty colleagues eager for an expansion of academic resources in women's studies, and by the vision of Tulane University president Eamon Kelly (1981–98). Kelly sought to make Tulane one of the foremost research universities in the country. Willinger reasoned that if the Center were to survive and thrive, its mission had to support the new administration's goals and objectives, with priority given to research and teaching. Moreover, it was increasingly apparent that the Center could and should represent more than the interests of white, upper-middle-class women.

In January 1983, Dr. Sara Chapman was hired as dean of Newcomb College. Chapman recognized the Center's potential to contribute to the creation of a body of knowledge about women, particularly women in the South. With her support, the resources allocated to the Center increased, and Willinger's appointment was made permanent.

Despite the increased support for the Center, it became impossible for a staff of two (director and secretary) to continue the services for which the Center had become known and also move the Center toward a more academic focus. After thoughtful examination, all career services and eventually the art gallery were eliminated. Library acquisitions in women's studies were increased. In 1983, two programs supporting research were established: the Women's Studies Research Grants Program, a competitive program to encourage research on women and gender among Tulane students; and the Women's Studies Visiting Scholars Program, a nonfunded fellowship program for women's studies scholars. Funding requirements for these programs were nominal. Yet the outcomes were invaluable in promoting the Center's academic mission and creating a community of scholars whose use of the library and archives enlivened the daily life of the Center. Visiting Scholars, who gave at least one public presentation during their fellowship year and participated in the programs of the Center, often were recruited to move into paid positions on the Center staff.

A highly popular weekly series featuring an "oral history interview" between a woman of some prominence, usually local and often an alumna, and a faculty member brought together members of the New Orleans and academic communities to build a solid base of support for the Center's efforts. The success of these programs convinced the administration to grant the Center a part-time position for a program coordinator. Kathryn Carter, at the time a Center Visiting Scholar, was the first to hold this position. Notable among the series of programs Carter planned were "Women in Communications," "Women in Politics," "Women and Peace," "Women Artists," and "Women Graduates of the University" (in celebration of Tulane's sesquicentennial in 1984). The tape-recording of these conversations formed the beginning of the Center's archival collection of oral histories. Dr. Maryann Valiulis continued the programming excellence begun by Carter and introduced Center audiences to notable feminist theorists such as Gloria Anzaldua, Janice Raymond, Petrice Petro, and Bernice Sandler. Carolyn Ware, who also began her affiliation as a Center Visiting Scholar, followed Valiulis as program director. With a PhD in folklore, Ware expanded awareness and understanding of women's involvement in maintaining cultural traditions such as women's roles in community gardens, and the Cajun and New Orleans Mardi Gras. The importance of these programs was twofold: first, by expanding knowledge about women's lives and experiences, the programs introduced the field of women's studies as a serious academic enterprise; second, the programs brought women to campus as producers and transmitters of knowledge. No longer were the all-male speakers at "Directions," Tulane University Center Programming (TUCP), or the Mellon Symposium the only invited campus lecturers.

As more and more of the Center's activities were directed toward research and teaching in women's studies, the Center staff determined that a name change was needed to reflect this academic focus. Thus, on the occasion of the Center's tenth anniversary in 1986, the name of the Center was changed from the Newcomb Women's Center to the Newcomb College Center for Research on Women (NCCROW). The public announcement of the change in title, made by Newcomb interim dean Mary Ann Maguire in the presence of the University president and other administrators, established the Center more firmly within the University community as a unit whose mission enhanced the mission of a research university. These efforts were recognized particularly when, in 1987, the undergraduate schools at Tulane were restructured and the faculties of Newcomb College and A&S were merged as the Faculty of the Liberal Arts and Sciences. Provost Francis Lawrence led the Administrators in resolving: "The Newcomb College Center for Research on Women shall receive an enhanced budget to enable it to add to its library collection, host lectures and conferences, offer improved research support to graduate students and Center Fellows as well as to other faculty committed to the mission of Newcomb College and allow for its development as a major research center."[34]

A key event that solidified the Center's mission as a research center was the receipt of a two-year grant from the National Historical Publications and Records Commission (NHPRC) in 1988. The award recognized the historical importance of Newcomb College records and formally established the archives of the College with Susan Tucker (NC 1972) as archivist. Internally, the process of writing the grant helped to articulate both immediate and long-range Center goals; externally, the grant led to the Center's credibility as a valuable resource for scholars. In her permanent position on staff, Tucker has developed the library and archives to their present standing as the centralized repository for women's studies books and periodicals at Tulane, and as an outstanding collection of primary-source materials focusing on the records of the College, and the manuscripts of its alumnae and other southern women. Hundreds of national and international scholars have acknowledged the Newcomb Archives and Vorhoff Library as the source of their research on topics ranging from credit discrimination to a biography of Lillian Hellman.

NCCROW also has engaged in conducting several original research projects. Noteworthy among them is a four-year project, led by Dr. Barbara Moely of the Department of Psychology, and Willinger, to study the moral development of Newcomb and A&S students. These research activities led in 1989–90 to NCCROW's membership in the National Council for Research on Women, a consortium of independent and campus-based women's centers that focus on feminist research, advocacy, and policy. The affiliation brought NCCROW into a valuable network of national and international centers conducting research for and about women.

Despite efforts to build a strong research component, NCCROW remains best known on campus and in the community for its programming. Especially popular are the Zale Writer-in-Residence Program and the Arons Poetry Forum, which have welcomed more than thirty outstanding women writers to campus, among them Maxine Kumin, Ann Patchett, Edwidge Danticat, and Sonia Sanchez; and the Adele Ramos Salzer Lecture Program with notable visionaries such as Jill Ker Conway and Helen Caldicott.

In 1996–97, NCCROW experienced an expansion of facilities and function. First, NCCROW's request to assume the occupancy of the first floor of Caroline Richardson Hall, more than 4,500 square feet, was approved. Rather than moving NCCROW to smaller quarters as had been proposed in 1982, the University now allocated almost an entire building to the advancement of feminist scholarship, a visible demonstration of the administration's commitment to the enterprise. The Vorhoff Library and Newcomb Archives moved into the space, transformed into the Seltzer-Gerard Reading Room by a gift from the M. B. and Edna Zale Foundation honoring Newcomb alumnae and cousins Dana Zale Gerard (NC 1985) and Karen Landsberg Seltzer (NC 1983). Then, with a grant from the Louisiana Education Quality Support Fund, spearheaded by education coordinator Crystal Kile, NCCROW established a computer laboratory that would serve both to connect Newcomb students to the Internet as competent users and producers of knowledge and as a means of disseminating knowledge about women through online exhibits and research reports.

In 1998, Willinger and her "Research in Women's Studies" class collaborated with the Washington, D.C.–based Institute for Women's Policy Research to publish *The Status of Women in Louisiana*. Publication of this report, which placed Louisiana women in the bottom 10 percent on all health and socioeconomic indicators nationally, led to increased visibility for NCCROW on the state level. The report also was instrumental in leading then governor Mike Foster to establish the Louisiana Women's Policy and Research Commission and appoint Willinger a member. This ongoing research on the status of Louisiana women, including research on New Orleans women post-Katrina, has made NCCROW the state leader in providing reliable data for policy and program development benefiting Louisiana women.[35]

Administrative support for the Women's Studies Program would come more slowly. Although the women's studies academic minor was approved by the faculty in 1986 and the major in 1990, funding for faculty to teach in the program was not forthcoming. The majority of courses required for the major were taught by NCCROW's director and program director with no additional compensation. When Dr. Marsha Houston was hired by the Department of Communication in 1990, she requested a joint appointment with the Women's Studies Program and thereby became the first professor in women's studies. However, a full-time faculty position was not funded until fall 1997. Dr. Suzanne Dietzel, a NCCROW Visiting Scholar who had been teaching "Introduction to Women's Studies" for several semesters, assumed the position; after several years, she accepted an appointment as director of the Women's Resource Center at Loyola University, New Orleans.

Thus almost from the beginning of the Women's Center, efforts were made to build simultaneously both a center for research on women and an academic program in women's studies. The activities of the latter involved the NCCROW director and staff in gaining approval for the academic major and minor in women's studies, teaching courses, advising students, sponsoring and facilitating faculty development seminars, establishing the Women's Studies Faculty Associates program, and the Women's Studies Student Association. Willinger served as director both of NCCROW and the Women's Studies Program for more than ten years. However, the merger of the Newcomb and A&S faculty in 1987 removed all academic and administrative responsibility for faculty from the dean of Newcomb, leaving the Women's Studies Program, as a division of NCCROW, with no authority for faculty appointments or curriculum. In 1996–97, discontent among the Women's Studies faculty associates concerning the lack of University resources committed to the program, including a dedicated leadership position, pushed Kelly to convene a faculty committee to evaluate the mission and direction of NCCROW. At that time, thirty members of the faculty had been accepted as Women's Studies faculty associates, and the Women's Studies Program offered approximately twenty core and cross-listed courses annually; more than thirty current students had declared either a major or minor in women's studies; and more than twenty students had graduated with a women's studies major.[36] The recommendations of the faculty committee, as well as the recommendations of external evaluators and NCCROW's self-study, called for the appointment of a director of women's studies who would report to the dean of Liberal Arts and Sciences. These recommendations led to a search for a director of the program and resulted in the appointment of Anne McCall, associate professor of French at Tulane, as director in 1999.[37]

Nationally, few centers have attempted to serve as both an academic department and a research center, and those that have, like NCCROW, have been severely underfunded. Yet there were positive aspects of blending the two functions. Women's studies courses, taught mainly in the Center lounge, brought students to NCCROW in growing numbers. Not only then did students seek out NCCROW for the Vorhoff Library, but also for course work; interest in courses led to greater interest in the programs sponsored by NCCROW; and cosponsorship of programs with academic departments brought NCCROW into the academic mainstream. The involvement of NCCROW staff in the teaching mission of the University kept NCCROW's work immediate and vital. And the involvement of students, faculty, and community members in NCCROW's programming brought about an intellectual excitement that became one of its distinguishing features.

After twenty-five years of leading the Center from a resource center to a nationally recognized research center, Willinger retired as executive director of NCCROW in 2007. Her work promoting feminist scholarship was recognized by her selection as the 2003 "Humanist of the Year" by the Louisiana Endowment for the Humanities. Nancy Mock, with a Tulane doctorate in public health and an appointment as associate professor at the Tulane School of Public Health and Tropical Medicine, assumed the reins as acting executive director. In January 2010, Sally Kenney began her tenure as executive director of the Newcomb College Institute and also assumed the duties of directing NCCROW.

The Relationship between Newcomb College and NCCROW

Recall that it was the frustration of former students and the complex pattern of women's lives that first led Joseph Cohen to propose a center for women. One of the special features of Newcomb has always been this engagement between the College and its alumnae. NCCROW certainly has benefited from this involvement. From the first campaign to renovate Caroline Richardson Hall to the present, the support of alumnae has made it possible for NCCROW to build the library and archives, offer grants for research, and bring in nationally acclaimed speakers and writers. NCCROW's first endowed fund was established by the class of 1930 in celebration of their sixtieth anniversary. Willinger was sharing the news of this $10,000 gift with Peggy McIntosh, associate director of the Wellesley Center for Research on Women, when McIntosh received a call notifying her of her Center's first $1 million endowment. Instead of dampening Willinger's spirits, as McIntosh worried it would, the news brought Willinger to a new awareness of women's giving potential. The increased attention to engaging stakeholders in NCCROW's mission resulted in an array of endowments helping to make NCCROW one of the leading centers for research on women in the country.[38] Perhaps at no time was support more welcome than in 2005, when the first floor of Caroline Richardson Hall was inundated with floodwaters following Hurricane Katrina. The M. B. and Edna Zale Foundation called with an offer to restore the Seltzer-Gerard Reading Room, and the Society of Southwest Archivists, as well as the National Endowment for the Humanities, provided grants for the remediation of library and archival materials.

At the same time, not everyone associated with the College has supported NCCROW. A number of alumnae and students simply are not committed to the mission of the Center, while others have feared that NCCROW might become stronger than the College itself and, like the Pembroke Center for Research on Women and the Ann Ida Gannon Center for Women and Leadership (Mundelein College), become the only remnant remaining. The 1999 reincarnation of Radcliffe College as the Radcliffe Institute for Advanced Study, a consortium of the four existing research centers, did little to assuage this fear. In fact, this apprehension almost proved prescient when, in 2005, the University shuttered Newcomb College as part of the University's Renewal Plan following Hurricane Katrina. Only through the combined efforts of alumnae and students did the H. Sophie Newcomb Memorial College Institute emerge with NCCROW as one of its departments.

A sentiment persists that women's centers, and the struggle for women's equality, are no longer relevant to the lives of young women. Yet new campus-based women's centers are established each year. Many, like the Newcomb College Institute, are assuming the role of earlier women's colleges in providing a place where women faculty and staff serve as mentors, and where women's ideas, scholarly achievements, advocacy, organizing, and friendships are allowed to develop unfettered. Centers now emerging have the benefit of the experiences and visions of those who have come before them, several professional associations (the National Council for Research on Women and the National Women's Studies Association–Women's Center division), and important critical resources to help guide the way.[39]

The long and difficult conversations and debates among the Newcomb faculty, students, alumnae, and administrators over the mission and goals of the Newcomb Women's Center created an outline that, more than thirty years later, has been realized. The Newcomb College Center for Research on Women is unique among the seventy-some campus-based centers of the National Council for Research on Women, not only for its focus on women in the South, but also because of its fourfold mission to preserve, document, produce, and disseminate knowledge about women. Perhaps most importantly, NCCROW is distinctive among research centers in its continuing efforts to bring traditional-age undergraduate students into the mission of NCCROW through teaching and course projects, grants for research, opportunities for students to work on programs and projects with NCCROW faculty and staff, and collaborations between NCCROW and student organizations.

NCCROW thus continues and expands Newcomb's historical mission to educate women by providing students with the resources and opportunities to become educated *about* women. NCCROW supports the mission of Tulane University, a major research university, by bringing together students, faculty, and visiting scholars in the production and dissemination of new knowledge about women.

NOTES

1. James F. Davidson to the Newcomb Executive Committee, February 8, 1972, Joseph Cohen Papers, Box 9 (hereafter cited as JC), Newcomb Archives, Newcomb College Center for Research on Women (hereafter cited as NA NCCROW).

2. James F. Davidson to Professor John Clemmer, Chairman, University Senate Committee on Physical Facilities, Subject: Proposal for Use of the Upper Floor of Caroline Richardson Dining Hall, September 25, 1972, JC, Box 9, NA NCCROW.

3. University Center Governing Council memoranda to University Senate Committee on Physical Facilities, Dean of Newcomb College, *Tulane Hullabaloo*, n.d., Newcomb Women's Center Papers (hereafter cited as NWC-P), NA NCCROW. Resolution passed November 9, 1972.

4. "Davidson Defends Proposed Lounge," *Tulane Hullabaloo*, December 1, 1972.

5. James F. Davidson to David Deener, Provost, June 11, 1973, NWC-P, 1972–74; James F. Davidson to Dr. Clarence Scheps, Executive Vice President, October 9, 1973, NWC-P, NA NCCROW.

6. "Proposal for a Newcomb College Educational Center for Women," Joseph Cohen to James Davidson, August 7, 1973, JC, Box 9 (hereafter cited as Cohen Proposal), NA NCCROW.

7. James F. Davidson to Committee on Caroline Richardson Hall, November 16, 1973, NA NCCROW.

8. Announcement sent to University Relations, July 2, 1974, "Newcomb Women's Center Fund Drive," NWC-P, NA NCCROW.

9. Newcomb Women's Center Committee, 1974–75, NWC-P, NA NCCROW.

10. U.S. Census Bureau, *Statistical Abstract of the United States: 2000*, www.census.gov/.

11. "Public Affairs Report," *Bulletin of the Institute of Governmental Studies, University of California, Berkeley* 14, no. 6 (December 1973) (regarding the *Report on Higher Education* March 1971), Wendy Delery Papers (hereafter cited as WD), NA NCCROW.

12. Linda Eisenmann, *Higher Education for Women in Postwar America, 1945–1965* (Baltimore: Johns Hopkins University Press, 2006), 180–82; Mariam K Chamberlain, ed., *Women in Academe: Progress and Prospects* (New York: Russell Sage Foundation, 1988), 63.

13. Public Law 78–3346 regarding World War II education benefits states that "to be eligible, an individual must have served on active duty between September 16, 1940 and October 6, 1946. An individual was entitled to 1 year of full-time training plus periods equal to the time on active duty, up to a maximum of 48 months. . . . VA paid educational institutions a maximum of $500. a year for full-time tuition, books, fees and other training costs" (www.gibill2.va.gov/ "Ask a Question").

14. The Radcliffe Institute for Independent Study was renamed the Bunting Institute in 1978 to honor Mary Ingraham Bunting, and in 1999 renamed the Radcliffe Institute Fellowships Program (see www.radcliffe.edu/fellowships) ("History of the Fellowship Program").

15. See www.umich.edu/~cew.

16. www.radcliffe.harvard.edu/schles/index.php ("About the Library").

17. Chamberlain, *Women in Academe,* 85.

18. Catharine R. Stimpson, *Women's Studies in the United States: A Report to the Ford Foundation,* with Nina Kressner Cobb (New York: Ford Foundation, 1986). See also, for Wellesley College, www.wcwonline.org/ ("Who We Are").

19. In 1966, courses on women were offered for the first time in the United States. Of the three courses offered, one of them was taught by Cathy Cade and Peggy Dobbins at the New Orleans Free School (Marilyn Boxer, "For and about Women: The Theory and Practice of Women's Studies in the United States," *Signs* 7, no. 3 [1982]: 663).

20. Cohen Proposal.

21. Ibid. The Colloquium involved more than ten faculty members who provided an overview of the scholarship on women in their discipline or discussed a topic such as women's rights.

22. To Joe from Jean, n.d. (handwritten, then typed for distribution to committee members), "Women's Center Proposal," JC, Box 9, NA NCCROW.

23. Ibid.

24. The proposal was submitted by Florence Andre, Mary Dott, Meneve Dunham, and Edward Morse on April 12, 1975 ("Women's Center Committee Meeting Minutes," WD, NA NCCROW).

25. To Advisory Committee of the Women's Center from F. Andre, M. Dott, M. Dunham, E. Morse, April 21, 1975, "Women's Center Committee Meeting Minutes," WD, NA NCCROW.

26. The May 28, 1975, minutes of the Women's Center Committee state that a "revised draft of the original proposal" written by the University Development Office would be submitted to foundations and corporations for funding (JC, Box 9, NA NCCROW).

27. Kathryn H. Brooks, "The Women's Center: The New Dean of Women?" *Initiatives* 51 (1988): 17–21; Jodi Wetzel Clevenger, "Women's Centers: The Frameworks," *Initiatives* 51 (1988): 11–16; Florence Andre, "Many Visions/Twenty Years," NCCROW Anniversary Panel, Newcomb College Center for Research on Women, New Orleans, March 15, 1996 (also on the panel: Elaine Spurlin Tomlinson Corum, Alice Maxfield, and Beth Willinger), NWC-P, NA NCCROW.

28. James F. Davidson to Florence Andre, July 9, 1974 (Proposal for Newcomb Education Center for Women), NWC-P, NA NCCROW.

29. *Womantalk,* November 1975, WCP-P, NA NCCROW.

30. *Tulane Hullabaloo,* January 1977, NWC-P.

31. "Director, Newcomb Women's Center," n.d., NWC-P.

32. Anna Many was the first woman to serve as dean of Newcomb College, 1951–53. She was promoted from her position as counselor to women.

33. Beth Willinger Papers, NA NCCROW, nonprocessed; and recollections of the author.

34. "Resolutions of the Board of Administrators of the Tulane Educational Fund Adopted on November 19, 1987 Regarding the Reorganization of Newcomb College and the College of Arts and Sciences."

35. Beth Willinger, ed. *Katrina and the Women of New Orleans.* December 2008. (New Orleans: Newcomb College Center for Research on Women, 2008). Also "NCCROW" Fact Sheets," http://tulane.edu/nccrow.

36. Newcomb College Center for Research on Women Self-Study, 1996–97, 40, NA NCCROW.

37. Editors' note: In 2009, the name of the Women's Studies Program was changed to Gender and Sexuality Studies and the office moved to Fortier Hall.

38. In 2009, NCCROW received the Lifetime Achievement Award from the National Council for Research on Women, only the eighth center to receive this award.

39. Most notably Sharon L. Davie, University and College Women's Centers.

The Newcombus Ball held in Josephine Louise House, 1930. This was the most exclusive of all Carnival balls as only JL residents could take part. The "king" of Newcombus chose his queen, and half of the girls became perfect "gentlemen."

Chapel service led by graduating seniors, ca. 1950s. Prior to the construction of Myra Clare Rogers Memorial Chapel in 1976, chapel was held in a basement room of Newcomb Hall that was adorned with a wall mural painted by Newcomb art professor Xavier Gonzalez.

Homecoming court, ca. 1950s. Newcomb's status as a coordinate college held special appeal to students who wanted to take part in those activities and traditions of both a coeducational institution and a women's college.

The Daisy Chain, 1966. The Daisy Chain tradition was begun in 1909 and continues today as members of the junior class weave daisies through vines in the early-morning hours of commencement and then, wearing white dresses, form two aisles for the passage of the seniors, members of the faculty, and members of the fifty-year class who return as alumnae to again receive recognition from their alma mater.

The 2001 senior class speaker, Amanda Leiker, and class president, Mara Karlin (*right*), with the diploma of the University. The two senior-class dignitaries wear the brown academic gowns of Newcomb College, which are embroidered in blue each year with the date.

A coeducation classroom, ca. 1960s. Coeducation began between Newcomb and the College of Arts and Sciences in 1911, when men gained access to Newcomb's courses in music. By the early 1970s, all Newcomb and A&S courses were open uniformly to women and men.

Centennial Celebration, 1986. Students hold balloons reading "JL Newcomb—The Spirit Lives On" in celebration of the one-hundredth anniversary of the H. Sophie Newcomb Memorial College.

Spring Arts Festival Committee members publicize their event on a New Orleans streetcar, 1991. As one of the annual activities sponsored by the Newcomb College Senate, Spring Arts features the works of student and alumnae artists and writers.

The Newcomb Dance Company twenty-fifth anniversary performance, 2010. The Dance Club began at Newcomb in the 1940s under Frances B. Bush, continued under the direction of Minnette L. Starts (NC 1950), and expanded to become the Newcomb Dance Company in 1984. The Company is an integral part of the Newcomb Dance Program that offers a BA and BFA in dance and regularly sponsors residencies and master classes with nationally acclaimed guest artists. Photo by Tulane University, Paula Burch-Celentano.

The Class of 1928 at the 1953 Alumnae Association banquet. Posing in their period costumes for their class stunt are alumnae identified in the *Tulanian* as follows: *front row (left to right):* Kathryn Hanley, Robbie Lang Lloveras, and Villa East Cox; *back row:* Dorothy Daspit, Katherine Clement Koerner Jr., Mary Rollins, Edith Fasterling McGee, Sarah Thorpe Ramage, Audry Bate Stephens, and Esther Brandao McDill.

The Class of 1937 views their thirtieth reunion through rose-colored glasses at the Newcomb Alumnae Association's 1967 banquet.

Newcomb Alumnae Association banquet, 1972. From the time of its founding in 1891 to the present day, the Newcomb Alumnae Association has held a yearly banquet. Each reunion class also holds its own individual celebratory event.

Newcomb Alumnae Board meeting held in the faculty lounge of Newcomb Hall, 2000. *Back row (left to right):* Margee Gandolfo Farris (NC 1951); Winifred Kelly Delery (NC 1949); Carolyn Shaddock Woosely (NC 1971); Lizzie Horchow Routman (NC 1986); Irene Siragusa Phelps (NC 1975); Nancy McDaniel Galkowski (1980); Amy Burr (NC 1993); Maryanne Graham Hoskins (NC 1995); Ann Salzer (NC 1978); *middle row:* Andrea Arons Huseman (NC 1982); Martha McCarty Kimmerling (NC 1963); Valerie Greenberg, Newcomb dean; Sue Bernie (NC 1972); *front row:* Cassie Steck Worley (NC 1985); Heather Pelofsky Rittenberg (NC 1989); Jaimee Hongola Carreras (NC 1994); Paula Teles Picker (NC 1968). From its inception, the Newcomb Alumnae Association has been active in sponsoring programs and activities to advance student learning and foster student-alumnae partnerships.

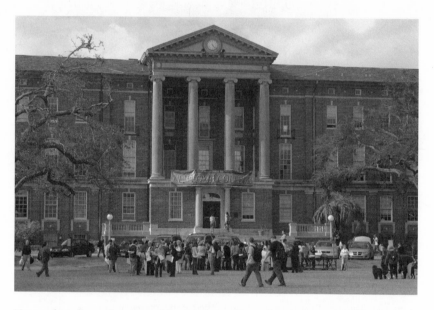

Newcomb students, alumnae, and faculty meet in front of Newcomb Hall to rally in protest of the 2005 merger of Newcomb College and Tulane College as Newcomb-Tulane College. Photo by Tulane University, Paula Burch-Celentano.

Forum sponsored by the Newcomb/Tulane Task Force of the Tulane Board of Administrators to hear views on enhancing Newcomb's name and legacy in the aftermath of its closing. *On stage from left*: Paul Barron, Tulane law professor; Yvette Jones, senior vice president for external affairs; Linda Smith Wilson (NC 1957); Daryl Berger (L 1972); Jeanne Olivier (NC 1975); Richard Schmidt (E 1966); Sybil Favrot (NC 1956); and Carol Downes Cudd (NC 1959). Photo by Tulane University, Paula Burch-Celentano.

Students and alumnae line up to express their views in favor of retaining Newcomb College as the women's coordinate college at the Forum, January 27, 2006. Speaking at the microphone is Mignon Faget (NC 1955). Photo by Tulane University, Paula Burch-Celentano.

A 2011 gender and sexuality studies class meets in the Seltzer-Gerard Reading Room housing the Newcomb Archives and Nadine Vorhoff Library of the Newcomb College Center for Research on Women. The first women's studies class was offered in 1972, and the major adopted in 1990.

Inaugural Newcomb Scholars Class of 2013. The first group of students accepted to the Newcomb Scholars Program pose in front of Gibson Hall, 2009. *Back row (left to right):* Taylor Geiger, Mariah Bullock, Frances Roche, C. Grace Sprehn, Kelsey Moran, Haley Ade, Briah Fischer; *middle row:* Alexa Schwartz, Amelia Conrad, Nicolette Guillou, Gisele Calderon, Jackie Schornstein, Katherine Ryan, Katie Weaver; *front row:* S. Rebecca Chen, Julia Chen, Melanie Harris, Meagan Knowlton, Victoria Troeger, Alexandra Yarost. Photo by Tulane University, Sally Asher.

Daisy Chain at the Under the Oaks award ceremony, Dixon Hall, 2011. *Left to right:* Christine Remby, Suzannah Schneider, Amy Holiday, Margaret Francez, Christina McLennan, Miranda Larsen, MaryKate Romagnoli, Emily Cardarelli, Laura Cannon, Taylor Geiger, Cassady Adams, Shannon Williams, Amy Leonard, Mary Penn, Katie Weaver, Julia Chen, Ariel Noffke, Katie Lucky-Heard.

III

LIVES

"W hen I finally got to Paris, I was disappointed because it was not like New Orleans," Ann Quin Fournet (NC 1952) wrote as she recalled her life's passages in a Newcomb College reunion survey.[1] For Fournet, as for generations of students speaking to one another across the boundaries of time and space, New Orleans and Newcomb were linked as one of the high points of life. For many alumnae, the College and the city represented a period of their past that held the privilege of thought and the colorful complexity of a city culturally rich yet economically poor. From Tulane president William Preston Johnston's first appreciation that the modern languages of the city should be emphasized to the present-day appreciation of the opportunities in service learning, the symbiotic relationship of the College and the city has been inscribed in course work, discussed at every turn, and folded into the consciousness of the College community. A 1930 pamphlet written to attract prospective students asked, "What special advantages has Newcomb to offer?" The answer was, "The City of New Orleans . . . one of the most interesting cities in the world . . . [and] one of the few cities of America with a distinct and unique personality."[2]

Just as New Orleans' rich cultural traditions and diversity have been used to lure students and faculty to Newcomb, so, too, has the College been a vital force in influencing the culture of the city. One can readily find something of Newcomb's giving back to its hometown by looking to the prestigious *Times-Picayune* Loving Cup award, offered to "residents who have worked unselfishly for the community without expectation of public acclaim or material reward." Since 1901, ten of the twenty-nine women who have been selected as recipients of the award have had a Newcomb College education. One of these was Rosa Keller, who entered Newcomb in 1928. In1953, Keller was the first woman to be appointed to the Public Library Board, and was largely responsible for the desegregation of the city's public library system. She also stretched both the city and Newcomb by exercising a strong hand in the desegregation of Tulane.[3] One of the most recent recipients, Ruthie Jones Frierson (NC 1962), formed "Citizens for One Greater New Orleans" in the aftermath of Hurricane Katrina. The *Times-Picayune* described this group as "the engine of the region's recovery" for organizing successful campaigns to consolidate levee board districts and reduce the seven municipal assessors to one.[4] Anne Milling (NC 1962), who was awarded the Loving Cup in 1995, was responsible for establishing another of the city's major hurricane recovery organizations, "Women of the Storm," bringing many U.S. Congress members to New Orleans and the Gulf Coast to educate them about the area's needs for greater federal funding.[5]

The lives of the women who appear in this volume represent but a few of the more than twenty thousand women who would benefit from Mrs. Newcomb's desire to "advance the cause of female education in Louisiana." By and large, the alumnae whose contributions are documented in this section have spent all or most of their adult lives in the city. They alone justify Mrs. Newcomb's "deep personal sympathy with the people of New Orleans," which was, with Johnston's influence, one of the reasons she chose to locate her memorial within Tulane University.[6]

Making a College Culture for Women

New Orleans also accommodated Mrs. Newcomb's "cautious generosity." Her initial donation allowed for the purchase of just a single building. New Orleans, then the eleventh-largest city in the United States, had a population large enough and affluent enough to have young women who could spend their days in learning rather than labor, and who would not require boarding. In this way, Newcomb College was established as a day school and differed appreciably from the residential women's colleges such as Agnes Scott, Vassar, or Mount Holyoke that were built in remote areas and were, by necessity, self-contained campus communities.

The recruitment of students from out of town also initially was viewed warily by Newcomb president Brandt Dixon, who was uncertain of the quality of instruction that would be offered by this "experiment" in women's education. The success of the special students in art, and the strength of the first eight students who earned the baccalaureate degree in 1890, made Dixon "greatly interested in the high schools of this and adjoining states" as feeder schools for sending well-prepared students to Newcomb. To accommodate these out-of-town students, he oversaw the donation of Mrs. Newcomb's additional gift for the first College residence, Josephine Louise House, three years after the move to the Washington Avenue campus in 1891.[7] Students by this time numbered 188, with just twenty coming from outside New Orleans and of these, only six from outside Louisiana, primarily from Mississippi and Texas.[8] Dixon's 1897 tour of "important schools" in the "Gulf states . . . asking for co-operation in building a great women's college for the South" led to an even greater need for campus housing.[9] Another residential house, "The Gables," was purchased with this purpose in mind. In 1901, with the death of Mrs. Newcomb, her home became a third campus residence known as "Newcomb House." Shortly after, in 1903–4, two other houses were added as campus residences, providing what Dixon described as "a total capacity for about one hundred inmates."[10] So the dream of Newcomb as more than a city college was born early, even though, by 1917, residence hall students comprised about one-fourth of the total student body, not more than forty students in any given year.

For most students, then, the responsibilities of family life and the influence of family members continued to take precedence over collegiate life.[11] An amusing example of parental consideration of a daughter's proper role can be found in a letter to Mr. Durel (chair, French department) from Ruth Dreyfous (NC 1923) requesting special arrangements be made for her to take a mandatory College exam required for her reenrollment in fall semester: "Father has purchased a machine up here [Chicago] and expects me to drive them to Atlantic City. We cannot leave here until the second of September and it will break up the families' [sic] summer plans entirely if I have to go home [New Orleans] the early part of the month. Please try to let me have the special examine [sic] for not only would I appreciate it but likewise Mother and Father would be greatly relieved."[12]

Mr. Durel responded by asking Miss Dreyfous to decide herself the importance of academics. Despite the continuing pull by family and community on the loyalty of Newcomb students, a student culture began to take shape. Dixon reported that the move to the Washington Avenue campus in 1891 prompted a burst of "new aspirations" and "desires to assume the manners and practices found in the established colleges. The class of 1891 decreed that their colors, bronze and blue, should become the College colors, and it was so."[13] Memorial services commemorating Sophie's birth and death, as requested by Mrs. Newcomb, also quickly became traditions linking students to the campus. May Day, Gym Night, Big Sisters, Spring Arts Festival, and "Little Commencement" became other rituals of the academic year.[14]

Student organizing exhibited a second burst in 1909. With the court case contesting Mrs. Newcomb's will settled in favor of the College, the future was secured. Pamela Tyler's essay attributes to three members of the class of 1909—all New Orleanians—the creativity and leadership in forming several activities that would be the foundation of student life for years to come. Perhaps the greatest creation of this period was the establishment of the quarterly literary magazine, the *Newcomb Arcade*, named after the students' favorite building connecting College Hall and the Academy (high school). In the *Arcade*, students reported on the books they were reading, current affairs, and the events of the College and alumnae. They also wrote stories, essays, and poems, and designed the block prints for which Newcomb artists became well known.[15] In a very real sense, within the *Newcomb Arcade* as a literary magazine and the actual Arcade as a place they "owned," the students created ways of imprinting their own social and intellectual engagement onto the landscape of the College.[16]

The Class of 1909 was responsible for establishing the 1909 Prize, which continued for nearly one hundred years as the highest award bestowed upon a senior by the College. The popular Daisy Chain tradition also appears to trace back to 1909,[17] as does the founding of the national honor society Phi Beta Kappa, with two Newcomb students admitted in the next year.[18] At Newcomb in general, the number and variety of student activities increased over the following years. Newcomb students sponsored all-women dances, presented plays, worked as artists designing the graphics for University-wide publications and invitations for many events in the city, participated in athletic events, and formed clubs around their course work. In their own student government, they were required to vote some thirty years before this privilege would be given to women in society at large.

Chapters of national sororities also arose quickly at Newcomb. Pi Beta Phi came first in 1891; Alpha Omicron Pi, 1898; Chi Omega, 1900; Kappa Kappa Gamma, 1904; Phi Mu and Alpha Delta Pi, 1906. Nah Sukham, a local sorority was founded in 1908, likely as a society for Jewish students who were excluded from membership in the predominantly Christian national sororities.[19] Subsequent early sorority chapters include Kappa Alpha Theta in 1914; and

Alpha Epsilon Phi, which absorbed Nah Sukham in 1916.[20] Dixon allocated five rooms in the basement of the main building for the use of the sororities and was pleased with their conversion "into charming society homes."[21] But the sorority house as a residential "home" to members, and as a symbol of the prominence of the Greek system in campus social life, never materialized at Newcomb, even in the move to Broadway. In 1919, Newcomb administrators and faculty moved to abolish sororities, a not unusual step among college administrators nationally, who often opposed the sororities' policies of exclusion. Newcomb administrators quietly yielded to the collective protest of the sororities and then withheld any official recognition of Greek life for more than forty years when a description of the work of the Panhellenic Council as "the governing body of nine sororities on campus" appeared in a College publication.[22]

Numerous explanations exist as to why no more than a few sorority members have been permitted, even in the twenty-first century, to live in sorority houses. One explanation points to city blue laws prohibiting unrelated women from living together as a means of preventing the development of brothels. Evidence suggests, however, that the strongest opposition to the sorority house as a college residence came from the University administration.[23] The outcome, whether or not intended, was that Newcomb students who have lived together in the residence halls, regardless of sorority affiliation, had a shared experience that served to disrupt some of the cliquishness often associated with membership in Greek societies.

In general, early boarding students had greater restrictions than their New Orleans classmates. While the majority of nonboarding students were quite free to come and go as permitted by their parents, residence hall students were held to a strict schedule: Rising bell at 6:30 a.m.; Breakfast, 7:15; Chapel 8:45; Lunch 12:00; Dinner 5:30 p.m.; Study hour 7:00; and Lights-out at 10:15. Special permission was required for a resident to leave the dorm, and other rules intended for her "proper care and security" were strictly enforced. Permission to go out or to receive callers was given only for Friday evenings, and only then when the women would be in the "company with a suitable chaperone." Rules changed very little over the first forty years and grew in number as infringements took place. For example, permission from parents was extended to cover the occasions "to remain all night with friends, to go swimming, and to go in a boat."[24] Curfews remained in place until 1969.

The initial construction of three buildings on Newcomb's Broadway campus in 1919 included Josephine Louise Residence Hall, which was designed to house approximately two hundred students.[25] The next residence halls to be built were Doris Hall, named for Doris Zemurray and constructed in 1925, and Warren House, named for Warren Newcomb and constructed in 1927. Domesticity was institutionalized in Doris, which was designed for students of "moderate means" who were willing "to help reduce the cost of their college education by co-operative effort," such as working in the dining room or answering the telephone.[26]

As outsiders to the New Orleans social establishment, boarding students founded their own masked ball, one "even more exclusive than the most exclusive of Carnival organizations, in so far as only resident students take part." During the event, held on the Friday evening preceding Mardi Gras, the "king" of the Newcombus Carnival Ball chose his queen, and "half of the girls bec[a]me perfect gentlemen."[27]

The *Register* for 1928–29 announced a new policy by the Board of Administrators that required residence in the College dormitories of all Newcomb students not living in the New Orleans area.[28] As the rule applied only to female students and limited their number, some alumnae and faculty thought the policy a deliberate attempt to maintain Tulane as a university for men, or an unspoken determination to keep a two-to-one male-to-female undergraduate ratio. Not until 1986 did the number of undergraduate females equal the number of males.[29]

Beginning around 1940, Newcomb was forced to address why a number of out-of-town students were refused admission. In some years, more than two hundred applicants were turned away, prompting Tulane University president Rufus Harris to pronounce: "The question is no longer whether Newcomb can afford to construct additional dormitory facilities, but whether we can afford not to do so."[30]

In 1949, a fund-raising drive was begun for the construction of a new dormitory, with Newcomb alumnae targeted as the primary donors. This successful drive allowed the construction of Johnston Hall, named in honor of William Preston Johnston. Like Johnston, who had much earlier promoted the education of women as crucial to regional development, Dean Logan Wilson (1943–51) announced that the new building was an "investment in brains and character that would be good for the whole of the South."[31] He noted that "aside from the case to be made for more students, an increase in the proportion of resident students would result in a considerable improvement in the quality of our student body. Since we are not restricted to the immediate location in the admission of dormitory students we are able on the whole to get higher type individuals, as is specifically indicated by their higher average score on entrance examinations and by their higher scholastic average throughout their four years in college. . . . We still admit some local applicants who are known in advance to us to be very dubious college material."[32]

To a certain extent, local students shared this belief that the recruitment of out-of-town students would enhance the reputation of the College. Competition for limited campus housing raised Newcomb's admission standards and was one reason Newcomb students always considered themselves smarter than Tulane men. Another reason was the requirement begun in 1927 that candidates for the BA or BS degree take a comprehensive examination in their major field.[33] The same was never required of A&S seniors. Lastly, beginning in 1948, Newcomb required College Entrance Board Examinations for admission, a policy not adopted by A&S until 1956.[34]

The construction of Johnston Hall (1950) was followed by that of New Doris (1958) and Butler (1963, named for Newcomb dean Pierce Butler), increasing the available space for boarding students. A "new air-conditioned dining room building," Caroline Richardson Hall, was completed in 1958.[35] During this period of expansion, students living on campus increased in number from 400 to approximately 2,400, marking "the beginning of a very radical change in the nature of the university" from "an institution with a definitely local orientation to one which attracts students from all parts of the country."[36]

In these, the baby-boom years, Newcomb slowly became a Louisiana school, rather than a New Orleans one, and then, a southern school. By the late 1960s, other southern states represented 40 percent of the enrollment, with the largest contingents coming from Florida and Texas, and slightly fewer (37 percent) from Louisiana.[37]

Beginning in the mid-1980s, Tulane again undertook an ambitious program of residence hall expansion.[38] This allowed Tulane to require all first- and second-year students (not just females) to live on campus unless approved to reside in their family's home in the New Orleans area. In the first decade of the twenty-first century, Tulane has fourteen residence halls, only one of which remains all-female—Josephine Louise Residence Hall.

The expansion of residence halls not only increased the proportion of out-of-town students relative to New Orleanians, it also allowed even local students to live in the dormitories and to gain the experience of a residential college. In the 1980s, a local student whose mother insisted she go away to college argued convincingly that going to Newcomb *was* going away from home because Tulane students came from all over the United States and also from other countries.[39] Today Tulane advertises that its students "travel farther to school than those of any other college or university in the nation (more than 75 percent of entering freshmen come to Tulane from farther than 500 miles away), making the student body geographically diverse—and socially and academically multidimensional."[40]

Inclusion and Exclusion

Still, Newcomb mirrored the elite of the city for most, if not all, of its history. As a private college situated within an affluent neighborhood and regulated in part by the belief systems of that community, Newcomb was neither founded on nor expected to serve democratic purposes. The College was not always open to even the most-qualified students, and policies of inclusion and exclusion based on race, class, religion, and age have taken years to come to the surface, and even longer to change.

The ability of families to forego the earnings of one of its members for four years, let alone provide for the costs of tuition, fees, books, and possibly boarding and long-distance transportation, meant that higher education itself very often was available only to the rich. A sampling of parents' occupations listed by Newcomb students in 1909 includes cotton broker, merchant, manufacturer, pastor, foreman, grocer, planter, physician, realtor, and inventor. The majority of these and other occupations listed would be considered professional or managerial positions and would place the families in the upper-middle to upper social classes.

The social standing of families often belied an underlying need. Dixon noted "the want of prosperity in the Southern country" and the need for the "lowest possible prices . . . for tuition, fees and board."[41] Ida A. Richardson, who referred Tulane president William Preston Johnston to Mrs. Newcomb, was the first to endow a scholarship in 1891.[42] By 1919, 76 students out of a student body of 518 (approximately 15 percent) held scholarships. In 1946, 18 percent of Newcomb students received full scholarships or tuition reductions. It is likely, however, that these early scholarships were used to assist prominent but impoverished families in sending their daughters to

Newcomb, rather than in providing educational opportunities to promising young women of the lower classes. Policies that waived tuition for the daughters of journalists and clergy, for example, helped to perpetuate the idea that Tulane, and by extension Newcomb, was a "rich man's school."[43]

Alumnae mention frequently, both in casual conversation and in oral history interviews, that they were able to afford the costs of attending Newcomb only because of this financial assistance. The stories of several of the scholarship recipients—Bessie Margolin, Sarah Towles, Mildred Christian, Dorothy Seago, and Rena Wilson—appear in this volume. Others, such as Sarah Reed Atkins (NC 1932), who established the Award for Study in Germany, have given back to the College in gratitude for the opportunities provided them through Newcomb scholarships.[44] In the late 1950s and again in the late 1990s, financial aid was expanded in large measure to implement academically selective admissions policies instituted by the Board of Administrators.[45] Funding would be used to attract students with high academic records, not only those with financial need.[46]

Opportunities for enrollment in any colleges of the University were unavailable to African Americans until the 1960s.[47] However, the Free Drawing School of Tulane University, established in 1884–85 by William and Ellsworth Woodward, was open to all "bread-winners" in the city with "the only restriction placed upon entrance" being "immaturity of age or incompatible duties." It is unknown if any persons of color attended these evening and Saturday classes, but catalogue descriptions appear to offer a thinly disguised and early challenge to Paul Tulane's restriction of a Tulane education to "white young persons." The Saturday classes were "intended principally to aid the teachers in the Public Schools" and were "attended by both women and men, chiefly by women."[48] The Free Drawing School ceased its offerings in 1894, but it seems fair to say that the Woodwards attempted to "take energetic steps for the enlightenment and improvement of all who aspired to a better intellectual condition" regardless of race or sex.[49]

While the desegregation of the University was formally achieved in 1963, many years of spirited discussions among the Administrators, the faculty, and students preceded the event.[50] Although conservative members of the College faculty and administration often declined to go along with the push for integration by national organizations such as the YWCA, the National Council of Jewish Women, and the League of Women Voters, there existed pockets of students and faculty who questioned the racial restrictions long before the decision to desegregate was made by the board.[51] New Orleanian Hilda Arndt (NC 1932), who attended Newcomb at the height of the Depression, noted that her psychology professors Dagmar Sunné and Dorothy Seago were active in promoting understanding between African Americans and whites, and in teaching about the Creoles of Color of New Orleans. These teachers took her to hear lectures by educated African Americans around the city, illustrating another benefit of being in New Orleans.[52] Shannon Frystak's essay on the lives of four Newcomb alumnae provides ample evidence that a sense of activism was nurtured at the College even as it was muted.[53] Dean Hubbard reported to the alumnae: "Although it [integration] broke sharply with tradition, it was greeted with undisguised relief by our faculty, which by a unanimous vote supported and commended the board for its action."[54]

In the fall of 1963, Deidre Dumas Labat (NC 1966) became the first African American to enter Newcomb. Labat, a New Orleanian, remembered her days at Newcomb as a lonely time, the cleaning staff being her primary lunch companions.[55] Labat went on to earn a PhD in biology and later became senior vice president for academic affairs at Xavier University of Louisiana. By 1966, the year she graduated from Newcomb, funding from the Rockefeller Foundation to encourage the enrollment of African Americans at Tulane had increased the number to forty-two.[56] Various other efforts by the University to increase diversity on campus have met with moderate success.[57] An Office of Multicultural Affairs was established in 1988 to sponsor student activities and provide support services to ensure the academic success of students of color. In 1990, Alpha Kappa Alpha became the first historically African American Greek letter sorority to be founded at Tulane. Thirteen years earlier, however, in 1977, a small group of Loyola students were granted a citywide charter of Delta Sigma Theta and invited several Newcomb students to become members. Delta Sigma Theta continues as a sorority serving the two campuses. In recent years, African American women also have joined the historically white sororities on campus. Membership of African American women in either historically white or black sororities, however, remains on average quite low. For example, among the approximately 1,300 women members of the Tulane Greek letter community in the 2010–11 academic year, only about 20 are African American. In 2006, Delta Xi Nu Multicultural Sorority was formed at Tulane and has approximately ten active members.[58]

In the first decade of the twenty-first century, approximately 10 percent of Tulane's undergraduate enrollment is African American and 80 percent

Caucasian.[59] Given that more than 60 percent of the city's population is African American, the perception persists among a large segment of the New Orleans community that the doors to the colleges of the University remain the prerogative of white upper-class women and men. The relative homogeneity of the student body coupled with the predominance of white males on the board appear only to strengthen this perception.[60] Women, and especially African Americans, remain distinct minorities among the faculty.

In contrast to segregationist policies regarding race, neither Newcomb nor Tulane had similar policies regarding religion. Dagmar LeBreton and Bobbie Malone experienced Newcomb's religious, though nonsectarian traditions as favorable to campus life and intellectual growth. Invitations to religious leaders to participate in College events helped to shape a small part of the early and continuing history of the College, though such invitations were more likely to be accepted by Protestant and Jewish leaders than Catholic ones. Dixon observes that the prelate of the Roman Catholic Church declined the invitation to participate in the dedication of the Chapel in 1895, noting that "it was against the policy of the church he represented to accept such invitations."[61]

Although "chapel services" were held every morning from 8:15 to 8:30 and originally were mandatory for students living on campus, attendance soon became voluntary. Daily services continued until at least the late 1930s, but very little else can be found in the records about religion at the College. Faculty minutes report only the need for chapel readings of various types and a preference for the same faculty member to serve as reader over a whole semester. Students from the 1940s and 1950s most often remembered the murals painted by the renowned artist and Newcomb art professor Xavier Gonzalez in the basement classroom where the services were held in Newcomb Hall.[62]

Policies of the Catholic Church and the existence of alternative educational opportunities for the city's Catholic girls and young women may have limited early interest in Newcomb among Catholics. Education in New Orleans beyond high school, for example, was offered in scattered years at Ursuline Academy (founded in 1727, with a day school founded in 1867), Academy of the Sacred Heart (established 1887), and St. Mary's Dominican College (established 1910). There existed also some bias among Newcomb's students and alumnae. As one alumna asked when she heard of a new Catholic group on campus, "Has Newcomb ceased to be undenominational?"[63] The ever-energetic Florence Dymond (NC 1891), Newcomb's longtime representative to the Tulane board, also felt the need to be reassured that the new club was "not violative [sic] of any of Newcomb traditions." Though she was "for religious tolerance, being a Unitarian from youth," she felt the need to state that there was some danger since "that particular religion [Catholic] grants nothing to other religions."[64]

Dean Pierce Butler, on the other hand, replied that the activities of the club should be interpreted favorably without reservation since "our Catholic population has been growing (in spite of the outspoken hostility of some of those formerly in charge, like Archbishop Janssen) until Catholics now outnumber others. This is surely gratifying testimony to the fact that this most conservative body of the public no longer regards Newcomb as a danger to sound religion or good morals."[65]

The early Newcomb student body was predominantly Protestant, while Jewish students were always among the student leaders and came from a wide cross-section of the city's population, from the most affluent homes to orphanages. In the period following World War I, the women's colleges of the Northeast, with the exception of Barnard, developed policies limiting the number of Jewish students.[66] No such policies existed at Newcomb. In 1919, 12 percent of Newcomb students reported their religion to be Jewish, compared to 20 percent Catholic and 62 percent Protestant. Ten years later, the enrollment of Jewish students slipped to 10 percent, but by 1939, nearly 14 percent of students declared their religion to be Jewish.[67] Tulane's various efforts to recruit students from outside the city and region had the effect of encouraging the enrollment of Jewish students from the Northeast as well as Florida and Texas, as Bobbie Malone attests. Malone's essay begins with her guidance counselor suggesting Newcomb as a college favorable to Jewish students and continues as a story unveiling numerous sites of learning and sharing between Newcomb and Tulane and the New Orleans Jewish community. In the past several decades, College and University administrators often mentioned with a sense of pride that Tulane students always have been one-third Catholic, one-third Jewish, and one-third Protestant. This claim appears to be an "urban myth," however, as students' religious preferences remain largely undocumented. A rare report from 1946–47 lists the religious affiliation of the study body as follows: "Baptist 61; Catholic 252; Christian 11; Christian Science 10; Congregational 1; Episcopal 140; Hebrew 159; Greek Orthodox 1; Latter Day Saints 1; Unitarian 8; Anglican 1; Disciples of Christ 1; No preference 7."[68] Only through sorority membership records was religious affiliation consistently documented.[69] Two of Newcomb's sororities—the already mentioned Alpha Epsilon Phi formed in 1916 and Sigma Delta Tau in 1955—were founded as Jewish national sororities. For a number of years, a separate "rush," or membership recruitment, was held for students wishing to join the traditionally Jewish sororities. A separate rush no longer exists, and religious crossover in membership between Jewish and Christian sororities has become common. For example, in 2010–11, a historically Jewish sorority elected a Christian woman to the presidency, while a historically Christian sorority elected a Jewish woman president.[70]

Another example of the complexities of inclusion and exclusion is centered in Newcomb's mission to educate women. The College was not always a place where, in the words of Sara Chapman, Newcomb dean (1983–85), "women come first."[71] Neither equity nor equality of women with men ranked highly. In 1920, when the Newcomb Alumnae Association applied for membership in the national Association of Collegiate Alumnae, they were denied because of the unequal treatment of women faculty: "One of our requirements is that there shall be equal pay for equal work as between men and women and that there shall be equal opportunity for women to advance to the higher positions. From what our Committee was able to learn about the policy at Sophie Newcomb, it is believed that this condition is not met."[72]

The Alumnae Association then made a series of recommendations concerning academic standards, and sent three to the Tulane Board of Administrators, two of which were ratified. None made mention of the discrepancy in pay and promotion between the women and men of the faculty.[73]

The first woman hired on the faculty of the Newcomb political science department, Jean Danielson, came from the Midwest in 1965 with new ideas about women's education. In the early 1970s, she organized a course for fifteen students that fostered an interdisciplinary approach to study the lives of women.[74] Danielson acted as part of a national movement that manifested itself at Newcomb in ways that opened doors for women in coeducational classes and graduate school programs, while closing other doors. One particular problem was the reticence of women to act as leaders in classes where they no longer dominated in numbers. Anthropology professor Arden King worried that his women students "deferred to men."[75]

This restrained participation on the part of women students, later defined as "a chilly climate," was quite different in women's colleges—whether an elite women's college of the Northeast, a southern women's college, or a

Catholic women's college—where there were more female role models and greater encouragement of women students' leadership skills.[76] Miller-Bernal has argued that the coordinate colleges offer women many of these same advantages.[77] This would be true, but not wholly so, at Newcomb. Until the 2006–7 academic year, the presence of Newcomb's own student government gave leadership roles to women students outside the classroom that they did not have in the larger University. However, as has been emphasized through much of this volume, Newcomb was a women's college, a coordinate college, and a coeducational college at different periods, and different times, and even to different students at the same time. As the late-twentieth-century college promotional literature stressed: "'How much will Newcomb College as a women's college affect my college experience?' It depends on you. For some students, Newcomb is the focal point of the college years, and their development is enhanced through significant involvement in Newcomb activities and leadership responsibilities. For others, the total University experience is more meaningful, and their involvement expands well beyond the college to University-wide contact and contribution. Maybe that's why some students say 'I go to Newcomb' and others claim Tulane as their alma mater."[78]

At least some University officials believed that the women students were not as bright as their male colleagues, as Clarence Mohr's essay in this volume points out. This belief was in direct opposition to what the Newcomb students themselves thought, and also in opposition to the many creative programs, successful alumnae, and contributions to the city and, ultimately, the nation that the College made, even in comparison to Tulane's male divisions. These perceptions rarely were cast in the open for discussion. Rather, as Tulane history professor Sylvia Frey found, there was "a subtle but pervasive subtext" of a "culture of gender inequality."[79] The initial presence of a small number of women did not change the maleness of the University environment, nor did the presence of a mass of women later produce a community of equals.

"The Interest and Devotion of Its Alumnae"

If the choice were theirs alone, any number of students would not have chosen either the College or the University, as Ida Kohlmeyer and Monique Guillory discuss. Rosa Keller, one of the Loving Cup recipients mentioned above, was another who was not so sure about Newcomb. After two years at the College, she finally convinced her parents to let her go away to Hollins College.[80]

However, for all these women and many others like them, Newcomb offered opportunities later in life. They found in the College a way to "return" again and again—as graduate students, as professors or members of the staff, as nontraditional-age "returning students," as community members involved with programs and public lectures offered by the College, and as alumnae connected by mail, reunions, and reunion surveys.

For some, Newcomb's presence created unprecedented employment opportunities. In 1900–1902, ten alumnae were counted among a Newcomb faculty of twenty-five. In 1909–10, seventeen Newcomb alumnae served on a faculty of forty-seven.[81] In part, this was to be expected as graduates of the College were among the best-educated people, women or men, of the city. During the period from World War I to the 1960s, Newcomb graduates continued to be represented in steady numbers of some five to seven faculty members every year. Even in the 1970s through the present, Newcomb alumnae among the faculty and staff have numbered at least four in any given year. Six of the essays included in this section touch upon the role of alumnae as members of the faculty or were written by those who eventually returned as faculty: Dagmar Renshaw LeBreton, Ida Kohlmeyer, Caroline Durieux, Mildred Christian, Tania Tetlow, and Monique Guillory.

The Alumnae Association was formed less than three years after the first class had graduated and has consistently provided a vehicle for alumnae to maintain affiliations made at the College. One of the first projects was the founding of the Newcomb Alumnae Loan Fund to lend "moderate sums of money to Newcomb students standing in need of such aid."[82] About 1909, the Newcomb Alumnae Association joined with the Tulane Alumni Association to establish an Alumnae Employment Bureau.[83] In more recent years, similar opportunities for Newcomb and Tulane students to connect with alumnae mentors and employers have been handled through an online network service monitored by the University Career Center. In addition, the Newcomb Alumnae Association and Newcomb Student Programs often cosponsor programs to facilitate networking between students and alumnae for both career information and advice.

Over the years, a host of publications by the Alumnae Association have connected Newcomb alumnae to one another.[84] Early Newcomb postings tended to focus on the lives of Newcomb artists, teachers, social workers, missionaries, lawyers, doctors, plantation owners, car dealers, antique store owners, and librarians. An astute Dionjsia de la Cruz Dawson (NC 1916) drew attention to the absence of information on mothering in 1935: "It is interesting to note the many fields of endeavor in which Newcombites are engaged, but I wonder why we who are engaged in the oldest and perhaps the most noble as well as stable of women's careers are never mentioned! Isn't it something to be rearing a family of seven children?"[85] Dawson's framing of the question exposes the dilemma posed by many women and the College that educated them. What was more important in the public presentation of self: family or work achievements?

By the 1970s, such questions became more focused when Adele Ramos Salzer (NC 1940) and Lou Hutson Finke (NC 1940) wrote to their classmates asking them to fill out "information sheets" about "yourself" your "children, grandchildren, offspring who attended Newcomb or Tulane . . . work or main interests, employment, hobbies, civic involvements, club involvements."[86] Alumnae were asking one another to define themselves through a broad array of activities, through movements between public and private selves.

The freedom to ask such questions had not always been afforded. When her parents made the College her only choice, Sylvia Sterne (NC 1954) was dismayed because "Newcomb was in the Victorian era. Newcomb was like a finishing school." An English major, Sterne wanted to take a course with Robert Lumiansky, a noted authority on Chaucer and a professor at A&S. She was denied this opportunity because of the possibility that Lumiansky might say curse words that young women should not hear. But she came to like that Newcomb offered a coeducational side. Slowly, too, she began to feel that Newcomb "had much higher academic standards than Tulane." By the time of her graduation, as she "started to get interested in what" she was "learning," she became "terribly sad": "Because I knew I was going to have to get married. And that was the way it was. You just knew. Your time comes. By the time you graduate, if you don't have a husband or a fiancé, your parents are not going to make your life easy. They are going to make your life miserable. . . . [There was] that kind of pressure, and it was on everyone [who was graduating]."[87]

Tensions concerned with the expected path for Newcomb graduates as charming wives and competent mothers reached a peak in the late 1960s and early 1970s. The questions designed by Salzer and Finke were different from those posed in earlier surveys in that they were explicitly born of the second wave of feminism. The class of 1940 would have been invited to hear

Simone de Beauvoir speak at the College in 1948.[88] The English translation of *The Second Sex* appeared in 1953 and launched new ideas about feminism and women's roles in society. In 1963, Betty Freidan published *The Feminine Mystique* based on a survey of her own Smith College classmates' lives. Quickly the popularization of such ideas spread via magazines such as *McCall's* and *Ladies' Home Journal,* which Salzer and Finke drew upon to construct their questionnaire.[89] Another source of guidance was a questionnaire designed by the National Commission on Working Women. The survey was entitled, "How Do *You* Feel about Working?"[90]

The questionnaires and their answers point to the fact that although Newcomb alumnae enjoyed the social status associated with being educated women, their education had little impact on their economic status, particularly before women in greater number entered the well-paying fields of law, medicine, and business. Nationwide, middle- or upper-middle-class jobs considered appropriate to educated women—nursing, teaching and secretarial work, or something related to the arts—gave them an income comparable to working-class wages, sometimes even below those wages.[91] In 1973, 23.5 percent of all Newcomb graduates from the Class of 1971 worked as teachers, and the same percentage worked as secretaries.[92]

Throughout the years, patterns of underemployment and ambiguity about women's education and working lives, whether as a mother or paid worker, were eased by the friendships that began at Newcomb. The Alumnae Reunion Surveys relate the importance of ongoing connections between alumnae and their classmates as well as the memories of the wisdom of their teachers.[93] Oftentimes alumnae fully realized the import of a Newcomb education only years after leaving the College.

Continuing Legacies

President Johnston's nineteenth-century goal of creating an educated workforce, especially of teachers, for the South is also documented in the alumnae publications. From Newcomb's earliest beginnings, graduates entered public, private, and parochial schools as teachers. In 1905, the Newcomb Alumnae Association organized a Free Night School for "poor servant girls and factory workers" that operated until 1911. Although Newcomb's School of Education was in existence for little more than ten years, from 1909 to 1921, countless Newcomb students pursued a straight academic program and became teachers.[94] The lives of many in this volume show that the reach of Newcomb-educated teachers continued well into the end of the twentieth century.

Newcomb alumnae also were instrumental in changing traditional notions *about* teachers. As Leslie Parr notes, Sarah Towles Reed changed the marriage bar against teachers only in that she was reinstated as a widow. It was not until 1936 that she was ready to the challenge the law requiring female teachers to sign contracts stating they were not married and would not marry. This challenge also was assumed by two other Newcomb alumnae, Mary Irvine (NC 1925) and Yvonne Crespo LaPrime (NC 1932). Irvine lost her case against the Ursuline Academy in 1926; LaPrime won her battle against the Orleans Parish School Board in 1936.[95]

Reed's efforts on behalf of teachers were recognized with the naming of both a New Orleans public high school and primary school in her memory. Another Newcomb alumna whose civic efforts were recognized by the naming of a New Orleans public school in her honor was Marion Pfeifer Abramson (NC 1925). In the early 1950s, Abramson began planning educational programming for public television. In 1957, she founded WYES, which more than fifty years later remains the primary public educational television station in New Orleans.[96]

Newcomb alumnae also were some of the first women to enter city government. Under Mayor deLesseps Morrison (1946–61), Lillie Nairne (NC 1917) served as head of the Department of Welfare, the first woman to head a city department, and Inez Crane Prendergast (NC 1949) served as director of the Upper Pontalba Building Commission, the first woman to direct a Non-Charter Agency. Mildred Fossier (NC 1935) followed Nairne as head of the Department of Welfare. In the 1970s, as director of the Parkway and Park Commission, Fossier became the first woman to serve as director of a City Boards and Commission department. The woman who followed Fossier in this position was Florence Schornstein (NC 1956), who served from 1982 to 1997.[97]

In 1954, the year the mayor-council form of government was adopted in New Orleans, Martha Gilmore Robinson (NC 1909) ran for a city council seat, the first woman to do so, and perhaps the first woman to run a campaign for any city office. She lost her bid for election as did Felicia Schornstein Kahn (NC 1948), who also made an early run for a council seat. It was not until 1986 that the first women were elected. Suzanne Haik Terrell (NC 1976) was the fourth woman elected to the New Orleans City Council (1994–99),[98] and the first woman elected commissioner of the Department of Elections and Registration for the State of Louisiana. In the 2010 mayoral race, Nadine Ramsey (NC 1977), a civil court judge for the Parish of Orleans, was the only woman candidate and only the second woman in recent history considered to be a serious contender for the position. Lindy Boggs (NC 1935) is likely the most well-known Newcomb alumna elected to public office, having served eight terms in the U.S. House of Representatives from 1973 to 1991, and then serving as ambassador to the Vatican from 1997 to 2001. Tania Tetlow's (NC 1992) essay in this section reveals one of Boggs's less official, but equally important roles—that of mentor. These are just a handful of the hundreds of Newcomb graduates who have been active in the political process in New Orleans. Many, like Felicia Kahn, who is discussed in Shannon Frystak's essay, have been actively involved in the League of Women Voters, the Committee of 21, and other political-action groups—assuming the "intended roles" that College administrators always envisioned for alumnae.

Newcomb-educated artists and writers have brought beauty and insight into the city in countless ways. As mentioned in the preface, Newcomb artists deserve a book of their own. Angela Gregory (NC 1925), daughter of Selina Bres Gregory, a well-known Newcomb potter, was one of the city's first female sculptors. Gregory sculpted the relief on the Criminal Court Building on Tulane Avenue, and also the statues of John McDonogh, and Bienville standing with a priest and Native American. Mary Lou Christovich (NC 1949), Sally Kittredge Reeves (NC 1965), Betsy Swanson (NC 1960), and Roulhac Toledano (NC 1960) have focused on the unique splendor of New Orleans' architecture and influenced the way New Orleanians think of their homes and their city. Among the city's writers, Betty Carter (NC 1931), with husband Hodding Carter, published the *Hammond Daily Courier*, one of the few newspapers to stand against Huey Long, and the *Delta Democrat-Times* in Greenville, Mississippi, which promoted civil rights through various editorials that won the paper a Pulitzer Prize in Editorial Writing in 1946. Returning to New Orleans, Betty promoted the work of numerous women writers and, indeed, encouraged the early work on this anthology. Shirley Ann Grau (NC 1950) remains one of two New Orleanians to win the Pulitzer Prize in Fiction. Grau, along with Sheila Bosworth (NC 1971) and the children's book author and illustrator Berthe Amoss (NC 1946), are among the writers whose works are explored in *Louisiana Women Writers* by scholars such as the historian Patricia Brady (NC 1965).[99]

To return to the idea of the reciprocity between the College and the city, other professionals found inspiration *from* New Orleans culture. Earl Retif describes how Durieux found the subjects of her satirical prints in her Uptown neighborhood; LeBreton's upbringing amidst the city's several languages led to her life's work with language; Kohlmeyer's residence in the city allowed her to return to Newcomb and discover a passion for art that established her as a nationally renowned artist. Christian, who wished to go away for graduate school but could not afford to, found in the University's coordinate system a way to achieve a graduate education. In doing so, she remained a Newcomb stalwart and influenced generations of Newcomb students as Emilie Griffin so poignantly describes.

In these and other more subtle ways, the College and the city influenced one another, leaving the legacies of achievement (and legacies of failure), but more importantly the legacies of continual learning. The lives of Newcomb alumnae form a memorial of their own, as well as a testament to Mrs. Newcomb's desire to ensure that the memory of one life, that of her daughter, Sophie, "would go on year by year doing good."[100] As she stated, "Such a memorial . . . [remains] better than statues or monuments."[101]

NOTES

1. Ann Quin Fournet, Reunion Survey, Class of 1952, NAC 176b, NA NCCROW.

2. *Newcomb College, Pictures and Practical Information, May, 1930:* 5 (hereafter cited as 1930 brochure), NA NCCROW.

3. Rosa Freeman Keller: A Legacy of Southern Activism, exhibit of the New Orleans Public Library, ca. 1996, http://nutrias.org/~nopl/exhibits/keller.htm.

4. "Post-Katrina Activist Gets TP Loving Cup," *New Orleans Times-Picayune,* February 18, 2007.

5. See Women of the Storm, www.womenofthestorm.net.

6. Josephine Louise Newcomb to Tulane Board of Administrators, October 11, 1886, quoted in Brandt V. B. Dixon, *A Brief History of the H. Sophie Newcomb Memorial College, 1887–1919* (New Orleans: Hauser Printing, 1928), 10.

7. Dixon, *Brief History,* 92.

8. *Catalogue, 1893–94* (Newcomb Announcement for 1894–95): 118–23.

9. Dixon, *Brief History,* 101.

10. Ibid., 128.

11. Lynn Gordon, *Gender and Higher Education in the Progressive Era* (New Haven: Yale University Press, 1990), 175–76.

12. Ruth Dreyfous student file, NA NCCROW.

13. Dixon, *Brief History,* 78.

14. Traditions file, Reference Files, NA NCCROW.

15. The history of the *Newcomb Arcade,* http://tulane.edu/nccrow/newcomb_archives/newcomb-arcade.cfm.

16. The reading community they formed can be explored through lists in the student records and the book reviews in the *Arcade.* The *Arcade* reviews show diverse reading, but a preponderance of titles by women authors.

17. Georgen Coyle to Martha Giordano and Margaret King, April 2, 1990, and other file clippings, "Customs–Daisy Chain," NA NCCROW.

18. Hortense Shlenker and Leah Herold were the two elected that year.

19. *Tulane Weekly,* November 25, 1908, 5.

20. Leslie Brown Shiffman, National Historian, Alpha Epsilon Phi Sorority, to Mary-Allen Johnson, March 6, 2010.

21. Dixon, *Brief History,* 133.

22. Ibid.; John P. Dyer, *Tulane: The Biography of a University, 1834–1965* (New York: Harper and Row, 1966), 159; *Newcomber 1970–71,* 22.

23. Dyer, *Tulane: The Biography of a University,* 160.

24. *Catalogue, 1901–2:* 26–27.

25. *Catalogue, 1918–19:* 4

26. *Catalogue, 1925–26:* 10. This followed an earlier experiment with a cooperative dormitory called the Newcomb House (*Newcomb Announcement 1924–25:* 10).

27. *Newcomb College, Pictures and Practical Information, May, 1930:* 25, NA NCCROW. "Newcombus" is a play on Comus, a very elite men's krewe.

28. *University Register, 1928–29:* 175–76.

29. Newcomb Admissions Committee Annual Report, Fall, 1979, Newcomb Admissions Committee Annual Report, Fall, 1981, F. Sheldon Hackney Papers, Box 23 (hereafter cited as FSH Papers), Admissions reports, Reference Files, NA NCCROW.

30. Quoted in Dyer, *Tulane: The Biography of a University,* 268. See also Extracts from the Report of President Harris to the Administrators of the Tulane Educational Fund, December 7, 1948.

31. Logan Wilson, "Newcomb in Balance: The Need and the Opportunity at the 'Start the Dorm' Dinner," Josephine Louise House, April 24, 1950, typewritten speech, Dean's Records, NA NCCROW.

32. Logan Wilson, Extracts from the Resolutions of the Board pertaining to Newcomb, NAC 008, December 16, 1948, NA NCCROW.

33. *Announcement 1926–27.* A handwritten note inside front bindery leaf verso notes that the requirement was added for graduation (*Announcement 1928–29:* 39–40).

34. Dyer, *Tulane: The Biography of a University,* 249.

35. Fields, ed., *Potpourri: An Assortment of Tulane's People and Places,* 135, 138–40; Dyer, *Tulane: The Biography of a University,* 268–69.

36. Dyer, *Tulane: The Biography of a University,* 269.

37. Report of the Dean of the H. Sophie Newcomb Memorial College, Session, 1967–68, Newcomb Dean's Records, Faculty Files, NAC 020, NA NCCROW.

38. Construction of residence halls at this time included Aron Residences, Mayer, Willow Residences, and Wall Residential College (2005). All were built as coed facilities.

39. Kristen Calonico to her mother, Beth Willinger, 1985.

40. Tulane University, "School Says: Admissions," www.entrpreneur.com/colleges/ugrad/1022808.html. See also Undergraduate Admission, "Scholarships & Aid," http://admission.tulane.edu/aid/index.php.

41. Dixon, *Brief History*, 171.

42. Tulane University of Louisiana, *Catalogue, 1890–91; Announcement, 1891–92:* 78.

43. Scholarship Records, Card Files, NA NCCROW; Dagmar LeBreton, Oral History interview, this volume.

44. Financial advisor for Sarah Reed Atkins to acting dean Beth Willinger, 1992.

45. Clarence L. Mohr and Joseph E. Gordon, *Tulane: The Emergence of a Modern University, 1945–1980* (Baton Rouge: LSU Press, 2001), 32.

46. These include: Dean's Honor Scholarships (the most prestigious with full tuition for four years, with approximately one hundred granted annually); Presidential Scholar Award; Distinguished Scholar Award; Founders Scholarship; Academic Achievement Award; and Community Service Scholarship (http://financialaid.tulane.edu/idxscholarships.htm).

47. LeBreton interview.

48. *Catalogue, 1887–88, Announcement for 1889–89:* 72–77.

49. Ibid., 72. Meghan Freeman correspondence with Beth Willinger, February 2011.

50. See Mohr and Gordon, *Tulane: The Emergence of a Modern University, 1945–1980,* for a lengthy discussion of the process of integrating the University.

51. For work with the YWCA, see the index to the *Newcomb Arcade*. The YWCA student organization was particularly active between 1910 and 1930.

52. Hilda Arndt, Manuscript notes, Biographical Files, NA NCCROW.

53. The Alumnae Class files also give a sense of this activism (see Class Agent Files, NAC 118 and 119, NA NCCROW).

54. John R. Hubbard, dean, *Newcomb Alumnae Newsletter* 12, no. 1 (Winter 1963):1.

55. Deidre Dumas Labat, Oral History interview by Joan Bennett, February 20, 1987, NA NCCROW.

56. Mohr and Gordon, *Tulane: The Emergence of a Modern University, 1945–1980,* 307.

57. Report from the Diversity Action Taskforce, Spring 2008, tulane.edu/liberal . . . /Appendix_5_SLA_Diversity_Task_Force_Report.doc.

58. Elizabeth Schafer, Director of Fraternity and Sorority Programs, to Beth Willinger, February 3, 2011.

59. Office of the Registrar, Tulane University, "Tulane University Profile," http://registrar.tulane.edu/enrollment_profiles/enrollment_profiles.

60. Tulane's most recent presidents, Eamon Kelly and Scott Cowen, made efforts to diversify the board by race, sex, and region by increasing the number of board members. The 2009–10 Board of Administrators is comprised of thirty-six members, ten of whom are women.

61. Dixon, *Brief History,* 95.

62. *Newcomb College: Pictures and Practical Information, May, 1930,* NA NCCROW. The first mention of religion appears in Faculty Minutes concerning Saturday examinations for Jewish students (see Faculty Minutes, May 16, 1906); Helen Lefkowitz Horowitz, *Alma Mater Design and Experience in the Women's Colleges from Their Nineteenth-Century Beginnings to the 1930s* [New York: Knopf, 1984], 259; and Barbara Miller Solomon, *In the Company of Educated Women: A*

History of Women and Higher Education in America [New Haven: Yale University Press, 1985], 143–44).

63. Mary Hewitt to Rufus Harris, December 9, 1937, Pierce Butler Vertical Files, University Archives, Howard-Tilton Memorial Library (hereafter cited as UAHT).

64. Florence Dymond to Pierce Butler, December 8 1937, Pierce Butler Vertical Files, UAHT.

65. Pierce Butler to Florence Dymond, December 7, 1937, Pierce Butler Vertical Files, UAHT.

66. Horowitz, *Alma Mater,* 259; Solomon, *In the Company of Educated Women,* 143–44.

67. Newcomb Matriculation Reports, 1919, 1929, 1939, NA NCCROW.

68. Registrar's Report, Newcomb College 1946–47, NA NCCROW.

69. Sorority records generally have been found to be thorough. For Newcomb, see Marianne Sanua, *Going Greek: Jewish College Fraternities in the United States, 1895–1945* (Detroit: Wayne State University Press, 2003), 181.

70. Elizabeth Schafer, Director of Fraternity and Sorority Programs, to Beth Willinger, February 3, 2011.

71. Newcomb College Convocation, August 1983.

72. *Newcomb Arcade* 13, no. 3 (April 1921): 208.

73. Ibid., 213–19.

74. Mary Ann Travis, "Women's Studies' Original Organizer," *Inside Tulane,* January 1, 2004. See also Jean Danielson, Biographical Files and Oral History Collection, NA NCCROW.

75. Arden King quoted in Newcomb College Committee on Excellence, August 16, 1966, Newcomb Dean's Records Faculty File, NAC 020, NA NCCROW.

76. Roberta M. Hall and Bernice Sandler, *The Classroom Climate: A Chilly One for Women?* Project on the Status and Education of Women (Washington, D.C.: Association of American Colleges, 1982); M. Elizabeth Tidball, "Women's Colleges: Exceptional Conditions, Not Exceptional Talent, Produce High Achievers," in *Educating the Majority: Women Challenge Traditions in Higher Education,* ed. Carol S. Pearson, Donna L. Shavlik, and Judith G. Touchton (New York: American Council on Education; London: Macmillan, 1989), 157–72.

77. Leslie Miller-Bernal, "Conservative Intent, Liberating Outcomes: The History of Coordinate Colleges for Women," in *Gender in Policy and Practice: Perspectives on Single-Sex and Coeducational Schooling,* ed. Amanda Datnow and Lea Hubbard (New York: Routledge, 2002), 156–71.

78. *Tulane's Newcomb College,* undated brochure, ca. 1986, NA NCCROW.

79. Sylvia Frey, "Newcomb College: Prologue and Epilogue," paper presented at Women and Learning Conference, September 22, 2007, Newnham College, Cambridge, England, copy in possession of volume editors.

80. The quotation used as the subheading is taken from Dixon, *Brief History,* 134.

81. Newcomb *Bulletins* for years indicated.

82. The first reference to the Loan Fund in the *Bulletin* appeared in 1906–7.

83. *Newcomb Announcement 1923–24:* 128.

84. See, for example, various issues of the *Newcomb Arcade, Newcomb Alumnae Newsletter, Newcomb News,* and *Under the Oaks.*

85. Elizabeth Kell, "Newcomb's Women," *Newcomb Alumnae News* 1, no. 2 (May 1935): 3.

86. Reunion Survey Collection, Class of 1940, 1980 reunion, NAC 176a, NA NCCROW.

87. Sylvia Sterne, February 10, 2006, Oral History interview by Rosalind Hinton, NA NCCROW.

88. Simone de Beauvoir spoke at the College on Tuesday, April 1, 1947. See Extracts from the "Board Resolutions Affecting Newcomb," April 16, 1947.

89. In 1956, *Ladies' Home Journal* published, for example, "The Plight of the Young Mother"; in the same year, McCall's published "The Mother Who Ran Away."

90. Lou Hutson Finke and Adele Ramos Salzer to Newcomb Classmate, February 1, 1979, Reunion Survey Files, Class of 1940, NA NCCROW.

91. Solomon, *In the Company of Educated Women,* 127–28.

92. Career Patterns Survey, Newcomb Class of 1971, 4, Reference Files, NA NCCROW.

93. The Reunion Surveys and the Oral History tapes and transcriptions are a good source for memories on the life of the mind (NA NCCROW).

94. Dyer, *Tulane: The Biography of a University,* 142, 203.

95. *Newcomb Alumnae News* 2, no. 4 (October 1936). Yvonne Crespo LaPrime, Biographical Files, NA NCCROW. LaPrime used the arguments first proposed by Sarah Reed; Mary Hunter Irvine, Oral History interview by Diane Manning, June 15, 1995, NA NCCROW; Sarah Towles Reed Biographical File, NA NCCROW. Women involved in the case included Sarah Towles Reed, Martha Wegert Comeaux, Nellie May Pearce Cupit, Gladys Castell de Be Majeau. Yvonne Crespo LaPrime, Oral History interview by Beatrice Owsley, January 19, 1988, Box 1, Earl K. Long Library, University of New Orleans.

96. Marion Pfeifer Abramson Papers, Louisiana Historical Center, Louisiana State Museum, New Orleans.

97. City Archives, New Orleans Public Library, Louisiana Division Public Fact Finder, "Women in New Orleans City Government," http://nutrias.org/~nopl/facts/women.htm.

98. City Archives, New Orleans Public Library, Louisiana Division Public Fact Finder, "New Orleans City-Council Members, 1954–2000," www.nutrias.org/~nopl/facts/council.htm.

99. Dorothy H. Brown and Barbara C. Ewell, eds., *Louisiana Women Writers: New Essays and a Comprehensive Bibliography* (Baton Rouge: Louisiana State University Press, 1992).

100. JLN to the Administrators of the Tulane University, quoted in Dixon, *Brief History,* 13.

101. Quoted in "Brief on Behalf of Respondent Brandt V. B. Dixon," 251, Dixon Papers, NA NCCROW.

13

SARAH TOWLES REED, CLASS OF 1904

LESLIE GALE PARR

Everyone who knew Sarah Towles Reed held a strong opinion about her. To her teacher colleagues, she was a "guardian angel."[1] Members of the Orleans Parish School Board considered Reed "disobedient, argumentative, obnoxious and contrary."[2] Throughout her long public life as a leader in teachers' associations and founder of the first teachers' union in New Orleans, Reed constantly outraged authorities and emboldened supporters. From the time she graduated from Newcomb College in 1904 until her retirement in 1951, Reed identified herself with the chief concerns of liberal reformers: women's rights, educational reform, the plight of labor, civil liberty, and racial justice. Her story presents an opportunity to reevaluate both the strength of liberalism and the intensity of women's activism in the South—and in New Orleans in particular—during the first half of the twentieth century.

In 1900, Sarah Butler Towles won a competitive scholarship to Newcomb College. Because of its large endowment, Newcomb could keep tuition relatively low at one hundred dollars a year and give scholarships to about 25 percent of its students.[3] Without a scholarship, Sarah never could have attended Newcomb. Her cash-strapped family had moved to New Orleans from their small plantation in St. Francisville, Louisiana, five years earlier, when her father was forced to give up farming or face financial ruin. He eventually found a job at the U.S. Custom House in New Orleans, secured through the influence of Governor Murphy S. Foster, his brother-in-law.

Like nearly all Newcomb students at the time, Sarah lived at home. She took the streetcar from Uptown, where her family lived in a modest bungalow, to Newcomb, then located on Washington Avenue in the wealthy, beautiful Garden District. Sarah was an enthusiastic learner, who, like the rest of her family, took education seriously. As a student in a private college, Sarah knew that the cost of her education, even with a scholarship, strained her family's finances. As one of the only 2.8 percent of women aged eighteen to twenty-one who went to college in 1900, and as one of only twenty-two in her class, Sarah could easily see that she was part of an elite group of young women.[4] She recognized her privileged position and worked hard to justify the sacrifices her family made for her.

The turn of the century was a heady time to be a college woman. The suffrage movement was gaining momentum, and the "New Woman" was on the rise. Although it was not until about 1915 that women's suffrage attracted a large following at Newcomb and other colleges, the movement was already under way in New Orleans by the time Sarah Towles entered college.[5] In 1892, women organized the first suffrage association in New Orleans, the Portia Club.[6] Three years later, Susan B. Anthony visited New Orleans, inspiring women to start a second suffrage organization, the Era (Equal Rights Association) Club. Representatives from the Portia and Era clubs met in 1896 to organize the Louisiana Woman Suffrage Association.[7] During Sarah's junior year, in 1903, the National Suffrage Association held its annual convention in New Orleans, featuring such luminaries as Anthony, Alice Stone Blackwell, and Carrie Chapman Catt. New Orleans' own Kate Gordon served as program chair.[8]

Sarah's comments in college papers reflect her support for women's suffrage and the influence of social activists in New Orleans and at Newcomb. Several suffragists and women reformers worked at Newcomb, including the second president of the Era Club, Evelyn Ordway, who taught chemistry during Sarah's undergraduate years.[9] The example of so many competent, progressive women at Newcomb, with its predominantly female faculty, would have made a strong impression on students such as Sarah, who already loved learning, books, and politics.[10]

The example of New Orleans' civic-minded women was central to Sarah's development and the shaping of her philosophy and career. Her later ability to draw people into her causes and organize them depended, in part, on precedents established by the strong women who came before her. Although women in the Crescent City lagged behind those of the North in organizing women's clubs and associations, social feminism took root in New Orleans sooner than in most parts of the South. By the late nineteenth century, local women had already developed a strong tradition of community involvement.

In 1881, they organized the Woman's Social and Industrial Association to aid working women. The New Orleans Exposition of 1884 helped focus attention on women's work, and that year women created the New Orleans Woman's Club to help women find jobs and train them for better ones.[11] The Woman's Club soon joined the General Federation of Women's Clubs, a move that led its members increasingly into the public realm of politics and reform.[12]

Women stood in the forefront of the social justice wing of the progressive movement in New Orleans. In 1901, Laura McMain began her thirty-year career as director of Kingsley House, a settlement house in a poor Irish neighborhood. Kate and Jean Gordon participated in nearly every reform effort in town, including the Milne Home for Destitute Orphan Girls, the prevention of cruelty to animals, the treatment of tuberculosis, the admission of women to medical school, and myriad other causes.[13] Sarah joined these women in the public world of reform soon after she graduated from Newcomb and volunteered to teach at the Newcomb College Alumnae Association's Free Night School, which opened in January 1905. The school met three times a week from 7:00 to 9:00 p.m., with Newcomb graduates contributing their time to teach "poor servant girls and factory workers."[14] This yearlong experiment in the classroom may well have decided Sarah's future career. In addition to teaching in the Free Night School, she enrolled in graduate school at Tulane, from which she received an MA in 1906, with concentrations in English and Latin.[15]

That Sarah would take some kind of job after graduation was never in doubt. Her family's precarious economic situation undoubtedly influenced Sarah's decision to work. Four siblings still lived at home, and her parents needed the extra income. It was not uncommon for a woman college graduate to take a job in 1904. A significant number of Sarah's classmates either went on to graduate school or began working immediately after graduation.[16] Like most young women with degrees in the early twentieth century, Sarah chose teaching, and she made it her life's work.

It is impossible, of course, to say what her life might have been had her marriage worked out differently. Some time before 1921, Sarah married Elkerna "Eck" Reed, who ran a country store in West Feliciana Parish. When the marriage actually took place, no one knows. It was a secret Sarah Towles Reed never revealed. She omitted the wedding date in all family records while carefully noting the dates of her siblings' unions. According to family lore, Sarah told only her mother about her marriage. All that is now known is that the couple never lived together and that Eck was killed in an automobile accident in 1921.[17]

One overriding practical reason explains why Sarah kept her marriage a secret, at least as long as Eck was alive—married women were not allowed to teach in Orleans Parish public schools. Had her marriage been discovered, she would have been automatically fired from her teaching position at Sophie B. Wright High School. She had to choose between Eck and her family's economic needs, and there seems little doubt that the family claim was stronger. It was not until Eck's fatal car accident that Sarah's marriage became public, when it was revealed in his obituary. When school authorities read about Sarah's marriage, they immediately fired her. As Sarah's principal, Alice Lusher, explained to her, Sarah's position had been automatically vacated by her marriage, even though news of it did not reach authorities until she was already a widow. Lusher asked the president of the school board for Sarah's reinstatement, and he, in turn, requested a letter from Sarah explaining the circumstances.[18] In September the board allowed her to return to her classroom.[19]

Sarah never remarried after Eck's death. She spent the rest of her life living with her sister Roberta Towles, also a teacher in the Orleans Parish public schools and a close ally in her sister's educational reform efforts. In 1921, Sarah decided to enter night classes at Loyola law school.[20] She graduated in 1924 and passed her bar exams but never practiced law or professed any interest in becoming an attorney. Her lack of interest at least shielded her from the prejudice women faced in the legal profession. In 1920, women made up only 1.4 percent of the lawyers in the United States. Like Florence Kelley, Crystal Eastman, and Alice Paul, Reed used her legal knowledge informally to advance women's causes—in her case, the rights of the predominantly female teaching force in New Orleans.[21]

The teachers' organizations and unions she helped organize provided a base for Reed's political activism and the mechanism to help secure teachers' economic and intellectual independence. The economic dimension of Reed's activities on behalf of teachers linked her incipient feminism with her later dedication to the labor movement. Reed believed that all workers had the right to economic security and that women were the most vulnerable workers in this respect. Like many early-twentieth-century feminists, Reed assumed that political rights were intrinsically bound up with economic rights.[22]

Sarah Reed's first public activities for teachers involved a basic feminist demand: equal pay for equal work. When she joined the New Orleans women teachers' fight for equal pay in the 1920s, Reed encountered a salary disparity between men and women that was as great or greater than that found in the nonacademic labor market. Paying women teachers less than men had long been common practice in academia. Beginning with the salary-equalization struggle, Reed became the most visible and vocal activist in the women teachers' fight for economic justice. In 1925, she helped found a new teachers' organization, the New Orleans Public School Teachers Association (NOPSTA). In addition to fighting for equal pay—a battle that women teachers would not win until 1937—NOPSTA also worked for the recognition of teaching as a profession, one that was accorded the respect they believed it deserved. Members urged Reed to accept the presidency of the new organization, but she declined, choosing instead to head the salary committee, to edit the organization's magazine, and to serve as chair of the legislative committee, a position she would hold for nearly fifty years.[23]

The Great Depression marked a turning point in Reed's public life. NOPSTA's emphasis on obtaining professional recognition for teachers seemed less important in light of the economic problems teachers were now facing. The crisis triggered in Reed the realization that she and her colleagues shared the same concerns as the American working class. She also came to understand that the inequality of women was tied to larger societal injustices suffered by workers in general. As the Depression dragged on, Reed concluded that unionization was the key to correcting these inequities.

Like other workers everywhere in the country, teachers experienced a sharp decline in their standard of living during the Depression. Already overworked and underpaid, New Orleans teachers saw their class sizes swell and their salaries shrink in the early years of the financial disaster. Rapidly falling property taxes—the main source of school revenue—cut into the amount of money available to the school board, while enrollments climbed by some twenty-five thousand in the decade after 1925.[24] Teacher salaries fell 16 to 26 percent during the first two years of the 1930s.[25]

Reed realized that teachers needed an organization stronger than NOPSTA to protect their interests and was open to a suggestion that she help teachers organize an American Federation of Teachers local. The AFT picked the right person to lead the way. Reed had always been a "firm believer in the labor movement."[26] In 1934, Reed, her sister, and eight colleagues applied for a charter for a new union, the Classroom Teachers' Federation (CTF), Local 353, of the American Federation of Teachers, AFL. It was testimony to Reed's enormous popularity among her peers that she persuaded some of them to join her in a movement that most professionals, including teachers, scorned. Reed used her considerable rhetorical talents to persuade her colleagues to stand together in their fight for better schools and working conditions. Teachers stood and cheered when Reed exhorted them in public meetings. "Organization! More organization! And more organization!" she would proclaim. "Talk in corridors—in cloakrooms—at bridge tables won't get teachers anywhere. But action will—organized action!"[27]

Even after the Classroom Teachers' Federation had secured a number of gains for teachers, most teachers continued to resist the union's organizing efforts despite its assurances that professionals in many fields were beginning to appreciate the power of organization.[28] A few AFT locals, such as the ones in Chicago and Atlanta, represented a majority of their city's teachers, but most, including the New Orleans Classroom Teachers' Federation, represented only a minority. Until the late 1940s, fewer than 10 percent of the city's white teachers belonged to Local 353.[29] Still, like other small AFT locals, the New Orleans group was often able to exert influence that was out of proportion to its actual size.[30]

With the inauguration of the CTF, Reed and her colleagues entered a period of substantial progress for educational reform. Reed's political acumen and skillful lobbying of state legislators helped account for much of the teachers' success. One of their greatest accomplishments came in 1936, when the state legislature passed a tenure bill for New Orleans teachers.[31] Later that year, the legislature approved a similar bill giving teachers tenure throughout the state based on the same requirements established for New Orleans teachers.[32]

The passage of the tenure law allowed Reed to at last attack the prohibition against married women teachers. It was an inauspicious time to embark on such a campaign. The Depression saw a strengthening of the prejudice against working married women.[33] As one civic organization put it, married women ought to return to domestic life because "they are holding jobs that rightfully belong to the God-intended providers of the household."[34] A 1936 Gallup poll found that 82 percent of all Americans opposed giving jobs to women with husbands who were employed, leading George Gallup to conclude that he had "discovered an issue on which voters are about as solidly united as on any subject imaginable—including sin and hay fever."[35]

Long-standing pressures to exclude married women from teaching reached new levels of intensity during the Depression. By the beginning of the Second World War, the number of school districts that would not hire a married woman had increased to 87 percent, with 70 percent of all school systems automatically firing a woman who married while under contract.[36] It is little short of amazing that the marriage prohibition in the New Orleans public school system came down in 1936. In large part, this gain for the economic rights of women was testament to the influence and legal perspicacity of Sarah Reed.

It was also during the Depression that Reed began to pay more attention to racial issues. The beginnings of the civil rights movement in the 1930s transformed Reed's racial views and prompted her to join the emerging struggle for racial justice. This is not to say that Reed went so far as to advocate integration publicly. The educational color line was a fact of life, and no one sought to overturn the formal structure of school segregation in the 1930s. She did, however, begin working actively to promote interracial cooperation among teachers, thereby earning the animosity of many within the New Orleans educational establishment.

In 1937, an interracial delegation of fourteen teachers, headed by Reed and Veronica Hill, a prominent African American teacher, marched into the school administration building armed with a petition asking for raises and a "fairer deal" for black teachers. When an elevator operator told them he had been directed not to take them to the third floor, where a closed meeting of the board was in progress, Reed, Hill, and some of the other women climbed the outside fire escape, found an open window on the fifth floor, entered the building, took the stairs to the third floor, and slid the petition under the locked door of the meeting room.[37] The black teachers got their raises the next day.

A few days later, Reed met with a group of African American teachers in Jefferson Parish to urge them to form their own union of classroom teachers. The AFT's policy was to conform to local practices in matters involving race. If a community's schools were segregated, as New Orleans schools were, so, too, were the local unions.[38] In speaking to her black colleagues, Reed emphasized the importance of unionization for all teachers. The African American teachers passed a resolution to join the AFT and organize the League of Classroom Teachers, American Federation of Teachers, Local 527.[39] Locals 353 and 527 formed a liaison committee that met once a month, worked together on common issues, and occasionally appeared before the board together.

In the 1930s, a conservative backlash against the labor movement, radical political activity, and New Deal legislation gave rise to an anticommunist movement that foreshadowed the McCarthyism of the 1950s. "Red-baiters" of the 1930s paid particular attention to the schools and initiated a loyalty oath movement that specifically targeted teachers. By 1936, twenty-one states and the District of Columbia required teachers to take loyalty oaths as a condition of employment. Some states prohibited communists from teaching in the public schools; others banned teacher membership in supposedly subversive organizations.[40]

As the new school term in New Orleans got under way in the fall of 1940, school superintendent Nicholas Bauer ordered all the public schools in the city to devote a minimum of ten minutes a day to an "Americanism program." Bauer specified that all schools would be required to use as their slogan: "Americanism—the Blessings and Responsibilities of a Democracy." Every principal and every teacher in the system, Bauer said, would be expected to use this motto; no exceptions would be made. "We are not afraid to touch on isms," Bauer told the New Orleans Principals' Association, "but we want you to come back always to the thought that the American way of life is the grand way of life."[41]

The campaign to ensure a teaching staff free from the taint of any "isms" picked up steam in 1940, when the Coalition of Patriotic Societies of Louisiana revived a campaign it had begun in 1936. The Coalition wanted to make "un-American" activities by teachers illegal. Despite protests from teachers and other community groups, the school board passed an "Americanism" rule that prohibited teachers from belonging to or participating in any organization that advocated the overthrow of the government and the abolition of private property, promoted class or religious hatred, or attempted to thwart conscription. Teachers also had to pledge they would not persuade their students to join any prohibited group.[42]

It is not surprising that Sarah Reed became the first target of the Americanism rule. She had engaged in many activities that rendered her suspect to conservative southerners. In addition to working with African American teachers and affiliating with organized labor, she participated in several liberal and even radical organizations, including the Southern Conference for Human Welfare and the League for Industrial Democracy. She was, moreover, an outspoken advocate of academic freedom for teachers and equal rights for women. Her record of liberal activism was anathema to New Orleans conservatives, who used the new rule to make their first attempt to discredit the veteran teacher, citing her outspoken views and liberal affiliations as evidence of "un-Americanism," the catch-all category for virtually any doctrine or policy that seemed to threaten the status quo. She was, in her own words, "a marked woman."

In 1940 and 1941, seven of Reed's civics students at Fortier High School filed affidavits with the Association of Commerce's National Defense Committee, one of the most vocal supporters of the Americanism rule, which questioned their teacher's patriotism and criticized her unorthodox teaching methods. The superintendent called Reed into his office and showed her the unsigned affidavits, indirectly warning her that the board was keeping an eye on her classroom. Reed protested to the Orleans Parish School Board that the affidavits were "so obviously false and malicious that they do not merit consideration." She had no idea what she was expected to do about them, she said, but "I believe that 30 years of devoted service to the schools of Orleans Parish is ample evidence of my patriotism and abiding faith in American principles and institutions, and entitles me to your confidence."[43]

The board took no action against Reed over this incident, but two years later the charges resurfaced after a conflict erupted between Reed and her Fortier High School principal, John Conniff. The incident seemed innocuous at the time, but the school board and Conniff seized upon it as a pretext for removing Reed from the teaching force and discrediting the CTF. In February 1943, Reed refused an order from Conniff to fill out a questionnaire sent to teachers by the board concerning their after-school activities. Reed left the questionnaire blank, except for her signature, refusing to participate in an effort to weed out teachers who were moonlighting in war industries. When Conniff saw Reed's empty form, he immediately wrote the school superintendent to complain that Reed had refused to follow his instructions.[44] A few days later, Conniff sent for Reed and suspended her.

After hearing evidence in the case, the school board found her guilty of willful neglect of duty and then proceeded to reinstate her anyway, despite her continued refusal to fill out their questionnaire. The board did assert some measure of authority by withholding her pay during her suspension. Reed took her case to court, but Judge Frank Stich found in favor of the board. "The plaintiff not only failed, but she deliberately, willfully and militantly refused to fill in the questionnaire," Stich said. "Her testimony in open court and her demeanor and action on the witness stand are conclusive of the fact that she did not ever intend to comply with the request of the School Board." Her attitude, he said, clearly indicated that she did not think the board had any right to inquire into her time after school. However, he ruled, it did have that right.[45]

The verdict reflected the establishment's scorn for Reed's attitude as well as her politics. Reed's social outlook was unpopular in itself, but her independent and combative public posture had also rankled school officials for more than thirty years. The school board alleged that Reed, "for many years past, has been disobedient, argumentative, obnoxious and contrary in the performance of her duties; that she has systematically and consistently sought to embarrass the members of respondent Board, the Superintendent of Orleans Parish Schools, and the principals of the schools at which she was teaching, by willfully refusing and neglecting to obey orders and instructions and by publicly and adversely criticizing actions of the Superintendent."[46]

The board maintained that its members were "business and professional men of high standing in this community." Nevertheless, Reed had, "time after time, sought to override the wishes of the electorate of this community by annoying, humiliating and embarrassing the members of the respondent Board, the Superintendent . . . and her principals . . . in an attempt to impose her will, her thoughts, her ideals, her opinions, her doctrines and her methods of teaching upon this community." The board would have brought charges against Reed earlier, it claimed, but decided not to "because of her long tenure of office, her age, and the hope that she would adjust herself to conditions prevailing in the Nation and cease her system of activities above delineated."[47]

Five years later, the board once again attempted to silence Reed and the Teachers' Federation. Now, in the wake of World War II, with the Soviet Union no longer an ally, charges of "un-Americanism" first leveled against Reed in 1940 were brought out again, and this time they carried more weight. There is good reason to conclude that the school board decided to take advantage of growing anti-Communist sentiment to rid itself of a longtime problem in the person of Sarah Reed. The Cold War presented the board the perfect pretext for discrediting Reed's outspoken advocacy of teacher rights and academic freedom. At the very least, the targeting of Reed can be explained as the board's effort to show the community that it was diligently guarding the schools against Communist influence. Someone as liberal as Reed, with her long-standing labor affiliation and ties to the political Left, presented an ideal target for anti-Communist crusaders.

The new campaign against Reed began on May 5, 1948, when Dr. John Kieffer, a Tulane political science professor, told the Young Men's Business

Club he had heard a report that some New Orleans students were following "the party line."[48] Five days after Kieffer made his allegations, Superintendent Lionel J. Bourgeois submitted to the board a summary of evidence he had collected regarding Reed's commitment to "Americanism." This material consisted of "unsolicited" statements from five of Reed's current students, plus material from her file, including the 1940–41 affidavits. The superintendent reported that after hearing Kieffer's statement, he had sent a questionnaire to every white high school student. The results, he said, indicated that there were no grounds for the Tulane professor's charges that New Orleans students had been infected by communism, with the possible exception of a few Fortier students. Bourgeois interviewed these students, who had answered the questionnaire "in such a manner as to cast serious doubt about the teaching of Communism in the Fortier High School."[49]

Bourgeois presented to the board excerpts of testimony given by a few of Reed's civics students. One reported that Reed had pointed out some of the "superiorities of Communism over the Democratic way." Another said that she advocated an equal distribution of the nation's wealth, while another complained that she favored repeal of the Taft-Hartley Act. "She always brought out the bad points of our government," he alleged. One student reported that Reed had voiced her support for Henry Wallace for the presidency. "The student asked if she was aware that he was being supported by Communists, to which she replied that she was for Henry Wallace regardless."[50]

Bourgeois also presented the seven student affidavits from 1940–41. He reminded the board of "the many difficulties it had encountered in its past official dealings with Mrs. Reed," recalling specifically "her refusal to obey a board directive," her suspension and subsequent lawsuit against the board, which, he pointed out, she had lost. He also reminded the board that two of Reed's principals had requested her transfer from their schools because of her "uncooperative" attitude. He included a 1940 letter from John Conniff in which the principal complained that "Mrs. Reed is antagonistic to all recognized authority, exerts a damaging influence upon the patriotism of the student body and handicaps the school's Americanism program, etc."[51]

Bourgeois wanted to transfer Reed from civics to another, less dangerous, subject unrelated to social studies. In her new position, Bourgeois informed Reed, she would be prohibited from mentioning communism, socialism, "or any other foreign 'ism' in dealing with the children on school property and during school hours." Bourgeois further admonished Reed "that in any case where the American way of life is brought up in your class it will be your bounden duty to extol the merits of the American system." Although he did not directly accuse Reed of advocating communism, Bourgeois told her that "there is too much doubt as to whether or not you have done all that you should have done to proselytize for the democratic way."[52]

After thirty years in the New Orleans school system, Reed was nearing retirement in 1948. It is doubtful that she would have accepted a transfer in any case and particularly not now, when she was already sixty-seven years old. She insisted on a public hearing. In August 1948, the same month that Whitaker Chambers appeared before the House Un-American Activities Committee and publicly accused Alger Hiss of supporting communism, Sarah Reed appeared before the Orleans Parish School Board for a hearing on charges of "not stressing the American way of life as superior in every respect to Communism or other 'isms.'"

Bourgeois' accusation of "un-Americanism" was a serious one to make against a schoolteacher. In a Cold War climate, any taint of a foreign "ism" would be enough to destroy a teacher's career, especially the career of a teacher who already was closely identified with organized labor and civil rights for blacks and women, and who was known for her irreverent attitude toward established authority. The ploy failed, however. In the six-hour session, Reed's students and colleagues overwhelmed the board with protestations of her commitment to democracy. Eight students spoke on Reed's behalf; only three testified against her. At least forty more students and twenty teachers waited outside the hearing room prepared to come to Reed's defense, and nearly two hundred students volunteered to do whatever they could to help their teacher.[53]

The students who testified against Reed were all former Fortier students from her civics class who had signed affidavits against her in 1940 and 1941. One of these was Kenneth Muller, who told the board that, as he recalled, Reed was opposed to military training at the high school; she was opposed to saluting the flag; and "she spoke highly of the Communistic Movement." She also said that the South was an unfit place to live, Muller reported. "We had a little pamphlet known as 'Economic Conditions of the South,' and we had to break this down and give a lengthy speech on it and bring out just what was wrong with the South from it." Muller did not know who published the pamphlet and could not say whether it was "Communistic" literature or not. When asked what facts the class discussed about the South, Muller replied:

"Well, the thing is we were pretty well handicapped by a Civil War, held down in that respect. I think as a teacher she should realize that that shouldn't be harped upon. We are doing as well as we possibly can. The fact that she brings out and made us go through this little pamphlet, 'Economic Conditions of the South,' I don't see where that has any bearing on teaching . . . high school students Civics."[54] Evidently, Muller did not think that the 1938 government publication *Report on the Economic Conditions of the South*, commissioned by President Franklin Roosevelt and written by his National Emergency Council, was appropriate reading material for students.

Reed's pedagogy was a shining example of liberal-left educational pro-gressivism. Her students did not get a traditional education in her class. She unbolted the students' desks from the floor to encourage a more participa-tory, democratic classroom. She initiated lively discussions on labor unions, race relations, and politics. A teacher who taught controversial subjects in an unorthodox classroom made an ideal target for red-baiters. Reed's case presents a nearly textbook example of how the 1940s Red Scare was used against liberal and controversial teachers for reasons entirely unrelated to communism.

As much as the school board members wanted to pluck this thorn from its side, it had little choice but to exonerate Reed in the face of such over-whelming support for her. Admirers both inside and outside the educational community hailed her success and celebrated at a victory party at her house. Having won a major battle for academic freedom, Reed immediately resumed her fight for teachers' rights. Even after she finally retired in 1951, she con-tinued to work for teachers' interests, particularly retirement benefits. Well into her nineties, Reed served as executive secretary and legislative chair for NOPSTA until illness finally forced her to give up her cherished job. During all this time, from 1924 to 1972, she did not miss a single session of the state legislature, traveling from New Orleans to Baton Rouge by bus.

After forty-five years as a teacher and nearly sixty on the front lines of battle for teachers' rights, academic freedom, and quality education, Reed died on May 8, 1978, at the age of ninety-six. She had served as spokeswoman and role model for teachers her entire adult life. Her consistently left-leaning political stance caused many New Orleanians to consider her a radical, a label she deserved within the context of her time and place. Her commitments to women, blacks, and labor were enough to mark her as subversive, unsouth-ern, even un-American in the minds of conservative antagonists. Indeed,

Reed's career illustrates just how radical a liberal might appear to a society joined to the twin idols of patriarchy and white supremacy.

Viewed from a more hopeful perspective, the record of Reed's accomplishments presents a valuable reminder that not all southerners shared the values associated with the "southern way of life." Her political battles contradict conventional generalities about southern traditionalism and parochialism. Reed's struggles to secure equal rights for women and blacks and her insistence upon academic freedom, economic justice, and unionization aroused intense opposition, but they also garnered impressive support at the grassroots level and among civic leaders, academics and political figures. Allies in the community protected her from critics who periodically tried to discredit her. Teachers, members of women's clubs, labor unionists, and other concerned citizens rallied to her side time after time.

Reed emerges as a southern liberal who frequently stood in the forefront of social activism, occupying a minority position while seeking to rally others to her cause. Although Reed had a plethora of opponents, she also had numerous supporters, and virtually all of them were southerners. Her story attests to the long tradition of civic activism among New Orleans women, especially Newcomb alumnae, and constitutes an important chapter in the ongoing story of southern liberals' efforts to transform their society from within.

NOTES

1. Yvonne LaPrime to Sarah Towles Reed, August 2, 1951, Sarah Towles Reed Collection, Archives and Manuscripts Division, Earl K. Long Library, University of New Orleans (hereafter cited as STR).

2. Civil District Court for the Parish of Orleans, State of Louisiana, no. 249–672, Division "E," Docket 3, *Mrs. Sarah Towles Reed versus Orleans Parish School Board,* Answer, STR.

3. Lynn D. Gordon, *Gender and Higher Education in the Progressive Era* (New Haven: Yale University Press, 1990), 173.

4. Barbara Miller Solomon, *In the Company of Educated Women: A History of Women and Higher Education in America* (New Haven: Yale University Press, 1985), 62.

5. Ibid., 112.

6. Carmen Lindig, *The Path from the Parlor: Louisiana Women, 1879–1920* (Lafayette: Center for Louisiana Studies, University of Southwestern Louisiana, 1986), 57; Elna Green, "The Rest of the Story: Kate Gordon and the Opposition to the Nineteenth Amendment in the South," *Louisiana History* 33 (Spring 1992): 172.

7. Lindig, *The Path from the Parlor,* 60–61.

8. Ibid., 132.

9. Gordon, *Gender and Higher Education in the Progressive Era,* 177.

10. *Newcomb Bulletin 1901–1902:* 4–5; Pamela Tyler, *Silk Stockings and Ballot Boxes: Women and Politics in New Orleans, 1920–1963* (Athens: University of Georgia Press, 1996), 15.

11. Anne Firor Scott, *The Southern Lady: From Pedestal to Politics, 1830–1930* (Chicago: University of Chicago Press, 1970), 122–23.

12. Ibid., 160–61.

13. *Newcomb Arcade,* June 1909, 34; Katy Coyle, "Women of Sympathy and Truth: Newcomb Women and the Communities They Forged, 1887–1918," unpublished paper, Tulane University, December 4, 1992, 12, Newcomb Archives, Newcomb College Center for Research on Women; Brandt V. B. Dixon, *A Brief History of the H. Sophie Newcomb Memorial College, 1887–1919: A Personal Reminiscence* (New Orleans: Hauser Printing, 1928), 135.

14. Kathryn W. Kemp, "Jean and Kate Gordon: New Orleans Social Reformers, 1898–1933," *Louisiana History* 24 (Fall 1983): 390.

15. Tulane transcript, STR.

16. *Newcomb Arcade,* June 1909, 34.

17. Nora Marsh, interview by the author, November 30, 1993.

18. Alice Lusher to Sarah Towles Reed, August 30, 1921, STR.

19. Nicholas Bauer to Sarah Towles Reed, September 8, 1921, STR.

20. John Towles to Sarah Towles Reed, n.d., STR.

21. Solomon, *In the Company of Educated Women,* 131.

22. Nancy F. Cott, *The Grounding of Modern Feminism* (New Haven: Yale University Press, 1987), 117.

23. Papers of the executive board of NOPSTA, 1925–26, STR.

24. Theo Hotard, farewell speech, December 8, 1944, STR.

25. Donald E. DeVore and Joseph Logsdon, *Crescent City Schools: Public Education in New Orleans, 1841–1991* (Lafayette: Center for Louisiana Studies, University of Southwestern Louisiana, 1991), 169–70.

26. Allie Mann, vice president, American Federation of Teachers, to STR, "My dear Mrs. Reed," May 5, 1934, STR.

27. Sarah Towles Reed notes, n.d., STR.

28. The New Orleans Classroom Teachers' Federation, Local 353, *American Federation of Teachers 1937–38 Yearbook,* STR.

29. American Federation of Teachers, Monthly Reports to the Secretary-Treasurer, selected dates from September 1935 to June 1956, AFT Archives. In December 1935, the CTF had 26 members. The figure rose dramatically in 1947 to 225, declining again to 182 in June 1956. Its largest membership was achieved in July 1953 with 425 members.

30. William Edward Eaton, *The American Federation of Teachers, 1916–1961: A History of the Movement* (Carbondale: Southern Illinois University Press, 1975), 171.

31. "Legislative Digest," *New Orleans Times-Picayune,* June 9, 1936.

32. "Teacher Bill Passed," *New Orleans Times-Picayune,* July 24, 1936; Guy Clifford Mitchell, "Growth of State Control of Public Education in Louisiana" (PhD diss., University of Michigan, 1942), 411.

33. Claudia Goldin, *Understanding the Gender Gap: An Economic History of American Women* (New York: Oxford University Press, 1990), 166; Philip S. Foner, *Women and the American Labor Movement: From World War I to the Present* (New York: Free Press, 1980), 298.

34. William H. Chafe, *The Paradox of Change: American Women in the 20th Century* (New York: Oxford University Press, 1991), 116.

35. Foner, *Women and the American Labor Movement: From World War I to the Present,* 298; Chafe, *The Paradox of Change,* 116

36. Goldin, *Understanding the Gender Gap,* 162.

37. *New Orleans Item,* September 1, 1937; Veronica Hill, interview by the author, April 1, 1996, Gretna, La.; Orleans Parish School Board (OPSB) Committee Minutes, Aug. 31, 1937. Earl K. Long Library. University of New Orleans. Another version appeared in the *New Orleans Times-Picayune,* September 1, 1937.

38. Eaton, *The American Federation of Teachers,* 62.

39. Record Book and Minutes of the New Orleans Federation of Classroom Teachers, AFT Local 527, September 9, 1937, Box 7, William H. Davis, Sr. Collection, Archives and Manuscripts Division, Earl K. Long Library, University of New Orleans.

40. David Tyack, Robert Lowe, and Elisabeth Hansot, *Public Schools in Hard Times: The Great Depression and Recent Years* (Cambridge: Harvard University Press, 1984), 63; Marjorie Murphy, *Blackboard Unions: The FT and the NEA, 1900–1980* (Ithaca: Cornell University Press, 1990), 179; David Caute, *The Great Fear: The Anti-Communist Purge under Truman and Eisenhower* (New York: Simon and Schuster, 1978), 404.

41. *New Orleans Times-Picayune,* September 5, 1940.

42. OPSB minutes, January 10, 1941.

43. Sarah Towles Reed to President and Members of OPSB, April 21, 1941, STR.

44. OPSB Committee minutes, February 9, 1943.

45. *New Orleans Times-Picayune,* July 12, 1944; *New Orleans Item,* July 12, 1944.

46. Civil District Court for the Parish of Orleans, State of Louisiana, No. 249–672, Division "E," Docket 3, *Mrs. Sarah Towles Reed versus OPSB,* Answer, STR.

47. Civil District Court.

48. *New Orleans Times-Picayune,* May 6, 1948.

49. Lionel J. Bourgeois, Superintendent, to the President and Members of the OPSB, August 9, 1948, OPSB General File.

50. Bourgeois, August 9, 1948. In 1940, Henry Wallace was elected vice president of the United States on the Democratic Party ticket. Because of his progressive ideas, he was dropped by the Democratic Party as Franklin Roosevelt's running mate in 1944 and replaced with Harry S. Truman.

51. Ibid.

52. Lionel J. Bourgeois, OPSB, to Sarah Towles Reed, Alcee Fortier High School, May 24, 1948, STR.

53. *New Orleans Item,* August 27, 1948.

54. OPSB, Hearing in the Matter of the Alleged Failure of Mrs. Sarah Towles Reed, Teacher at the Fortier High School, to Adequately Stress Americanism in Her Civics Classes, 56, STR.

14

HILDA, MARTHA, AND NATALIE
Newcomb's Furies

PAMELA TYLER

Edith Hamilton's *Mythology* identifies an intriguing trio of female creatures called the Furies. Greek poets in antiquity thought of them as punishing sinners on Earth, where they were inexorable, but just. As long as there was sin in the world, the Furies could not be banished.[1] Hilda Phelps Hammond and Martha Gilmore Robinson, members of Newcomb's Class of 1909, might be called Newcomb's Furies. As activists, they made unpaid but nearly full-time careers of hounding "evildoers" in the sordid world of Louisiana politics. Though their Newcomb education had exposed them to rigid standards of decorum and Victorian notions of gender propriety, Hammond and Robinson were neither retiring nor "proper" as they made forays into political matters in the 1930s and 1940s. Instead, they frequently displayed a surprising assertiveness, occasionally an abrasiveness, which bespoke their rejection of the prevailing codes of gentility and deference for women.

Legend holds that wise Athena later changed the Furies from fearful avengers, with snakes for hair and eyes that wept blood, into the Benignant Ones, the Eumenides, protectors of the suppliant. This mythological transformation rendered them beings who enforced a law of mercy rather than of vengeance.[2] It is with the Furies-become-Eumenides that her tolerant, broad-minded views place Hammond and Robinson's best friend, Newcomb 1909-er Natalie Vivian Scott. Scott's life trajectory unfolded differently from that of Hammond and Robinson. While Scott was not a wife, a mother, a political activist, or crusading reformer, her genius lay in living a bohemian life of adventure, which meant rejecting norms and conventions, and this she did with zest. Hammond, Robinson, and Scott began a lifelong friendship at Newcomb and ever after spoke of the College as having formed them in important ways.

They thought of themselves and were viewed by others as a sort of triumvirate, a female version of the Three Musketeers. This essay examines the bonds that joined the three great friends to Newcomb College and to each other for more than forty years.

During his decades at the helm of Newcomb College, President Brandt Dixon attempted to forge a first-rate college for women.[3] He struggled to boost academic standards in the face of a prevailing local attitude of general indifference to higher education for women and labored to overcome the desire for mere "accomplishments" that he felt many parents and their daughters manifested.[4] Gradually, his insistence on stricter admission standards and intellectual rigor bore fruit, though the process was glacially slow.

Dixon enjoyed quicker and more obvious success in nurturing the development of a college culture. During the first decade of the twentieth century, he detected a definite, positive shift, caused, he believed, by "the beautiful college spirit which, in time, came to abundant life in the student body." He noted with pleasure that relations between faculty and students became intimate and cordial; he glowed when reporting the variety of extracurricular activities, such as plays, debates, and sororities, that sprang to life. Because of the changed climate, Newcomb students remained on campus for longer and more interested participation, friendships flourished, and a new campus spirit bloomed. Much of the credit for this shift goes to Hilda Phelps, Martha Gilmore, and Natalie Scott, who embodied Dixon's idea that "the building of the college was their task."[5]

In the summer of 1908, rising seniors Hilda, Martha, and Natalie had led the senior class in a purposeful undertaking to reorganize and invigorate campus life. Abandoning their summer vacations, they met in each other's homes and on the old Washington Avenue campus to plan. The highly satisfactory outcome saw Newcomb's faculty and administrators embrace their suggestions for reform, bringing a modern energy to campus life. A debate program, glee club, student government, athletics (tennis, basketball, track, and crew), and literary magazine were either revived or created for the first time at Newcomb. A scholar who has examined women's colleges in the Progressive Era concurs that Newcomb did in fact develop "an absorbing collegiate culture resembling that at the eastern women's colleges."[6]

Hilda Phelps was her classmates' choice as president of the Class of 1909. Martha Gilmore emerged as the editor of the *Arcade*, the new literary magazine inaugurated in January 1909. Both young women pledged sororities,

Kappa Kappa Gamma and Pi Beta Phi, respectively. Natalie Scott, already exhibiting traits of egalitarian iconoclasm, did not join a sorority but instead founded the Student Club, a nonexclusive body "where all students meet on an equal footing," open to all and designed to encourage "the spirit of good fellowship." In their final year at Newcomb, all three enjoyed dramatics and frequently took roles in student presentations. The invigorated student life their efforts had wrought included, in 1908–9, dramas in English, French, and German. Hilda later recalled that the constraints imposed by propriety meant "Orlandos, Petruccios, and Romeos wearing men's apparel from the waist up and skirts from the waist down!"[7] In her old age, Martha boasted, perhaps accurately, that she had been the first Newcomb student to don trousers for a dramatic role.[8]

Concerns over female propriety also circumscribed athletic and artistic aspects of college life. When Hilda and Natalie played on the Newcomb basketball team, they performed under restrictive rules that prohibited female players from bouncing the ball more than three times before passing and discouraged much running on the court. In art classes, the code of decorum prohibited nude models, prompting Hilda to note that "classes in the nude were an accepted part of the curriculum of Eastern schools."[9]

Arguably the most significant contribution the 1909-ers made to a richer campus life was the creation of a literary magazine to serve as the official organ of students and alumnae. Christened the *Newcomb Arcade* in reference to the structure on the Washington Avenue campus where young women congregated between and after classes, the publication printed campus gossip, current jokes, and the usual student fiction and poetry. It distinguished itself by editorials and coverage of student and alumnae activities. An unsigned editorial, almost certainly penned by editor in chief Martha Gilmore, revealed the incipient feminism of its author. The writer vigorously supported placing a Newcomb alumna on the Board of Administrators of Tulane University. She argued that because of Newcomb's size and quality, justice demanded female representation. She deplored the low level of female faculty pay, "a wrong that demands speedy righting," arguing that female professors should "be valued at their proper worth and . . . be paid salaries equal to those of the men professors of the same standing." Her outspoken language indicates a testy intelligence: "We recognize that it is the custom of the time to underpay women for the same grade of work men perform, but an unjust commercial practice should not be carried into use in such a center of culture and uplift as a great twentieth century University."[10] Six years later, the Tulane board finally added its first female member, Florence Dymond. Newcomb students celebrated by singing, to the tune of "There Is a Tavern in the Town":

> There is a woman on the Board, on the Board,
> To which long years our hopes have soared, hopes have soared,
> But at last the thing we want has come our way
> So now there's nothing more to say.[11]

Not by coincidence, the editorial urging female representation and fair pay for female faculty followed close on the heels of a January 1909 campus visit by the noted suffragist Maud Wood Park. Under the auspices of the Newcomb College Equal Suffrage League, Park had addressed a Newcomb assembly on the merits of women's rights and woman suffrage. Her arguments impressed Martha Gilmore favorably. However, Martha's father, attorney and soon-to-be-congressman Samuel Gilmore, refused to be converted. "I disagreed with him on woman suffrage," she recalled. "We had wonderful arguments."[12] After the passage of the Nineteenth Amendment in 1920, Martha went on to become a lobbyist, a political activist, and a force for reform. She always credited her years at Newcomb College with awakening her interest in political roles for women.

A Newcomb education advanced the concepts of urban progressivism and municipal housekeeping, less strongly perhaps than was the case at Vassar or Smith, but uniquely among southern women's institutions. Her students could look to capable women on the faculty as role models, but more typically, Newcomb students looked to Newcomb alumnae as examples of engaged womanhood in the Progressive Era. A regular feature in the *Arcade* was a letter from an alumna who described her life and work since college. These biographical vignettes offered a tempting range of possibilities of service and usefulness to the impressionable students and helped them to answer a question posed by many in the first generations of women in higher education: "After college, what?"

Josephine Louise Newcomb died in 1901. Upon learning that the eccentric Mrs. Newcomb had left her entire estate to the college she had established as a memorial to her daughter, disappointed relatives brought suit to have her will set aside. Legal proceedings dragged on until 1909. When the matter was ultimately resolved in the College's favor, her generous legacy made major expansion possible. With a bequest of $3.6 million, Newcomb College moved forward with plans to relocate to a larger campus adjacent to Tulane University.[13]

News of the proposed move excited apprehension among Newcomb students and alumnae in 1909. They worried over loss of identity, cohesiveness, sisterhood, and unity. Could the promise of expanded facilities and modern laboratories in faraway Uptown ever replace the idyll of the sequestered and tranquil Washington Avenue campus? Would Tulane devour the College and obliterate its identity and independence? To preserve a sentimental connection between old and new, the Class of 1909 staged a ceremony for planting acorns from the old campus in beds specially prepared on the new campus site, symbolizing their hope that the spirit of old Newcomb would live on in the new location. "Arbor Day" became an annual tradition from its first observance in 1909 until the College finally occupied its new home in 1918. Hilda, Martha, and Natalie were among the students who planted some of the Newcomb oaks that shade the campus today.[14]

The homosocial culture of Victorian America flourished at women's colleges.[15] It was certainly an aspect of life among the pioneer generations of Newcomb women who formed intense lifelong ties with each other whether they married or not. A poem in the 1909 *Arcade* alluded straightforwardly to the well-known penchant for what the girls called "smashing."

> C is for Crush which girls have on each other,
> Quite unhealthy, you know, for the lungs nearly smother.[16]

One cannot know whether any of the "crushes" ever found sexual expression, but on a campus where approximately 80 percent of the students were commuters who lived at home, it would have been less likely than at a full-fledged residential college. Nevertheless, the emotional attachments could be deep and intense, as this cryptic note, written from a Newcomb student to Martha Gilmore a year after her graduation, attests. "I write you many pillow letters, but they never reach—perhaps fortunately," her correspondent begins.

Sometimes lately I have wanted you very much. I have made such a mess of things. . . . You do things of to-day with such a whole heart that you forget, perhaps. That's fortunate, but I can't forget. The present is so intolerable— the one thing that compensates is that it's interesting—the problem—our problem. You will probably think me crazy & indeed I hardly know what I am writing. You see it is terrible. There is no one to talk to. It's queer how few people understand! The thing that distresses me is that we are leading half a life when we might be leading a whole one. That's wicked.[17]

When this letter was written, Martha, aged twenty-one, was in the midst of her courtship with the man who would become her husband; they married the following summer. Her feelings toward the letter writer are unknown.

A few years later, when Natalie Scott, in France, received a telegram from Hilda Phelps informing Natalie of Hilda's impending marriage in the terse language mandated by wartime restrictions on telegraphic use ("marrying Hammond, January 23, love Hilda Phelps"), Natalie's response was close to distraught, indicating the emotional closeness that the marriage threatened. In letters to her mother, she declared herself "stunned" and "simply thunderstruck," unable to imagine her friend settling down to a wedded life based on routine. "Hilda," she mused, "whom I think of always as restless, seeking new fields and pastures green, in things and people." At the reception, the bride decreed that the first slice of wedding cake belonged to her absent friend. Natalie's mother duly sent it to her daughter in France, from where Natalie reported, "I swallowed my tears with the cake, and thought my thoughts."[18]

Perhaps because each woman had come from a birth family in which her only siblings were male, she found in her Newcomb friends the sisters she had never had. Fond campus nicknames coined early in the twentieth century clung to each woman for the rest of her life. Among themselves, the adults Hilda, Martha, and Natalie were Whildoo ("Will Do"), K-Marfoonie, and K-Nat. Their children knew them as Aunt Hilda, Aunt Martha, and Aunt Natalie. Among themselves, the three friends continued to use language they had invented during Newcomb days. Ten years after their graduation, for example, Natalie sent a birthday letter to Martha in which she referred to herself as "your monstrous big and entirely grown-up friend" and playfully sent "big, long, soulful kerfectionate kisses."[19]

Through the vicissitudes of life, all three women maintained a deep loyalty to and interest in Newcomb College. In the early years, Hilda and Natalie returned regularly to campus for "stunts" on Class Day during commencement week. Each spring brought the 'baby show," at which "alumnae spinsters" entertained the children of the married alumnae and their mothers. In 1910,

Hilda headed the entertainment, leading the tots in a rousing game of "Pin the Woman on the Board," allowing the blindfolded little ones to pin a sketch of a Newcomb woman in the midst of a photo of the male Tulane Board of Administrators. Martha, living with her husband in a lumber camp in the wilds of southern Mississippi, was of necessity less a participant in Newcomb alumnae affairs in the years immediately after graduation, but her interest remained keen. Correspondence with her Newcomb classmates helped to sustain her in her isolated situation.[20]

The vibrant Newcomb Alumnae Association fostered and nourished identity, keeping alums informed of each other's progress, soliciting funds for campus improvements, and embracing worthy causes, most notably sending the Newcomb Relief Unit to France in 1918. Hilda, Martha, and Natalie were "Newcomb girls," not only in their years as students on Washington Avenue, but ever after. A round sung to the tune of "Three Blind Mice" captures the spirit of the special bond.

> Newcomb girls, Newcomb girls,
> See how they come, see how they come,
> They start as such in the freshman class,
> And after the course is completely past,
> They join the alumnae and end, at last, as
> Newcomb girls, Newcomb girls.[21]

Love of self-expression and of argument formed an integral part of the campus personalities of Hilda, Martha, and Natalie. Hilda and Natalie shone as collegiate debaters. In 1909, Newcomb's Odds and Evens debated whether universal disarmament would be a benefit to civilization, whether a lie is sometimes justified, whether Japanese schoolchildren should be admitted to California public schools, and whether woman suffrage should be adopted.[22] As a senior, Hilda won the coveted Agonistic Award, the honor bestowed upon the school's best debater. From 1910 until 1915, she represented her alma mater in the alumnae debates staged annually between Sophie Newcomb and Agnes Scott Colleges.

Martha's penchant for long-windedness earned her the distinction of being the target of a good-natured poetic parody of Poe's "The Raven," in which the bird croaked in refrain, "but Miss Gilmore has the floor." The concluding stanza jabbed wickedly at Martha's prolixity:

Onward still with simple reason, on from season unto season,

Martha talked upon her subject, talked and talked from boundless store,

Not a single sigh was uttered, not a single threat was muttered

Not a single eyelid fluttered, on the eyes which saw no more

For each girl was slumbering softly, seeming to avoid a snore

While Miss Gilmore held the floor.[23]

The subject of this witticism must have found the doggerel amusing rather than wounding, for it was she, the editor of the magazine that published it, who held gatekeeper's powers to determine what would be printed. The magazine also twitted Hilda for similar tendencies to "run on." "Anyone in need of a subject for an epic poem need only apply to Miss Phelps '09 to be fully satisfied," joked an anonymous *Arcade* staffer, suggesting that in Hilda's telling, "the collision between her and the gym door would afford an admirable subject."[24]

A year after graduation, Hilda made her debut to society at the French Opera House, but the customary ritual of courtship and marriage did not ensue at that stage in her life. Instead, she and Natalie enjoyed a single life in New Orleans. They taught for a time in the Newcomb Alumnae Night School for working women and earned master's degrees in literature from Tulane. When the First World War plunged the country into a ferment of patriotic activity, Louisiana's governor named Hilda Phelps to chair the women's division of the Council of National Defense, in which role she urged the state's women to greater efforts of food conservation and voluntary service. Hilda promptly appointed Natalie Scott secretary of the organization, so the two friends continued to work together daily.[25]

This changed when Natalie went to France, in September 1917, to serve as executive secretary to the medical director of the American Red Cross in Paris. Her organizational skills and proficiency in French fitted her for the work. During the German offensive in the spring of 1918, while serving in a French evacuation hospital to help English-speaking patients communicate with French medical personnel, she endured nightly German air raids and behaved with conspicuous courage in evacuating wounded men from their bombarded hospital. She continued to serve after the Armistice, working with wounded doughboys until they were transported home, then working again as translator while Red Cross offices decommissioned and closed up shop. This extraordinary wartime service earned for her the French nation's highest medal for heroism, the Croix de Guerre.[26]

Natalie Scott made a triumphant return to New Orleans in the fall of 1919, greeted by a crowd of well-wishers at the railroad station. News reports noting that she emerged dressed in her service uniform, epaulets, trench coat and all, carrying a riding crop (!), sporting her Croix de Guerre "inconspicuously" on her lapel, and hailing the crowd with, "Hello, folks," indicate an unmistakable swagger in her manner.[27] For Natalie, a life of doing the unexpected had begun in earnest. Her path had already carried her far from the sheltered Newcomb campus and would carry her much farther in decades to come. Newcomb College was thrilled to claim her as its own.

Meanwhile, Hilda Phelps and Martha Gilmore became wives and mothers and lived conventional and comfortable lives in New Orleans until the 1930s. Then, with their youngest children safely enrolled in school, both exercised the resultant maternal freedom by becoming deeply involved in political reform movements.[28] Both led reform groups that they founded; both courted press attention; both were outspoken and sometimes acerbic. Hammond suffered a serious economic setback when Governor Huey Long fired her husband from state employment, plunging the couple into financial hard times and making necessary a long period of household retrenchment. Robinson's husband's lumber business flourished on two continents, affording her the luxuries of a capable staff of household servants, frequent travel, a vacation home in the North Carolina mountains, and a generous budget for clothing and entertaining.

Wordsworth's observation that "the child is father to the man" has a female parallel: one discerns clearly the outlines of the adult Hilda and Martha at Newcomb in 1909. The confidence born of unassailable social standing and stylish appearance typical of many women activists was amplified in both women as adults by their undeniable verbal abilities. In adulthood, they were articulate, verbally nimble, and in love with words. Hilda Phelps Hammond took on the formidable Huey Long in the 1930s, heading a statewide anti-Long women's movement. She traveled six times to Washington to confer with senators and President Roosevelt and addressed many audiences on the evils of Longism. Going unescorted in the nation's capital, locating Senate offices, and buttonholing officeholders may have been daunting, but she never lacked for words when she encountered her quarry. In her own telling, Hammond sometimes came across as blunt, abrasive, and even discourteous in her dealings with U.S. senators, so fervently did she press her case for ousting Huey Long from their august body. During Senate hearings into election irregularities in New Orleans, she rose repeatedly from her seat to address the committee without waiting for recognition from the chairman, hectoring the senators, chastising them for foot-dragging, and even courting citation for contempt.[29]

Hammond's daughter later recalled of her mother that "she didn't cook, she didn't sew, she didn't garden." Instead, she remembered a woman who read the New York Times daily and thrived on discussion and vigorous debate. When asked by an interviewer what her mother's hobbies had been, Hammond's daughter was interrupted by her husband, who said emphatically of his mother-in-law, "Your mother liked to argue." A veteran New Orleans journalist recalled that while he had admired Hammond for her principled stand against the excesses of Huey Long and his machine, he had found her humorless and grimly serious: "[Hammond] could be unpleasant . . . she could be short with people who disagreed with her. . . . I don't ever recall seeing her smile."[30] Crescent Carnival, a 1942 novel set in New Orleans, included a character that readers recognized as a thinly veiled Hilda Phelps Hammond. Being critical was "a lifetime habit" with this character, the leader of a fictional women's movement in Louisiana who grew "grimmer and grimmer . . . more and more exclusively the zealot."[31]

That argumentative side extended to public occasions as well as family gatherings. During World War II, a local reporter offered a glimpse of Hilda and Martha in full throttle at a public lecture: "There's never a chance of a dull evening at a lecture in New Orleans even if the lecturer is dull, when Mrs. Martha Robinson and Mrs. Hilda Hammond are both in the audience. . . . Well informed and extremely vocal, they like to put the speaker on the spot and frequently take over the argument from the floor, firing verbal challenges at each other as well as the speaker."[32]

Martha Gilmore Robinson acknowledged that she and Hilda did sometimes "wrangle like nuts when we get together," but, through it all, she maintained of her Newcomb classmate and friend, "I never leave her—sometimes exhausted, I'll confess, without the thought that she is so much more interesting and worthwhile than most of the people you encounter in life."[33] Robinson's activities in adulthood, focused through the prism of leadership of the state League of Women Voters, included leading voter registration campaigns, pressing for civil service reform and permanent voter registration, lobbying in person at the legislature, and monitoring polling places in New Orleans to insist on enforcement of laws banning alcohol and boisterous behavior at voting precincts. She believed fervently in the need for "good government" and worked for decades to defeat those she saw as practitioners of graft and corruption. After an unsuccessful campaign to become the first woman on the city council, Robinson dedicated her remaining years to historic preservation, winning some notable victories. Of particular satisfaction was the 1966 defeat of the proposed Riverfront Expressway, a U.S. Department of Transportation scheme that would have beset the city with a gigantic elevated highway directly bisecting the historic French Quarter.[34]

Robinson lived long enough to develop a reputation as one of the grande dames of her city, and also something of an *ancien terrible*. A local reporter noted her "smart clothes," "natural flair for colors and styles," "her very feminine personality," and "patrician assurance," but also observed: "She . . . speaks her mind at any gathering she attends. This has made her the subject of some barbed remarks from more timid or less well-informed women, but Mrs. Robinson goes blithely on, not at all perturbed by any controversy she may stir up."[35] A political columnist acknowledged that over the years many politicians had felt her "whip-like scorn."[36] Another reporter claimed to have seen her "in a tizzy" at a public meeting when things had not run as she had anticipated. The incensed Robinson had "descended from the stage like an avenging fury . . . reading the turncoat off and shaking a menacing finger" in the face of one who had upset her plans until "the mortified backslider was slumped crimson-faced in his seat." Thereupon, she regained the podium and resumed her meeting.[37]

If Hilda and Martha were Newcomb's Furies, boldly avenging wrongdoing and displaying a fearsome visage at times, then Natalie Scott belonged to the Eumenides, merciful judge and protector of the weak. Evidence for this interpretation comes chiefly from her correspondence with longtime friend Martha Gilmore Robinson, in which Natalie revealed over the decades broad streaks of leftist liberalism, humanitarianism, and appreciation and awareness of multiculturalism. Natalie's circle of acquaintances was wide; she counted among her friends artists, writers, and homosexuals in the French Quarter; intellectuals and theater people from New York's Greenwich Village; art collectors from the Southwest; and cosmopolites from all corners of Europe. She once brought a very dark-skinned Mayan elder home with her for a Louisiana Christmas, leaving tongues wagging. After a decade of life in New Orleans writing a column for the newspaper, she chose a self-imposed exile in Mexico, residing there from 1931 until her death in 1957. The expatriate life satisfied her love of the exotic and her desire to be free of convention, while also ensuring a comfortable standard of living on relatively little money, with house servants aplenty. When Mexican leader Cardenas expropriated the American oil industry in Mexico in the late 1930s, she applauded his action enthusiastically. This "Bolshevik" stand prompted Martha Robinson's husband, who deplored the collectivist tendencies of the New Deal and later hated FDR energetically, to forbid their daughter to visit Natalie. "Is he afraid the bandits will get her," Natalie jibed, "or that she she'll become a Socialist???" When Robinson failed to forward a letter from Natalie to his wife, Natalie wondered if he were stopping her letters "because he considers me a Red!"[38]

During the Second World War, Natalie again served with the Red Cross. She enlisted the Newcomb Alumnae Association to send parcels of comfort articles and recreation materials (cigarette lighters for burn victims, news magazines, model plane kits) for the wounded men at the North African hospital where she worked. Their generous outpourings earned thanks from the director of the Red Cross field unit, prompting Martha, who organized the Newcomb efforts, to crow, "Who said we were not ready to stand behind our Natalie." Subsequently, Natalie requested a release from that assignment because the hospital had adopted a policy of not giving comfort articles to German patients. "Why should we take even a fraction of an inch of a motion in their [Nazis'] direction, by inflicting little deprivations on little people, worst of all on the sick and wounded?" she demanded.[39]

Finding no official sympathy for her generous views, Natalie left the Seventh Station Hospital in North Africa and spent a leave in the States before her reassignment to the Pacific. To her dismay, it was not a happy interlude for her. "The States almost broke my heart," she reported. She had hoped to find "an awareness of the horror and extent of the tragedy of war . . . [and] a violent insistent demand . . . for a way to peace, for tolerance and understanding. Instead I found everything interpreted in personal terms, 'my loss,' 'my son's handicap,' and so on. And a carping, carping—against Russia against England—always *against!*"[40]

The energetic Martha took the lead during the war in organizing relief for Britain in New Orleans, but Natalie expressed disappointment that there was no parallel effort for the Russian people. She understood that American suspicion of communism colored feelings toward our Soviet allies. "If our government is run ultimately so as to give the masses of the people a fair chance," she opined, "I don't see why we need ever fear communism. Only

under-privileged and resentful peoples offer soil for growth of foreign ide-
ologies."[41] As the war crawled toward its fiery finale, both she and Martha
worried over the dangers of postwar isolationism. Unlike Martha, Natalie
harbored deep suspicions of British imperialist tendencies and hoped that
Churchill would be turned out in the postwar elections. She told her friend:
"He is not the man for a constructive program for his country. I fear that if he
is elected, war with Russia might be on the schedule."[42]

As the Cold War chilled the American scene in the immediate postwar
years, Natalie remained with the Red Cross, stationed in Seoul. Her reactions
to the announcement of the Truman Doctrine and the rising Red Scare were
rapid and negative.

> Our house of democracy needs a lot of cleaning, while we are so busy inflicting
> it wily-nily [*sic*] on the rest of the world! Poor Greece, almost as fascist now
> perforce as under the Jerrys and we virtuously going in to help hold down those
> who resist it! The catastrophic war will inevitably come from our course, and
> O the vast pity of it! Had we let Russia alone, let her get ahead to economic
> security, her people once industrialized would inevitably demand increasing
> freedom. Our big brains know that perfectly well, but they do not want Russia
> to have economic security with the resulting cut in our dollar supremacy. So
> they wave this menace of communism and blind our misguided people.[43]

Martha, the recipient of this fervent outpouring, had a solid understanding of global issues. She was neither uninformed nor provincial, supporting,
for example, Lilienthal's appointment to the Atomic Energy Commission and
civilian control of all forms of atomic energy and criticizing the reactionary
drift of the Republican Party. Finding her good friend naïve, however, she
took Natalie to task for being too sentimental toward the Russian people and
overlooking their government's menace. "Millions of Americans feel for the
Russian people," she wrote, "not because of what America will do to them,
but for what the Politburo is doing to them. I can't say your thinking seems
unmixed with sentimentality and the Party Line." She enclosed clippings of
comments by Norman Thomas and Albert Einstein in the hope of changing
her friend's liberal view of the Soviet cause. She closed her letter: "Humans
are the components of America, pretty decent ones. Don't forget."[44]

Spirited disagreements were a vital part of the friendship that Hilda,
Martha, and Natalie prized. Natalie had once complained, "I can keep my

most conservative friends in other places, even while diametrically opposed to them intellectually, but in New Orleans intellectual disagreement seems to be considered personal treachery!"[45] But, among the threesome, that was not so. They "wrangled like nuts" with others and each other, a reflection of their strong intellects and strong opinions, yet they retained until death the highest regard and affection for each other.

The year 1949 found Natalie once more in residence in Mexico, now sponsoring a day care center for the children of the impoverished working women of Taxco. Hilda, her crusade against Huey Long a thing of the distant past, was reading, debating, occasionally writing, but taking little part in public affairs. Martha by 1949 had emerged as the premier female civic figure in New Orleans, leading the League of Women Voters and spearheading efforts for historic preservation. Her opinions were routinely sought and quoted; she was a presence. The year brought the three friends together again for a happy time in New Orleans, their fortieth Newcomb reunion. Through Martha's interventions, Newcomb's president offered Natalie a temporary position as director of alumnae solicitations, chief fund-raiser in Newcomb's capital campaign to raise $200,000. She spent a busy month in 1950 visiting alumnae chapters in Louisiana, a popular speaker because of her record of dynamic accomplishments.[46]

Hilda, Martha, Natalie, and their 1909 classmates established the Class of 1909 Prize. It is awarded each year at the closing exercises of Newcomb College to the senior who has "best combined scholarship with effective and unselfish service in student activities,"[47] a definition that typified their experience at Newcomb. In the nurturing setting of a single-sex college, without the distractions and intimidations of young men, they had flourished, developed native abilities to the maximum extent possible, and stretched to grow intellectually, socially, athletically, emotionally, and spiritually. Natalie's reminiscences from a distance of nearly four decades strike a nostalgic tone: "I can see us all at old Newcomb, our gay times, our wild discussions, our plans and bafflements and exaltations. And Miss Imogen. And Ann Hero. Tewsie, Miss Harkness. And the chapel. And how life has knocked us about, one way or another, but also given us a lot. But sometimes I feel that I've assimilated pitifully little. How far still from the Spinoza goal—'to live under the aspect of Eternity.'"[48]

Death came early for Hilda Phelps Hammond and Natalie Scott, claiming them while they were in their sixties. Martha Gilmore Robinson lived to be ninety-two, a vigorous part of her city until the very end. Whether avenging

Furies or benevolent Eumenides, the three friends were always Newcomb products and very proud of their connection. Urged by their beloved professor Imogen Stone to become voters and to be "strong and fine," they responded.[49] Commanded by their alma mater to pursue "honest thought and high endeavor," to cultivate "shapely souls" and "ample lives" as opposed to fashion and form, to be above all "women noble, consecrated—each unto her calling true," it would seem beyond dispute that Newcomb's daughters Hilda, Martha, and Natalie succeeded.[50]

NOTES

Editors' Note: Pamela Tyler's essay first appeared as "Newcomb's Furies: A Tale from the Class of 1909," *Louisiana History LII* (summer 2011): 300–323.

1. Edith Hamilton, *Mythology* (Boston: Little, Brown, 1948), 44.

2. Ibid., 362.

3. Brandt V. B. Dixon, *A Brief History of H. Sophie Newcomb Memorial College1887–1919* (New Orleans: Hauser Printing, 1928), 132.

4. Ibid., 29.

5. Ibid., 34.

6. Lynn D. Gordon, *Gender and Higher Education in the Progressive Era* (New Haven: Yale University Press, 1990), 166.

7. Hilda Phelps Hammond, *Let Freedom Ring* (New York: Farrar and Rinehart, 1936), 23–24.

8. Martha Gilmore Robinson, oral history interview by Dorothy Schlesinger, August 6, 1972, Friends of the Cabildo Collection, Howard-Tilton Memorial Library, Tulane University.

9. Hammond, *Let Freedom Ring,* 23.

10. "Newcomb Rights," *Newcomb Arcade,* March 1909, 64–65.

11. Untitled poem, *Newcomb Arcade,* August 1915, 79. Dymond, longtime president of the Newcomb Alumnae Association, served on the Board of Administrators until 1951.

12. Undated *New Orleans Times-Picayune* clipping, Martha Gilmore Robinson scrapbook, Newcomb Archives, Newcomb College Center for Research on Women (hereafter cited as MGR Scrapbook).

13. Dixon, *Brief History,* 124, 128.

14. Ibid., 142–1 43.

15. This phenomenon forms the subject of considerable solid scholarship. See, for example, Carroll Smith-Rosenberg, "The Female World of Love and Ritual," *Signs: Journal of Women in Culture and Society I* (1975): 1–30; and Martha Vicinus, "Distance and Desire: English Boarding School Friendships," *Signs* 9 (1984): 600–622.

16. ETC, "The Newcomb Alphabet," *Newcomb Arcade,* January 1909, 48.

17. Illegible to "Marfoonie," June 27, 1910, Martha Gilmore Robinson Papers, Jones Hall Louisiana Research Collection, Tulane University (hereafter cited as MGR Papers).

18. Natalie V. Scott to "Muddie," January 23, 1918, and February 25, 1918, both in Natalie Scott Papers, Jones Hall Louisiana Research Collection, Tulane University (hereafter cited as NVS Papers).

19. Natalie Scott to Martha G. Robinson, August 8, 1919, MGR Papers.

20. See, for example, Martha G. Robinson to "Weechie" (Mrs. Thomas D. Westfeldt), September 11, 1911, MGR Papers.

21. Esther F. Harvey, "The Newcomb Round," *Newcomb Arcade,* April 1915, 37.

22. *Newcomb Arcade,* January 1909, 58.

23. "A Student Body Meeting," *Newcomb Arcade,* June 1909, 16.

24. *Newcomb Arcade,* January 1909, 58.

25. Isoline Rodd Kendall, *Brief History of Woman's Committee, Council of National Defense: New Orleans Division* (New Orleans: n.p., [1919]), 5–7; Hammond, *Let Freedom Ring,* 27.

26. John W. Scott, "Natalie Vivian Scott: A New Orleans Lady Goes to War," manuscript, passim, NVS Papers.

27. John W. Scott, *Natalie Scott: A Magnificent Life* (Gretna, La: Pelican, 2008), 220, 229.

28. Ibid., 228–29.

29. Hammond, *Let Freedom Ring,* 155–56, 185–86, 240–41, 270–73; Pamela Tyler, *Silk Stockings and Ballot Boxes: Women and Politics in New Orleans, 1920–1963* (Athens: University of Georgia Press, 1996), 50–51, 70, 76.

30. Hammond's daughter and son-in-law quoted in Tyler, *Silk Stockings,* 64; James H. Gillis interview by Pamela Tyler, January 24, 1986.

31. Frances Parkinson Keyes, *Crescent Carnival* (New York: Franklin Watts, 1942), 8–9, 610.

32. "She Leads in Labor for Peace," *New Orleans Item,* November 30, 1944, MGR Scrapbook.

33. Martha Gilmore Robinson to Natalie Scott, February 22, 1947, MGR Papers.

34. See Tyler, *Silk Stockings,* chap. 5, for the complete story of Robinson's 1954 campaign for a seat on the New Orleans City Council. Robinson's key role in defeating the expressway project is told in Richard O. Baumbach Jr. and William E. Borah, *The Second Battle of New Orleans: A History of the Vieux Carre Riverfront-Expressway Controversy* (University, Ala.: published for Preservation Press, National Trust for Historic Preservation in the United States, by University of Alabama Press, 1981), esp. 38, 74, 100–101, 171, and 204.

35. "She Leads in Labor for Peace."

36. Undated clipping [probably 1966], MGR Scrapbook.

37. Howard Jacobs, "Remoulade," *New Orleans Times-Picayune,* July 17, 1949; Clipping in MGR Scrapbook.

38. Natalie Scott to Martha Gilmore Robinson, August 14, 1938 and September 21, 1938, both in MGR Papers.

39. Katherine Parsons to Martha G. Robinson, May 17, 1944; Scott to Robinson, May 16, 1945, NVS Papers.

40. Scott to Virginia Withers Reese, December 1, 1945, NVS Papers. Reese was also a member of the Newcomb Class of 1909.

41. Scott to Robinson, September 1, 1942, MGR Papers.

42. Scott to Robinson, June 5, 1945, MGR Papers.

43. Scott to Robinson, April 15, 1947, MGR Papers.

44. Robinson to Scott, July 27, 1947, MGR Papers.

45. Scott to Robinson, August 30, 1938, MGR Papers.

46. *Tulanian*, March 1950, 2.

47. "The Class of 1909 Prize," 1, Newcomb Archives, Newcomb College Center for Research on Women.

48. Scott to Robinson, September 2, 1946, NVS Papers.

49. Imogen Stone, "Address to the Class of 1921 on Cap and Gown Day," *Newcomb Arcade*, December 1920, 52.

50. "Alma Mater," *Newcomb Arcade*, January 1909, 16.

15

FROM SOUTHERN LADY
TO STEEL MAGNOLIA

Newcomb Women and the Struggle for Civil Rights in New Orleans

SHANNON L. FRYSTAK

S treetcars wind quietly through the "silk stocking" district in New Orleans, past hundred-year-old homes, ancient oak trees draped with
Spanish moss, and, arguably, two of the city's oldest and most respected universities—Tulane University and Loyola University New Orleans.[1]
Tucked behind these prestigious institutional facades lining Saint Charles
Avenue lies the H. Sophie Newcomb Memorial College, where southern genteel families sent their daughters to learn the liberal arts. For many years,
these southern ladies also were expected to "finish" at Newcomb—find husbands to marry, have families, and rear fine girls and boys of the South. After
World War II, however, educational experiences for women, in particular, began to take a different form. Although institutions such as Newcomb College
remained entrenched in the traditional southern notions of gender, race, and
class, the young women attending these institutions of higher learning often
looked past their parents' expectations and searched for experiences beyond
that of wife and mother. For many young, white southern women, the social
protest movements of the 1950s and 1960s broadened their experiences and
provided their lives with greater meaning.[2]

This essay explores the highly controversial political activities of five Newcomb alumnae who challenged the traditional stereotype of "southern lady"
by actively working toward greater equality and the ideals of American democracy during the civil rights movement of the 1950s and 1960s.[3] Longtime
New Orleans residents Anne Moore Dlugos (NC 1944) and Felicia Schornstein Kahn (NC 1948) largely credit their sensitivity to issues of racial justice
and their subsequent activism during the 1950s and 1960s to their experiences at Newcomb. Similarly, Connie Bradford Harse (NC 1963), Margaret

Leonard (NC 1963), and Jill Axler Finsten (NC 1964) defied traditional notions of southern womanhood still present on southern college campuses in the 1960s and actively participated in the student-led phase of the civil rights movement in New Orleans.

In recent years, a number of histories have chronicled the significance of white female activists to the southern civil rights movement.[4] The historian and civil rights activist Sara Evans noted: "When the revolt of southern blacks began in 1960, it touched a chord of moral idealism and brought a significant group of white southern women into a movement that would both change their lives and transform a region."[5]

In this light, this essay is significant to the history of Newcomb College in that it alters our conceptions of the role of a traditional southern, white women's institution of higher learning in the mid-twentieth century. Despite the perceptions of the families who sent their daughters to Newcomb to "finish," and often to the dismay of Newcomb administrators, Newcomb unwittingly produced women who stepped out of prescribed gender and class roles to effect change in the Deep South during a period of intense racial strife. Indeed, the lives of these five women illustrate that for many southern, white female students, the postwar college experience broadened their knowledge of the world and enhanced their perceptions of their place in expanding democracy and equality in America.[6]

Born in 1926, Felicia Schornstein Kahn grew up in a traditional elite, southern genteel family. Like many of New Orleans' privileged families, her family owned a large house on St. Charles Avenue where they employed black servants. Kahn recalled her "nurses and maids" as "some of the most influential people in my life."[7] Despite Kahn's upbringing in the Jewish faith, a belief system often considered to hold greater sensitivities to social and racial injustice, she does not remember anyone challenging the racial status quo. "In this community," she stated, "I never heard anything questioned."[8]

Kahn believes that her real education in race relations began while attending Newcomb in the mid-1940s. Classes in history and sociology enlightened Kahn on social divisions due to race and class. One course on race relations taught by Newcomb dean Logan Wilson introduced her to the writings of the anthropologist Gunnar Myrdal, whom she described as "the intellectual expert on those issues."[9] In another class, Kahn learned of Democratic Party politics. Though these courses were never taught "in a way to challenge the status quo," Kahn noted that "the political interests of mine were carried through with some of the professors . . . who were political activists."[10]

Her early observations of race relations are evident in a paper she wrote for a sociology class entitled "A Southern Negro's Attitude on the Race Problem." In this paper, Kahn chronicled the experiences of what she deemed a "typical conservative middle-class" black female servant who had worked in their home for fifteen years. The sociology assignment gave Kahn an opportunity to talk with "Edna," Kahn's longtime servant, and admittedly, family friend, about topics not usually broached between the two, and appears to have had a long-ranging affect on Kahn's views concerning the expectations of the black community. For example, Kahn learned that "Edna" and other "typical conservative middle-class blacks" did not aspire to equality as she had expected. In fact, "Edna" believed that segregation was good for the black community. "Edna's" reflections shaped Kahn's conviction that only through education could the African American community understand their "lot in life."[11] While still a student at Newcomb, Kahn joined the well-respected educational organization the League of Women Voters of New Orleans (LWVNO or League). In later years, the majority of Kahn's activities would focus around her work with the League.

Kahn recalled the societal expectations for women graduates in the 1940s: "I knew that I was going to get married; I never thought of a career. I think that's one of the saddest [things], but that was part of the times. Why didn't I have equal opportunity to pursue whatever I wanted to as males did? But it was always women go to college to have the 'MRS' degree. You were supposed to get married, and you were supposed to have children, and you weren't supposed to work."[12]

While attending Newcomb, Kahn's attitudes on the role of women in society changed: "I was determined that I was going to work." After graduation, Kahn secured a job at the welfare department where, she stated, "Newcomb graduates went to work." It was her first racially integrated experience, although she recalled that there were "different rooms [for blacks and whites] for eating and recreation." Kahn married in 1949, and contrary to expectations for married women of the time, she continued to work for the welfare department. Her interviews and welfare visits to poor blacks and whites in the Iberville and St. Thomas public housing communities, as well as in the French Quarter, increased her already budding interest in racial and class divisions in America.[13]

Kahn's membership in the LWVNO provided her with a milieu for focusing her attention on these issues. In the mid-1950s, the League played a pioneering role in efforts toward racial justice.[14] Kahn often led in these efforts.[15] She not only advocated openly for the League's integration in 1953, but she also held integrated meetings in her home, a dangerous act for an elite, white woman in the 1950s South. Undaunted by the risk associated with being labeled a pro-integration liberal, Kahn served as chair of the League's education committee during the melee that erupted over the school integration crisis of 1960 and 1961. Through the League, she developed literature advocating desegregation of the New Orleans public school system and held meetings on integrated education and open schools. After the public school crisis abated, Kahn continued to work on racial issues with the New Orleans Urban League and the Community Relations Council, an integrated organization created to address wider issues of civil rights in the city. Moreover, Kahn was one of the first women to run for a New Orleans city council seat, albeit unsuccessfully; nevertheless, it represented a significant achievement for an independent-thinking Newcomb alumna. In the late 1960s, Kahn, along with fellow League member Betty Wisdom, cofounded Carrollton Central, a unique housing/employment/day care/health-care facility located in a poor black neighborhood in New Orleans.[16]

Kahn today remains active in the New Orleans community working on issues ranging from education and race to the American democratic system. Reflecting on her life, Kahn stated: "My philosophy about myself is that since I am so inbred in this community I have to reach out. Otherwise I'm going to be sunk. Otherwise I am going to be just like everybody else who lives in a tiny little piece of the world and doesn't know anything about the rest of the world."[17]

Anne Moore Dlugos's life parallels Felicia Kahn's in a number of ways. She, too, belonged to an established, elite southern white family. Although her parents raised her as a traditional southern lady, Dlugos recalled growing up in a family that espoused the virtues of "complete acceptance, complete freedom, [and] complete tolerance." Her mother was a member of the New Orleans Young Women's Christian Association (YWCANO), which as a more liberal organization, was in the "forefront of racial progress in New Orleans and all over the country." During the YWCANO integration in 1944, Dlugos's mother served as acting president, and although she recalled that her mother "wasn't exactly for it, she made sure it went smoothly."[18]

Dlugos lived much of her early life riding segregated streetcars and in other ways living a life separate from the New Orleans African American community. It was in college, she recalled, that she began to question southern race relations. Dlugos transferred to Newcomb her sophomore year, from Judson College, an all-white Baptist school near Selma, Alabama. Like Kahn, Dlugos learned about the politics of race at Newcomb. She remembered two professors in particular, Mary Allen and "Miss Labouisse," greatly influencing her perceptions of life in the South. As had Kahn, Dlugos took a sociology course that dealt "in detail" with racism. She recalled that Allen, an active participant in the civil rights movement and "registered communist," focused on race and labor history "in all of her lectures." After college, Dlugos became friends with the two women. In remembering Mary Allen, Dlugos explained: "[It] was the examples that she held up, the things that she described in a changing world, revolutionary movements, social change, human betterment. All the things that she [thought] that Christians should be involved in. She belonged to a church that became interracial. The more I knew her, the more I loved her, and the more she came the closest to living out her Christian beliefs."[19]

Despite the effect a Newcomb liberal arts education had on Dlugos's political sensibilities, like many American women in the 1940s, she married after graduation. "My ambition was to find a husband and raise children," she explained. "As far as 'mother' was concerned, that was the most fulfilling life a woman could have, but part of it was that you did community service, a responsibility."[20]

Dlugos's commitment to community service was particularly strong in the 1950s and 1960s. After returning to New Orleans from a short move to New York, Dlugos joined the LWVNO and the YWCA. It was within the confines of the League and a historically significant spin-off group, Save Our Schools (SOS), that her values and activism found expression. During the 1950s, Dlugos spoke to various groups around the city about what she deemed to be problematic about McCarthyism. Dlugos believed that "the number one problem in the country was civil rights and racial discrimination," and in the 1950s, the two were interrelated. She credits that belief to her friend and former teacher at Newcomb, Mary Allen. When the LWVNO began working toward integrating its own organization, Dlugos organized unit meetings and study committees and worked on voter registration by helping to simplify the registration process for undereducated African Americans.

In 1957, Dlugos committed her first "real act against segregation" by accompanying George Dreyfous, a lawyer for the ACLU and the husband of fellow League member Mathilde Dreyfous, to the state legislature to testify on behalf of school desegregation. Shortly thereafter, another League member, Gladys Cahn, asked her "if she would call a group of people to a meeting to organize support for keeping the schools open." In 1959, a group of elite white women, Dlugos included, organized SOS, arguably the most significant organization formed during the New Orleans school desegregation crisis. From the outset, SOS provided Dlugos with "an organization through which I could work . . . to bring about change. It was the most intense experience, second only to childbirth, that I ever had." Dlugos "ferried" the children to the newly integrated schools, held meetings in her home, and generated educational materials in an effort to change community opinion on the ways integration could work in New Orleans.[21]

After the integration crisis abated, Dlugos, like Kahn, continued to work on race issues in the community, albeit mainly with the League. Dlugos, like other southern white women of her generation, stand out for their actions during a time of intense racial strife. Unwilling to abide by prescribed gender, race, and class norms, Dlugos and Kahn used their privileged positions as respected white educated women to achieve a more equitable society. As Dlugos explained: "The fact that I didn't stand by and do nothing when the city was in crisis . . . [gives me] a sense of achievement."[22]

While Kahn's and Dlugos's activism played out after they left Newcomb, a new generation of women attending college in the 1960s would leave their mark on the institution's history and on the history of the civil rights struggles in the South. In early 1960, four African American college students in Greensboro, North Carolina, entered a local Woolworth's and sat down at the "whites only" lunch counter. The following day, twenty-seven students returned to the lunch counter and "sat-in." Within two weeks, sit-ins had occurred in eleven cities in four states, and by April, in seventy-eight southern cities.[23] The sit-ins ushered in a new phase of the southern civil rights movement: the student-dominated, nonviolent direct-action movement.

News of the sit-ins spread precipitously across the South, and soon colleges and universities in Louisiana joined the movement. In the summer of 1960, black and white students from around the city met and formed a New Orleans chapter of the Congress of Racial Equality (CORE). At the organization's inception, membership was comprised mainly of students from the city's black colleges and universities—Dillard, Xavier, and Southern University of New Orleans. Within a few weeks of the sit-ins, however, white students from Newcomb, Tulane, Loyola, and Louisiana State University of New Orleans (now the University of New Orleans) would join CORE. Three Newcomb students—Margaret Leonard, Connie Bradford Harse, and Jill Exler Finsten—joined CORE and the southern student civil rights movement.[24]

The experiences of Leonard, Harse, and Finsten typify those of white female student activists. For these three women, involvement in the southern civil rights movement, and their years at Newcomb, were transformative experiences. Leonard grew up in Georgia in a not-so-typical southern family. Although her family had owned slaves on her father's side, both parents— journalists—were extremely liberal for their time. Leonard noted that her father was more liberal-minded than her mother, despite the fact that her mother wrote a "pro-integration" column for the *Macon Journal*. Leonard's grandmother apparently had similar liberal tendencies for Leonard recalled her once remarking on the status of the family's black cook, stating, "Ida's real smart and the only reason she has to be a cook is because she's colored." Leonard's early learning and predisposition to liberal ideals played out during her time at Newcomb.[25]

Leonard received a scholarship to attend Newcomb in 1959, a year before the onset of the southern student movement. In the fall of 1960, a local newspaper article about a black student from Dillard University involved in the sit-ins prompted her to write him a letter. When the student, Lanny Goldfinch, invited her to attend a CORE meeting, she immediately joined. The following Saturday, police arrested Leonard and the other protesters for sitting-in at a lunch counter on Canal Street in downtown New Orleans. Undeterred, Leonard continued to affiliate with CORE, sitting-in and picketing on the weekends while attending classes at Newcomb. Her actions garnered the attention of Newcomb administrators, who admonished Leonard for her activities. She recalled the repercussions as "pretty severe." Leonard was "called-down"—an action akin to being grounded—by the dean of students when she sat-in and picketed with CORE. On another occasion, Leonard brought a black female friend of hers to campus and found herself once again in trouble with the dean for breaking Newcomb's segregation policy.[26]

When news of the Freedom Rides began to circulate, Leonard called Dr. Martin Luther King Jr. and expressed her interest in participating. She joined the rides in Atlanta and rode to Montgomery, Alabama, and then on to Jackson, Mississippi, where police arrested the integrated group as they attempted to enter the bus station's "whites only" waiting room. Leonard stayed in the Hinds County jail for nine days before being transferred to Parchman Prison Farm, an institution located in rural Mississippi well known for its harsh treatment of the civil rights activists interred there. While imprisoned, Leonard taught the other women French, participated in Bible-study groups, and sang freedom songs. At one point, jailers asked the women to stop singing freedom songs. When they refused, the jailers removed all of their personal belongings from the cells, including the mattresses and bedding they used for sleep. Leonard stayed at Parchman for sixteen days until members of CORE secured her release.[27]

After she left Parchman, Leonard returned to Atlanta. In the fall of 1961, she began a year of study at the Sorbonne in Paris. Upon returning from Europe, Leonard continued her work with the student movement in Atlanta, affiliating herself with the Student Non-Violent Coordinating Committee (SNCC). "When I came back," stated Leonard, "I had a real different point of view about the world. I thought it was important that southern whites make it real, real clear that a lot of us know it's [segregation] wrong, and that we're not all bigots. I thought it was important in the South, for a lot of [white] people to say 'No.'"[28]

Like Leonard, Harse arrived in New Orleans in 1959 on a scholarship to Newcomb. Unlike Leonard, however, Harse was raised with traditional southern values concerning racial segregation. Growing up in Birmingham, Alabama, she attended segregated schools and had no contact with African Americans in her community. In fact, her family boasted close ties to the infamous Eugene "Bull" Conner who brutalized civil rights activists in Birmingham in the 1960s. Indicative of her family upbringing, upon arriving in New Orleans, Harse accepted a part-time job handing out flyers on Magazine Street for the White Citizen's Council. She recalls having friends that first year who participated in the movement, despite her disagreements with them regarding their involvement.[29]

The circumstances surrounding Harse's association with CORE and subsequent civil rights activism are full of irony. In the fall of 1960, Harse attended a CORE meeting intending to prove to the students in attendance that segregation "was the best thing" for the South. At the meeting, however, Harse met young black students much like herself. "I shook their hands and talked to them," she recalled. "My head was turned around instantaneously." She immediately joined CORE and remained active with the organization for the next few years. As she explained: "We would go to meetings and we would talk and talk and talk. It was just very interesting to me. When I went to Newcomb I had never had a real date. So I was just fascinated to meet people who were willing to be my friends. I was fascinated to find out that black people were just the same as white people. In fact, I had been raised to think that the black skin color might rub off on me."[30]

Harse not only attended meetings, but she also sat-in, picketed, and took pictures for CORE, chronicling the New Orleans student movement. She was arrested, spit on, yelled at, and at one point had a cigarette put out on her back. Refusing to be deterred by this intimidation, she continued to work in the movement during her summers at home, affiliating with the Alabama Christian Movement for Human Rights (ACMHR), SNCC, and another student organization, the Student Union for Racial Equality (SURE).[31]

Although Harse suffered no serious reprisals at the hands of Newcomb administrators, her relationship with her family deteriorated. Because of her affiliation with CORE in New Orleans and her work in Alabama with the ACMHR, SNCC, and SURE, her father banned her from the house: "I was very unpopular with the white people there [in Birmingham]. My parents were very angry with me." In fact, her parents were so dismayed by her civil rights activities that they attempted to have her institutionalized at a mental health facility in Tuscaloosa. When friends of hers from SNCC heard of her predicament, the Reverend Fred Shuttlesworth "whisked her away" one night and took her to stay with Anne Braden in Louisville, Kentucky, for the rest of the summer. That fall, Harse attended school overseas in Scotland.[32]

Harse returned to Newcomb in the fall of 1963, only to discover a CORE organization in disarray. The black students had purged white students as early calls for Black Power began to surface. According to Harse: "I was kind of sad about it [the purges] because I really enjoyed what I was doing. I always thought that if that was the way they felt, it was probably appropriate not to have so much white input." Harse subsequently turned her attention to the peace movement, aligning with Students for a Democratic Society (SDS) in New York and, later, the women's movement in the 1970s.

Harse's change of beliefs is certainly not unique, but it is telling. "I was thrilled that there was something I could do to help," she stated. "I just thought that if I could show people that what I believed, that if I touch a black person their skin color would not rub off on me, maybe more people would come to the realization that I had come to. Normally you don't get those opportunities. It really caused me to do the same thing all through my life. I didn't have any spectacular moments like then, but I did try to follow that way all through my life. I trusted and appreciated all the people I met there. We were working for something."[33]

Many white women involved in the southern civil rights movement did not come directly from the South. According to Jill Finsten, "I was the quintessential outside agitator." Finsten grew up in Toronto, Canada, and moved to Florida when she was fourteen years old. Finsten feels that despite what Americans believe, Canada—much like America—*truly* was a segregated and racist society. Finsten's knowledge of a segregated world stems from growing up as a Jew. "Jews were very much a separate culture," she stated. "My attitude about injustice is very much shaped by being chased home by girls who called me a 'dirty Jew.'" From these experiences, Finsten believes that the line is very fluid between being Jewish and being black. That belief subsequently affected her participation in the southern civil rights movement.[34]

Finsten applied to Newcomb at the behest of her father, who researched the College's background and "found out that it . . . was a 'good girls' school.'" She arrived in New Orleans in the summer of 1960 to study art history. Initially, Finsten attempted to join "the sorority crowd," but soon realized that she did not fit in there. She had heard of the civil rights movement, the sit-ins, picketing, and later the Freedom Rides, and decided she "wanted to make a contribution." After reading an article about Margaret Leonard's involvement with the movement in a local paper, Finsten knocked on her dorm room door and expressed interest in joining CORE.[35]

Finsten attended her first CORE meeting alone, and like Leonard and Harse, she immediately immersed herself in the movement's structure. She recalled that the groups were "smallish," mostly black, and that they sat and talked for hours about how they needed to dress well, look nice, and act proper. Every Saturday, Finsten and other CORE members picketed and sat-in at the Woolworth's on Canal Street. She recalled: "I was terrified every time I went. Every Saturday morning I had diarrhea." Finsten also worked on voter registration and recalled feeling extremely frustrated at the apparent apathy of the people that either "wouldn't vote, or didn't feel that their vote made a difference. I could feel the sense of hopelessness," she said. "I felt that here we are busting our butts, pounding the pavement and trying to help people and the reaction was total nothing. It really took awhile to sink in that a lifetime of being treated a certain way, . . . well, you don't want a bunch of little bright-eyed, bushy-tailed kids coming in and bossing you around. They had seen an awful lot more than I had and to them, voting was certainly not going to change their lives."[36]

Like Leonard, Finsten remembered that her political activities prompted reaction from Newcomb administrators. On one occasion, the dean called her into his office and said, "I know that you're involved with CORE and I want you to know that there are a lot of us who admire what you're doing, but we can't take responsibility for you." Just knowing that the dean "admired her" made her feel very brave. When the dean then called her parents, they responded by saying that they knew of her involvement and that they were very proud of her. The main problem for Finsten, however, was that as a result of her activism she became a social pariah. "Being friends with me," she stated, "was like social poison." When her roommate asked her to move out, a girl across the hall, Mary Bell, a sorority girl, bravely let Finsten move in with her. The two remain friends to this day. In another incident, the mother of a boy Finsten dated begged her, on hands and knees, to end her involvement with CORE. She did no such thing, of course.[37]

Like Leonard and Harse before her, Finsten often found herself in precarious situations. While sitting-in at the local Woolworth's one Saturday, nervously chatting with a young black male sitting next to her, Finsten noticed three white men milling around. In an instant, one of the white men grabbed a hot coffeepot and poured the coffee all over her black companion. "It was just so deliberate," she recalled. "It was my first real inkling, the first time I was really scared. Nobody lifted a finger to help." On another occasion while picketing, Finsten noticed a white woman lean down and whisper in her young son's ear. The boy promptly walked up to Finsten and called her a "Nigger lover." She recalled her "shock" and her realization of the ways that people "learned racism."[38]

Like Leonard and Harse, Finsten participated in Newcomb's Junior Year Abroad program. When she returned from Italy, Finsten played only a marginal role in CORE, protesting rather sporadically her senior year. Yet she described her time at Newcomb as "the single most powerful, transformative experience, but for all the wrong reasons. There was no support for someone trying to think independently." In the end, she explained, "it was still just a 'finishing school' for girls." Still, Finsten believes that her role in the movement was important; her presence "as a clean-cut, nice white woman, lent some credibility to the movement."[39]

It is obvious that through the years, Newcomb provided a unique place for southern white women to gain a liberal arts education, to learn to think independently, and, subsequently to challenge the southern social structure at its core. The revolutionary nature of the civil rights movement itself, as well as other social movements that arose from the southern civil rights movement, provided women a vehicle in which to express their independence and to work toward a more racially and socially inclusive society. Yet even before the civil rights movement of the 1950s and 1960s, Newcomb women played significant roles in transforming the New Orleans community, if not southern society as a whole. These women continue to this day to effect change in their families, in their workplaces, and in their community structures. Although Tulane is now integrated and Newcomb no longer considered a "finishing school," for the women who attend, one wonders if without the foresight and actions of an older generation of women, the change would have come so soon. As these women so aptly demonstrated, Newcomb students brazenly applied "the lessons of the classroom to the world outside."[40]

NOTES

1. I wish to thank Elizabeth Palumbo and Emily Schoenbaum (NC 1989) for their comments on earlier drafts of this chapter. I am also grateful to the women who allowed me to interview them, sometimes more than once and often for many hours, about a time in their lives that is often difficult to revisit. The term "silk stocking" refers to the Uptown area described in Pamela Tyler's *Silk Stockings and Ballot Boxes: Women and Politics in New Orleans, 1920–1963* (Athens: University of Georgia Press, 1996), 1.

2. See Amy Thompson McCandless, *The Past in the Present: Women's Higher Education in the Twentieth-Century American South* (Tuscaloosa: University of Alabama Press, 1999).

3. This essay is part of a larger study on black and white women's activism in Louisiana's black struggle for equality (see Shannon L. Frystak, "'I Woke up This Morning with My Mind on Freedom': Women and the Black Struggle for Equality in Louisiana," [Ph.D. diss., University of New Hampshire, 2004]).

4. See Constance Curry et al., *Deep in Our Hearts: Nine White Women in the Freedom Movement* (Athens: University of Georgia Press, 2000); Sarah Mitchell Parsons, *From Southern Wrongs to Civil Rights: The Memoir of a White Civil Rights Activist* (Tuscaloosa: University of Alabama Press, 2000); Catherine Fosl, *Subversive Southerner: Anne Braden and the Struggle for Racial Justice in the Cold War South* (New York: Palgrave Macmillan, 2002); and Gail S. Murray, ed., *Throwing off the Cloak of Privilege: White Southern Women Activists in the Civil Rights Era* (Gainesville: University Press of Florida, 2004).

5. Sara Evans, "Women's Consciousness and the Southern Black Movement," *Southern Exposure* 4. no. 4 (1977).

6. Interviewees suggest other Newcomb alumnae actively participated in the New Orleans civil rights movement. I have been unsuccessful in locating them but suggest that the experiences of Kahn, Dlugos, Leonard, Harse, and Finsten are representative of other Newcomb students who participated in the movement.

7. Felicia Schornstein Kahn, interview by the author, November 28, 2001.

8. Ibid.

9. See Gunnar Myrdal, *An American Dilemma* (New York: Harper and Brothers, 1944).

10. Kahn interview.

11. Felicia Schornstein, "A Southern Negro's Attitude on the Race Problem," May 26, 1947, copy in possession of the author.

12. Kahn interview.

13. Ibid.

14. Nancy Neuman, *The League of Women Voters: In Perspective, 1920–1995,* League of Women Voters Publication no. 995 (Washington, D.C.: League of Women Voters, 1994).

15. For more information on the integration of the League of Women Voters of New Orleans, see Shannon L. Frystak, "The Integration of the League of Women Voters of New Orleans, 1953–1963," in *Searching for Their Places: Women in the South across Four Centuries,* ed. Thomas H. Appleton Jr. and Angela Boswell (Columbia: University of Missouri Press, 2003).

16. In March 1960, U.S. District Court Judge Skelly Wright ordered the desegregation of Orleans Parish public schools to take place on November 14, 1960. Four girls integrated the first grade in November 1960, and white families largely boycotted the schools; Kahn Interview.

17. Kahn interview.

18. Anne Dlugos, interview by Kim Lacy Rogers, June 30, 1988, Kim Lacy Rogers–Glenda Stevens Collection, Amistad Research Center, Tulane University, New Orleans. See also Kim Lacy Rogers, *Righteous Lives: Narratives of the New Orleans Civil Rights Movement* (New York: New York Press, 1993) and "Oral History and the History of the Civil Rights Movement," *Journal of American History* (September 1988): 567–76.

19. Dlugos interview.

20. Ibid.

21. Ibid. See also Shannon L. Frystak, "Elite White Women and Civil Rights in New Orleans," in *Throwing off the Cloak of Privilege: White Southern Women Activists in the Civil Rights Era,* ed. Gail Murray (Gainesville: University Press of Florida, 2004).

22. Dlugos interview.

23. Harvard Sitkoff, *The Struggle for Black Equality* (New York: Hill and Wang, 1981), 62–63.

24. August Meier and Elliot Rudwick, *CORE: A Study in the Civil Rights Movement, 1942–1968* (Urbana: University of Illinois Press, 1973), 101.

25. Margaret Leonard, interview by the author, March 29, 2003.

26. Ibid.

27. Ibid.

28. Connie Bradford Harse, interview by the author, March 19, 2003.

29. Ibid.

30. Ibid.

31. Ibid.

32. Ibid.

33. Ibid.

34. Jill Axler Finsten, interview by the author, May 23, 2004. For a discussion of the role of Jewish women in the New Orleans civil rights movement, see Debra Schultz, *Going South: Jewish Women in the Civil Rights Movement* (New York: New York University Press, 2001); and Clive Webb, *Fight against Fear: Southern Jew and the Black Civil Rights Movement* (Athens: University of Georgia Press, 2002).

35. Finsten interview.

36. Ibid.

37. Ibid.; John Randolph Hubbard was dean of Newcomb College during the early 1960s (1953–66); the Tulane dean of students was John Henry Stibbs (1951–75).

38. Finsten interview.

39. Ibid.

40. McCandless, *The Past in the Present.*

16

CAROLINE WOGAN DURIEUX
A True Original (1896–1989)

EARL RETIF

C aroline Wogan Durieux was a petite, proud Creole woman with piercing, hawk-like eyes who did not suffer fools gladly. Born of a Roman Catholic father and an Episcopalian mother, she developed a deep spiritual sense and a strong interest in things religious but with a sharply critical eye for all organized religion. She inherited a strong independent streak from her mother along with a burning desire to be an educated woman at a time when that was not the norm. Always intellectually curious, she constantly sought out new ideas and was reluctant to stay too long with what was tried and true. Learning new things and teaching others was as much a part of her life as being an artist. But from her earliest memory, she knew she saw things in a different way.

She began to draw at the age of four when her grandmother gave her a slate tablet with slate pencils. She soon discovered that by spitting on the slate and whisking the pencil around, she could create something that resembled smoke. This resulted in a series of pictures of smoke-spewing chimneys until her mother informed the budding artist that spitting was not a proper activity for young ladies.[1]

While in grammar school, Durieux took art lessons on Saturdays from Mary Butler, a member of the Newcomb College faculty. Durieux remembered Butler fondly as a teacher who taught her the basic rules of art, like perspective, without imposing restrictions on what she drew. Durieux had been working in watercolors since the age of six and was exhibiting great promise under Butler's tutelage.[2] Some of those very early efforts from 1907–8 depicting the Ursuline Convent, the French Market, and the Morphy Courtyard are now housed in the Historic New Orleans Collection.

Upon Durieux's graduation from high school at the bilingual private Cenas Institute for Girls, her mother insisted that she continue her education at Newcomb College in the Art School then headed by Ellsworth Woodward. Durieux received a broad education in both the fine arts and the liberal arts, but the one thing that Woodward drilled into all of his students was the importance of drawing.[3] She once commented, "If I can draw at all, it's because for four years every day we drew for four hours."[4]

Although Woodward and his star pupil were not always on the best of terms, Durieux respected him for the strong foundation that he and her other Newcomb teachers gave her. Woodward discouraged any exposure to modern or European art and had very set ideas on what constituted true art. Durieux commented: "He was a precise man who expected his students to copy his work exactly. This didn't sit very well with me, so I decided that I would do what he wanted even to copying his signature. Woodward always signed his work with his initials in block form. His EW and my CW (for Caroline Wogan) were as similar as I could make them."[5]

Durieux was interested in satire, and she often used humor in her art. Woodward thought art was a serious matter into which humor should not intrude. Her independent spirit often roused the fiery temper of the legendary professor. Durieux recalled: "One day Professor Woodward gave us the theme, 'To him who hath, more shall be given.' I made a black and white line drawing that showed a man in a hospital surrounded by his five children being presented with a new set of twins by a nurse. It brought down the house because it was the only one that was funny. All the other students had chosen to work more solemnly. Woodward couldn't take my drawing seriously. He would have if he could have; he just could not do it."[6]

Durieux earned a bachelor of design in 1916 and a bachelor of art education in 1917 from Newcomb. Her subsequent attendance at the Pennsylvania Academy of Art from 1918 to 1919 was something of a coup for it was highly unusual in that period for parents to finance advanced studies for women. It was the custom in New Orleans for prominent families to formally introduce their young daughters into society via a season of lavish parties. Caroline, however, was able to convince her parents to use the funds set aside for her debut to continue her studies. She often stated that being a woman worked to her advantage since, as she said "my father would have never allowed a son to go into a career so impractical."[7]

The Pennsylvania Academy was elevated to the forefront of American art education when Thomas Eakins (1844–1916) taught there from 1876 to 1886. Students from all over flocked to the school that educated the likes of Robert Henri (1856–1929), John Marin (1870–1953), Charles DeMuth (1883–1935), Charles Sheeler (1883–1965), and John Sloan (1871–1951). When Durieux attended, it was led by Henry McCarter (1866–1942), who had studied directly with Eakins. McCarter was a less rigid man than Woodward, and Durieux blossomed under his encouragement of individual expression.

Upon her return to Louisiana, Caroline married Pierre Durieux (1889–1949) in April 1920. Pierre was a childhood friend and neighbor who worked in his family's business, "importing laces, embroideries, white and colored dress goods and mosquito nettings." His job gave Pierre the opportunity to forge friendships and relationships with many associates in the Latin countries. He learned their customs and spoke Spanish fluently. Shortly after their wedding, Pierre took a position with General Motors as part of its Cuban operation.[8]

The Durieuxs lived abroad in Havana in the early 1920s except for a short period when they returned to the Wogans' summer home in Bay St. Louis, Mississippi, to await the birth of what was to be their only child, Charles Wogan Durieux. Caroline describes her Cuban stay as one of "quiet artistic growth." She thought Cuba was a very beautiful place, one that heightened her sense of color. Most of her paintings from the period were oils of still lifes, flowers, and landscapes.[9]

In the mid-1920s, New Orleans' French Quarter became home to an extraordinary gathering of creative and talented people including the author William Faulkner, who lived across the alley from Durieux. Faulkner's roommate at the time was William Spratling, who later moved to Mexico, where he created beautiful designs for handmade silver jewelry and one-of-a-kind art objects. Faulkner and Spratling would publish a privately printed book satirizing their circle of friends called *Sherwood Anderson and Other Famous Creoles*.

In 1926, Pierre was named the chief representative of General Motors for all of Latin America, and the family moved to Mexico City. He traveled extensively throughout the region while Caroline stayed in Mexico City and painted. Frans Blom (d. 1963), a professor in the Middle American Institute of Tulane University, provided Caroline with a letter of introduction to Diego Rivera (1886–1957), who eased her entry into the local community of artists. An artistic fervor was sweeping through Mexico at this time, with all the

Figure 1. Diego Rivera (1886–1957), *Portrait of Caroline Durieux*, 1929. Oil on canvas. Collection of Louisiana State University Museum of Art, Baton Rouge, Louisiana. Reproduced with the permission of Artists Rights Society (ARS).

leading artists being encouraged to create public murals that would educate the masses about the history and achievements of the Mexican Revolution. The artistic leaders of this movement were José Clemente Orozco (1883–1949), David Alfaro Siqueiros (1896–1974), and Rivera.[10]

Durieux was impressed with the artistic genius of Diego Rivera, but as usual she stayed true to her own individual style. Rivera once remarked to Caroline, "I like your work, because it's nothing like mine."[11] In 1929, Rene d'Harnoncourt (1901–1968), an important figure in the art world and later the director of New York's Museum of Modern Art, organized a solo exhibition of Caroline's oils and drawings at the Sonora News Company. Diego Rivera wrote a favorable review of his friend's exhibition and then chose the occasion to paint her portrait (Figure 1).

Again, a promotion for Pierre marked an important development in his wife's career. This time they moved to New York, where Caroline forged a lifelong friendship with Carl Zigrosser (1891–1975). Zigrosser would champion Durieux's career first as director of the prestigious Weyhe Gallery on Lexington Avenue, then as the curator of prints at the Philadelphia Museum of Art and by including her in his many books on prints and their creators. It was Zigrosser who recognized Durieux's talent and eye for satire and encouraged her adoption of lithography as a primary means of artistic expression.[12] The result was her first print, the 1931 *Teatro Lirico,* which depicted a Mexican chorus line of less than fatal attraction.

In 1931, the Durieuxs again were transferred to Mexico City. Caroline was eager to learn more about lithography, and she enrolled in the Academy of San Carlos (now the National University of Mexico) to study with Emilio Amero (1901–1976). Amero had a passion for lithography and was a major influence on Durieux as well as many other artists in Mexico and the United States.

In 1934, Durieux experimented with etching, a technique she learned from Howard Cook (1901–1980). Her images are very moving yet, for her, rare examples of overt political commentary. Caroline wrote to Carl Zigrosser: "All my etchings are harrowing. I think it is because the medium is such a precarious one—the least slip and all is lost. I can't be funny on a copper plate. I feel tragic the moment I think of doing an etching."[13]

Also in 1934, the first major exhibition of her lithographs, etchings, and drawings was held at the Galeria Central in Mexico City to unanimous critical acclaim. Zigrosser wrote: "Her most outstanding quality is her individualism. This work is all hers—original, personalized, without foreign influence. Her observations about human weakness are strong, satiric and ingenious. She is a creator of types, to which she gives the truth of life, making them a part of enduring and memorable art."[14] The Mexican poet Jose Gorostizo (1901–1973) remarked on her ability to balance comedy and pathos and declared her part of "the spiritual family of Charlie Chaplain."[15]

In 1937, Pierre Durieux was diagnosed with severe cardiac disease, and his doctors ordered him to return to the United States. The couple left Mexico reluctantly and returned to New Orleans. Caroline was coming home in style, a celebrity not only feted for her own art but as a colleague of Diego Rivera and the other great artists of Mexico. In the June 1937 edition of the national literary magazine *Coronet,* eight lithographs depicting North Americans visiting Mexico were illustrated.[16] In the article accompanying the illustrations,

Harry Salpeter wrote: "She strips people no less remorselessly when they're fully attired at the opera as at the beach, where they help by stripping themselves. Maybe the truth is that people are their own caricaturists waiting for a Durieux or a Peggy Bacon [1895–1987] to come along and tell on them. Perhaps, it is a little too early to say that she is a modern Goya, but whether this is a prophecy or exaggeration, it proves what an impact her work has made."[17]

From March through September 1937, Caroline worked as a consultant on the Federal Writers' Project, creating drawings for the *New Orleans City Guide* and the book *Gumbo Ya-Ya*.[18] She wrote to Zigrosser: "The drawings will amuse you—Negro spirituals, Creole ladies, whores and cemeteries. We have a Negro on the project who knows everything and everybody on the dark side of New Orleans. Nothing goes on that we miss—prominent church men and women, sportin' ladies, voodoo queens, he gets them all to pose for me."[19]

The dean of Newcomb College, Pierce Butler, hired Durieux to teach in the art department for the 1937 fall term. Durieux always credited Woodward and Newcomb for her drawing skills, and she placed particular importance on ensuring that her students could draw before advancing to other classes.

Durieux took on a second job as director of the Federal Art Project (FAP) of the Works Progress Administration in February 1939. In a state where segregation by race remained legal until the 1960s, Caroline's Louisiana division of the FAP was the only project not to practice segregation. Caroline always expressed great pride in that accomplishment: "I had a feeling that an artist is an artist and it doesn't make any difference what color he or she is."[20] Robert Armstrong Andrews, associate director of the national office, praised Durieux's work: "It is my observation that the people in Louisiana have more concern with the potentialities of the Negro and less for his limitations than the people of any other state."[21] Some of the notable artists who created works for the Louisiana FAP were Clarence Millet (1897–1959), John McCrady (1911–1968), Charles Reinicke (1906–1983), Laura Blocker Lewis (1915–), Knute Heldner (1886–1954), and Lawrence Arthur Jones (1910–1996).

In 1941, Durieux took a six-month leave from Newcomb and the FAP at the request of the Rockefeller Foundation to travel throughout Latin America with a special exhibit titled North American Paintings. The Museum of Modern Art and the Metropolitan Museum of Art, in conjunction with the federal government, sponsored the exhibition in an effort to promote President Franklin Roosevelt's "Good Neighbor" policy. By the time Durieux returned to New Orleans, America had entered World War II. Many of the artists who had been on the FAP had left to fight overseas so Durieux enlisted those who remained in a silkscreen project that turned out posters supporting the war effort.

Louisiana State University offered Caroline a position in their art department in 1942. She decided to leave Newcomb because she thought, "it would be more challenging to be at a state university where you could teach both men and women."[22] Another lure was LSU's more extensive printmaking facilities, which enabled Durieux to be more productive in her own lithographic output. The move also marked the first time she taught printmaking.

The 1940s saw the completion of three major projects by Durieux. She created ten lithographs to serve as illustrations for the book *Mardi Gras Day,* which also featured works by John McCrady and Ralph Wickiser.[23] She oversaw the publication of a book by LSU Press titled *Caroline Durieux: 43 Lithographs and Drawings* with an introduction written by Carl Zigrosser. In addition, Durieux earned a master's degree in fine art from LSU using her own lithographs as the basis of her thesis titled "An Inquiry into the Nature of Satire: 24 Satirical Lithographs." This thesis is a treasure trove of information because it affords a rare look into the thought processes of a creative artist on twenty-four of her most important works. The illustrations *Visitors* (Figure 2) and *Revelations* (Figure 3) are two of the lithographs from her thesis.

Durieux's lithographs of the 1930s and 1940s rank as some of the finest satirical pieces ever made. In *Visitor,* death is portrayed in the French fashion as feminine seductress rather than as grim reaper. Durieux's ladylike skeleton in all her finery comes to pay yet another call in wartime New Orleans. Her contribution to Carl Zigrosser's Artists for Victory exhibition was *Bourbon Street,* in which Durieux chose to portray our servicemen in a rest-and-relaxation setting listening to the jazzy vocals of two singers in a local club. Religion was a recurring theme in Durieux's work, as portrayed in the lithographs *Priests, Benediction, First Communion 1 and 2* and *Nuns on Orleans Street.*

In October 1949, Pierre Durieux, overcome by the health problems that had plagued him since the couple's return from Mexico, boarded a bus to New Orleans from Baton Rouge, checked into the St. Charles Hotel, and took his life. Caroline rarely spoke of this, but she made a pencil drawing of Pierre that calls to mind a death mask. Caroline's way of dealing with her husband's death was to throw herself even more into her work.

During the 1950s, Caroline traveled to Europe to work at Desjobert and Lacourierre, two of the great ateliers of Paris, where she created several series of color lithographs as well as etchings. *Insomnie* contrasts an initial

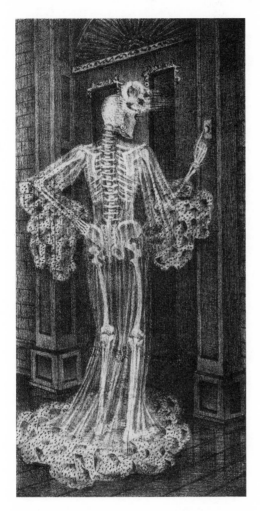

Figure 2. Caroline Durieux, *Visitor,* 1944. Lithograph. Courtesy of the author.

humorous impact with a most serious underlying message, which challenges the idea of death as that final, peaceful sleep. *Deep South* is the artist's statement on the Ku Klux Klan, complete with white-hooded figures and stylized crosses all rendered in a subtle red, white, and blue motif. The lithographs created in Paris represent the first time Durieux used color in printmaking. At first, her use of color was almost incidental to the lithographs she created, but soon she began to produce color-rich images.

Perhaps it is most important to know that Durieux was an innovator. Never content with her past accomplishments, she always strove to create

Figure 3. Caroline Durieux, *Revelations*, 1945. Lithograph. Courtesy of the author.

exciting new images in interesting new ways. In the early 1950s, Durieux began her experimental work on electron printmaking, demonstrating the peaceful use of atomic technology.[24] When she showed her electron prints to Arthur Heintzelman, then keeper of prints at the Boston Public Library, he drew a historical parallel with the cliché verres of the French artist Camille Corot (1796–1895), which he brought out to show her.[25] Her curiosity piqued, Durieux began to explore the possibilities of creating cliché verres in color. She successfully produced the first color cliché verres while simultaneously perfecting her technique for electron prints.

Durieux might be less widely known today precisely because of her pioneering creativity in these avant-garde fields. Though Carl Zigrosser championed her prints in all media, the general public remained hesitant to accept the new methods to which she devoted the last thirty years of her artistic life. Zigrosser, writing about *Impasse* in *The Appeal of Prints*, stated: "Electron prints . . . are true prints which indeed have a direct and intimate connection with the artist's own handiwork."[26] *Impasse*, Zigrosser continued, "depicts our constant struggle to overcome professional or emotional inertia in everyday life. We often become so bound by daily activities, so familiar and secure, that we fail to break the binds that prevent us from achieving our true potential."

By 1964, Durieux had retired from active teaching but was named professor emeritus and continued to work with individual students at her home and studio on the fringe of the LSU campus. During her teaching career at both Newcomb and LSU, she influenced the lives and careers of innumerable students who would go on to artistic careers of their own. Most notable among the Durieux students were Jesselyn Zurik (1916–), Robert Gordy (1933–1986), George Dureau (1930–), Elemore Morgan, Jr. (1931–), and Aris Koutroulis (1938–). In an oral history interview, Koutroulis talked about Durieux the professor: "And of course the major person who had a lot to do with my life was Caroline Durieux, the printmaker. She was fantastic. I learned from her not only about art but also learned about life. She was just absolutely amazing in her way of life and her way of thinking, the clarity of her mind and her presence of knowing what is and what isn't, what's real and what's illusion. . . . She imposed a certain discipline about working, about the process of working, somehow about the beauty of working."[27]

The ten years between 1964 and 1975 seemed to be less active in Durieux's career. She concentrated on her work with both electron printing and cliché verre, producing thirty-five images in that period. However, less attention was being paid to her work: nothing new was being written and there were no big exhibitions. Except in her local community, Caroline Durieux seemed to be an artist relegated to the history books. She and her art were out of fashion.

The late 1970s saw a resurgence of interest in the art and artists who had begun their careers in the early part of the twentieth century. All of a sudden, Caroline Durieux and her art were again relevant. In 1976, the Historic New Orleans Collection (HNOC) mounted a major retrospective of her work at their Royal Street gallery—the first exhibition ever held in that institution for a living artist. In 1977, Loyola University mounted a retrospective that complemented the one held earlier at HNOC, and LSU Press published an expanded version of its 1949 book on Durieux's lithographs with added illustrations and additional text. In 1978, at the age of eighty-two, Durieux conducted a three-day seminar on cliché verre printing in connection with Wayne State University and the Detroit Institute of the Arts. A full description of Durieux's role in the development of this process can be found in *Cliché Verre*, published by the Detroit Institute in 1980. At that time, the only cliché verre in the collection of the Museum of Modern Art was Durieux's *Frail Banner*. The LSU Museum also mounted an exhibition in 1978, Art, the Atom and LSU: An Exhibition of Electron Prints, showing only the artist's electron prints.

June and Norman Kraeft of the prestigious June 1 Gallery mounted an exhibition, Caroline Durieux: Three Lifetimes in Printmaking in 1979, in both their Washington, D.C., and Connecticut locations. The Kraefts later included Durieux's work in their book *Great American Prints*. In a 1980 ceremony, the Women's Caucus for Art chose Caroline Durieux to receive a lifetime achievement award for Outstanding Achievement in the Visual Arts.[28] Newcomb College mounted a retrospective entitled Caroline Durieux, Five Decades in Printmaking, just one of five exhibitions of the artist's work held that same year to coincide with the award.[29]

Howard Mumford Jones, a Pulitzer Prize–winning writer on American culture, wrote in the March 1978 edition of the *New Republic:* "I suppose Caroline Durieux of Louisiana was born too far South (and continues obstinately to live and work in and around New Orleans) for the critical telescopes of the New York art critics. There is now . . . another opportunity to consider the worth of this artist. Some satirists go to work with a meat-axe and some with a stiletto, but Durieux prefers the finest and sharpest of needles."[30]

Durieux's artistic career was ended in the early 1980s by a stroke that impaired her hand-eye coordination. She refused to draw or paint after that, even avoiding the art therapy that was prescribed as part of her recovery. She retreated into a world of books and had the library deliver seven new books each week. She read voraciously, seeming to prefer works in her first language, French, or her adopted language, Spanish. She liked to keep her language skills sharp, and this was her way of doing so. When friends visited, she would often be armed with things she had read that she would strongly insist they read. Her visitors often left looking for translators so that they could keep up with their frail friend. Hers was indeed a lifetime of learning until the day she died in 1989.

Artist, teacher, innovator—these were words often used to describe Caroline Durieux. While all are true, this daughter of Newcomb might have preferred to be remembered most as a learned and fiercely independent woman unafraid to speak her mind. She was a true original.[31]

NOTES

1. Much of this essay is based on the author's conversations and friendship with Durieux over many years. See also Ann Michelle Moore, "The Life and Work of Caroline Spelman Wogan Durieux (1896–1989)" (master's thesis, Tulane University, 1992), 12.

2. Caroline Durieux, interview by Lois Bannon, Baton Rouge, 1975, in possession of the author.

3. Moore, "The Life and Work of Caroline Spelman Wogan Durieux," 15–16.

4. Caroline Durieux, interview by Dennis Barrie and Marilyn Symmes, *Archives of American Art,* June 1978.

5. Moore, "The Life and Work of Caroline Spelman Wogan Durieux," 19–20.

6. Caroline Durieux, "An Inquiry into the Nature of Satire: Twenty-Four Satirical Lithographs" (master's thesis, Louisiana State University, 1949).

7. Durieux interview by Bannon.

8. Moore, "The Life and Work of Caroline Spelman Wogan Durieux," 37.

9. Ibid., 39–40.

10. Ibid., 44–46.

11. Cynthia Lamey, "The Graphic Art of Caroline Durieux" paper, n.d., 2.

12. Lithography is a form of printmaking that utilizes the principle that grease and water do not mix. The process involves the production of an image on a flat metal or traditionally limestone surface by treating the items to be printed with a greasy substance to which ink adheres, while treating the nonimage areas to repel ink. Impressions of this are then printed onto paper and can be used for multiple productions.

13. Carl Zigrosser, *The Artist in America: Twenty-four Close-ups of Contemporary Printmakers* (New York: Knopf, 1942), 128.

14. Ibid., 131.

15. Richard Cox, *Caroline Durieux: Lithographs of the Thirties and Forties* (Baton Rouge: Louisiana State University Press, 1977), 11.

16. Moore, "The Life and Work of Caroline Spelman Wogan Durieux," 73.

17. Harry Salpeter, "About Caroline Durieux: A Southern Girl Whose Pictures Have No Languor, but an Icy Bite," *Coronet,* June 1937, 50.

18. Lyle Saxon, *New Orleans City Guide* (Boston: Houghton-Mifflin, 1938); Lyle Saxon, *Gumbo Ya-Ya* (Boston: Houghton-Mifflin, 1945).

19. Zigrosser, *The Artist in America,* 130.

20. Durieux interview by Barrie and Symmes.

21. Robert Armstrong Andrews to Caroline Durieux, June 26, 1939.

22. Durieux interview by Barrie and Symmes.

23. Ralph Wickiser, Caroline Durieux, and John McCrady, *Mardi Gras Day* (New York: Henry Holt, 1948).

24. An electron print is made by creating an image on a flat surface with ink that contains radioactive isotopes. The radioactive image is placed in contact with a sheet of photographic

paper in a light-tight envelope. The envelope is then placed between two pieces of glass, ensuring absolute contact between the photographic paper and the matrix. The radioactive image reacts with the photographic paper to produce an exact print of the image onto the paper. The original image is radioactive; the final electron print is not (*Caroline Durieux Gallery Guide*, LSU Museum of Art, 2010).

25. A cliché verre print has the characteristics of both printmaking and photography. The process involves two basic steps. In the first step, the artist makes an image on a matrix (as in printmaking) that is transparent or partially transparent. This involves coating a transparent glass plate or sheet of plastic film with an opaque emulsion, such as printer's ink, on which the artist then draws an image with an etching needle or other sharp instrument to reveal the glass plate surface. The hand-drawn matrix is then used in a manner of a photographic negative when it is superimposed on light-sensitive paper and exposed to light. The light acts as the printing agent as it passes through the drawn areas of the glass plate to darken the corresponding portions on the photographic paper below, replicating the image as a positive print as in photography (http://arts.jrank.org/pages/9550/Clïch%C3%A9-verre.html).

26. Carl Zigrosser, *The Appeal of Prints* (Kennett Square, Pa.: KNA Press, 1970), 78.

27. Aris Koutroulis, interview by James Crawford, *Archives of American Art,* January 1976.

28. Ida Rittenberg Kohlmeyer (NC 1933) also received an award the same year (see the Ida Kohlmeyer interview in this volume).

29. A posthumous exhibit, From Society to Socialism: The Art of Caroline Durieux, was held at the Newcomb Art Gallery, in spring of 2008, with the author as curator.

30. Howard Mumford Jones, "Books Considered," *New Republic,* March 1978, 34–35.

31. The largest collection of Durieux works may be seen in the following museums: the Philadelphia Museum of Art, Philadelphia; the Historic New Orleans Collection, and the Louisiana State Museum, both in New Orleans; the Museum of Art at Louisiana State University and the Louisiana Art and Science Museum, both in Baton Rouge; and the Meridian Museum of Art, Meridian, Mississippi.

17

DAGMAR ADELAIDE RENSHAW LEBRETON (1891–1994)

Oral History Interviews from the 1980s by Adele Ramos Salzer, Anneke Himmele, and Susan Tucker

EDITED WITH AN INTRODUCTION

BY SUSAN TUCKER

Introduction

Dagmar Adelaide Renshaw LeBreton's associations with Newcomb spanned almost the whole of the twentieth century. She entered Newcomb as a freshman art student on the Washington Avenue campus in 1908 and retired as a professor of French and Italian on the Broadway campus in 1956, remaining an active alumna until the early 1990s. Her memories, recorded in interviews conducted when she was in her late eighties and early nineties, are especially representative of the changes that occurred in the interwar years (1919–41).

Besides her Newcomb undergraduate studies (Class of 1912, diploma in art, and Class of 1919, bachelor of arts), LeBreton earned a master's degree in French and Italian from Tulane (1923) and studied at the University of California at Berkeley, Columbia University, and universities in France and Italy. She was the author of a number of publications on Louisiana as a French colony, including *Chahta-Ima*, a biography of the Jesuit missionary Adrien-Emmanuel Rouquette that describes his work with the Choctaw Indians. She was a founding member of France-Amérique de la Louisiane and was an active leader in a number of professional, civic, and Catholic organizations.

LeBreton's enrollment at Newcomb and her subsequent teaching career exemplify the kind of students and the curriculum of the College that Tulane president William Preston Johnston had envisioned in 1886 and 1887. Describing the cosmopolitan, still then bilingual or trilingual air of New

Orleans, the early catalogues announced: "The city affords large facilities for acquiring a thorough knowledge of the modern languages, and board can be obtained in families where French, German, or Spanish is correctly spoken."[1] The Renshaw family was such a family, and Dagmar's recollections present remnants of the world that Johnston saw in the early 1880s.

Among the eleven children of Judge Henry Renshaw and Marie Eugenie Deynoodt, only the four youngest of the eight daughters were given the opportunity to attend Newcomb College. These would be Dagmar, Gladys, Solidelle, and Mildred—all born in the 1890s. Older sisters Marie, Yvonne, Yolande, and Marguerite (born between 1879 and the mid-1880s) were needed to help in the family or married early in life, circumstances vaguely recalled by LeBreton as reasons for foregoing an education at the College. In addition, the College was not immediately trusted by all New Orleanians, the Renshaws included, who may have considered an education at home in their father's library a superior alternative.

Thoughts on the need for women's higher education in a place such as Newcomb changed very slowly over Newcomb's first decades. Rumor long held that French-speaking families were wary of the College. Two exceptional Creole students in the 1880s and early 1890s, Amélie and Desirée Roman, might have convinced the skeptics to change their minds. The Roman sisters attended Newcomb because of the influence of their guardian, the Tulane French professor Alcée Fortier, and because they had attended the Saturday art classes taught by William and Ellsworth Woodward during the Cotton Exposition of 1885. Two other Creole sisters from the 1890s, Marie and Emilie de Hoa LeBlanc, worried their families when they had to take the "dangerous" streetcar ride out to the Garden District from the French Quarter.[2] Among the fifty-nine students registered as academic or art students during 1898–99, none was educated at bilingual schools, which until the 1920s included Ursuline Academy and the Academy of the Sacred Heart. Dagmar LeBreton attended another bilingual school, Picard Institute. By 1911–12, among the 180 academic students at Newcomb, seven students came from families living in the French Quarter or along Esplanade, the historic homes of most Creoles and the location of most of their schools.[3]

Besides the dividing line of language, religion was also an issue for Creole families considering some form of postsecondary education for their daughters. The Academy of the Sacred Heart and Ursuline Academy were thought to offer a better choice for most Catholic young women. LeBreton would be one of a few professors and students to organize a late-1930s Catholic club on campus, a development that highlighted the novelty of Catholics at the school.

One senses also the tension between the Creole residents and the early students and administration when LeBreton discusses her beginning years at Newcomb. As a French teacher, she followed a teacher long revered among the Creoles, Clarisse Cenas (1840–1927), who began teaching at Newcomb in 1907. Preceding Cenas was another acclaimed Creole and the first French faculty member, Marie Augustin, known especially for her book on the Haitian Revolution, *Le Macandal*. This volume was one of twenty-five books representing the history of Louisiana at the Woman's Building of the 1893 Chicago World's Fair.[4]

Given that LeBreton would continue teaching at the College until the mid-1950s, the ladder of influence of these Creole women was a long one, leading indirectly to the founding of the Junior Year Abroad Program. The Renshaw family itself touched generations of Newcomb and Tulane students through foreign languages and travel. Besides LeBreton's work in French and Italian, her sister Gladys (NC 1914) taught Latin, Spanish, and French for many years at Newcomb. Both sisters, along with Professor Adele Drouet, led tours in the summers of the 1920s and late 1940s, taking Newcomb students to see various cities in France, Italy, and England.[5] Another sister, Marguerite (called Margot), worked as a reference librarian and specialized in languages and literature at Tulane's Howard-Tilton Memorial Library.

The community of the College and especially its evolution is also glimpsed in LeBreton's mention of her colleague and math professor Marie Johanna Weiss (the first woman to receive a doctorate from Stanford), who felt Newcomb's high standards should be better publicized to the nation as a whole. Though Weiss's vision for a nationally based student body would not be realized until the 1960s, enrollment during the 1920s through the 1930s grew to reflect other circumstances of LeBreton's narrative. During the interwar years, even during the Depression, more and more middle-class families sent their daughters to Newcomb. The College came to be considered an affordable school and no longer the home for only the daughters of the city's elite. Indeed, the elite began more and more to send their daughters farther away. The Godchaux family, for example, mentioned in both this interview and the following one with Ida Kohlmeyer, sent all of their daughters born between 1915 and 1930 to the northeastern women's colleges.[6]

Finally, besides these wide-ranging insights over such a long period of time, LeBreton gives voice to the gratitude she felt for her own growth in such a community. After the early death of her husband, it was her former Newcomb professors and fellow alumnae who encouraged her as a scholar and a teacher. Later, she found similar connections and the chance to nurture others through those alumnae who became teachers in the public schools and those students they sent to the College.

Narrative from the Interviews

I begin with this memory for you: Once, after I had become a member of the faculty at Tulane, I had a gathering here of professors. And one of the young men . . . I remember, actually looked into my library, saw the books we had there and said, "Where were you educated?" I replied, "At home." You see my father was a tremendous reader. . . . And he encouraged our reading and our education. Very early in my childhood, he had picked out books for us to read. He was very, very learned. . . . He was not only a great reader but he did some writing. . . . He was one of the first graduates of Tulane Law School. . . . I re-member when he gave me to read *The Stones of Venice* by Ruskin, and one of the Spanish philosophers. And then he saw to it that we read the Greek philos-ophers too. I remember reading *Pericles and Aspasia*. At the time, I remember that I thought, what is this all about? But later I knew . . . for the parties of my older sisters . . . they would ask Papa to read to them. Years ago, I remember one Mrs. Kerr, one of the Kerr girls, Mrs. Jackson I think her name was, said. "Oh, you know, I remember those beautiful evenings when your father used to read to us from Shakespeare."[7] So we were surrounded with that sort of thing you see and that's where most of our education came from.

Then, of course, we had the French opera that we went to. Always went to the opera. The French aunts, you see, would take us to the French opera. We had to climb way up top, *au troisième*. We heard the music, and then later, we'd sing it around the house. We especially liked Verdi and Wagner.

But in our family, we didn't go out very much because after the Civil War, people were not very prosperous. . . . Most of our entertainment was around the house, around the home, you see. Reading was how we spent our time, reading both in French and in English.

So, we went to school, at home . . . not in kindergarten, first grade or anything of that sort—nothing formal to begin with but a definite beginning at home, one that lasted.

Many young women were educated like this. I remember when one of my sisters was at Newcomb High School, along with the daughter of one of the presidents of Tulane University, and they had this remarkable English teacher, Miss Julia Logan. And Miss Logan gave an exercise; she wanted them to write a certain sentence that was going to illustrate something. And the two little girls chose as their sentence a sentence from Shakespeare. But even she, Miss Logan, just couldn't believe our little freshmen at Newcomb High School could quote Shakespeare to illustrate a grammar lesson. But that was the type of education that many of us had at home then. . . . We went to . . . one of those bilingual schools here in New Orleans, which came after the Civil War. There must have been ten or twelve private schools that were all bilingual. French and English, or English and German, or English and Italian. Maybe not Italian. I don't remember. But never Spanish. I do know that because the New Orleanians—we don't know Spanish too well. Here they [the French] really treated Spanish very badly. My sister Gladys, who taught Spanish all those years, wrote an article on the Spanish educational regime in New Orleans, and she said it was absolutely superior. But the French would have nothing to do with the Spanish. They wanted to cultivate the French. . . . But I know there were German and English schools too. And they prepared you all through elementary school and some of them through high school. . . . We [at the Picard Institute] had a dual program. In the morning all of our lessons were in French, the French language; in the afternoon, in English. And we had this remarkable French teacher whose method for teaching was extraordinary. I remember when I taught later at Scripps College, that my New Orleans teacher from 1905 had applied the same philosophy of teaching that Scripps did much later. And that was to connect your education with everything else that's happened in that particular time—*les faits historique et les faits divers.* You learned both. You had your particular subject, for example, you had Roman history, well then you had what happened in Rome and what happened in the other countries, what happened daily and what happened on the large scale.

Now in our household, our two grandmothers lived. One was of French descent, and one, Grandma Renshaw, was thoroughly English and Scotch descent. So we children grew up speaking the two languages to the two grandmothers just as we did in school. And there were ever so many families like that in New Orleans. . . . We called some families *American families* and others we called *French families.* The two intermarried, you see, but a great many people in New Orleans were bilingual. . . . French was thought to be superior.

New Orleans always had this idea, and sometimes the French curriculum was very advanced. The interesting thing was—when Newcomb started out, the students from Sacred Heart College were given sophomore standing when they came to Newcomb. Because in those days, the old convent was evidently under the French college program, you see. And they had studied beyond what we taught for the first year.

Three of my sisters and I went to Newcomb. There was no question that we would not go there, though the older ones stayed home because one married early and the others—my mother died in 1906, so they helped at home. We four came to Newcomb because it was here, and because then we could afford it. . . . People were not very rich after the Civil War. And we were a family of eleven children. We couldn't have considered anyplace else but also we didn't do so because, being from New Orleans, we were very conservative. Girls, and even boys, should stay close to home—that was the conservative thought . . . keep the family together. So Newcomb met that standard and it was affordable. At the same time, it was really quite a thing to go to Newcomb. It was a privilege. Though it was affordable to us, we were also told that a great many people considered Newcomb a rich man's school. . . .

Newcomb, then, was on Washington Avenue. We'd ride the streetcar. We were living downtown in the Quarter by that time, and we'd catch the Carondelet car and come up on Bourbon Street to Canal Street then we'd continue up Carondelet Street. . . .

Old Newcomb, this is called now. And this, the physical place of Newcomb, left quite an impression upon the students. . . . Old Newcomb in itself may have lent the air of a rich school. The old Robb mansion, a glorious place. And around it, the very pretty campus, with its chapel and its pottery building, and stately music building, and a fountain. Inside the main building, I remember a sort of Chinese urn that was there. And they had had this marvelous big table that the library inherited. It was a beautiful hand-carved table that came from the Howard Library.[8] But here particularly the Arcade was lovely. . . . I can remember sitting on those big steps that were under the Arcade, the famous arcade that connected two parts of the building. We called the wonderful little magazine that was published, the student publication, the *Arcade*. There are some excellent things in that publication. I remember there were the remarkable illustrations by the artists who made Newcomb famous. . . . But all through Newcomb there were people of that sort: Sadie Irvine and others.

The [Newcomb] High School was really an excellent high school. Some of the people later went over into the College. For example, there were the two Spencer sisters, Miss Adelin Spencer and Miss Mary Spencer.[9] One taught mathematics; the other one taught chemistry, I think, both in the High School and later the College, and they had advanced degrees from the East. There was Myra Rogers for whom the chapel is named. She was a Latin teacher; she was an excellent Latin teacher in the High School, and after she received her PhD, in the College.[10]

And in the High School, there was Miss Julia Logan, the one who I mentioned had the freshmen who quoted Shakespeare. But when the standardizing committee decided that a College could not have a high school on the same campus, the High School was abandoned.[11]

Now in 1908, I was an art student. . . . They had the remarkable faculty, wonderful people in that department, such as the old potter Joseph Meyer. And then we had another remarkable teacher there, Mrs. Gertrude Roberts Smith, who also came from the Northeast. Oh, she was a terror. We were terribly afraid of her. Every Friday we had to bring in an original composition and oh, ooh, you would think she might slay us, we were that afraid of her. Because she didn't mince her words. She told you whether it was trash or whether it was worthwhile.

I think Mr. Woodward really taught me how to appreciate literature as well as art. He was remarkable; he was so sensitive to beauty. There was in my class a beautiful girl. She had dark, dark hair; dark, dark eyes; fair, fair skin; and rosy, rosy cheeks. She was beautiful. And very popular with boys and so on. . . . And during one of his lectures, Mr. Woodward said: "Young lady, will you please go and sit on the back row? You are so beautiful that you distract me as I deliver my lecture."

But so many things I remember about my art from him. The first time I went to Europe so much of what he had taught came to light. I'll never forget my excitement when I came face to face with Michelangelo's *Moses*—I almost passed out. This was in San Pietro in Vincoli, the famous church in Rome. I lost my breath, I couldn't get over it. Mr. Woodward had shown [it to] us through so many beautiful pictures. And I remember his description of the Sistine Madonna, who seems to be standing on top of the world, with the winds of the sphere grazing her veil—with sort of loops around her. Mr. Woodward made these things so alive, so real.

The language department and the English Department at Newcomb were very good, as well. They always had a remarkable language department. We had native French, and we had some very, very distinguished Frenchmen who came, but after a while, as salaries went up, they could get more elsewhere.

Mr. Durel, I remember was teaching at a loss of a thousand dollars a year.[12] And when I was there, too, Mr. Wespy was another very good teacher. He was the old German professor, and Miss Stone was a remarkable woman, the English teacher. And another was Mildred Tonge. She taught English. She was English and she was very bright, very smart, and she introduced a lot of very interesting features. She oversaw lovely class plays. Very English, and we did *Alice in Wonderland* in 1912. . . .

Oddly enough I remember orientation. I remember getting a letter before I came to Newcomb, talking about orientation. Or maybe it was called something different, but that is where I met my friend Elizabeth McFetridge. She was in the academic program. In that class was Amy Hinrich, who became a school principal in Orleans Parish schools, and Juliette Godchaux and a number of others—Janey Marks, Louise Nelson, Evelyn Kahn—a number of remarkable women. Elizabeth McFetridge taught at McGehee's. She was a skilled and creative teacher all her life.[13]

Most of my very closest friends were my sorority sisters. I was an Alpha Omicron Pi. And we all had rooms in the first floor of this great big building, the Robb Mansion. So we would have our sorority meetings [there]. But overall, I belonged to the studious group.

When I left the Art School, I was married the year I graduated. I was married and I was widowed the following year. I had a child to support so I taught for a while at Miss Finney's School because I could draw. Then I came back to work at Newcomb. Mr. Woodward was awfully nice, awfully nice. He offered me a position in the Art School. But he said: "But my dear, I would suggest that you specialize in something else. Because I don't think that you could make a life's work of art." So I went into language. That's when I studied language. I returned to Tulane and got my master's degree. And then I taught again. I taught for a while in Newcomb High School. I taught for a while in the public school. Oh I enjoyed my public school teaching. I learned a lot from my public school teaching. I really did.

We had never gone to public schools, you see, and I met all of these nice children, well-behaved children who I would never have met. I was still living downtown, and taught at the John McDonogh High School. Times had changed, and I knew it because I had children of Italian descent. We had children of French descent. We had children of German descent. And I would ask each one of them as they came in, "Do you speak German?"

"No ma'am!" In a southern accent, they would say this.

"Do you speak Italian?"

"No ma'am!"

Their fathers or mothers did, but they didn't. But they were some lovely, lovely girls, girls who later became my personal friends, whom I taught at John McDonogh High School. Too, then there was quite a group of interesting teachers, mostly Newcomb graduates, you see. . . . That was really an educational experience for me as much as for them. Because not only was there this difference about languages, but also in the olden days, people were so much more class-conscious. And in my traditional New Orleans, people didn't appreciate public schools. I was privileged to learn that the students there were lovely girls. Many of these went on to Newcomb. I remember a class on Browning, we were studying Browning when one little girl, with big blue eyes, she asked me about the emotions Browning had described, "Do people really act that way, Mrs. LeBreton?" I said, "Yes they do." You really feel that you give something to high school students.

I enjoyed my college teaching too because there I felt I was educating myself too, but in a different way: where I was expanding the world of knowledge. But in high school teaching, I was expanding too something within each child. In high school, you had to be somebody to interest the children.

[My career at Newcomb] . . . to give you an idea of the long history of Newcomb as well as my own, consider that I followed there, Madame Cenas. She was in the family that ran another of the bilingual schools, this one on Esplanade right at Rampart. And she was a typical, typical French-Creole instructor of her time. One who was terribly strict. Mr. Dixon, the first dean of the College, said to me, "In hiring you, I think, I must say that I don't think the older French quite understand our new American children." He said, "Now that Madame Cenas is going to retire, I will say that the students have complained that they couldn't even sneeze in her class." He said, "They have to always be overly conscientious and perhaps too very respectful, very rigidly composed in a way they are not used to being."

So I began at Newcomb, taught art one year and then French for four years, during which time I earned my bachelor of art. I had to do that, as in 1912, the art students earned only a certificate and to be a true college graduate, to earn more money, to support my child, I returned to school. The second degree came in 1919, and then I taught in public schools for many, many years and during those years, I earned a master's degree in French and Italian from Tulane.

Then I went to teach at Scripps College in the fall, what year was that?—
Must have been in the 1940s somewhere, and spent a year there.

I came back to Newcomb, to the College, where I taught until 1956, when
I retired. I taught French and Italian. By then, Newcomb had instituted a Department of Italian, for the girls who had completed their language requirements. They required three years of language at Newcomb and they taught
then Latin, French, Spanish, Portuguese, and Italian, and then later again
Russian and German. But German, you might like to know, was discontinued
during World War I. It had been taught from the beginning at Newcomb. But
then the war came and the frenzy over the Germans occurred, and they cut
German from the curriculum, which of course was a great mistake. They felt
that you shouldn't have a thing to do with the Germans. For Mr. Wespy, the
German teacher, and so long a part of Newcomb—many of the people here
were heartbroken for him.[14]

In looking back, though, in other ways, Newcomb followed no set pattern of events or ideas. For the whole of the first period up until the 1940s,
Newcomb was very insulated in a way. Yet, in a way it was very advanced. A
Newcomb education prepared you well because you met other people, you
were on your own, you had to—you had to make good. It was a chance of just
trying out yourself against the group. Mr. Dixon, the first president, had high
standards. He was a college man. And he set the standard for Newcomb, and
Newcomb held up pretty well. I remember after more and more classes were
allowed for both men and women in Tulane or Newcomb, one of the teachers
in the Tulane French Department said: "I can't understand it, I can't understand it. We have so few of the girls come over here. Why don't they come? All
of the men want to go to Newcomb!" Newcomb really held higher standards.
We emphasized, you see, the classics, and there was great emphasis on the
classics.

But in other ways, it was rather insulated. . . . For one thing, Newcomb
was a small school. It was Dean Butler who said he would never let the school
go beyond six hundred or maybe three hundred.

I remember one of the younger teachers, Miss Weiss, in math, who came
from California but had taught at Vassar, and she arrived and was delighted
with Newcomb.[15] And she wanted to tell others what a good school it was, so
she was just indignant because Newcomb didn't advertise. She said it made
her perfectly furious to think of other colleges like Sweet Briar and the rest
of them who would have big pages in the *New York Times* and nothing about

Newcomb. To people from outside New Orleans and the Deep South, you mentioned Newcomb and they didn't know what Newcomb was. But Mr. Butler drew himself up and said we will not advertise.

So it remained then a very intimate group, where most of the girls were from New Orleans or from the nearby states—girls who had the same sort of background that we had, and very few girls from very far away. And that made us very conservative because here we were in New Orleans. In my days as a student . . . you couldn't even have an unmarried man as a teacher at Newcomb.

But we managed pretty well. There was basketball—that was very well known. My sister was quite a basketball player for her team. And, we did some debating, and our most important debating was against Agnes Scott. . . . And even the Tulane professors often said that Newcomb students were smarter than Tulane students.

In the years that I taught, we had a perfectly remarkable dean of women, Miss Many, who was herself a Newcomb graduate. Even when Dean Butler was there, Miss Many saw that she kept in touch with what was going on in the other private schools, up in the East.[16] So Newcomb has always had a rather high level of education. . . .

Inside New Orleans, we were thought of as rigid and rigorous, and outside, no one thought of us at all. But Mr. Butler said that advertising was something for a finishing school to do, and we were not a finishing school. We were a college. And the only thing that ever might have been assumed to be less than rigorous or up to the same standard as a very difficult male college was the Department of Home Economics. And they dropped that because they felt that that was below the academic level. The standardization came in you see. And Newcomb got its first-class rating very promptly after dropping the High School. They dropped the High School on account of that.[17]

But then there was the problem of education [as a field of study]. For a long time, to study education was thought of as not an academic endeavor. You couldn't be elected to Phi Beta Kappa, for example, if you were in education. But what is amazing is to think of how many public school children and private school children were taught by graduates of Newcomb. Many, many.

And finally, the art department really shows both this first-rate education Newcomb could offer and some of the ways it could change and develop. The end of the Woodwards brought change, brought so much change, for example. For a while, the art school was under the man from—what was his name?

The man who came from Yale. . . . He was a controversial man who hated Mardi Gras. He thought Carnival was a terrible, terrible burden for New Orleans and for Newcomb.[18] But the art department always emerged as a strong department.

Even I would say that Newcomb could help one build one's social consciousness—I would never have heard about someone not liking Mardi Gras. I would never have taught in public schools, for example, if I had not gone to Newcomb. And integration, for example, was not a problem at Newcomb. One faculty meeting and it was done.[19]

And for Newcomb graduates—all of the leaders in community work, all of the women leaders in community work are Newcomb graduates. We were taught to take part in these community activities because it was showing a willingness to help.

Once I remember the College brought to campus the editor of the *Atlantic Monthly*—that must have been in the 1920s, and the editor, the former editor of the *Atlantic Monthly,* the old, old editor, I've forgotten his name, but he came to Newcomb and made a talk about the young writers at the time. And among this group was Faulkner. This editor told us in the 1920s that "Faulkner, of all of that group would be remembered, because Faulkner has a sense of sin." That is to say, that Faulkner knew that you have to confront the circumstances.[20] Then another speaker who impressed the students was a Frenchman, quite famous, but I remember his words and not his name. He said that a human act has so many infinitesimal reactions that no human act ever goes unmarked. It just encircles a lot of people and keeps growing wider and wider and wider. All these things I took away from Newcomb.

Of course, some things have changed. . . . There was that other controversy about what a chapel should be for. Newcomb has a very loyal alumnae, which means that some of the old conservatives, they have to have everything as it was, not as the younger people might need it, today. So, it was just supposed to be a chapel where people would come and pray and meditate. But the religious staff at the College felt that it could be a place for meetings and get-togethers and also for praying and meditating, but not be a strictly religious building. And I believe that they were correct. Because after all, even our attitudes have changed somewhat toward, not the actual liturgies, but toward the actual practice of religion, so our buildings have to change too.

I don't want Newcomb to become too liberal. I mean too liberal, too, too E.R.A. Because I think women have a special mission in life. And I think women who are trying to be like men are making a mistake. I think they're losing their way. . . . I think that if a woman is married, I think her special mission is her marriage that she cannot combine, that motherhood and wifehood and childbearing and child rearing are enough to do. Combining! Who would want to combine so much? Even I just had to combine one child and work. . . .

But to return to memory—I have lived now almost one hundred years. When my class left the College in 1912, we left a bench marked 1912, as a gift. A stone bench. Some years ago, one of the Woodward boys, a nephew of Mr. Ellsworth Woodward, gave me a preliminary sketch of that bench. A sketch by Mr. Woodward . . . and it may still be there, I really don't know, I haven't been to Newcomb in so long. . . . It was on the main campus as I remember it. It was on the main campus, right below the steps, facing you know, not facing Broadway, facing back. Would you look and see if it is there now for me?

NOTES

Note: These interviews are from the Oral History Collection, Newcomb Archives, Newcomb College Center for Research on Women (hereafter cited as NA NCCROW).

1. "H. Sophie Newcomb Memorial College for Young Women: Announcement for 1888–'89," in *Tulane University of Louisiana, Catalogue, 1887–1888* (New Orleans, 1888), 70.

2. Biographical Files, Newcomb Archives; Class of 1890 collection, NA NCCROW; Anita Breisacher, Oral History interview by Susan Tucker, May 1, 1998, Oral History Collection, NA NCCROW.

3. *Newcomb Bulletin, 1898–99:* 28–30; *Bulletin, 1911–12:* 147–51. Some (but not all) of the early bulletins list where the students had prepared for Newcomb, but after 1899, this information no longer appears.

4. "List of books sent by home and foreign committees to the Library of the Woman's Building, World's Columbian Exposition, Chicago, 1893," compiled for the United States World's Columbian Commission Board of Lady Managers under the direction of Edith E. Clarke, http://digital.library.upenn.edu/women/clarke/library/library.html.

5. *Special Newcomb College Tour of Europe,* flyer, 1940, Pierce Butler Vertical Files, University Archives, Howard-Tilton Memorial Library.

6. Catherine Wolf, conversation with Susan Tucker, July 10, 2008 (see note 5 of Kohlmeyer's essay in this volume).

7. Gertrude Kerr Jackmann, Class of 1899.

8. Newcomb's library was opened in 1892 (Gillian North, "A Definite Amount of Library Work Is Required: The Development of the Library at H. Sophie Newcomb and Other Women's Colleges across the South, 1886–1910," Gillian North Collection, NA NCCROW).

9. Adelin Elam Spencer, Class of 1890, and Mary Cass Spencer, Class of 1892, both earned master's degrees from Cornell (in chemistry and in mathematics, respectively) and returned to teach at the College.

10. Myra Clare Rogers, Class of 1896, earned a master's degree from Tulane in 1898 and a PhD from the University of Chicago in 1928, and taught Latin for many years at Newcomb.

11. The High School operated from 1888 until 1920.

12. Lionel Charles Durel was known to generations of students as Papa Durel; his tenure spanned the years 1919 to 1949.

13. Elizabeth McFetridge, a classmate of Dagmar's, seems to be here confused with her sister, Katherine McFetridge, Class of 1919, who taught at a private girls' school in the city, McGehee's, from the 1920s to the 1970s. Elizabeth earned a master's degree in Latin from Tulane in 1916 and taught for a few years at the College. She became a medical writer and co-authored with Michael DeBakey a surgical history of World War II (see Biographical Files, NA NCCROW).

14. See Brandt V. B. Dixon, *A Brief History of H. Sophie Newcomb Memorial College 1887–1919* (New Orleans: Hauser Printing, 1928), 181.

15. Marie Johanna Weiss, a member of the faculty from 1931 to 1952 (see also above, and the introduction to part 2 of this volume, "Distinctions"). Weiss actually left the College to teach at Vassar, rather than coming to the College from Vassar.

16. Anna Many, Class of 1907, was counselor of women, 1919–51; acting dean, 1944 and again in 1951; and dean, 1951–53.

17. For more on the discontinuation of domestic science, see Nancy Rogers, "Household Economy at Newcomb College" (history honors thesis, Tulane University, 1990, NA NCCROW).

18. She is probably speaking of John Canaday, whose tenure at Newcomb spanned the years 1934–36, and another period, 1950–53.

19. The Newcomb College Faculty Minutes, December 7, 1962, show little discussion of this matter and a simple unanimous vote in favor of admitting all qualified students to the College and University (see also discussion in the introduction to part 3 of this volume, "Lives").

20. This was probably Ellery Sedgwick, editor at *Atlantic Monthly* from 1909 to 1938.

18

IDA RITTENBERG KOHLMEYER
(1912–1997)

Oral History Interview from 1986 by Adele Ramos Salzer

EDITED WITH AN INTRODUCTION
BY SUSAN TUCKER

Introduction

I n some ways, I didn't leave because I began teaching at Newcomb," Ida Rittenberg Kohlmeyer reported as she talked about her years as a Newcomb student and a teacher. Kohlmeyer received a bachelor of arts degree with a major in English literature in 1933. She returned to Newcomb nearly twenty years later and earned a master of fine arts degree in 1956. Immediately thereafter, she began a career teaching painting in the Newcomb Department of Art. For Kohlmeyer, as for many women in New Orleans, Newcomb was omnipresent, and whether Newcomb was a default option as it was for the young Ida Rittenberg, or a magnet, as it was for the mature Ida Kohlmeyer, the College provided educational opportunities for women throughout their lifetimes.

Although a relatively late starter in pursuing a career in art, Kohlmeyer became a prolific artist whose paintings and sculptures drew national acclaim as representative of modernism, abstract expressionism, and minimalism. Her studies with Hans Hofmann, Mark Rothko, and Clyfford Still place her among a handful of influential artists to emerge in twentieth-century America. In 1980, she was honored by the national Women's Caucus for Art with their second annual Outstanding Achievement in the Visual Arts Award. Other recipients that year included Anni Ablers, Louise Bourgeois, Lee Krasner, and another outstanding Newcomb artist, Caroline Durieux.[1] This award placed Kohlmeyer at the top of her profession, and within that profession, among the top ten women artists in this country. Kohlmeyer's and

Durieux's achievement of this award among the giants of the art world speaks to their extraordinary talents, and also to the place of Newcomb College in art education.

Ida Rittenberg was born and raised in New Orleans. The family's residence at 1 Rosa Park was just a short walk from the College. Ida's father was active in real estate and, significantly, a generous and enthusiastic person. One memory of him is that in his will, he left the family cook, an African American woman, enough money to start her own catering business. She then became one of the cooks most sought after by elite Jewish families of the city.[2]

Student records show the family in agreement about the education of girls in the family. Ida's sister, Mildred, had attended the College before her, registering in 1924. As Kohlmeyer relates in this interview, her two older brothers went to Harvard, but her parents wished for her to stay at home and attend Newcomb.[3]

During her undergraduate years, the only art classes in which she enrolled were "Art Appreciation" and "Aesthetics," causing one to wonder why the College with its specialization in art was unable to excite her curiosity in art. Ida remembers being too popular to be intellectual, but willing nonetheless to learn and to participate in athletic competitions. At the time of this interview, she listed her Newcomb College activities as: "Cheerleader—1930–33, AEPhi sorority, Glee Club, basketball, [and] volleyball teams."[4]

Kohlmeyer's first job was with her sister-in-law Kay Pollack Rittenberg (NC 1929), as co-owner of a small gift shop in Godchaux's—a family-run department store with an exclusive image. The store was owned by the Rittenbergs' friends, the wealthy Jewish Godchaux family who had sent generations of daughters to Newcomb.[5]

Kohlmeyer credits her experiences as a World War II army wife with the life-changing perspective that motivated her to pursue her interest in art. In her return to Newcomb and her continued contacts with the College, Ida's journey paralleled the Newcomb "craftsmen" before her who maintained lifelong friendships with their Newcomb professors and fellow artists and who used Newcomb as a home base from which to study in other places or to which to return as teachers. She often stressed the importance of studying with Pat Trivigno and the work she did with students such as Lynda Benglis, with whom she produced a large installation for the exhibition Five from Louisiana at the New Orleans Museum of Art in 1977. She lived in a fashion similar to those less famous and less well-to-do Newcomb graduates. Her cultivation of roses, her early passion for golfing, and her long marriage to a man she had known since she was fifteen, for example, endeared her to many locals as much as did her art.[6]

One cannot help but wonder if Kohlmeyer's abilities as an artist would have sprung forth more readily if her parents had allowed her to attend Wellesley College as she had wished. Conversely, would she, as a married woman with two children, have found the encouragement and the guidance to pursue the MFA and her artistic career if she had lived elsewhere, if she had not had the opportunity to return to Newcomb?

Her work was celebrated with an exhibit at the Newcomb Art Gallery in 2004, and a volume by the Tulane University art historian Michael Plante explored Kohlmeyer's art and life.[7] This oral history narrative serves as a brief supplement to that visual and critical study, and gives some of Kohlmeyer's own reflections in response to questions about her life from around the time of her seventy-fourth birthday.

· *Narrative from the Interview*

I was born November 3, 1912, the fourth child of Rebecca Baron Rittenberg and Joseph Rittenberg. My parents were Polish immigrants to this country. My father came over when he was about fourteen years old, and my mother when she was somewhat younger. They did not know each other, interestingly enough, although they came from the same town. They met again in San Francisco in 1900, where they married, and my older brother Leon was born a year later.

And they ultimately came to New Orleans. My father had, by this time, earned enough money to pretty much traverse the United States to select where he really wanted to put down his roots and raise his family, and he had decided upon New Orleans. And I think he made a very good decision.

I went to elementary school at Henry W. Allen. I was able to walk to school for those eight years, kindergarten through seventh grade. In those days, you might like to know, it was fashionable to skip the eighth grade if, academically, you were up to it. Well, I guess I was up to it, because I did skip the eighth grade and then went to Isidore Newman Manual Training School, which is now [Isidore] Newman School. And there, I really think I learned the love of literature and studying. There were a number of teachers there; I remember some of them distinctly. Miss Murphy, who taught me Latin and always had a little string hanging from the part in her hair—it never occurred to me then that she might have had a wig, but I'm, I'm quite sure she did. And had I thought of it then, I might have told her, but she didn't seem to notice . . . and everyone loved her so much, they wouldn't have embarrassed her by mentioning it. Mr. Kalin was the principal. I think, he and Mr. Henson. Those are two names that pop back. I spent a great deal of time in the gym. I was, also at Newcomb, very athletic.

When I was ready for college, my two older brothers were at Harvard University, and my mother didn't want to be bereft of another child. I had taken exams for Wellesley, and had passed the exams, but really much to my regret at the time, my parents decided they wanted me to stay at home. In those days, girls were just barely sixteen who went through the normal course of events to being a freshman at college, and I guess I was pretty immature, and maybe they made a very right decision. And now, I'm not sorry, of course I'm not sorry. I spent four wonderful years at Newcomb.

[ARS: And you made many friends there?]

Some were lifelong friends—not only New Orleanians but girls from other states. Bobbi Kahn from Milwaukee comes quickly to my mind, and several girls from Chicago with names I don't remember. But, I can't really recollect names.

I suppose my favorite teacher was Dr. Lee. He taught philosophy. You know I returned to Newcomb twenty-three years later, and I was quickly thinking of those teachers, in the second go-round, who were so poignant in my memory. But umm, [remembering her undergraduate teachers] Miss Frotscher . . . I'm sure you've heard of her.[8] Of course, there was Dr. Butler. And Clare Rogers, who was the athletic . . . head.[9] She's in my mind because we remained friends over many years.

I studied English literature. That was my major. And [I took] Latin, German, biology, and . . . what else . . . . I don't know, it was the love of literature that stayed with me, although I'm more interested now in American writers than English.

There's nothing I can think of that was so outstanding. All I know is our basketball team was the champion team in the state. We went to Shreveport, and Monroe, and Baton Rouge, and Alexandria. You know, one of the girls who played on the team with me lives just about a half block from me now; we were together just a few days ago. We were both forwards on that team.

When I graduated from Newcomb, I got married.[10] Just like that. I think I was the first girl in the class to marry. I'm not positive, but I'm pretty sure.

And then my sister-in-law and I—Kay Rittenberg, my brother Phillip's wife—opened up the gift shop at Godchaux's, in an elevator shaft.[11] And I stayed with that enterprise until my husband decided it was time to fulfill his obligation. He lost forty pounds so as to be eligible to be taken into the army. This was now 1941, and he went into basic training. He was [a] first lieutenant, I think he went in as a first lieutenant, and was stationed at Fort Bragg, in North Carolina, Fayetteville. And I sold the business, because my sister-in-law had gotten out of it a couple years earlier, and joined him at Fort Bragg, and we stayed there four years. He was subsistence officer for the camp, and well suited for the job because food was his business. One of the few men I knew who was properly placed—my husband and a veterinarian!

Four years had passed, and at the end of that time, I came home to have my first child, Jane. And this was in '44, I guess, yes, the fall of '44. And that was the year my father died. Three years later I had my second daughter, Jo. And those are the only two I have had. They are today enterprising young women, and I'm very proud of both of them. They both went to Newcomb.[12] But I didn't do the things mothers did. I didn't. And that had been a source of great worry to me until I grew up enough to realize that I was probably doing the best thing I could for my children, which was doing the thing I felt I was compelled to do, with a tremendous compulsion, and not taking out frustrations on them, which I saw many mothers do to their children. And I do think the quality of time I did spend with them was good.

[ARS: And then you had a second college career.]

Yes, well, life during the war years was a great education to me. Simply in meeting people whom I might never have had the good fortune to run into had I remained at home. I met people who had a very serious sort of attitude toward life, and up until then, I really didn't. I was typical—a fortunate, young American woman, who didn't have to worry too much about where the means were coming from for any kind of fun. Even my livelihood was provided for. And so I was dancing through life and playing tennis and playing golf, and I suppose had the war not come along, I never would have had children, because we were high-flyers.

Meeting the people I did during those four years, and beginning to realize the seriousness of taking advantage of life and using it in a worthwhile way, everything about me changed. My friends, my desires, my hopes, how I spent my time, and I wanted to—I guess I wanted to use what I was given. I wanted, I guess, to show gratitude for everything that I had been granted. And I, up until then, was just receiving everything and giving very little.

So I went back to school, and that has certainly been the most worthwhile thing I have ever done in my life.

I went to the Art Department, simply because I'd always loved to look at art, in a very dilettante way, and I had had one really meaningful experience in an art class that was given by Alice Hoch,[13] who was, during my undergrad work, I think the only art historian on the art school faculty. And it was a survey of art history, and I remember this one slide being flashed on the screen, and of all things, it was Rossetti's *The Blessed Damozel*. And if you look at my work today and think of Rossetti's *Blessed Damozel*, you would never know what an inspiration that painting was to me.

So I went back to school. I had always loved to look at art, so I thought I would try my hand at doing it. And I began spending so much time there, at the school, that it was suggested that I work toward a master's degree, which I did. I did my master's thesis under the title of "The Mood of Loneliness in Children"—portraits of children and studies of children, whom I borrowed mainly from my own home, my two children, and from the Protestant School for Children off of Magazine Street and Jefferson Avenue.[14]

And it took four years for me to accomplish that, because as I've said before, I wasn't the most promising student. I had no background, and I did have to spend some time with my two children, and there was no reason for me to rush, so I had those four wonderful preparatory years before teaching and going out into the art world professionally.

In some ways, I didn't leave because I began teaching at Newcomb. I taught the fall of 1954, no, 1955. I replaced Mr. Trivigno, who was my painting instructor and my first inspiration, incidentally. I replaced him teaching his University College night class. I think he was either on sabbatical or just didn't want to teach that fall. And I remember my fear and trepidation in that first class, but I learned an awful lot from doing that little stint, and then that same September, I started in teaching drawing and painting on the faculty. Daytime students. And I continued there from '56 to '65, nine years.

I did figurative work, mainly. You see, being six years, it took me four years to get the degree . . . no, actually six, because I simply went to classes from '50 to '54, but I suppose most of that time I was working toward my degree, which I received in '56. That very summer that I was given my MFA, I went up to Provincetown to study with Hans Hofmann, who is considered the most influential teacher of this century. He taught for about forty-five years, and touched the lives of so many people and fine artists in their own names today and yesterday. It was a remarkable experience I had there. Overnight almost, I turned into an abstract painter. It suited my temperament much more. I'm volatile and emotional, and abstract expressionism was the mood and mode of the day. And I seemed to fit into it.

[ARS: How did you find out about Hofmann?]

Well, I'll tell you how. David Smith, the great sculptor, who's now about ten or twelve years gone, came to Newcomb for a couple days as a visiting professor, and I was about to receive my degree, and I wanted to go on. I wanted to get in as much as I possibly could before starting on my own. And he said, "There's only one man to go to, and only one place to go." I went home that day, telephoned Hofmann's studio, spoke to one of his assistants, got in on the tail end of the class—it was almost full, and left about a week after. And never regret . . . it was one of the most stimulating experiences of my life, if not the most stimulating. Everybody there was on fire, and he put everyone on fire. A great man.

I studied with Hofmann for three months and then right away came back and went immediately into teaching, back at Newcomb. I learned more and more from my students, and loved teaching, probably too much. I think a teacher who loves teaching too much is probably not a good teacher, because he or she solves problems that should be left to the student, especially in creative work.

After nine years of [teaching], I realized I had to make up my mind what I wanted to be. I couldn't be both—I couldn't be a full-time artist and a teacher. Others can. I couldn't. By this time, I was, let's see, 1965, I was forty-four years old, and I had come to a point where I had to make a decision, I felt.[15] So we built a studio in our backyard. It was just a single room at first, but over the years, we extended it.

[ARS: Can you recall your first showing, or the first piece you sold?]

I certainly can recall both. The first piece I sold was to Dr. Griffin, who was a professor at Tulane, and it was out of my master's thesis; it wasn't the only piece I sold, but darn near.[16] And I heard from him just a couple years ago, after a period of how many years—'56 to maybe '83.

It was wonderful to hear from him, and he still had it [the painting]. He wanted to know how I was doing, and I told him I had never forgotten him and never would, because that was certainly a great thrill, to actually have someone put up money for one of my efforts.

And the first show I, well, the first show I had was my graduate show. But the real first show I had was at the New Orleans Museum. And I think that was about 19 . . . um . . . 1957, 1967, excuse me—no, I'm wrong, 1957, of course, it was just the year after I started teaching. And Alonzo Lanzpi was the director there. And I couldn't believe it. He came to the studio and saw my work and said, "I think you're ready for a show at the museum." And I often think if that happened to so-called "young" painters—although I wasn't young in years, I was young in experience—how wonderful it would be if more young artists were given that opportunity today. I don't know, I guess there are many, many more young artists today, so it's more difficult to choose, but it was certainly a tremendous boost for me, both to my ego and to those people who never could believe and still don't that I am a full-time, hard-working, agonizing artist. I still have old friends who say to me, "Are you still painting?" And I say to them, "Are you still breathing?"

[ARS: You're completely consumed by it, or it completely consumes you.]

Yes, that's quite true. I don't understand how it could be otherwise with artists, and I think if it is, then calling themselves artists is presumptuous. And I know that sounds high and mighty, but I honestly believe it. I think it is the kind of endeavor that is all-consuming, or, it is, or you're just not in tune with yourself. You're doing something you don't have to do. I think art becomes something, or is something, you have to do. I feel guilty when I don't work, and Lord knows I need not. I've done it now for thirty-seven years. That is more than half my life, but I can't stop.

[ARS: What do you think about women's colleges?]

I don't think I would want to go to an all-girls' college now, in 1986.

I remember when I started teaching, several young men came to take the class, the painting class, and the drawing class, from the architecture school and from the medical school, and I must say, those young men enlivened the group a lot. I don't think it was anything except that they were a bit more serious than the majority of the Newcomb students. This was in the '50s. I'm sure things have changed radically since then, as far as the attitude of the students at Newcomb. I would imagine it's changed. Our lives, everything is so changed over the past thirty, thirty-five years, what with women's rights. You know I'm not really a feminist. I don't think I am, although I'm very self protective—I mean, I can fend for myself, but I don't know, and I've been honored by the Women's Caucus [for Art] a number of times, and I keep telling them I'm not a feminist, but they tell me I live my life as though I were, and if they want to call it that, then that's fine with me. But I'm sure a great deal of good has come out of it; and I'm not so sure a great deal of harm has come too.

[ARS: Are there any other statements you would like to make?]

Yes, I'd like to end up with the happy thought that I have a grandchild. Jane's son, Benjamin, is twelve years old, he is the pride of our lives, and I just want him to know if he ever listens to the tape of this interview that he was in my mind the entire time.

NOTES

1. The Women's Caucus for Art, www.nationalwca.com/Framesets/laaframeset.htm. Recipients of the first awards were Isabel Bishop, Selma Burke, Louise Nevelson, and Georgia O'Keefe.

2. Lucy Ater, oral history interview by Dorothy Schlesinger, Friends of the Cabildo, 1974, original tape at New Orleans Public Library, transcription available at Newcomb Archives, Newcomb College Center for Research on Women (hereafter cited as NA NCCROW).

3. Student Records, NA NCCROW.

4. Mimi Read, "Ida Kohlmeyer," *New Orleans Times-Picayune, Dixie Magazine,* April 3, 1983: 9–14; Ida Kohlmeyer file, NA NCCROW.

5. Several of the Godchaux family members who attended Newcomb include Carrie Godchaux Wolf (NC 1905), Justine Godchaux Eiseman (NC 1910), Juliette Godchaux Trautman (NC 1912), Jeanne Godchaux Newman (NC 1917), Adele Godchaux Dawson (NC 1926), and Sally Godchaux Endom (NC 1961). In addition, many of the Godchaux men married Newcomb alumnae. The store was founded in 1840 by Leon Godchaux, who also owned several sugar plantations and whose life is one of the great American rags-to-riches stories; the store closed in 1986.

6. Read, "Ida Kohlmeyer," 9–14; Chris Waddington, "Renowned N.O. Artist Ida Kohlmeyer Dies," *New Orleans Times-Picayune,* January 25, 1997.

7. Michael Plante, *Ida Kohlmeyer: Systems of Color* (New York: Hudson Hills Press, 2004). The book was issued in conjunction with the exhibition, October 21–December 19, 2004.

8. Comment by ARS: Miss Frotscher had a PhD and taught German and English. She was formidable and very wise about learning. Students called her Miss Frotscher, but we always knew she had her doctorate.

9. Myra Clare Rogers was a professor of Latin. Kohlmeyer likely means Clara Baer, who was head of the physical education program, but retired in 1929, about the same time Kohlmeyer entered Newcomb.

10. Her husband was Hugh Kohlmeyer, who became active in a family business, Gerde Newman Institutional Food Service.

11. Kay Pollack Rittenberg graduated from Newcomb in 1929.

12. Jane Kohlmeyer Lowentritt graduated from Newcomb in 1966, and Jo Ellen Kohlmeyer Bezou Wohl graduated from Newcomb in 1969.

13. We have been unable to identify an Alice Hoch. Correspondence with Sally Main, curator of the Newcomb Art Gallery, August 9, 2006, suggests that Kohlmeyer was referring to Alice Stirling Parkerson. Parkerson received her bachelor of design from Newcomb in 1919, returning in 1933 to teach studio and art appreciation classes in the School of Art. Working successive

summers at the Harvard Summer School, she received a master of arts degree from Columbia University in 1937. She taught her first art history class in 1940. She stepped in as acting chair of the then named Department of Art in 1949–50, 1953–54, and 1957–58.

14. The Protestant School for Children no longer exists.

15. In 1965, Kohlmeyer would have been fifty-three, not the forty-four she mentions.

16. It is uncertain who Dr. Griffin was. John Dyer lists Max Liles Griffin, a professor of English, as a faculty member from 1951 to 1953. However, this was several years prior to Kohlmeyer's thesis show. Dyer also lists a William Joyce Griffith, a professor of history who became a full professor at Tulane in 1955 and was still on the faculty in 1966 at the time of Dyer's publication. As Dyer lists only full professors, Dr. Griffin might have been someone else altogether (John P. Dyer, *Tulane: The Biography of a University, 1834–1965* [New York: Harper and Row, 1966], 339).

19

ADMIRING MILDRED CHRISTIAN

EMILIE DIETRICH GRIFFIN

Whenever I go into Newcomb Hall, I steal along the main-floor corridor to a certain lecture room. I take a moment in the doorway to remember the charm and brilliance of my favorite Newcomb professor: Dr. Mildred Gayler Christian.

I was not alone in looking up to Miss Christian. Over her many years of teaching she earned a great following. Many students remember how she made scholarship exciting; how she delighted in us and our achievements; and how she helped us to grasp the idea of the life of the mind.

Miss Christian was a diminutive woman, yet she ruled the lecture hall with humor, broad knowledge of her subject matter, and a sure feminine hand. Courageous souls who had accepted her rod of discipline admired her toughness and revered her for the near-impossibility of her demands. The fact was, she had achieved high competence in several different specialties of English literature: seventeenth-century poetry and prose, including the Cavaliers and the Metaphysicals; the work of John Milton and Edmund Spenser; and the English novel, including the Brontës.

Charlotte Brontë became Miss Christian's focus during the second half of her eighty-eight-year life. Miss Christian died without achieving her major goal of publishing two significant works on Charlotte Brontë, but she was acknowledged as an authority among Brontë scholars worldwide.

I believe I first came to admire Mildred Christian as a sophomore (1954–55), when I took her survey course in English literature. Impressed by her vigorous lecture style and her remarkable knowledge, I signed up the following year for her "Poetry and Prose of the Seventeenth Century." Though I knew Miss Christian would be tough and demanding, I kept thinking about how much I would learn.

Miss Christian began the course by tracing the literary outlines of the seventeenth century and by giving us a comprehensive historical account of those troubled times. To attend one of her lectures was to risk an advanced case of writer's cramp. Almost everything she said was worth writing down. Notebook after notebook was filled to overflowing as we dealt with the works of Francis Bacon, Ben Jonson, George Herbert, Andrew Marvell, Isaak Walton, John Donne, and their contemporaries.

Once I had discovered this eloquent teacher, I signed up for every course she taught. One was a full semester of John Milton. Through Miss Christian's diligence, we covered nearly all of Milton's poetry and prose in a single semester. She introduced us to Milton's character and personality as well. I came to appreciate tales of Milton's having been *rusticated* (suspended) from Cambridge because he constantly quarreled with his tutor. I even began to identify with some of Milton's personal traits—his high ambition, his deeply studious ways, his sense of humor, and, in some sense, his worldview. I appreciated his noble imagination (remember, I was just nineteen or so) and his high ideals. Once I had decided to "choose the marketplace" over a university career, I justified my choice with Milton's words: "I never could admire a fugitive and cloistered virtue."

In my senior year, I signed up for Miss Christian's course in the English novel, so demanding that we covered Fielding, Richardson, Jane Austen, Charlotte and Emily Brontë, George Eliot, Charles Dickens, George Meredith, Thomas Hardy, William Makepeace Thackeray, James Joyce, and Virginia Woolf. The pace—a novel a week—left us breathless. Many of us had tried to read ahead the previous summer so that we would not have to cover a 400–600-page novel each week. However, Miss Christian defeated our plans to get ahead in this way. "Have you already read *Vanity Fair*? Then I suggest you try *Henry Esmond*."

It was rare in those days for undergraduates to socialize with faculty members. We were addressed by our last names in the classroom. I was "Miss Dietrich" to all my Newcomb professors; Miss Christian never used my first name. However, there was a *kind* of informality in that we students addressed her, not as Dr. Christian or Professor Christian (she was both), but as Miss Christian.

Shortly after my graduation, Miss Christian and I began, awkwardly, to develop a sort of friendship. Only after I had my degree and when it became clear that I would not pursue a university career, did we begin the first attempts at knowing each other. These trailed off and were renewed many years later when my first book was published in 1980. As part of this later friendship, I learned new things about Miss Christian's life. She told me, for instance, how her family's financial circumstances would not have permitted her to go to college at all without the benefit of a scholarship to Newcomb College.

A graduate of Sophie B. Wright High School in New Orleans, she entered Newcomb in the fall of 1918 and received her BA in 1922. Her formal work in Milton studies began with her MA at Tulane, for which she wrote a thesis titled "Satan in English Literature Prior to Milton," sketching out the many conceptions of Satan in Spenser and other writers that had influenced Milton in his writing of *Paradise Lost.*

Upon receipt of the MA in 1924, she was appointed a Teaching Fellow in English and began a forty-three-year teaching career on the Newcomb College faculty. (There must have been a pause for her doctoral studies at the University of Chicago.) In 1949, she became a full professor and was named to the Pierce Butler Chair of English in 1965, only two years before her retirement.

My mother, Helen Russell Dietrich (NC 1933), remembered Miss Christian as a young teacher (newly possessed of a doctorate awarded in 1932); she recalled that Miss Christian was beautiful. So Miss Christian seemed then, to undergraduates not much younger than she. She was still beautiful later on, in the eyes of my generation, when her hair was white, her manner formal, and her style charming. Never one to lose her dignity, Miss Christian nevertheless joked and turned witty phrases from the lectern. She rarely spoke of her own work, always putting the scholarly task ahead of any personal anecdotes or chatter. Still, she inspired her classes with her way of bringing poetry and fiction to life.

In the late 1940s, she began her work on the Brontës and became one of the few American scholars to acquire an international reputation in Brontë scholarship. Extensive research on the correspondence of Charlotte Brontë and the influence upon her of Ellen Nussey eventually led to her planning two volumes for publication by the Clarendon Press of Oxford University. Because her findings were incomplete, Dr. Christian was unwilling to offer either volume for publication, waiting now for this, now for that piece of the elaborate scholarly and critical puzzle to come into place. In later years, with her work still unfinished, she was invited to become a vice president of the Brontë Society in Keighley, West Yorkshire, England.[1]

In 1986, at the Newcomb Centennial, Dr. Christian was honored as an outstanding graduate and praised as a "beloved representative of early New-comb graduates who as professors returned to Newcomb to inspire other Newcomb students as they themselves had been inspired."

She recalled vividly the Newcomb of her undergraduate days, especially Dr. Pierce Butler and his personal influence on the College. So it seems fitting that Miss Christian was the first to occupy the Pierce Butler Chair in English.

"Dr. Butler had very sharp convictions," she said in an interview given to the Newcomb College Center for Research on Women. "He was a fine teacher and a fine reader. We just expected him to read beautifully. And he read a passage from the Bible every day. That was according to Mrs. Newcomb's request."[2]

She remembered, too, the women of her Newcomb years and spoke of their example as mentors and role models: Miss Caroline Richardson among them, whom she remembered as "an old-fashioned lady . . . a New Orleanian" and "one of the most effective of the teachers" because of her command of the English language.[3]

Miss Christian spoke passionately about poetry and faith. For her, the great poets and thinkers were those who lived by faith and made it shine for others. In an interview given in the late 1960s, she quoted Tennyson's line, "There is more faith in honest doubt, believe me, than in half the creeds." Wordsworth, she said in the same interview, could console us with his view that "the child is father of the man" and provide solace in a time of personal despair with words such as these from his poem "Michael": "There is a com-fort in the strength of love / T'will make endurable a thing which else / Would overturn the brain or break the heart."

In an essay of my own about John Milton, I mention Miss Christian's in-fluence on me: "No one in Miss Christian's classes could fail to notice her love of John Milton; nor could anyone fail to notice her personal resemblance to an angel. . . . And her voice, speaking or singing, was glorious. To excite us about Milton as artist and songwriter, she sang the songs of his *Comus* from the lecture platform. For us as students, she personified something Miltonic: a blazing core of goodness, a flash of understanding and humor, a breadth of knowledge and memory for detail."

Even now I can hardly read a passage of Milton's work without recalling some insight of hers. She knew the man, and she painted him, warts and all. She let us know he was not the best of politicians, no genuine diplomat; flawed as an orator despite his gift of rhetoric. Even so she showed us a man worth admiring, a poet whose lyric vision soared, whose love of God was passionate and deep. This was a man who conceived a life's work courageously and set about it fearlessly; a man to follow and imitate.

In the 1980s, I had several long visits with Miss Christian in her home on Lowerline Street. She told me about her frustration at not having finished her work on Charlotte Brontë, of the dilemmas she had faced in attempting to complete the work. I recall that we went together to hear a talk on C. S. Lewis given at Trinity Church on Jackson Avenue by someone who had known Lewis personally. (After all, wasn't it Miss Christian who had first introduced me to the work of C. S. Lewis? "You must read *The Allegory of Love*," she had said. Years later, I did.)

One lovely afternoon Miss Christian came to visit in my mother's apartment at 1441 Jackson Avenue. There, among the teacups and the family portraits, as we reminisced about many aspects of Newcomb College, I felt a sense of tradition taking hold. Both my mother and I had been Mildred Christian's students. Now all three of us were Newcomb alumnae together. My husband, William Griffin, who had been a Macmillan editor, had also corresponded with her. We recall a memorable lunch with her at the Pontchartrain Hotel. Still intending to publish, she asked his opinions about dealing with Clarendon Press.

Now I realize that my mother also influenced me where both Newcomb and English literature are concerned. When I was a small child, we lived on Zimpel Street, very close to the Newcomb campus. My mother often took me to the Newcomb campus to feed the goldfish in the Newcomb fishpond. She snapped my picture—when I was three or four—near the front gate on Broadway. She was certainly introducing me to the College. As I grew older, my mother taught me to love Wordsworth, Keats, Byron, and Shelley—quoting snatches of their poetry from memory. Was it at least partly Mildred Christian's influence? I am sure it was.

Since Mildred Christian's death in 1989, I still think of her often. Many things bring her back to me: Jane Austen films; Jane Austen novels; anything Shakespearean; reading George Herbert; watching that remarkable television play, *Wit*, in which Emma Thompson portrays a John Donne scholar. I am also reminded of Mildred Christian during my own random visits to Oxford and London. My notion of what Newcomb is, what English literature is, and what it means to be an accomplished woman, all that is part of remembering Mildred Christian.

NOTES

1. Among her many services to Tulane and Newcomb, Dr. Christian served on the Tulane Graduate School Faculty, as chair of the Newcomb Scholarship Committee, and as a member of the Tulane University Scholarship Committee. She was listed in *Who's Who of American Scholars* and *Who's Who of American Women (and Women of Canada)*. Besides the Brontë Society, she was also a member of Phi Beta Kappa, the American Association of University Women, the Tulane University Women's Association, the Quarante Club, Kappa Alpha Theta, and Rayne Memorial Methodist Church of New Orleans.

2. Mildred Christian, oral history interview by Florence Bass, April 21, 1986, Newcomb Archives, Newcomb College Center for Research on Women, Tulane University, New Orleans.

3. Ibid.

4. The essay "John Milton: Sing Heavenly Muse," in *More than Words: Contemporary Writers on the Works That Shaped Them*, ed. James Calvin Schaap (Grand Rapids, Mich.: Baker Books. 2002), 92–100.

20

LINDY AND ME

TANIA TETLOW

I f you are very lucky, you meet by chance the one person who makes all the difference in your life. In my case, it was entirely premeditated.

For as long as I can remember, I have wanted to be Lindy Boggs, the most famous of Newcomb's graduates. She was my congresswoman in New Orleans, a powerful politician of unquestioned integrity and famed charms. Along with every other sensible little girl in New Orleans, I worshiped her.

The trick was figuring out how I could convince her to take me under her wing and teach me everything I needed to know to save the world, preferably before I finished college. The first step, clearly, was to meet the congresswoman, but how? During my freshman year at Newcomb in 1988, Professor Jean Danielson, director of the Honors Program, suggested I try writing a letter and simply ask to meet her. This seemed far too obvious a plan to work, but my more elaborate fantasies of accidentally saving her life were not panning out.

"Dear Congresswoman, I would like to be you when I grow up. Could I please meet you?"

Shockingly, her secretary called me to set up an appointment. The anxiety! The excitement! When the day finally arrived, my parents dropped me off at the federal building downtown for my appointment with destiny. I wore stockings, I think, and something approaching a suit. The walls in her lobby were lined with photographs of the congresswoman with presidents and popes and other rulers of the universe. She seemed omnipotent.

It turned out that she was also small and loving and nice. She had pale blue eyes just like mine and sat with her feet demurely crossed at the ankles, back straight, bright scarf tied around her neck. I don't remember exactly what we talked about other than that she seemed sincerely interested in me, which even then seemed ridiculously generous. I do remember that she instructed me to join various women's political groups, which I did promptly, though I had to wait a year to turn eighteen to join the League of Women Voters.

Two summers later, I got to intern for her in Washington, D.C., carefully stuffing envelopes and answering phones, hoping to catch her in conversation. That month, on July 20, 1990, she announced her retirement from Congress, at the age of seventy-four, to pass the torch to a new generation. More importantly, her daughter Barbara Boggs Sigmund was dying of cancer, and she wanted to be at her side.

Barbara died in October 1990, and when the 101st Congress ended, Mrs. Boggs returned to New Orleans. She came to Tulane University with an office and a title, special counsel to the president. I went across campus to the Tulane president's office to ask about a student worker job in her office, maybe to do research for speeches or whatever her staff might need. It turned out that she had no staff, so they agreed to hire me. I was thrilled, though poor Lindy got a teenage college student to replace her entire congressional staff.

I did my best to keep her schedule and to keep things vaguely organized. Her supposed retirement was nonexistent; she gave hundreds of speeches a year all over the world, and did an annual tour of university graduations to accept honorary degrees. She joined countless nonprofit boards and made every appearance requested of her around the country. It would have been an exhausting schedule for someone a third of her age. As I put the latest plaque on the looming pile of awards in her office, I teased her that her new career was accepting awards full-time. I loved to ask her, "Mawmaw" (that's what I called her), "how many honorary degrees do you have now?" "I have no idea, darling."

Lindy did constituent services as if she were still in office. Senior citizens would call with their Social Security problems. She would listen to their entire story and then spend hours on the phone with the Social Security Administration to get it solved. I am fifty years younger than she is, but I could barely keep up. I never knew whether to try harder to protect her time, or just to stand back and admire her stamina.

Every ring of the phone promised a new adventure. Lady Bird Johnson would call to schedule their annual spring vacation together. (They liked to go to Acapulco.) When I asked her what I should wear for her fund-raiser for presidential candidate Bill Clinton, she said: "We can wear whatever we like, darling. We're the hostesses." She took me to mass on holy days of obligation and insisted on giving me a dollar for the collection plate.

She was the dearest grandmother you could have, but one who had the kind of power you wish your grandmother could have had. She had befriended world leaders, hiked in Antarctica, and chaired the 1976 Democratic Convention, the first woman to do so. She took me with her to the 1992 Democratic Convention. She has known presidents from Teddy Roosevelt, who visited her family when she was a child, to Barack Obama.

I shuttled between two worlds in college: one where I listened to professors lecture about American history, and another where I could ask Lindy what *really* had happened. She would tell me about the Washington wives and daughters who did much of the work of government behind the scenes.

Lindy carefully tutored me about women in politics, about power and conscience, about the purpose of a life's career. We spent lots of time debating the models of women in power. Are women inherently more virtuous? Must women always exercise power through sweetness and gentle tact, or should they be allowed to act more like powerful men?

Lindy operated in an era when her nonthreatening charms and graciousness were the most effective way for a woman to wield power. Congressmen marveled at her ability to whisper in the ear of the Speaker of the House, Tip O'Neill, and get whatever her district needed. A staff person for Louisiana senator J. Bennett Johnston told me that they dreaded his meetings with Lindy because he would return sheepishly, having promised her the world.

At the time Lindy entered politics, as the wife of a congressman in 1940 and elected in her own right in 1973, she probably had no choice about how to be effective. But even given the option of other models, Lindy would not have changed. She builds consensus by showing sincere respect for the best in others. She invokes fear only in the possibility of disappointing her. She is insistent in asking others to do the right thing, but pushes them without feeling anger.

Her perspective and her stories transformed my college experience. She made me feel part of the unbroken chain of young women who enter Newcomb each fall and graduate each spring. I could squint at the oak trees and imagine Lindy Claiborne as a teenager on campus in the 1930s, wearing her white gloves and heels, "cutting a rug" on Saturday nights, and politely refusing bathtub gin.

Lindy started Newcomb in 1931, a fifteen-year-old girl from the country and an only child raised by a houseful of women. The nuns at her convent school graduated her first in her class, though she was too young to be admitted to Newcomb College. So Lindy traveled to New Orleans from her plantation home in New Rhodes, Louisiana, to convince Newcomb dean Pierce Butler to let her enroll early. She had one piece of information to her advantage: she knew that he loved Shakespeare. When he sternly asked her age, she replied with her utmost attempt at charm and sophistication: "To be or not to be, that is the question. I cannot tell a lie, to thine own self be true, I am only fifteen, but . . ." She started that year.

The Depression changed everything, even for those privileged enough to go to college. Until then, college meant finding a husband and educating oneself enough to grace him with sparkling conversation. Newcomb, unlike many women's colleges, did not have a rule that prohibited married students from attending. Still, the Depression postponed marriage for young men who could not afford it. For Newcomb women, striving for an actual career suddenly seemed both possible and a matter of survival.

Because no one could get serious too quickly, students dated casually and often. Lindy tells stories, with laughs and winks, of scheduling multiple dates on the same night and struggling to get back to the dormitory in time for the next boy to pick her up. Two of her suitors got so tired of splitting time with her that they finally decided to take her out together.

Lindy wanted to be a professional photographer like the famed photojournalist Margaret Bourke White, who immortalized bridge builders and factory workers. Although she discovered at Newcomb that she was absolutely no good at photography, she kept working toward a career as a journalist and became the Newcomb editor of the *Tulane Hullabaloo*. At that time, women were not allowed to be the editor in chief of the paper, and that post was filled by Hale Boggs. Hale courted Lindy by leaving an apple every day on her desk to ward off the medical student she was dating: An apple a day keeps the doctor away.

Lindy took the art classes for which Newcomb was renowned, but found her own way to shape them. One of her professors, a handsome young man, had the annoying habit of expounding endlessly about rococo—the elaborate gaudy style abundant in New Orleans architecture. He hated it and would not stop talking about it. Lindy and her friends found his views a little pompous and his tirades tiresome, so they wrote a letter pretending to be an anonymous student expressing her love for him. The imaginary student knew she could never expect the professor to return her love, they wrote, but if he could give her any hope at all, all he needed to do was to mention the word "rococo" during class. Flummoxed, the professor would occasionally let the forbidden word slip and then blush and change the subject. Lindy tells this story with a smirk and great professions of embarrassment.

She graduated from Newcomb in 1935 and scrambled with everyone else for one of the few jobs available. She was hired by Saint James Parish to teach history and English, and moved into a house in Romeville, Louisiana, with three others. This would become the first of about five careers, and possibly her favorite. Of her many suitors, Lindy would eventually pick Hale Boggs, handsome, fun-loving, and fiercely intelligent. She married him in 1938 and moved to New Orleans, where Hale worked as general manager and director of the Tulane Alumni Association and became a leader in the movement to reform local politics.

In 1940, at the age of twenty-four, Lindy became a congressional wife. She spent the next three decades raising a family, being ready in case Hale brought the president home for dinner, organizing the Kennedy inaugural ball, managing Hale's campaigns, helping him agonize over his unpopular votes for civil rights, and traveling with him all over the world.

Hale's plane disappeared over Alaska in 1972. In the midst of her grief and uncertainty, Lindy was forced to decide whether to run for his seat. In a 1973 special election, Lindy was elected to Congress by an overwhelming margin and instead of merely holding the seat for a designated male successor, she served with great distinction for eighteen years.

Lindy always recites what the nuns taught her, "You can get anything done in life as long as you are willing to give someone else the credit." Sometimes I bristled at that advice as it applied to her, though, because as much as people adore Lindy, she does not always get credit for the things she accomplished.

Lindy never brags. She has a way of sincerely claiming that she just *happened* to be in the right place at the right time and was lucky enough to be able to help. She tells the story of her greatest legislative accomplishment that way, the inclusion of women in the Equal Credit Opportunity Act at a time when women had enormous difficulty getting business loans, mortgages, or even credit cards in their own names. When she was first elected in the early 1970s, a bill was making its way through Congress that would forbid lenders from discriminating by race or national origin. When the bill came through her banking subcommittee, Lindy quickly added in "sex and marital status" and told the committee members sweetly, "I am sure you all just overlooked this issue." The amendment passed unanimously and signs prohibiting gender discrimination now hang on the walls of every bank in America. Lindy, however, gives credit for this accomplishment to the women's business organization that met with her and educated her about the problem, and the luck of being in the right room at the right time.

Lindy does have a postscript to this story, however, in which she expresses uncharacteristic delight in what she accomplished. Soon after the Equal Credit Act passed, she bought a condominium closer to the Capitol. Her bank denied her a mortgage, one she clearly qualified for, without any explanation. Lindy looked at the banker and explained sweetly that the bank was quite clearly breaking a law that she authored. She got her loan.

After my graduation from Newcomb in 1992, Lindy sent me off to Harvard Law School with hugs and urgings of caution about that "Yankee Protestant school." She then embarked on yet another adventure. In 1997, President Clinton asked a favor of her, to serve as ambassador to the Vatican. Only half-joking, I offered to go with her and she said, "Oh no darling, we would get into too much trouble together." If diplomacy is all about nuance and consensus, she was the perfect choice for a crucial position. She helped foster the relationship between the most powerful nation in the world and a church that influenced (and had intelligence about) every country in the world.

I spent a week visiting Lindy in Rome in 1997, wandering around cafes during the day and following her to diplomatic parties at night. At breakfast in the formal dining room of the embassy residence, a butler in a white coat and brass buttons served us espresso. As soon as he was safely out of sight, Lindy pulled out a hidden jar of instant Louisiana coffee with chicory to add to her cup.

We headed out every day in her bulletproof Mercedes with police escort. Lindy would liven up the ride by making me sing opera to the Italian driver and making him sing back. The driver careened around Rome, driving even through ancient pedestrian squares. Elderly ladies, their heads covered in black, wagged their fingers at us for being so rude. Noting my discomfort, Lindy leaned over and told me: "Either look very important or very ill."

Even when she could not understand a word that people were saying to her in Italian, she responded in English, smiling and bowing while they babbled praise. Being eighty allowed her to flirt with cardinals with impunity, to the astonishment of the State Department staff and the delight of the cardinals. In almost every picture of Lindy and Pope John Paul II, he is holding her hand. We teased her that the pope, several years her junior, had a crush on her. She would blush and deny it.

Lindy came back to New Orleans in 2001, and I got to spend time with her again, going to dinner and finding jazz to sing along to. (We have some pretty good harmonies.) Four years later, her heart was broken by Katrina, but she cut down the tree that fell on her Bourbon Street home and kept fighting for all of the people who called her for help. On her ninetieth birthday, in 2006, she received handwritten notes from the president and the new pope, Benedict XVI. She spends most of her time in Washington now, with her daughter, Cokie Roberts, and son, Tommy Boggs, with her grandchildren and great-grandchildren. In March 2011, she turned ninety-five, still sharp and funny and generous. She tells me that former president Bill Clinton calls regularly to check on her.

I have never heard an introduction of Lindy at an event that did not include the word "gracious," but I worry that people mistake that quality for mere good manners. Lindy's charm does not stem from a disciplined politeness, but a sincere delight in every person she meets. She exudes goodness—not the pure, cloistered virtue of those who manage to avoid the evils of the world, but the integrity of one who has fully participated in the struggle for social justice.

And as for me, Lindy has made all the difference. I have met some very successful women who are weary of mentoring, resistant to the expectation that they assist every young woman who comes along. They understandably resent the ingratitude of a younger generation oblivious to how much better they have it, and wonder if they are not better off making their own way.

Lindy thrives on connecting with each of the multiple generations that have benefited from her hard work. She pushes us most by her example and her high expectations. Once I complained to her wearily about politics; she sighed and answered, "I know darling, but someone has to do it." She taught me that the point of life is to use all of the gifts you have been lucky enough to receive. The point of life is to spend your life trying.

21

GROWING UP UNDER THE OAKS

BOBBIE MALONE

I entered Newcomb College as Barbara Jean Scharlack in the middle of my sophomore year. Nearly a half century and four degrees later, it occurs to me that almost every significant connection of my adult life took shape within a limited geography, bound by Broadway, Calhoun, Willow, and St. Charles Avenue. Accompanying this reflection is a sense of gratitude for those who nurtured this slow coming to maturity under the oaks.

My path may not be unusual for a woman who came of age in the era marking the transition between the conforming 1950s and the rebellious 1960s. When I graduated from high school in 1961, the first-born daughter of an upper-middle-class Jewish family in a San Antonio suburb, parental and cultural expectations defined the proper parameters of my future. As a perennial overachiever, I was bound and determined to fulfill them: to become an attractive, well-educated wife who would enhance the career of an up-and-coming young Jewish man. The choices for attaining such a goal seemed just as clearly illuminated. I would choose a university that would make such an achievement a foregone conclusion—an excellent school with a large number of Jewish students. Although I didn't realize it at the time, I was about to ricochet between my desire to fulfill my sense of the woman I thought I ought to be and the then-unimaginable alternative of self-actualization.

The road to Newcomb began inauspiciously enough. I had been torn between the idea of attending a large state university or a small, prestigious liberal arts college for women, such as Vassar. In the fall of 1960, during my precollegiate counseling session at Alamo Heights High School, my guidance counselor pronounced that I would be ideal for Sophie Newcomb. Miss Bunyan felt I would find the Northeast too socially anti-Semitic, while Newcomb could provide the same kind of intellectual stimulation in a much friendlier atmosphere. I responded that New Orleans was not for me! As someone sensitive to discrimination (and, equally, creature discomfort) of any kind, I knew that New Orleans was more racist than San Antonio, and with its heat and humidity, my hair would kink, my face would break out, and I wouldn't be able to breathe. Newcomb was not really a choice that I entertained seriously, but a year and a half and two universities later, I found myself in New Orleans, just where Miss Bunyan thought I belonged.

After high school graduation, I headed for the University of California at Berkeley, my mother's alma mater—far from San Antonio and the South—but as it turned out, too far from my father's vision of the young woman he expected me to be. Perhaps he intuitively divined that the campus was about to be overtaken by the free speech movement. Perhaps it was my interest in a young man who, although Jewish, did not pass the test of "up-and-coming" in parental eyes. The following fall, I was eighty miles from home at the University of Texas in Austin.

In the meantime, I had started dating a Tulane student, Stephen Sontheimer, a Jewish native New Orleanian who won the hearts of all my family members. By New Year's we were pinned, and I'd applied to Newcomb for the fall term of 1963. Still, my father worried that absence does not always make a heart grow fonder. He suggested that Stephen might speak to someone in the admissions office about an earlier transfer. The next day and one month into the semester, Stephen called to tell me there was an extra bed in Josephine Louise House, the freshman dormitory. "Pack your clothes. I've ordered your weejuns (the loafer then popular on the Tulane campus). You're coming to Newcomb." I arrived twenty-four hours later.

This essay exploring my intellectual and personal journey to adulthood traces the ways I was shaped by the milieu that was at once Newcomb College *and* Tulane University, alongside its intersection with the distinctly small Uptown New Orleans Jewish community—and my desire to gain a perspective that both honored and transcended that world. Ultimately, Miss Bunyan would be correct in stating that Newcomb fulfilled its mission to educate women much as did the elite women's colleges of the Northeast. True, Newcomb was known for its acceptance of Jewish students—the statement bandied about was that the student body was one-third Jewish, one-third Catholic, and one-third Protestant.

The "someone" in admissions turned out to be Associate Dean Joe Cohen, and I became a student in his sophomore English literature class, where it was a thrill to hear him read Eliot and Yeats. But my real interest at the time was in art and architecture, so when I arrived at Newcomb and learned about the strong reputation of the art school, I declared myself an art history major. At nineteen, I was fairly sure about what life had in store for me: a lovely marriage, lovely children, and plenty of travel. As an art history major, I'd know just what to see on extensive trips abroad to the capitals of Europe. *That* was the subtext for choosing my major. The rationale might have been faulty in the extreme, but my love for art history was genuine, and the professors I encountered unwittingly seeded an appreciation for research and historical context that was much deeper than they or I could have imagined.

I had only the spring semester of 1963 as a typical "Newcomb girl," single and living on campus. Texas girls had a dubious reputation at Newcomb, where many matriculated on what was known as the "Texas plan"—two years at Newcomb and then, if no prospect for marriage seemed in sight, back to the University of Texas, closer to home and much less expensive. Of course, my own profile differed markedly from the stereotype except in one respect: Stephen and I married that summer. In the early 1960s, as before, women who married before completing their undergraduate careers simply dropped out of school or were not permitted to return. My new mother-in-law, Marion, told me that she married her husband, Maury, in January so she wouldn't have to take winter-term finals. She never completed her Newcomb education.

I had no intention of dropping out, however, and returned to school for my junior year as a young matron, which was fairly atypical at the time. I cannot say that I missed un-air-conditioned dorm life or the shared bathrooms at the other end of the hall. But I did miss the camaraderie of women friends that on-campus life in general had provided. Luckily, two Newcomb graduates who had just begun graduate school at Tulane lived in the same Garden District apartment building as Stephen and I. None of us had Thursday classes, so we spent most of those Thursdays kibitzing over coffee.

During the 1963–64 school year, I attended Newcomb full-time, with both memorable classes and remarkable professors, especially Prudence Meyer, from whom I took Greek and Italian baroque art, and who (like my advisor later, Jessie Poesch) constructed provocative final exams, so much so that I felt the exhilaration of an intellectual awakening as I wrote out my heart and soul. I can still recall specific questions that made me reconceptualize the material I had studied.

That year I also took an introductory psychology course with Dorothy Seago, certainly the most demanding and challenging professor I encountered during my entire educational career. Although I studied harder than I ever had and still could not manage to get an A, I was proud of my effort and thoroughly appreciated the discourse she fostered among the students in the class. I admired her unbending standards of excellence and found that her intellectual toughness was not without warmth.

I met another one of my future mentors that year in "Art Fundamentals," a course that was mandatory for all art and art history majors—six weeks of each medium then offered at the art school—printmaking, ceramics, painting, sculpture, design. Design was the one class I truly enjoyed, thanks in no small measure to the efforts of Franklin Adams, who both stimulated and criticized with an eye toward each student's needs and aesthetic development. Years later, that introduction to design and to such a nurturing personality made a difference in my orientation to life.

In the spring semester of 1964, I cross-registered in the School of Architecture for the first time so that I could take architectural history. Bernard Lemann taught all the architectural history courses, and I couldn't seem to get enough of him or them. As much as I enjoyed my Newcomb classes, I was self-conscious about asking more questions than most of the other undergraduate women in art history. In the School of Architecture, I was typically quiet, the only woman and the only non–architecture student in the class. I learned by listening to the answers of complex structural questions asked by the students that I never could have formulated. And the library in Richardson Memorial was blissfully peaceful, with its high windows providing just the right kind of light for study, especially in the late afternoon.

That first year of marriage, Stephen was a senior in the business school. We took turns cooking dinner with other young couples, most of whom were recent graduates of Newcomb or Tulane. Mary Lynn Silverson Alltmont (NC 1964) and I were the only ones still in school. Mary Lynn, along with Edie Levy Rosenblum (NC 1962), Linda Cole Rothschild (NC 1965), and Mathile Watsky Abramson (NC 1962) were key figures in my Reform Jewish "young marrieds" social circle and have remained my good friends for more than forty-five years. A few of the women were New Orleanians; the others, like me, hailed from out of state, but all married native sons.

But being married to an extremely extroverted and socially connected man put a strain on my status as a full-time student. By the time Stephen graduated, I decided I couldn't handle studying and socializing at the same level of intensity, and I became a part-time student for the duration (a really long duration) of my undergraduate career. That decision left plenty of time for community volunteer work, especially through the auspices of the Greater New Orleans section of the National Council of Jewish Women. Many of the leaders whose commitment to civil rights, social justice, and social action so impressed me had gained their self-determination and direction through their experiences at Newcomb College. More than anyone, Irma Moses Isaacson, a graduate of Newcomb (1923) and the Tulane School of Social Work, demonstrated the professionalism that so many of these volunteers brought to their positions. She was my first mentor in Jewish community work. In the early 1960s, women of her social milieu typically were married to "successful," often more conservative, attorneys or businessmen. With husbands who provided financially, these uptown matrons had housekeepers to take care of many domestic responsibilities, freeing them to maintain flexible schedules. While at home raising their families, they simultaneously volunteered their time to raise the civic consciousness of New Orleans. Irma exuded warmth, strength, a passion for social justice (the apex of Reform Jewish idealism), and a spiritual depth that I found singularly engaging and inspiring.

The decision to attend Newcomb part-time also worked well since we soon had two children, both boys. I have vivid memories of the semester before my younger son, Matthew, was born. I used to park my car on Audubon Place in front of the home of Stephen's aunt, Johnnie Levy Heymann (another Newcomb alum), to avoid hunting for a spot on campus. One sticky May morning when I was about eight months pregnant, I managed to park and puff to a final exam in the art building, only to realize that I had left my blue books behind. I rushed back to the car and then returned to the exam to find the second slide flickering off the screen. Dripping with perspiration and exasperation, I endured the swift kicking of my unborn child as I tried to identify eighteenth-century German cathedral floor plans and other artifacts of the Northern Baroque period. Yet I felt pleased and privileged to be able to both complete my courses and raise a family.

At the time, the pre-Columbian art course provided the counterbalance of intellectual immersion to the preoccupations of mothering. In his shiny-from-wear green blazer and with a cigarette dripping ashes as he lectured, art history professor Donald Robertson demonstrated passion and scholarship. He began the course by telling students to identify topics for a research paper. A photograph of the so-called Pyramid of the Niches at El Tajín near Veracruz captured my imagination, and I asked if that pyramid might work. Dr.

Robertson told me there would be insufficient information available on the pyramid, but I could research the entire archaeological site of El Tajín since little had been written on the subject.

A prompt visit to Tulane's Latin American collection confirmed Dr. Robertson's observation: little had been written on El Tajín—*in English*. The leading archaeologist at the site, García Payón, had written exacting descriptions of the excavated or extant portions of the site in Spanish. I perused his writings with the help of a bilingual dictionary and found so much information that I took my first "incomplete" in a course to allow me sufficient time to translate and paraphrase Payón's descriptions.

By the time I turned in the paper, I had written far more than Dr. Robertson had anticipated, and he wondered why I had expended so much effort on such an extensive topic. I reminded him that it was *his* suggestion and asked why *he* had expanded my original idea. I still laugh when I recall his reply: "Mrs. Sontheimer, how could I know that you would turn out to be such a little scholar?" In another time, this "little scholar" designation might be considered patronizing, but I prefer to think of his comment as validation of my ability. Dr. Robertson was the first Newcomb professor who helped me realize that I could *be* a scholar, until then a word I could never have applied to myself. All the while, I was a mother, with my intellectual journey informing the lives I shaped for my children and my understanding of them. As a baby and toddler, Benjamin was easy. He slept regularly and well, loved to listen to and look at books from the time he could sit up, and his hours at rest gave me time to study. But Matthew was full of restless energy and slept only intermittently, so the only hours I could concentrate were just before daylight. I would sit at the kitchen table with the art books spread in front of me until a pajama-clad boy climbed into my lap demanding attention. Just as Benjamin had been enthralled by the sound of words, Matthew adored pictures. I entertained him by telling him about the paintings, sculpture, and architecture that I was studying. Before long, he could identify artists and their work, just as his older brother could recite poetry. I still feel that those early mornings in the Nashville Avenue kitchen nurtured the soul of the visual artist he became.

Once I had dispensed with general requirements, almost all of my course work revolved around art history. The only exceptions were a class titled "Intellectual Backgrounds to English Literature" and creative writing, which I studied under Marvin Morillo. From him I learned how to nurture intellectual growth, no matter how tentative. For example, although both my poetry and my short essays were undoubtedly more cathartic than creative, Dr. Morillo responded objectively, professionally, and kindly. His gifts as a teacher and sensitive critic became even more apparent to me years later when I began my own career as a teacher.

Not all aspects of my life reflected the golden harmony of Dr. Morillo's well-rehearsed lectures. My marriage was cascading as my intellectual life and my pleasures with motherhood were ascending. Even though Stephen and I earnestly tried various forms of counseling, we were headed for divorce, and in February 1973, we separated. Stephen told friends that he found it hard competing with William Blake. William Blake *was* my obsession and current research topic about the time of our separation. I could lose myself in Blake's illustrated poems and sublimated passions, and I identified with his romantic courage, especially since I felt estranged from those safe uptown Jewish moorings that had sustained me. No longer Mrs. Stephen Sontheimer, I was unsure about the exact direction in which I was heading.

During this difficult personal transition, Jessie Poesch, from whom I was taking a course in American art and architecture, became the Newcomb mentor who helped me balance my intellectual yearnings and emotional upheavals. From her, for example, I learned to recognize that essential traits distinguish a colonial piece of furniture and reveal the city in which it was crafted. Dr. Poesch felt that the American vernacular was as important to understand as the American high-art exponent. That perspective helped me refocus my intellectual energies as I learned to appreciate the pursuit of the intellectual within everyday life.

In somewhat the same way, I struggled to look at divorce as another part of this journey of knowledge. As painful as it was, I was slowly gaining distance from the desire to fulfill the expectations others had of me and beginning to have intimations of myself as a person in my own right. Both Stephen and I adored our children, and we valiantly tried to balance our own becoming as separate individuals with keeping our children secure in knowing that they had the love of both parents. I tend to think we did so because of my growing happiness with learning, and his particularly New Orleans construction of a tenacious family bond.

I, too, came to practice a version of tenacity, both with family and with subject matter. Between the observations of Bernard Lemann and the wisdom of Jessie Poesch, I grew to believe that I *could* say something original about architecture that was within the purview of my own experience. Aesthetically,

New Orleans' architecture had always enticed me, and little had been written about its more pedestrian vernacular examples. Dr. Poesch had suggested that each person in the class choose a local structure to study. I found a block in the Irish Channel bound by Phillips, First, Constance, and Laurel, and decided to work on the entire urban symphony. I loved consulting the Notarial Archives at City Hall, and I walked "my" block many times. My paper became the subject of an article in one of the football programs the following fall, and Dr. Poesch became my academic advisor. I benefited from her patient, steady, and wise counsel as I drifted emotionally through turbulent waters. Staying focused on architectural research became increasingly difficult, however, when my father died suddenly at age fifty-eight. Architecture seemed somehow trivial next to the import and impact of his death in addition to the adjustments of single parenthood.

I carried around journals and a large number of felt-tip pens and doodled around the edges of thoughts or poems I was jotting down, as though I were taking my emotional/psychological temperature. When I shared one of the journals with Dr. Morillo, he counseled me, "Get the poetry off the page, and do something with those designs." Following his advice, I converted the independent hours of research I'd begun with Dr. Poesch into an independent study in design. I was wounded, unsure of myself, vulnerable, but my two mentors, Dr. Poesch and Franklin Adams, were unfailingly kind and gentle, providing a healthy critique that helped me liberate my designs from my notebooks.

I had started doing needlepoint when I was pregnant with Benjamin. Then I began designing my own canvases and teaching courses in needlepoint techniques at the Jewish Community Center (JCC). Friends, acquaintances, and then strangers were beginning to ask me to design canvases. The JCC asked if I wanted to mount an exhibit of my work in the center's lobby. Franklin Adams worked with me, and in May 1975, I had my first show in place of a senior honors thesis.

A few weeks prior to the show, I had decided that I wanted to try to complete my BA requirements over the summer and went into the Newcomb registrar's office to see if I could work out yet another independent study. The registrar was shocked (as was I) to find that I needed less than one hour of requirements to complete my degree. She suggested that if Mr. Adams would be willing to add the credit to the independent work I had done with him, I could graduate the following week with the class of 1975—ten years late, but cum laude! I had just enough time to be fitted for a cap and gown and have my name listed in the program. Eudora Welty, one of my favorite authors, spoke at graduation. Benjamin and Matthew, my mother, and Gussie Woodest, my dear friend and the children's babysitter, accompanied me, even though the boys worried that someone would think I was pretty dumb because it had taken me so many years to graduate.

The show at the JCC launched my first full-time career beyond the boys and home. The designs that Franklin Adams had helped me liberate from sketchbooks now expanded to cover entire walls. While I was volunteering at McDonogh #15, my children's elementary school, I met the school's artist-in-residence, Robin Halpren-Ruder. We clicked immediately and decided to go into business together designing and painting murals, something neither of us had ever attempted. Again, Franklin Adams provided priceless advice and guidance as Robin and I launched Artenvirons. Although we never made a great deal of money, I think that we made quite a few walls smile in medical and dental offices, hospitals, banks, residences, and other venues.

I was painting murals in the fall 1976 when I met Texas native and Tulane history professor Bill Malone, and we married the following May. When we decided to buy a home, I realized that we could use a more stable second income. I returned to Tulane for a master's in elementary education through an outstanding yearlong program of intensive study that included full-time student teaching. My placement at Trinity Episcopal School proved providential. I worked in the first-grade classroom of Felice Perrilliat Seavey, herself a Newcomb alumna (1957). Nurturing, well-organized, warm yet firm with her students, Felice was the best master teacher I could have had—the perfect mentor.

Over the next decade, I taught at Trinity for four years and then in Texas for another four. Benjamin and Matthew unexpectedly decided to follow the examples of their father and stepmother and attend boarding school, and Bill and I suddenly experienced an empty nest. We were smitten with the romantic notion of a return to Texas and reacted by selling our home and moving. There I taught gifted second- through fifth-graders at public elementary schools in Smith County. Bill had a sabbatical the first year, and we commuted the other three. As part of my teaching assignment, I introduced my students to independent research and directed more than sixty projects each year. Encouraging their initial experiences with inquiry, I realized how much I missed doing research myself. In spite of El Tajín, William Blake, and the

Irish Channel, I had never fully explored my own topic as I was encouraging my students to do.

Then, in the magical summer of 1987, I had an epiphany of sorts. Bill and I spent the summer in Berea, Kentucky, where he taught a seminar for teachers in Appalachian music at Berea College. I found my mind stretching with new ideas, new books to read, and new Kentucky venues to discover and explore. I also attended "Confratute," an institute for teachers of gifted students, and the combination of those experiences pushed me to consider a new career path. I decided that I really wanted to knit together both halves of my life by investigating and writing about the unique aspects of southern Jewish culture that had intrigued me. The last year in East Texas, I thought about returning to New Orleans, wondering if I should ask about vacancies at Trinity or whether I should pursue an academic rebirth. I chose the latter.

Our old friend and former Tulane history professor John Boles had become editor of the *Journal of Southern History*. For years, he had been feeding me articles on obscure or obsolete Texas Jewish communities, and he encouraged me to return to graduate school for a PhD in history. Even though it might be awkward with many of our old faculty friends now becoming my professors, I thought that southern history offered the best route to pursue my study of southern Jews, and that I could survive being a graduate student in my husband's department.

I not only survived, I thrived. The joy of returning to graduate school at forty-four was that I was completely focused and goal-oriented. The more deeply I immersed myself in southern Jewish history, the more I appreciated other topics and eras in social, ethnic, cultural, and economic history. Patrick Maney, Clarence Mohr, and Larry Powell, our closest social friends, now formed the triumvirate who became my trusted advisors and dissertation committee.

My first research paper under Richard Latner investigated the origins of Congregation Gates of Prayer, a synagogue whose initial decade (1850–60) fell under the purview of the course. My research on the group of German Jewish immigrants who founded the congregation included using the obituary files at the New Orleans Public Library assembled by the WPA in the 1930s and 1940s, rubbing gravestones in the old congregational cemetery on Joseph Street, and interviewing surviving descendants of the founders. I loved it all.

One of the sources I had uncovered was a slim history of Temple Sinai. Rabbi Max Heller, who served in Sinai's pulpit from 1884 to 1924, wrote the volume in 1922 to commemorate the fiftieth anniversary of the congregation. The elegantly written book—complete with footnotes to nineteenth-century sources—was much more than a congregational history: it related the development of the New Orleans Jewish community from its earliest member, Judah Touro. Some quirky references also indicated the rabbi's acceptance of Zionism (highly unusual for a Reform rabbi at that time). His recognition by Beth Israel—the city's largest Orthodox congregation—was also fairly unusual for the period. Having written an intellectual biographical study of Abraham Cahan—first editor of the Yiddish-language socialist newspaper the *Forward*—for Professor Bill McClay, I thought that Max Heller might be worth a paper for my second-semester writing seminar under Pat Maney.

The affair with Max Heller turned out to be more serious than my earlier flirtation with William Blake. The paper grew from a master's thesis to a dissertation and was finally published by the University of Alabama Press as *Rabbi Max Heller: Reformer, Zionist, Southerner, 1860–1929*. In sync with the other major players in my life, the rabbi and his family also had "under the oaks" connections: Max Heller taught Hebrew at Tulane, and both daughters, Cecile and Ruth, were Newcomb College graduates, in 1911 and 1918, respectively.

While I was researching Max Heller's life in the libraries of Tulane and at the American Jewish Archives in Cincinnati, I also was interviewing older members of the New Orleans Jewish community who remembered him. The rabbi's daughter-in-law, Mildred, was still alive when I began my research, and she recounted how she had met and married Isaac Heller while she was studying at Newcomb (NC 1927). Grandsons Theo and Edward Heller were also extremely helpful, graciously sharing photographs and other memorabilia and lending financial support to the biography's publication.

Other research informants I had known casually or at some distance now became wonderful friends—Ruth Dreyfous, a Newcomb graduate (1923), and Rosalie Polmer Cohen, who, as a journalism major, was one of the few female graduates of Tulane's College of Arts and Sciences (1930). These remarkable older women represented two very separate New Orleans Jewish spheres. I actually got to know Ruth when I responded to her request for a graduate student willing to read her the *New York Times* and help her write her memoirs. In her mid-nineties at the time, she was suffering from macular degeneration, but she wanted someone to keep her mentally stimulated. Ruth's paternal grandfather, Abel, had immigrated to New Orleans in the 1830s, and her father, Felix, was a Tulane law graduate and one of the city's leading progressives. According to Ruth, even though her parents were not "churchgoers," they were members of Temple Sinai, and Rabbi Heller had confirmed Ruth during the World War I era.

Rosalie's parents emigrated from Lithuania at the turn of the century, and she grew up in a deeply Orthodox and Zionist household where Max Heller sometimes shared Sabbaths and discussed dreams of restoring a Jewish homeland. Having lived during the most dynamic decades of Max Heller's career, the insights and vivid firsthand accounts of Ruth and Rosalie helped me visualize his life and times as otherwise I would have been unable to do. I later wrote an article on these two women for *Southern Jewish History* and gave a talk on their friendship at the Newcomb College Center for Research on Women. Ruth had already died, but thankfully Rosalie was able to attend.

When I began my course work in the fall of 1988, I had hoped that I would obtain a doctorate as a fiftieth birthday gift to myself—and I was able to fulfill that wish. On a hot, sticky late July morning in 1994, just as at my Newcomb graduation, I was joined by my children, Gussie Woodest, and my mother. Bill, along with my brother, my favorite cousin and his wife, my dearest friends, and Stephen—as proud as my father would have been—all gathered in McAlister Auditorium to witness my receiving my fourth and terminal degree from the University.

Writing and reflecting on my journey makes me ever more mindful that I had the luxury of becoming a lifetime learner. As a teacher, I often told students that there is more than one right answer, more than one role to fill, more than one imagination to satisfy. That a path may be circuitous does not make it less satisfying. The journey simply affirms the wonder of possibilities explored, possibilities rejected, possibilities sustained. An intellectual biography places achievement within a context that joins the personal and the professional as a narrative embracing both sides of a personality. I find that I was always weaving back and forth as I tried to navigate between competing images of myself. I feel grateful that I ultimately resolved this dilemma within the campuses of Newcomb and Tulane, in the many years it took to "grow up under the oaks."

22

NEWCOMB AND
THE NEW ORLEANS I KNOW

MONIQUE GUILLORY

I wasn't happy about staying home for college. I had my heart set on Columbia University in New York, the beginnings of a brilliant career in journalism that would take me to exciting, uncharted parts of the world. New Orleans?—Been there, done that. I had lived in New Orleans all my life and thought I had discovered all that the city had to offer. The cemeteries, Mardi Gras and the elusive Indians, Barsodi's eclectic coffee shop—the hodgepodge of hidden treasures that, at the time, had not yet come into their own with the tourists. Back in 1987, intimate knowledge of these people and places was as obscure to outsiders as the formula for a roux and the identity of Rex.

I have always loved being from New Orleans. I was never one of those restless women who longed to ditch their hometowns for the "anyplace is better than here" illusion. Early on, I knew that New Orleans was a tough act to follow. Few places in the world can offer a young person the lessons in beauty and tragedy that New Orleans has taught me. When you live in New Orleans, you learn how to live—you constantly remind yourself that things could always be worse; but sometimes, you actually feel that they could never be better. I was fortunate to appreciate this aspect of my hometown at a young age, but this recognition did little to quell my fascination with New York. It was one of the only cities, I thought, that could actually compete with New Orleans, and even then, I felt it was going to be a close call.

The disappointment of staying in New Orleans for school was tempered by the fact that my three best friends had decided to go to Tulane as well. We were the valedictorians and salutatorians of our respective high schools and received the "full-ride" scholarship that President Eamon Kelly offered for the top graduates from the local schools. This wonderful opportunity was the death knell to my dreams of college in New York, and my parents weren't interested in sending one dime to Columbia when I could go to "a perfectly good school" right there at Tulane. And the friends who had shared in the same early academic success experienced similar ultimatums—one had been accepted to MIT and one to Princeton—and now we were all in the same boat (thanks to serious conspiracies among our parents). We would make it work and looked forward to continuing the camaraderie that had sustained us through the perils of high school. For me, this consolation would be short-lived. As far as I was concerned, we were all going to Tulane. But while we would all be on the same campus, we ultimately ended up worlds apart. My three friends went to the Engineering School while I was on my way to Newcomb.

When I finished high school, I was ready to see the world. I was not, how-ever, ready to live with boys. Coming from an all-girls' Catholic school, living in a coed dorm where boys were but a brief elevator ride away seemed an impropriety I simply could not brave—one of the "near occasions of sin" I had steadfastly promised to avoid. My best friend from high school agreed with me, and we found a safe, single-sex haven in the stately elegance of Josephine Louise Residence Hall.

For me, Josephine Louise Residence Hall (JL) was one of the pillars of Newcomb College. While the rest of the campus buzzed with Frisbees and soccer games, bikes and skateboards whizzing past you on the narrow walk-ways, the most activity noted near JL consisted of languid young women sun-bathing in the sweltering New Orleans heat. At St. Mary's Academy, I had spent six years in a world of women, but JL offered me my first experience of what it was like to live in a sorority house.

My high school days couldn't have been more different from the world I encountered at JL. St. Mary's is an African American private school managed by the Sisters of the Holy Family, the second-oldest order of African American nuns in the country. This modest and austere institution instilled in young women of color a sense of pride and self-respect. The nuns dictated every-thing to us from the lengths of our skirts to the number of folds in our socks. The student handbook left little room for error, and where errors were made, they were not suffered lightly. In the wake of such discipline and structure, life in JL was like a carnival—rich with color, texture, and variety. Young women would play the piano in the sunlit parlor; young men fidgeted at the front door as they waited to be buzzed in; late-night study sessions resembled pajama parties with hair curlers, Cokes, and pizza. Although it was an all-girl, freshman dorm with curfews and visitation restrictions, JL was my window to the real world of responsibility, choices, and consequences.

It was also the first time I would ever really get to know white women. I had gone through most of my life telling myself that white girls were no different from me, particularly when I competed against them in debate and academic tournaments. But now that I lived with them, now that I talked with them at length, met their parents and their boyfriends, I realized that they were different from me and the other four black girls who lived in JL. They weren't different because they were white, but there was something about whiteness itself, like blackness, that amounted to obvious differences in class, education, socialization, economics, and general worldview. Having come of age through St. Mary's, where everything I learned was imparted by strong, intelligent, proud women of color, I never questioned whether I was as capable as any among my peers—woman or man. But observing these young women and living with them in the place we all called home opened my eyes for the first time to the ease, anonymity, and entitlement that are typically synonymous with white privilege.

White people weren't the only ones who broke through my safe little world. At Newcomb, I would also meet the remarkable phenomenon of black people who seem white in all respects except for their skin color. I marveled at how one young black woman moved so effortlessly with her white clique, pledged a sorority, and never sought the familial comfort of the African American student association. For this, among the black students on campus, she was secretly, and maybe not so secretly, dismissed, ignored, and vilified as the "Oreo"—black on the outside, white on the inside. As she circulated around campus, I surreptitiously watched her with an almost anthropological interest, having known that people like this existed but never having seen one up close. I now understand the threat this type of "passing" poses to the black psyche, especially in an environment like a majority white college campus where there are so few African Americans. For one to stray away from the fold seemed haphazard and brazen yet also demonstrated a type of courage and freedom that the rest of us, huddled together at lunch or gathering on our favorite bench, wouldn't dare.

In addition to this black/white anomaly, there were also foreign women who called themselves black even though they came from South Asia, North Africa, and England and did not appear to manifest the antebellum heritage I assumed was a prerequisite to self-identify as black in America. Again, I had never considered the implications of blackness from a global sense apart from the delineations of slavery, civil rights, and "the African-American experience." I learned how the British and Irish venerate soul music as much as my own parents and how there was a universal solidarity in the quest for freedom that was tethered to the civil rights movement but resonated beyond the South and the March on Washington. All of these realities compelled me to reexamine my own identity as an African American woman—a challenge that would follow me throughout my graduate career as I studied the dynamics of identity politics and the fluid parameters of race and gender. All this I learned before setting foot in a classroom at Tulane just from living among people I had never previously encountered. It is what college is all about, and while St. Mary's had been instrumental in teaching me who I was and the potential that lies within me, Newcomb gave me a glimpse of who I would become and the world where I was expected to compete.

I learned a lot more from the women of JL than just these abstract, theoretical forays into race and identity. One feisty redhead, the quintessential southern belle, introduced me to the hymns of Patsy Cline. She would saunter down the hall crooning, "I go out walkin', after midnight, out in the starlight, just hopin' you are out walkin', after midnight searching for-oor meeeee." She also had a gay friend, and it startled me to know that someone so young could be so sure and so confident about this unconventional aspect of himself. I was that naïve. Nadia was undoubtedly the envy of the hall. She had an accent, was brilliant, gorgeous, and about as nice as anyone could be. She was extremely classy, and you just had to like her even though you inevitably felt frumpy whenever she was near. As was typical of her remarkable nature, she went on to become a Watson Fellow and an amateur fencing champion. Georgia and Brooke had the best room in the house. They had a suite, much larger than our standard cells, and their own bathroom—a lush life by JL standards. These girls were undoubtedly privileged—Brooke was the daughter of a well-known prime-time actress, and Georgia exuded good breeding from every pore. Their lavish digs may have separated them from the rest of the JL flock, but other than that, these girls were warm and kind—just folks in the dorm like the rest of us, trying to finish a paper or cram for a midterm. I still see Georgia from time to time in New Orleans, and she remains sweet and pleasant to this day—one of those rare individuals who makes me think, for just a moment, that maybe all my fuss and fears about racism may be overblown.

My life at JL lasted a year, but to continue the charming existence to be found at all-women institutions, I chose a room in New Doris Hall—the women's dorm. The difference between the atmosphere at Newcomb and the School of Engineering ultimately took its toll on the relationship with my JL roommate. I was an English major, which seemed a frivolous undertaking compared to the rigors of the engineering curriculum. Indeed, the friends that initially came with me to Tulane were often squirreled away in labs or meeting constantly with study groups. The majority of my time went into reading books I wanted to read anyway, talking about them with friends, and then writing about them. It was a life I had always longed for, while it seemed like my friends in engineering were actually doing time in some punitive sense. Long live the liberal arts!

I eventually met other women at Newcomb whose ideas and aptitudes were more in line with my own, and surprisingly, these women were white. Karen Brandenburg and Laura Jordan are as much a part of my Newcomb education as any class I took. Their names should be somewhere on my transcript. Through them, I learned the truly essential lessons about life—how to be a friend, how to understand and see things from another's perspective, how to forgive. Laura is older than I, but we were in the same department and ended up taking several classes together. We had one of those friendships where you aren't really sure how and when it started. All you know is that one day, this person is just someone in your class, and the next, you're driving down the street together singing disco songs at the top of your lungs. Laura was dating a black football player and got a lot of hassle from black women on campus. I was an active member of the African American Congress at Tulane, and I knew how a lot of black people on campus felt about interracial dating. I knew how I felt about it, and before Laura and I were friends, I had been a part of that pack. Black women at Tulane resented these transgressions across the color line that seemed to heighten the difficulty of finding a suitable partner among the dismally low number of preprofessional black men who were our peers. We resented losing "a good one" to a white girl who seemingly had plenty of possibilities on the other side. Laura and I talked about this often—the two-way street of race, prejudice, discrimination, and fear. While I initially, and foolishly, tried to convince Laura that black women somehow had a right to be hostile about white women dating black men, I ultimately learned through our friendship that who people love is truly no one's business, and we really just need to be happy for the people we love when they find love—no matter what the package it comes in looks like.

Karen was my roommate during our semester at American University in Washington. We had become friends in a political science class with Dr. Nancy Maveety, who encouraged us to take advantage of the opportunity to spend a semester in D.C. Karen and I remain friends to this day—a bond that is earnest, solid, and dependable. In this new environment, however, my friendship with Karen was tested since a city like D.C. offered a bounty of black women with whom I could, and did, form friendships. I also sought to pledge a black sorority that was not yet on campus at Tulane and became very embroiled in the allure of the buppy bourgeoisie. I felt the tension between my attraction to the new friends who introduced me to the sophisticated, lively nuances of urban blackness and my relationship with Karen, which was rooted in the small-town provincialism of Tulane and New Orleans. I know that when my black friends would invite me to go out, I awkwardly avoided asking Karen to come, assuming she would feel out of place as we headed to a black restaurant or club. She probably would have enjoyed herself all the same, but we likely would have been overconscious of her presence and might have felt the need to modify what we said or did in fear of offending or alienating her. I now recognize that I was being oversensitive or cowardly—however you choose to see it—but these are the complexities of "code switching" that black people wrestle with on a daily basis. As we negotiate the realities of our identity and how we manifest ourselves in a white-dominant world, we constantly trip over our own self-consciousness, often shutting ourselves off from greater possibilities in the process.

Race was and is an integral part of all of my friendships, with whites as well as blacks. Even now I find it difficult to relate to people who don't at least attempt to understand how much race still matters. I don't consider myself to be an activist, nor do I keep the race card close at hand, but I fear that with globalization, multiculturalism, and the ubiquitous nature of hip-hop, folks get lulled into the notion that discussions about race are passé and archaic. Somehow, in the Tulane environment, race seemed so pervasive, yet so elusive. You couldn't really say that there was direct tension between the races. During my time at Tulane, we didn't have any particularly sensational racist incident occur that underscored some dormant yet persistent bigotry at the heart of the institution. Looking back, I think this was largely due to President Eamon Kelly and how deliberately he sought to diversify the student and faculty populations. At the same time, however, I felt there was an invisible wall that kept black and white students worlds apart even as we occupied the same campus. It was a type of separation that did not translate to my

New Orleans sensibilities, where blacks and whites famously come together, if only in the name of letting the good times roll.

Tulane was more segregated than most places I frequented in New Orleans, but I also found many students who realized that this fact about the school, and the world, was a problem. I was fortunate to attend Tulane with Timothy Wise, who today is one of the most respected race theorists in the country raising awareness about the pitfalls of white privilege. Tim was one of the most outspoken and radical students on campus, demanding that Tulane divest its holdings in companies that supported apartheid South Africa. He was bold and unwavering, but why wasn't he black? Why didn't one of "our own" students assume the responsibility of this mission that was so much closer to our reality than to his? I now understand that there are positive uses of white privilege and that whiteness has its role to play in the fight for freedom and justice from the abolitionists to the sacrifice of Schwerner and Goodman. Now that I am a college administrator, I cringe at the thought of managing a student like Tim Wise, yet Tulane should be proud of the contributions this alumnus has made to the world. Along with Tim, there were many professors and administrators I encountered at Tulane—Rebecca Mark, Felipe Smith, Molly Travis, John Patton, and Carolyn Barber—who, apart from the lessons detailed on their syllabus, modeled for me the value of doing the right thing even if the ultimate result seemingly made little difference in my own little life. Sometimes, the slightest differences make all the difference in the world.

Today, one of my closest friends in the world, Gwendolyn Thompkins, is somewhere in East Africa writing a news story about some global intrigue. She is a correspondent for National Public Radio and has led an inspirational and amazing life as a reporter and editor for various media outlets. Gwen is also a Newcomb alumna, and although we never crossed paths at our alma mater, she embodies the same Newcomb spirit as the women in my cohort— the drive, the worldliness, and sophistication that tell you that this girl is going places. Gwen started the Russian Club at Tulane and traveled through eastern Europe on a Watson Fellowship. She and I worked at the *New Orleans Times-Picayune* for several years together, and we shared our experiences about being black women in the mostly white world of Tulane. Her story is considerably different from mine. Having come from high school at Ursuline Academy, Gwen had already been baptized into the arena of academic competition with white and/or privileged students. Unlike me, Gwen did not necessarily find a refuge in the black student association but rather aligned herself with the students in the International House, no doubt an indication of the experiences that her future held. Gwen and I have been friends now for nearly twenty years, and even though we never spent one day together at Newcomb, I have little doubt that our Newcomb education is one of our strongest bonds. We share the same fierce love for New Orleans, and our years at Newcomb are an important part of that romance. Clearly, that is one of the more remarkable strengths of a place like Newcomb—the capacity to mold the hearts and minds of young women, regardless of how they came there; to instill them with the talents, skills, and self-determination to take them wherever their dreams can carry them but to always appreciate and return to the comforts of home.

EPILOGUE

I n 2005, the University addressed the challenges posed by Hurricane
Katrina and the subsequent levee failures with a renewal plan that called
for a single undergraduate college to be named Newcomb-Tulane College
"in recognition of the missions, histories, and values of these colleges."[1] Yet,
this did not bring the 120-year history of Newcomb College to an abrupt end,
and there is much about the closure of the College that still merits scholarly
study. In the years from 2006 to 2011, for example, a number of Newcomb
alumnae waged a legal battle focused on ensuring that Mrs. Newcomb's intentions for the College would continue to be honored. Since the reader has
learned that Mrs. Newcomb's relatives fought for the money against the University in the early 1900s, it is only fair to recall that between 2006 and 2011,
other relatives came forward to challenge the Administrators to uphold Mrs.
Newcomb's bequest, leaving her estate for "the present and future development of this department of the University known as the 'H. Sophie Newcomb
Memorial College.'"[2] This battle to prevent Tulane University from closing the
College and transforming it into the H. Sophie Newcomb Memorial College
Institute ended on February 18, 2011, when the Louisiana Supreme Court re-
fused to hear an appeal of a lower-court ruling upholding Tulane's position.[3]

Today, the bequest of Mrs. Newcomb benefits the Newcomb College Institute, an interdisciplinary center supporting all undergraduate women at
Tulane by providing academic and leadership programming, hosting speakers, symposia, and international summits, funding student research projects,
participating in community projects, and fostering mentor and networking relationships with Newcomb alumnae and other community leaders.
The Institute serves even more students than the College did; for example,
women in business and architecture had not been served by Newcomb College in many decades. The interpretation of ways to honor Sophie's memory

therefore continues. We hope that this volume, too, allows others to build upon a legacy concerned with women's education and its particular manifestation within a place created so that one mother could remember her own daughter through the lives of other learning women.

NOTES

1. "Complete Recommendations of the Newcomb-Tulane Task Force Approved by the Board on March 16 [2006]," http://renewal.tulane.edu/traditions_031606_board.shtml.

2. John Pope, "Newcomb Suit Continues as Women's College Merged with Tulane," *New Orleans Times-Picayune*, June 30, 2006; John Pope, "New Suit Filed over Newcomb Closure," *New Orleans Times-Picayune*, August 21, 2008; quote from Brandt V. B. Dixon, *A Brief History of H. Sophie Newcomb Memorial College 1887–1919* (New Orleans: Hauser Printing, 1928), 17.

3. Katherine Mangan, "Tulane U. Wins Donor-Intent Lawsuit over Closing of Women's College," *Chronicle of Higher Education*, February 21, 2011.

CONTRIBUTORS

ALICE GAIL BIER served as Tulane's first executive director of the Center for International Studies from 1998 to 2004. She guided the expansion of the Junior Year Abroad Program to encompass non-Western countries, independent studies, and semester study options. Currently, she is the senior director of International Education and Global Engagement at CUNY Brooklyn College.

SHANNON L. FRYSTAK is an assistant professor of African American history and women's history at East Stroudsburg University of Pennsylvania. She is the author of *Our Minds on Freedom: Women and the Struggle for Black Equality in Louisiana, 1924–1967* (2009).

LYNN D. GORDON is an associate professor of history at the University of Rochester. She specializes in the history of women and in American foreign relations.

EMILIE GRIFFIN (NC 1957), a Newcomb graduate and New Orleans native, writes about spiritual life. Her most recent books include *Souls in Full Sail: A Christian Spirituality of the Later Years* and *Small Surrenders: A Lenten Journey*. The series editor of the HarperCollins Spiritual Classics, she and her husband, the author William Griffin, live in Alexandria, Louisiana.

MONIQUE GUILLORY (NC 1991) has worked in higher education administration for the past ten years and currently serves as the special assistant to the administration at Xavier University of Louisiana. Her postdoctoral research focuses on questions of race, gender, and identity with a particular focus on contemporary literature of the African Diaspora.

KAREN KINGSLEY is a professor emerita of Tulane University School of Architecture. She has published widely on southern architecture, including *Buildings of Louisiana* (2003). Currently, she serves as editor in chief of the Society of Architectural Historians' Buildings of the United States series.

BOBBIE MALONE (NC 1975) recently retired from the Wisconsin Historical Society, where she directed the Office of School Services, creating publications for teachers and students, including coauthoring the state's fourth-grade textbook *Wisconsin: Our State, Our Story,* and *Thinking Like a Historian: Rethinking History Instruction.* She's now working on a biography of Lois Lenski, her favorite childhood author and illustrator. She and her husband, Bill, live in Madison.

JANE MILLER was a teaching assistant and faculty member of the Newcomb College Department of Chemistry. She retired as an associate professor of chemistry and education from the University of Missouri–St. Louis after twenty-seven years. Her published research has been in organic chemistry and biochemistry, chemical education, and the history of chemistry, particularly on women in chemistry and chemistry in St. Louis.

CLARENCE L. MOHR, the recipient of the 1986 Avery O. Craven Prize from the Organization of American Historians, was a professor of American history for seventeen years at Tulane University. After accepting a post at the University of South Alabama in 1998, he published *Tulane: The Emergence of a Modern University,* coauthored with Joseph E. Gordon.

LESLIE GALE PARR is a professor in the School of Mass Communication, the Shawn M. Donnelley Professor of Nonprofit Communication, and the director of the Center for the Study of New Orleans at Loyola University New Orleans. She is the author of *A Will of Her Own: Sarah Towles Reed and the Pursuit of Democracy in Southern Public Education* (1998; paper, 2010).

JOAN PAUL was a professor and department head at Southeastern Louisiana University before going to the University of Tennessee, Knoxville, as head of the Department of Human Performance and Sport Studies. She is now retired and resides in Knoxville, Tennessee. She has written extensively on Clara Baer.

JESSIE POESCH began her tenure at the Newcomb Art Department of Tulane University in 1964 as an assistant professor of American art history. When she retired in 1992 as full professor, an endowed art professorship was established in her honor. Shortly before her death on April 23, 2011, she completed a book on the Great Dismal Swamp. She wrote numerous books and articles on Titian Ramsay Peale, early Louisiana furniture, and the art of the Old South, but was best known for her work on Newcomb's arts and crafts.

EARL RETIF is a noted expert on the work of Caroline Durieux, whom he knew personally over many years. He curated an exhibit of Durieux's work, From Society to Socialism: The Art of Caroline Durieux, at the Newcomb Art Gallery in the spring of 2008.

HARRIET SWIFT, a researcher and former newspaper editor and reporter, is the author of Hidden New Orleans.

TANIA TETLOW (NC 1992) is the Felder-Fayard Associate Professor of Law and the director of the Tulane Domestic Violence Clinic. Before joining the Tulane faculty, she worked as a commercial litigator and served as a federal prosecutor.

SUSAN TUCKER (NC 1972) is the curator of books and records at the Newcomb Archives and the Nadine Vorhoff Library of the Newcomb College Center for Research on Women. Her research interests have extended from an oral history project on domestic workers, Telling Memories among Southern Women (1988), to projects on records and material culture, including the editorship of The Scrapbook in American Life (2006) and New Orleans Cuisine (2008).

PAMELA TYLER is the author of Silk Stockings and Ballot Boxes: New Orleans Women and Politics, 1920–1963, winner of the Kemper Williams Prize for best book on Louisiana history. She is currently an associate professor of history at the University of Southern Mississippi, where she teaches courses on the history of the American South and U.S. women's history.

TRENT WATTS is an associate professor of American studies at the Missouri University of Science and Technology. He is the author of One Homogeneous

People: Narratives of White Southern Identity, 1890–1920 (2010) and *White Masculinity in the Recent South* (2008).

MARSHA WEDELL (NC 1963) is the author of *Elite Women and the Reform Impulse in Memphis, 1875–1915* (1991). She lives in Tennessee and Argentina.

BETH WILLINGER began her Newcomb career as a visiting instructor in sociology in 1975 and in 1982 began her twenty-five-year tenure as the director of what would become the Newcomb College Center for Research on Women. In 1992–93, she served as interim dean of Newcomb College.

INDEX

Note: Italicized page numbers refer to figures.